AGENCY

MANIA

Harnessing the madness of client/agency relationships for high-impact results

BRUNO GRALPOIS

BEAUFORT
BOOKS

Saxe, John Godfrey. The Poems of John Godfrey Saxe: Complete in One Volume. Fields, Osgood, 1871. "The Blind Men And The Elephant"

Library of Congress Cataloging-in-Publication Data
Names: Gralpois, Bruno, author.
Title: Agency mania : harnessing the madness of client/agency : relationships
    for high-impact results / Bruno Gralpois.
Description: 2nd edition. | New York, NY : Beaufort Books, [2019] | Revised
    edition of the author's Agency mania, c2010. | Includes bibliographical
    references and index.
Identifiers: LCCN 2018045186 (print) | LCCN 2018046550 (ebook) | ISBN
    9780825308062 (Ebook) | ISBN 9780825308963 (pbk. : alk. paper)
Subjects: LCSH: Marketing--Management. | Strategic alliances (Business) |
    Customer relations--Management.
Classification: LCC HF5415.13 (ebook) | LCC HF5415.13 .G69 2019 (print) | DDC
    658.8/04--dc23
LC record available at https://lccn.loc.gov/2018045186

For inquiries about volume orders, please contact:
Beaufort Books
27 West 20th Street, Suite 1102
New York, NY 10011
sales@beaufortbooks.com

Published in the United States by Beaufort Books
www.beaufortbooks.com

Distributed by Midpoint Trade Books
www.midpointtrade.com

Printed in the United States of America

Interior design by Mark Karis
Photographer: David Doctor Rose
Book Cover Design: Evan Bross, Keslie Watts

Any views or opinions presented in this book are solely those of the author and do not imply any endorsement from Agency Mania Solutions or any of the book contributors.

Dedicated to the many talented agency and client maniacs around the world who are committed to building strong business partnerships and driving excellence in all they do.

CONTENTS

FOREWORD

"AGENCY MANIA"

What a fresh title—and what a fresh perspective! This book presents wonderful insights that will undoubtedly guide the marketing industry to pursue the next generation of client–agency relationships. We should all be grateful that Mr. Gralpois has brought the full extent of his experience to bear on this remarkably engaging and important subject.

Working with and managing agencies is, for marketers, one of the great pleasures and challenges of their jobs. It's a subject I love to discuss and debate because I think agencies are terrific and provide enormous value. They provide the strategic pathways and creative inspiration that enable marketers to continuously pursue effective brand development.

Unfortunately, over the past decade, agency management has become increasingly difficult and, in some ways, destructive. "Managing the agency" often consumes such an extraordinary amount of time and energy that marketers begin wondering why they hired these firms in the first place. Before marketers can begin addressing the challenges of creating great work for their brands, they must wrestle with issues like:

- What is fair agency compensation?

- How will the agency be evaluated?

- What agency talent will support the brand?

- What will the ongoing role of procurement be?

- Who will coordinate the efforts of multiple agencies to ensure that strategies and messages are fully integrated and supportive of the overall brand positioning?

Managing agencies should not be so difficult! Agency personnel should function as a seamless part of the brand or corporate management team, bringing their objectivity, strategy, creativity, media savvy, and experience grounded in the case histories of all their past relationships. Most importantly, client/agency relationships should be uncomplicated so that agencies can freely provide the valued skills that many marketers don't possess—skills that are crucial to building brands and building businesses.

Frustratingly, over the past decade, the business system for managing agencies in a way that affords marketers the full array of needed resources has become maddeningly complex. Just think about the array of agencies that populate some brand teams: General, Digital, Multicultural, Media, Sponsorship and Event Marketing, Social Media, CRM Agencies, Public Relations, and more.

While each of these agencies makes an important

contribution, it's ridiculously exhausting to organize this vast pool of talent and get everyone on the same page. And what does that "page" look like? Again, not an easy subject. At the Association of National Advertisers (ANA), we've developed a "blueprint" that outlines ten "marketing musts" for long-term marketing effectiveness. We call this document "The Marketers' Constitution." Here are the first seven of its ten articles, which provide a sound framework to guide effective client-agency relationships:

1. Marketing must become increasingly targeted, focused, and personal.

2. Marketing must build real, tangible, and enduring brand value.

3. Marketing must become more effective—more creative, insightful, and accountable.

4. Marketing must become more integrated and proficient in managing expanding media platforms.

5. The marketing supply chain must become more efficient and productive.

6. The marketing ecosystem—including agencies, media, and suppliers—must become increasingly capable.

7. Marketing professionals must become better, highly skilled, diverse leaders.

Can agencies and marketers fully embrace these principles and get to the finish line? Well, *Agency Mania* is the "kick in the pants" needed to make it happen! *Agency Mania* is a brilliant, insightful digest of how marketers and agencies can successfully navigate today's immense challenges and opportunities. It insightfully analyzes the current state of marketing and suggests ways the business system should transform to adapt to the dynamic marketing ecosystem of tomorrow.

Mr. Gralpois has a unique vantage point. With experience on both the agency and client sides, his personal history provides him the latitude to explore the entire landscape and devise new, sensible business practices that cut through the issues that handicap client/agency partnerships.

Our increasingly complex, technologically enabled world has many wonderful advantages and possibilities. However, it provides us with no footprints to the future. Mr. Gralpois suggests what the new footprints should look like. In doing so, he greatly helps us learn how to lead our respective organizations more confidently and more capably in the future.

I applaud this book—and recommend it to the entire marketing community. It will help you understand what's working and what's not within your organization. It will help you move to a better plane with your operations, strategy, creativity, and partnership. I am delighted Mr. Gralpois has given me this opportunity to share my perspectives and to express my whole-hearted encouragement for his superb work!

—**BOB LIODICE**, PRESIDENT AND CEO,
ASSOCIATION OF NATIONAL ADVERTISERS (ANA)

ACKNOWLEDGMENTS

The source of my knowledge and inspiration over the course of a career spent on both the client and agency side includes a vast number of anecdotal stories, professional experiences, and vivid conversations with colleagues, partners, and friends—a group of brilliant professionals and subject-matter experts who shared many success stories as well as failures—that ought to be told and are now included in this book. All of them are highly successful business executives and lifetime learners who share a common passion for harnessing the madness of client/agency relationships and, in the process, driving results. I would also like to acknowledge my friends and talented business partners, Teri Wiegman and Shaun Wolfe, and the entire Agency Mania Solutions team that apply these best practices every day to enable advertisers to realize the transformational value of their agency partnerships. Our team collaborates daily with the world's largest brands and remarkable leaders in a variety of roles ranging from agency relations, agency management, marketing operations and marketing procurement.

I would like to express much gratitude to Bob Liodice, President and CEO of the ANA, and his A-team—Bill Duggan, Tracy Owens, April Rueppel, Lisa Guhanick, Sandie Colon, Irene Pantazis, Shepard Kramer, Nick Primola, Morgan Strawn, Michael Palmer, Bill Zengel, Jeni Neiswonger, Brian Davidson, Marni Gordon, Sara Stein and many others—for their unwavering commitment to marketing excellence and successful partnerships. Other industry influencers include committee and conference chairs like Jim Wallace, Mary Ann Brennan, Brett Colbert, Kate Short, Francisco Escobar and others. I want to acknowledge the great work done by the 4As (American Association of Advertising Agencies) to broaden our understanding of the client/agency relationship under the leadership of President and CEO Marla Kaplowitz, as well as Stacie Calabrese, Manager of Research Services. I want to thank my friend Neal Grossman, Chief Operating Officer at Americas eg+ worldwide and the designory for his valuable perspective and insight on the often-controversial topic of compensation, as well as Tim J. Williams, Founding Partner of Ignition Consulting Group, for his continued efforts to broaden our understanding of what constitutes agency value. I also want to thank many important contributors: my friend Patricia Berns for her insights on the agency world, Allison Acton of Acton Creative, Laura Temple, Editor on Call Founder & Chief Editor, John Raffetto and Kara Lundberg from Raffetto Herman Strategic Communications, my book agent Bill Gladstone of Waterside Productions, Megan Trank and Karen Hughes of Beaufort Books, and Eric M. Kampmann of Midpoint Trade Books for their efforts, and the team of the former Seattle-based ad agency Wexley School for Girls—Ian Cohen, Christine Wise, Amy

Lower, Tara Cooke, Dee Dee Jones, Patrick Mullins, and Eric Roche for their terrific work on this book's cover. Other well-respected contributors, current and former colleagues, long-time supporters and friends that influenced my thoughts on many of these topics include Antonio Lucio (Facebook), Diego Scotti and Cathy Stanley (Verizon), Kevin Esposito (IBM), Sal Vitale and Tracy Allery (Mondelez International), Keecia Scott (Gilead Sciences), Lori Knutson (Bank of America), Jarret Hollier (Dell), Michele Dunn (Michelin), Dionne Colvin-Lovely (Toyota), Angela Robinson (Genentech), Antonio Humphreys (Adobe), Peter Stabler (Wells Fargo), Sarah Armstrong (McKinsey & Company), Deb Giampoli, Darren Woolley, John Hardy, and key industry icons like Maurice Levy, Sir Martin Sorrell, Arthur Sadoun, Marc Pritchard, Olivier Francois, Keith Weed—to name a few—quoted in this book. I want to thank Jillian Gibbs of APR, Olivier Gauthier of COMvergence, Philippe Paget, and Elizabeth Marks of AdForum, Emily Foster of In-House Agency Forum, and Laura Forcetti of the World Federation of Advertisers for their support promoting healthy client/agency relationships. I've been privileged to meet leaders in many aspects of the business and marketing world and in agencies and brand advertisers of all sizes—and many of them have been quoted or referenced in this second edition of *Agency Mania*. The business world and marketing community is a better and a more fulfilling, purposeful place because of their generous investment in time, creativity, and effort. Last, but not least, I also want to acknowledge my wife Christine for her continued support, love and patience at every step of this project.

PREFACE

When I wrote *Agency Mania* in 2010, the world of advertising was going through major disruption with the unstoppable advance of the empowered consumer, technology, and digital. For context, that was the year Apple Computer unveiled the iPad tablet computer and *TIME Magazine* announced Facebook founder Mark Zuckerberg as its 2010 Person of the Year. Much has changed in the past few years. In our industry, change is often the only constant. Nearly a decade later, the world of advertising and the marketing communication discipline are far more complex and demanding than they have ever been. I think we can all agree on that.

Brand advertisers, along with their agency partners, are under remarkable pressure to deliver business growth and marketing performance in cost-effective ways, so they compete successfully. As a result, all aspects of the client/agency relationship have drastically evolved, if not transformed in some instances, requiring us to revisit industry best practices and take into consideration new and upcoming trends in the advertising industry. Hence the absolute necessity to write the second edition of *Agency Mania*.

We are building from a sturdy foundation. The first edition of *Agency Mania* was warmly received by both brand advertisers and agencies alike. It became the single, most comprehensive reference book on how to practice effective client/agency relationships. It has been used around the world as either required training or reference material for anyone looking to get more from their partnerships. Luckily, it also led to the creation of Agency Mania Solutions in June 2013, a Seattle-based software company that provides streamlined and automated SaaS solutions to some of the largest brand advertisers in the world.

This second edition includes many helpful revisions based on feedback from various colleagues and thought-leaders who shared their valuable anecdotes and stories over the years. The advertising world experienced a range of seismic transformations, including disruptive media fragmentation, hyper-specialization of marketing talent, AdTech/Martech and digital innovation, the unstoppable rise of procurement in client/agency affairs, growing fiscal accountability and budget pressures, greater client expectations, and a flurry of alternative creative and digital solutions, ranging from in-house departments to publishers getting into marketing content, and the entry of big consultancies. These changes are not without severe consequences. Advertisers and agencies alike are watching the aftermath of these profound yet rapid changes as one might watch a life-threatening virus spread swiftly, wondering if the industry's condition is indeed curable and how to best prepare themselves for what is next. Under pressure to morph and adapt, the agency industry has been dangerously teetering on the edge of irrelevancy in recent years, a situation that has drastic implications for advertisers as well.

These important forces at play and their domino effect are creating a set of new challenges that both advertisers and agencies must confront. When you combine the increased distrust by clients that the lack of transparency has created in various spend categories clients rely on agencies for, including inaccurate time-reporting and confusion about the existence of media rebates along with new production concerns raised by the DOJ, you have a recipe to undermine trust, raise valid questions, and breed many competitive reviews. The increase in agency reviews in the past decade has an obvious impact on all agencies and their ability to serve advertisers: it creates uncertainty and fear that their accounts may also be put into review. The agencies then tend to take a more conservative approach to the work they do and avoid pushing too hard on clients, choosing the path of least resistance and less friction. The work becomes more tactical, and advertisers increasingly see agency deliverables as a commodity. As the perceived value goes down, so does the likelihood for clients to engage agencies in more strategic assignments. Clients push back on pricing and agency profitability goes down, preventing the agency from keeping or attracting the right talent. As talent quality suffers, so does the agency's ability to deliver strategic value. The "spiral of irrelevancy," as I refer to this phenomenon, is indeed circular, worsening as time goes on. Thankfully, these challenges have created new opportunities for innovative agency players to disrupt this dangerous, vicious spiral and find a healthy way to differentiate themselves and grow.

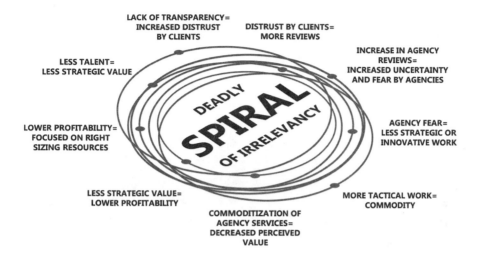

As in our personal lives, building a healthy environment is a wise investment, not an expense. The advertising industry must remain healthy to serve the interests of advertisers and agencies alike, and not let itself get caught in this spiral. Many of the underlying drivers can be found in the way advertisers' needs have evolved and perhaps how they involuntarily contributed to this current state. We need to eradicate the commoditization of advertising services and go back to a more relevant, stronger industry . . . one in which agencies thrive and one that advertisers need and appreciate. The second edition of *Agency Mania* explores the many facets of the evolving client/agency relationship and suggests a more rewarding, productive way to engage, partner, and realize tangible value. This book introduces a wide range of easy-to-follow principles and methods that have been tested and validated. They ensure both parties are building a partnership that is grounded in mutual accountability, understanding, respect, and business performance. Then, and only then, can we ensure that together, both advertisers and agencies can harness the madness of the client-agency relationship for high-impact business performance.

INTRODUCTION

In a world saturated with attention-grabbing advertisements targeted at fragmented in-control audiences, and delivered on a multiplying number of vehicles, brand advertisers are investing billions of dollars to address the ultimate challenge: how to successfully engage audiences, drive demand, build brand affinity, grow market share, and, in the end, boost profitability in their industry. Chief Executive Officers (CEOs) are answering the call by turning to their busy marketing departments to break through the media clutter and accomplish wonders with their brand. They count on their Chief Marketing Officers (CMOs) and their talented organization to come up with ideas that engage, educate, or entertain consumers and create differentiated value. Marketing leaders, in turn, rely on the vast expertise of talented advertising and communication agencies and their wide range of effective creative, media, digital, analytical, and specialized competencies to connect brands and consumers like never before. An estimated one trillion dollars is funneled through these agencies, which in turn stimulates a substantial portion of our global economy. Companies of all sizes, in all industries, are eagerly partnering with skilled professionals who understand their business and have mastered the art of creating and delivering magical moments for their brands.

The agencies that serve them deliver a wide range of communication solutions, from branding, creative, media, programmatic, digital, PR, sponsorship, retail, events, data, and many others. Why is it so important? The advertising profession requires marketers to build a diverse set of muscles to be effective at what they do. One of these critical muscles is the ability to work productively and collaboratively with an agency and deliver high-impact work. A well-managed relationship between an advertiser and its agency has been shown to multiply brand equity and the company's bottom-line profits, exponentially driving value from their partnership. Conversely, a poorly managed relationship is incredibly wasteful and seriously undermines a company's ability to compete effectively.

WHY IS THE BOOK DEDICATED TO THE SUBJECT OF CLIENT/ AGENCY RELATIONSHIPS?

Everyone gets one of these pivotal moments in their life, the type of epiphany that makes you do something out of the ordinary: finding a new vocation, changing career path, or dedicating years to research a topic of interest. I had mine on multiple occasions throughout my career. I became an avid student of the agency and client business. I learned from my experience on the client and agency sides and from my peers what makes two companies click and ultimately accomplish wonders together— and what makes them fail miserably at times. Advertisers often wonder: How do we best collaborate with agencies and get better work from them? What constitutes a strong relationship? How do we get greater value and return on investment from these partnerships? Agencies wonder as well: How do we get what we need from clients to deliver the best possible value to them? How can we best ensure their commercial success?

Over the years, I realized the frequent and rising gap in a company's knowledge and skills, despite the best intentions in the world, prevented even the world's leading advertisers from turning their agencies into the powerful competitive assets they were always meant to be. CMOs are looking for smarter ways to set up their organization for long-term success. Marketing professionals are looking for easy-to-follow steps on how to work more productively with agencies. Agency Management/Relations and their sister Marketing Procurement and Marketing Operations teams are looking for ways to enable client and agency teams to come together to deliver splendid work at reasonable value. Agencies are looking for ways to build stronger, long-lasting relationships with their clients. Starting in the 90s, the advertising world was profoundly changing, as well as the marketing discipline and its ever-important client/agency dynamic. Today, change is still the flavor "du jour" as they say back home. The advertising industry is still going through a profound paradigm shift fueled by the spectacular explosion of new competencies and fragmentation of media channels. We used to think that marketing wasn't rocket science. Well, that might have changed with the proliferation of data scientists and statisticians in every facet of marketing. If marketing can be mastered, then so can the art and science of building strong partnerships between advertisers and agencies.

AN INDUSTRY IN CONSTANT TRANSFORMATION

English biologist Charles Robert Darwin was attributed to say that, "It's not the strongest of the species that survives, nor the most intelligent, but the one most responsive to change." Based on that observation alone, I think you will agree that Darwin would have deserved to be a guest speaker at the next big advertising conference. The advertising industry is only forgiving to those who can quickly adapt to it. This is something that some learn the hard way. The radical changes in consumer preferences with the rise of new digital technologies, social media, influencer marketing, mobile, and user-generated content—to name a few—enable converged brand experiences and conversations that redefine the essence of the connection among agencies, media, and clients. Gone are the old ways of doing business and relationships built over martinis, as famously immortalized in the *Mad Men* series. How do you like your martini? Whatever your style or preference is, let's face it. It's likely to be shaken, not stirred. Even today, technology ranging from connected devices, self-driving vehicles, artificial intelligence, and virtual assistants, voice-activated interfaces, Virtual Reality and Augmented Reality headsets, and more, is drastically transforming business, media, consumer habits and therefore the way companies market to consumers. It's hard to keep up. During a past Advertising Week conference, former WPP CEO Martin Sorrell insisted that the definition of advertising is outdated, as the work done by agencies goes far beyond traditional vehicles. I think we all know that to be very true.

However, as the advertising industry searches for its new identity, Madison Avenue is now facing other, more significant challenges: it's increasingly squeezed between advertisers starting their own in-house agency departments and crowdsourcing vendors, while ad-tech giants like Google and Facebook go direct to clients, and large production studios and data players like Acxiom and Epsilon expand their offerings. Massive consultancies like Accenture, PwC, and Deloitte are venturing into advertising, and publications like the *Wall Street Journal,* Time Inc. (a part of Meredith Corp. since early 2018), and the *New York Times,* have built robust content and production capabilities that directly compete with agencies. What will the agency of tomorrow look like? What will the advertiser of tomorrow ask for?

Digital drastically changed the marketing discipline from customer consumption to strategy to execution, data, and analytics. Every aspect has been digitalized and the battle for marketing dollars is still under way as advertisers are shifting budgets from traditional to digital media. Companies like WPP's mPlatform and Omnicom's Annalect are on the offensive, trying to partner, but also compete, with the advertising, media, and data platforms of Google, Facebook, and Amazon. Adtech/martech is adding remarkable capabilities to the arsenal of brand advertisers, but also injecting much greater complexity, confusion, and various integration issues. When the first Marketing Technology Landscape chart from Chiefmartec. com was produced in 2011, there were only 150 companies in categories ranging from workflow management, content, social media, to analytics. It grew to 350 the following year. In 2014 the chart revealed 1,000 companies. In 2017 the chart had a total of 5,381 logos, up nearly 40 percent from the previous year. Imagine what it might look like by 2030. The relationship between brands and consumers is being redefined, and so is the relationship between advertisers and their supplier chain, including technology vendors and agency partners.

Content creation and distribution are coming together to

enable rich customer scenarios and draw in audiences. Brad Jakeman, the now former president of PepsiCo's global beverage group, claimed that it used to take four months and a budget of $2 million to create four pieces of content vs. the norm today being 400 to 4,000 pieces of content a year on a $20,000 budget. Advertisers are known to generate 20 times less content than brand fans are creating. Companies like Lego are encouraging user-generated content. For example, its Lego Ideas page invited people to propose their own ideas for new Lego sets, to recreate a Lego figurine and take pictures against diverse backgrounds all around the world. Mattel hired Tongal to crowdsource content from its community of 125,000 creators, including video specials, YouTube series, and television spots, in a two-year deal to promote Mattel's toy brands in partnership with its creative agency BBDO. At one point, Tongal's Hot Wheels video series resulted in 4 million plus YouTube views. Doritos launched a program called "Legion of the Bold," which involves asking the public for creative ideas throughout the year on everything from Vine videos to banner ads. Doritos "Crash the Super Bowl" consumer-generated ad contest, which started 10 years ago, ensures that the ad that wins the most fan votes will air during the Super Bowl. The maker of the winning ad also gets $1 million. Doritos receives over 4,500 submissions from 28 countries and it seems to pay off. Ad-scoring firm Ace Metrix ranked Doritos No. 1 on its list of the most effective Super-Bowl advertised brands from 2010-2015, ahead of Pepsi, Budweiser, and other brands that typically use big-name ad agencies.

Innovation is a big focus and will remain a competitive differentiator in advertising. Publicis launched an "innovation space" in London where it will connect startups with brands, joining similar programs launched by Iris and R/GA to fuel innovation and get ideas that expand their charter beyond advertising as we know it. Digital creative and ad buying agencies like WPP Mindshare and Possible are increasingly combining forces to deliver better solutions, reinforcing the importance of better, higher-performance content in advertiser efforts. We have also seen a record number of mergers and acquisitions in the marketing and communication sector in recent years, from the large holding companies strengthening their base to consultancies aggressively buying their way into the advertising sector.

Madison Avenue is reinventing itself as quickly as it can to adjust to client needs—both existing and future. In the process, marketing has become more measurable, and therefore far more accountable, than it has ever been. Marketers are getting increasingly more sophisticated, more demanding, and are expecting to do more with less. Will they still need agencies in the same capacity? Will they collaborate in entirely new ways to get better work? What type of agency will they rely on to compete and rapidly grow their business?

The last few years have been marked by many agency shifts, in some cases ending long term relationships (30+ year relationships that ended suddenly: Land O' Lakes and Mithun, Special K and Leo Burnett, Target and Haworth, McDonald's and Leo Burnett, Olive Garden and Grey, Accenture and MEC, Southwest and Camelot, American Airlines and TM, and Energizer and TBWA, to name a few). Advertisers are consolidating their agency roster, adding new partners, and constantly recalibrating their agency talent pool. There is also continued consolidation in the agency world, especially among digital, ad-tech, and analytics firms: holding companies and consultancies went on an acquisition spree in recent years, snatching talent around the world. Publicis's purchase of Digitas, Razorfish, and Sapient Corp. remains top of mind, showing that the convergence of digital marketing and technology requires agencies to broaden their offering to successfully compete with the big ad players.

THE SUSTAINED IMPACT OF SUCCESSFUL PARTNERSHIPS

As working with agencies becomes more complex, the quality of the partnership is also more critical than ever to a company's success, requiring client/agency relationships to reinvent themselves. Understanding what they need or expect from each other, and how they can work together isn't an insurmountable challenge. But even the most sophisticated companies are ill-prepared to make the best use of these valuable partnerships. This universal problem is about to get worse before it gets better. Until now, there wasn't any blueprint. No roadmap. No guideposts for clients or agencies to follow. How should companies harness that madness and get results? Today, small, medium, and large companies all face a similar challenge. They want to get the most from their agencies. They want business performance. Trust issues continue to be top of mind for clients, uncertain on how to address ad fraud and lack of transparency in programmatic advertising. The rate of change is unprecedented in our history. Contemporary trends have brought a new level of intricacy for brand advertisers attempting to adapt and take advantage of these new growth opportunities. More than ever, advertisers need to partner with agencies that can help them make sense of this cacophony, invest their limited resources into more impactful, measurable content, solve brand connection issues, break down barriers, better integrate their activities, and come up with new ways to strengthen conversations with consumers.

How can you tell whether your company's marketing budget is working as hard as you are? This is a question every budget owner and every business executive, whether in marketing, finance, operations, or procurement, must answer. Today, extremely sizable portions of company operating budgets are poured into agencies of every size. Budgets end up in the hands of agency executives given the task of turning them into gold. And they often do, even though there may be no other relationship structure in the corporate world today that historically has received so little oversight or been so poorly managed. Yet it flies in the face of decades of undeniable proof that successful brand advertisers have successful agency partnerships. Savvy companies, versed in the art of nurturing productive partnerships, know how to take full advantage of their agency resources to fulfill their vision. By efficiently leveraging such assets, they are able to drive greater return on investment (ROI) out of their campaigns. The less skilled will unavoidably be unsuccessful unless they engage in a set of universal principles and best practices that can apply to companies of virtually any size.

Over the years, I've seen many client/agency relationships fail. The successful ones have both the client and the agency engaged and invested in making the relationship work. This is what *Agency Mania* is all about. It's about viewing the partnership between advertisers and agencies as vital to their marketing success and nurturing and managing them as such. And I mean relentlessly, rigorously, and enthusiastically. The word "mania" comes from the Greek mania, "*to rage, to be furious.*" In Greek Mythology, a "mania" was the personification of insanity.

THE GUIDE TO ENDING THE INSANITY ONCE AND FOR ALL

It's insane to see so many otherwise sophisticated advertisers painfully fail over and over to fully leverage their agencies to further advance their marketing efforts and grow their business. It's heartbreaking to see the many opportunities lost on increasing the brand advertisers' bottom lines. It's distressing to see agencies failing to do for themselves what they preach to clients: Create differentiated value for their offering and get fairly compensated for their contribution, while under the pressure of disintermediation, zero based budgeting, and the growing involvement of procurement. It's upsetting to see sophisticated advertisers and their brilliant agencies go through trials and errors, unable to work effectively together and, as a result, lose themselves in today's "Wild Wild Waste." It's also disheartening to witness the swiftly declining levels of satisfaction and trust between advertisers and agencies. It's perplexing that while an agency is often a company's single largest marketing expense, and one of the most powerful and competitive weapons at a company's disposal, there are no formal rulebooks and few guidelines being followed on how to effectively make the best out of this unique type of partnership.

Agency Mania is such a guide. It's an invitation for advertisers and agencies to explore new ways to draw even greater value from their partnerships in today's new world order. It guides companies on how to achieve the multiplier effect of successful advertiser/agency relationships in both business performance and their mutual obsessive pursuit of marketing effectiveness. It advocates for a renewed interest on both sides to unleash this untapped force multiplier. In this business environment where consumers are more empowered than ever before, and harder to engage and motivate, advertisers are now demanding more from their agency partners. They are pushing the envelope and aggressively driving their agenda of effectiveness and efficiency through new forms of compensation, solid contract arrangements, and greater expectations. They want more rigor in the way creative and digital communications are produced and media channels are leveraged. Conversely, agencies are challenging the status quo to build new competencies and business models. They are embracing new opportunities and pushing advertisers to be innovative and to think outside the box to deliver compelling stories and consumer experiences.

Many books have been published over the years about the agency business or how agencies work. Although they offer different and valuable opinions on the subject, they don't provide a client's unique perspective. These books are often written by life-long consultants, or high-profile and iconic agency executives, but are written from an agency's viewpoint. *Agency Mania* gives companies the opportunity to be agency-savvy, to know how to get the best from an agency without necessarily having worked inside an agency. It also provides the agency profession a perspective rarely voiced about key client challenges and expectations. Marketing and procurement professionals—at all levels of seniority—are looking for ways to answer everyday questions about these important business partnerships.

There is limited training available to agencies and advertisers on this topic. There is no curriculum about the client/agency relationship at business schools. There are limited reference materials available on how to build and sustain relationships so vital to their companies' success. Yet everyone in marketing and procurement seems to unanimously agree that by failing to harness these partnerships, a company's marketing investment is at risk. After years on both the client and agency side, I experienced firsthand the tremendous challenges and opportunities associated with both well- or poorly-managed relationships and their profound impact on the bottom line performance. Later in my career, I've been privileged to create and lead Agency Management teams for some of the largest brands in the world. The world's largest brand advertisers would not be the successful companies they are today without strong agency partners. Yet, you don't need to be a Google, Microsoft, or a Pfizer to reap the benefits of these industry best practices. It sure helps to use technology to automate most client/agency-related processes. However, any advertiser, regardless of budget size, can apply these best practices. If you don't know where to start or what steps to follow, you are not alone. This book will provide answers to your most pressing questions and debunk common myths about successful client/agency partnerships. It will spur you to act and make a lasting impact. *Agency Mania* advocates for stronger, more effective partnerships that generate remarkable results. These valuable business partnerships must be based on mutual understanding, trust, collaboration, respect, and accountability. Consider yourself now one step closer to harnessing the mania.

HOW SHOULD YOU LEVERAGE THIS BOOK?

The book is organized in simple, intuitive, successive chapters that guide the reader through the process of building long-standing relationships. In the first part of the book, I describe the unique value agencies bring to their clients. I also provide some insight into the often multifaceted, rapidly changing, and confusing world of Madison Avenue. I then introduce what it takes to establish agency management as a marketing discipline and much-needed skill set. In subsequent chapters, I walk you through common-sense steps on how to choose the right agency model, how to conduct a successful search, how to set up a solid contract, how to choose the right compensation method, and how to manage expectations by scoping and briefing effectively. I also explain how to measure performance and hold both parties accountable. Along the way, I share the insight and experiences of my peers, friends, and industry experts who are some of the most brilliant minds and world-renowned leaders in the field. Their vast professional expertise and their opinions on the advertiser or the agency side provide a unique perspective that strengthens our understanding of the client/agency relationship. I also provide actionable ideas that can be applied immediately. The last chapter will describe where the industry is heading and what that means for advertisers and agencies. Knowledge alone, however, isn't the answer. It's ultimately what we do with it that matters. As you implement what you learn through these chapters, face new challenges, or celebrate successes, I encourage you to share your experience and voice your opinion at www.agencymania.com. This is a journey, and you are not traveling alone.

* * *

The industry is at a crossroad. Advertisers are experiencing a new array of challenges. The intricate nature of the consumer/advertiser/agency/media confederation is being re-examined as we see the power shifting. Similarly, the agency world is in rapid transformation, with new competencies and operating models emerging every day to adapt to new demands and energize the industry. The ecosystem is more diverse and intricate than ever before. The approach of past decades to working with agencies is now completely obsolete. Brand advertisers must find new, more effective ways to manage and partner with a multitude of agencies and priorities. In a world in which the old ways no longer seem to produce results, agencies and their clients must move toward a new level of strengthened partnership through mutual accountability and greater risk-taking. Fasten your seatbelt and prepare yourself for a wild ride. *Agency Mania* will show you the path to the advertiser/agency relationships of the 21st century, and how to get unprecedented value from these strategic partnerships. These best practices are not meant to be applied rigidly and blindly.

If the title of the book implies that a healthy level of obsession is necessary to turn agencies into powerful marketing assets, it's to underscore how little attention this critical relationship with advertisers has received over the years. It calls out some of the most common mistakes both make routinely. It sets the record straight on many topics that can damage previously productive relationships and handicap their chances for success. If you are excited about the opportunity to turn your existing relationships into productive partnerships, this book is for you. *Agency Mania* will help you draw the line between complacent relationships and energized partnerships, between weak and effective marketing, between success as a team or crushing failure.

aut vincere aut mori*

*Either to conquer or to die, in Latin

1

THE MULTIPLIER EFFECT

Why we need agencies

"The work of an advertising agency is warmly and immediately human. It deals with human needs, wants, dreams, and hopes. Its 'product' cannot be turned out on an assembly line."

—LEO BURNETT, ADMAN EXTRAORDINAIRE

Have you ever wondered what a world would be without advertising? Imagine a world with no commercials during the Super Bowl. No billboards on your commute to work. No slick video on your smartphone. No sponsored apps or "push to buy" button in your favorite social feeds. No advertising-supported free anything, for that matter. Well, don't hold your breath. While I doubt if there were signs carved into prehistoric cave entrances advertising "Ogg's Fire-Starting Service (We bring the heat!)," advertising probably goes back to whenever people first attempted to change perception and influence human behavior. Advertising remains an integral part of society. It is a sort of flamboyant window into our culture. If I've got something to sell and you perceive a need for it because of my messaging, a brand relationship has been born.

Advertising is also a synonym for FREE these days. Free makes advertising tolerable, even enjoyable at times, doesn't it? In this Free Economy we are now so addicted to, consumers are refusing to pay for content—on websites, mobile apps, and magazines. They are refusing to pay for entertainment—videos, music, games, software, and services of all types—when they can find them for free. Free everything. This contributed to the rise and domination of goliaths like Facebook and Google, which together collect most of every new dollar spent in digital advertising. Advertising will continue to increase in importance in a world where free content, free access, and free sharing is its new currency. And as long as modern enterprises need to engage, motivate, and sell, agencies that serve them will continue to flourish, drive intrinsic value, and innovate. For years, basic wisdom or simple survival instincts have led brand advertisers to use the services of external agencies—large and small—to strengthen their brands and improve their bottom line. This is their raison d'être.

A DEEPLY ROOTED SENSE OF PURPOSE

At the core of an agency's purpose lies the promise of an energetic group of individuals with common values who combine their creative and intellectual brainpower to form an agency and work together. They help clients express their purpose using various communication channels.

CLIENT VIEWPOINT

"Our customers rely on us every day to deliver the connections that matter to them and in turn, we rely on our most valuable agency partners to make it possible for us to express our purpose through a wide variety of communication vehicles." [1]

—**DIEGO SCOTTI,** EXECUTIVE VICE PRESIDENT AND CHIEF MARKETING OFFICER, VERIZON

Agencies possess unmatched expertise and specialty skills. They also share unique philosophies and methodologies. They are agents of change or renewal. They share a burning craving to take on new challenges, tell engaging stories, and come up with ideas that resonate deeply with their clients' audiences. They influence clients' marketing budgets and priorities. They are committed to driving measurable business impact. They are so much more than mere suppliers in the vast sea of the advertising supply chain. For that reason, the agency world has always been considered a desirable environment in which to learn, start a career, and make a reasonable living. For decades, it has attracted talent from a wide array of professions. In perhaps no other profession can you find a more eclectic group of gifted right- and left-brained individuals meshed together from the various cultural segments of our modern society.

WHAT ARE AGENCIES?

They are— Visionaries, Entrepreneurs, Intellectuals, Developers, Writers, Musicians, Technologists, Artists, Producers, Philosophers, Innovators, Brand Builders, Humanists, 3D Animators, Instigators, Strategists, Filmmakers, Psychologists, Researchers, Activists, Statisticians, Thought-leaders, Illustrators, Linguists, Anthropologists, Planners, Photographers, Designers, Data Analysts and Scientists, Engineers, Programmers, and Digital Czars, Media Mavens and Zealots, Geniuses and Wizards, and Gurus of all kinds —

REPRESENTING ONLY A FRACTION OF THE MANY AUDIENCES THEY REACH ON THEIR CLIENTS' BEHALF.

Agency leaders have often operated in diverse businesses and industries in their lives before advertising. They have dealt with every possible challenge that clients could throw at them. Don't be fooled by their eccentric and edgy names or offices. They are likely to be some of the most perceptive and well-rounded business people you might encounter. Of course, all that non-homogeneous talent sometimes vanishes on paper to more sterile job titles on business cards: please meet the account supervisors, account managers, strategists, creative directors, art directors, producers, production managers, planners, copy writers, data analysts, media directors, programmers, and many others who collaborate day in and out to serve clients.

CLIENT VIEWPOINT

"Innovation and disruption does not come from homogeneous groups of people." [2]
—**BRAD JAKEMAN,** FORMER PRESIDENT GLOBAL BEVERAGE GROUP, SENIOR ADVISOR & CONSULTANT, PEPSICO

They all share a common desire to create magic. They want to tell a story that deeply moves people. They want to build content and experiences that create brand affinities. They are resourceful innovators. They are passionate advisers. They are relentless advocates. They use all available media to make a compelling case and prompt consumers to act. Of course, there are many types of agencies. Yet, creativity is always core to an agency. Creative talent always symbolized the unconventional personal style, ponytails, and fashionable attire of the industry. Brilliant thinkers and creative minds like David Ogilvy made it possible for top brand advertisers to produce breakthrough work that sticks in the marketplace and changes the conversation with consumers. In a world where audiences are increasingly multitasking and overstimulated, with access to significantly more information than they can possibly assimilate, creative plays a vital role in engaging them in exciting, fresh, and compelling ways. Even in the digital world where data czars, scientists, and technologists now have a predominant seat at the agency table, a powerful idea well executed and filled with "oohs and aahs" is what prevails and wins consumers. The essentials of storytelling in the digital age have profoundly changed. The media agency, historically associated with big budgets, is producing rich insights about evolving media consumption and consumer behavior. The PR firm is now associated with earned media, influence, and social marketing. The digital agency is creating platforms and even product experiences for real-time brand and customer exchanges. These agencies all play a more active role at the client's table, earlier than they ever did before, because great ideas can come from anywhere these days.

CLIENT VIEWPOINT

"We needed to start with a clean sheet of paper. So we chose a strategic and planning partner, Assembly, which built its company on that very premise. We wanted the thinkers, the scientists, the technologists, and psychologists to help us revolutionize our media and marketing." [3]

—JULIE RIEGER, PRESIDENT, CHIEF DATA STRATEGIST & HEAD OF MEDIA, 20TH CENTURY FOX FILM

This is a unique business. Perhaps in no other industry can you attend an "Idea Conference" in which creative geniuses gather to discuss the genesis of creativity and idea-making. What clients truly want is ideas that persuade and engage their target audiences. Whether you consider it art or science, persuasion and engagement are difficult to create. These storytellers love to energize brands, and to come up with big, lasting ideas that speak to people with a distinct emotional voice. They have found a creative outlet in their professional life to express it and make a difference. They partner with other specialized disciplines to channel their creativity and turn ideas into powerful brand experiences like Leo

Burnett's "Like A Girl" for P&G's Always, Ogilvy & Mather's "Evolution" for Unilever/Dove, Fallon's BMW "The Hire," and Crispin Porter + Bogusky's "Subservient Chicken" Burger King video. Many of these noteworthy campaigns have been celebrated at the annual Cannes Lions Festival of Creativity in France, a sort of Academy Awards-style event for advertising.

AGENCY VIEWPOINT

"Clients should expect agencies to reformulate people's most basic perceptions about the world and a product or service in that world. To do that, the client must simply expect brilliance. Sometimes that brilliance comes from objectivity and fresh eyes, which is why outside agencies can be useful. But ideas can, theoretically, come from anywhere." [4]

—**JEFF GOODBY**, CO-CHAIRMAN AND PARTNER, GOODBY,

SILVERSTEIN & PARTNERS

HOW DO ADVERTISERS BENEFIT FROM AGENCIES?
Agencies in the various advertising and marketing communication disciplines are so prevalent that perhaps we take them for granted. To advertisers who have reaped the benefits of working with agencies for years, the question, "How do advertisers benefit from agencies?" seems silly and grossly irrelevant. If you are using an agency today, you might even be tempted to skip this chapter. Yet the question seems to boil down to this: Are agencies a luxury or a necessity? Stated differently: So, what makes them so valuable to their clients? What do agencies offer that is so unique that their clients cannot create it on their own?

Agencies are all about talent. Advertisers always look for top talent. As much as 75 percent of all agency costs are for people. Agencies, often considered a mere extension of their clients' marketing teams, a sort of outsourced workforce, fulfill many critical and diverse functions on a client's behalf: they help successfully promote products and services; they choose the right media mix to reach a quality audience; they compose persuasive copy and press releases; they produce elegant ads; they create memorable jingles as well as sharp and witty 30-second commercials. They also tap into their knowledge of industries (like Health Care), or a demographic segment (like Generation X or Hispanic) to come up with messages that truly resonate with an audience. They leverage technology to build tools and applications and produce highly engaging experiences and conversations. They persuade customers to become brand advocates and manage loyalty programs. They take an active part in the launch of new product lines and major events. They push clients to think "outside the box." They create branded games, online content and mobile services, and software applications. They write code. They write copy. They place media. They come up with new means to facilitate conversations between brands and audiences. They come up with breakthrough ideas, then bring them to life, using tools, processes, or even approaches that are unique to their agency. They collaborate. They consult. They guide.

AGENCY VIEWPOINT

"Digital has changed our industry completely. If you don't change, you are out of the picture." [6]

—**MAURICE LÉVY,** CHAIRMAN OF THE SUPERVISORY BOARD
AND FORMER CHAIRMAN, PUBLICIS GROUPE

The value proposition of agencies has historically been anchored into the right side of the brain where creativity, subjectivity, and emotional connections converge. As the world becomes digital in all aspects of our society and communication infrastructure, agencies' value proposition is increasingly more about the left side of the brain where the power of measurement, analytics, programmatic media buying, and the science of marketing come together to provide advertisers with more targeted, more scalable, and more accountable capabilities. In short, agencies can be a valuable think tank, and the amplified voice of the client. They bring together a mix of talent and experience in various disciplines. They do it better, more efficiently, more quickly, with greater depth and deeper insight than a client could.

While the average tenure of a relationship is shrinking rapidly due to insanely short CMO tenures, some of these relationships have exceeded 50 years. In the case of GE, their relationship with Omnicom goes back to the beginning of the 20th century, when BBDO became the agency for GE's lighting division in 1920. L'Oreal's relationship with Publicis Groupe goes back to the early 1930s with the company founders, Eugène Schueller and Marcel Bleustein-Blanchet. Some of these relationships thrive and survive the pressure of time. On the opposite end of the spectrum, sadly enough, we've all witnessed dysfunctional relationships that don't survive long enough to celebrate their first-year anniversary. Longevity of an account is often the sign of a strong relationship. Isn't this true in any business—including yours? Advertisers gain more value from their agencies over time as the agency resources assigned to the account develop a deeper institutionalized understanding of their business and ways of getting things done. They also build personal ties and friendships that they can rely on during difficult times . . . and those will come without a doubt. Business is personal, especially in the business of agencies. But to fully benefit from the role agencies play, clients must acknowledge what their unique competencies are.

REALIZING THE FULL VALUE AGENCIES BRING TO THE TABLE
Here are the most common benefits advertisers realize by working with external agency partners:

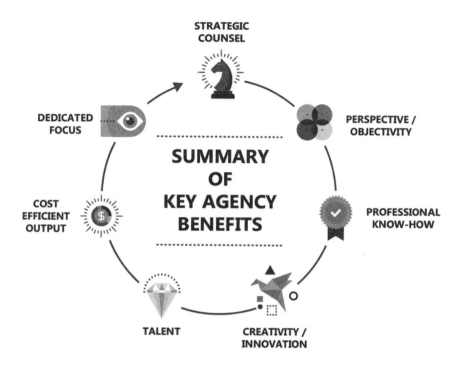

STRATEGIC COUNSEL

DEDICATED FOCUS

PERSPECTIVE / OBJECTIVITY

SUMMARY OF KEY AGENCY BENEFITS

COST EFFICIENT OUTPUT

PROFESSIONAL KNOW-HOW

TALENT

CREATIVITY / INNOVATION

Strategic Counsel: Advertisers get the most value when they view their agencies as strategic consultants and trusted advisors to their business. The essence of the agency business is to deliver fresh, strategically-grounded ideas based on consumer insight and forward-looking perspectives. Agencies employ talented resources such as strategists and account planners to confront and conquer challenging client situations. They take into consideration how consumers interact with brands. Consumer insight is vital to understanding and enhancing the relationship between consumers and brands. Agencies can be powerful think tanks that turn information into insight, insight into strategies, strategies into action plans, and action plans into measurable business results. As trusted advisors, agencies share their professional opinions, use benchmarks and best practices, suggest alternative courses of action, and come up with creative solutions for clients in need of answers.

CLIENT VIEWPOINT

"The value agencies bring to clients is their perspective, fresh ideas, benchmarking, and best practices. If they are constrained by their clients, as clients sometimes do, then they will not achieve the full value of the relationship." [7]

—MICHAEL E. THYEN, DIRECTOR OF PROCUREMENT, INTERNATIONAL BUSINESS UNIT, ELI LILLY AND COMPANY

But this role can be played successfully only by agencies that have earned the trust of their clients and have been invited to actively contribute to strategic agendas. They must be given the opportunity to come up with sound recommendations backed up by credible research and years of solid, relevant experience in their field of expertise. Agencies make a significant contribution by leading, guiding, or simply enabling better strategic client decisions.

Perspective/Objectivity: Not unlike management consultants before them, agencies bring a vast amount of collective experience from current and past clients. Obviously, experience comes in many different flavors. If an agency specializes in an industry, audience, or business category, it can significantly profit from having clients with similar interests. Agencies look for synergies in current and past client engagements. The larger the client portfolio, the richer and the more relevant are the agency offerings. The agency knows what works, what doesn't, and learns from past successes and failures, so clients don't have to at their own expense. Agencies may hire externally when they need deep technical knowledge. Agencies are well known for their ability to read and interpret the attitudes, behaviors, and preferences of customer audiences. They are valued for their aptitude to find ways to catch the customers' attention, build a positive connection to the brand, influence their perceptions, and persuade them to act.

AGENCY VIEWPOINT

"We continue to believe that our role as an agnostic consultant is key and allows us to provide clients with the recommendations and services that are best for their business." [8]
—**MICHAEL ROTH,** CHAIRMAN AND CHIEF EXECUTIVE OFFICER,
INTERPUBLIC GROUP

By leveraging their diverse portfolio of clients, agencies can deliver unique perspectives based on the wealth of knowledge accumulated one client at a time. They eliminate potential inefficiencies and increase chances of success for their clients. Too close to the trees, advertisers do not always see the forest and cannot act objectively. It can be quite difficult to remain truly objective when balancing priorities and facing business pressure. Acting as a neutral third-party, agencies are more likely to be unbiased when confronted with difficult business decisions.

Professional Know-How: Years of hands-on expertise translates into procedural knowledge, discrete methodologies, exceptional capabilities, and approaches that are worth gold to advertisers. Agencies employ talented individuals with specialized skills that come with years of practice. In the end, it doesn't matter how good or how fast the car is if the driver is grossly inexperienced. To create sustainable value that increases the client stickiness factor and monetizes their intellectual property, agencies often develop and refine innovative proprietary tools, unique approaches, structured processes, and measurement systems based on proven best practices.

CLIENT VIEWPOINT

"If you take a step back, agencies are outsourced marketing departments with specialties in things marketers don't do themselves." [9]
—BRIAN WIESER, SENIOR RESEARCH ANALYST, PIVOTAL

Here are a few examples: OMD's strategic planning process called *OMDCheckmate*™, Mediaedge:cia's *MEC Navigator,* Y&R's brand management tool, *Brand Asset Valuator®, and* Ogilvy & Mather's *360 Degree Brand Stewardship®.* Agencies use their know-how and these expert tools to become an extension of their client's marketing team, focusing on what marketers won't do themselves.

Creativity/Innovation: Agencies exhibit great ingenuity at solving marketing problems. Although this may vary slightly based on the type of discipline, there is always some element of creativity and innovation in what they do. Agencies are skilled creative storytellers by trade. Agencies have the unusual ability to distill the essence of an idea, blending their passion for solving business issues with a strong instinctive creative panache that leaves audiences begging. Some of these breakthrough ideas turned into hyped campaigns like DDB's and Budweiser's "Whassup," TBWA/Media Arts Lab's and Apple's "Get a Mac," and McCann Erickson's and MasterCard's "Priceless."

CLIENT VIEWPOINT

"The industry is changing so rapidly. Agencies must stay ahead of the curve. I look to our agencies to come up with new, breakthrough ideas. What's the next big thing in digital for example? The agencies must be the ones telling us what we should be doing in the next few years." [10]

—MARTINE REARDON, FORMER CHIEF MARKETING OFFICER,

MACY'S

They tell stories that move, connect, and captivate people. They must tap into cultural trends and find new, innovative ways to communicate and engage with their audience. They must come up with fresh, inspiring ideas that survive a swipe on their mobile device, the remote control, or the click of a mouse. The alchemy of creativity and innovation is a fundamental agency competency. This unique ability is often recognized at major industry events like the Clio Awards, Effie Awards, Reggie Awards, or the ANDYs to name a few.

Talent: The agency business, arguably like any other service industry, is a business of people. A strong talent base will determine the fate of an agency and its ability to attract clients. Big agencies can afford to hire big names across the board that then attract key clients. If you have been working with agencies for a while, you've noticed that the agency ecosystem is well contained. People tend to know each other.

CLIENT VIEWPOINT

"We need the talent and creativity of agencies. An in-house model can lead to brands becoming insular and self-serving and doesn't give a reality check on whether we are talking to consumers and tapping into cultural trends." [11]

—LISA WOOD, CHIEF MARKETING OFFICER, ATOM BANK

Talented agency staff blossom professionally when they are hired, trained, and managed by individuals with similar backgrounds. They benefit hugely from ongoing direct exposure to peers with similar skills and interests from which they can learn and improve their trade. They are given outlets to grow and enrich their skills. In such an environment, creative people have constant exposure or insight that only a diversified client portfolio can provide. It's not that less diversified companies do not attract top people, they simply do not have the type of talent that can be found mainly in major cosmopolitan and cultural epicenters like New York, San Francisco, LA, Chicago, London, or Paris, among other cities, where agencies with a large and diverse client base prosper. Agencies in major cosmopolitan areas can attract people of similar passion, professional interests, and career aspirations. Talent is a core part of the value agencies are responsible for delivering to clients.

Cost Efficient Outputs: The economic value of agencies is well understood, but not always easy to articulate. There are often substantial cost benefits realized by engaging with a certain type of agency rather than hiring resources internally, especially when dealing with media agencies. Media agencies can buy media in large volume, offering economies of scale that no client could replicate on his or her own. That benefit is passed on to the client and clients gladly pay for that service. Cost efficiency can also be realized when sharing resources, getting things done in less time and with fewer resources.

AGENCY VIEWPOINT

"We are in the business of selling creativity as quantified by the amount of time and the number of people. The success of our business is measured by numerical growth: revenue, margin, size, number of people and wins. But actually, the world is going in the other way. It's now about achieving the most with the least. It's about figuring out how to "Do More with Less." Less time, less money, and less people. Companies that will be successful—in 2020 and beyond—are those who will be smaller than their predecessors but can have bigger impact and influence." [12]

—REI INAMOTO, FORMER WORLDWIDE CHIEF CREATIVE OFFICER, AKQA

The flexibility that comes along with hiring external resources is worth highlighting as well. Advertisers can hire a portion of agency resources they couldn't afford otherwise. When budgets fluctuate, agencies can spread the impact of these fluctuations over multiple clients by adjusting staffing plans and managing the workload. Clients can more easily adjust the number and type of resources utilized, whether dedicated, partially dedicated, or freelance, leaving that responsibility and headache to their agencies. Global agencies can also provide access to international markets that would otherwise be cost-prohibitive for an advertiser to enter. Typically, clients call on their agencies because they are expected to do more with less than they would do on their own.

Dedicated Focus: Advertisers have their own business to worry about. It takes unique dedication, undivided focus, and long hours to compete successfully in any industry. A brand advertiser pours all it has into being the best at what it does. Similarly, agencies are laser-focused on developing their core expertise and being good at what they do: problem-solving. Companies often subcontract to third party firms in several business expense categories, and they should look at advertising services the same way.

CLIENT VIEWPOINT

"You have asked for their help for a reason, so why would you pretend you know the answer? They are problem solvers. And creative problem solvers, which you probably are not." [13]

—LESYA LYSYJ, FORMER CMO, HEINEKEN USA AND PRESIDENT US, WELCH'S

Advertisers want to work with agencies that have built deep expertise in areas that they don't master and probably never will. And with focus, comes speed, which is increasingly critical to companies that must respond in real time and on a constant basis to competitive situations or rapidly changing market conditions. Their dedicated focus pays off, and advertisers clearly benefit.

WHEN THE WHOLE IS GREATER THAN THE SUM OF ITS PARTS

What's keeping most CMOs up at night? Is it the volatile economic environment, or financial pressure and shrinking budgets? Is it the uncertainty of how to sail through a storm of technology innovations and new media? Or is it the unexpected marketing strike by a key competitor? Perhaps it's all of this and more. Companies are facing an insane number of business challenges, organizational pressure, and more intense competition. Marketers at every organizational level understand that the key to business longevity is not to sell commodities and compete on price, but rather to sell innovative products that can be differentiated and sold at a premium. This is what companies with strong brands do.

CLIENT VIEWPOINT

"It's always hard to speculate what the future will look like, but today we're very reliant on the expertise of outside partners."[14]
—ERIC REYNOLDS, FORMER CMO, NOW VP GENERAL MANAGER—EUROPE, MIDDLE EAST, AFRICA & ASIA, THE CLOROX CO.

Naturally, advertisers are anxious about keeping up with innovation, rapidly changing consumer habits, emerging media, and new technologies that the competition might already be tapping into. They are concerned about finding the right mix and getting a reasonable return on their marketing investment. They agonize about over-investing in some areas and under-investing in others. They wonder about a world where consumers are increasingly in control and content is harder to produce and manage. What content should be created, co-created or simply curated? Who should be on point? In addition, CMOs are under tremendous pressure by CEOs and CFOs alike. Budgets are tight, resources are limited, and there is never enough time. Balancing the need for short-term performance, such as revenue and share growth, without sacrificing brand building, can be tricky. This is where the agency comes in.

AGENCY VIEWPOINT

"If we want to continue to be a valued partner for our clients, we have to be able to face their challenges with them." [15]
—ARTHUR SADOUN, CHAIRMAN AND CEO, PUBLICIS GROUPE

They need the professional expertise and know-how of an experienced agency partner that will help them to tackle these burdensome questions side by side. I like to think about it as the *"multiplier effect"* of agencies on a client's business. First coined by the philosopher Aristotle, the expression, "The whole is greater than the sum of its parts, best summarizes the multiplier effect of agencies on their client business. In the military world, they refer to it as "force multiplier," a factor that dramatically increases the combat effectiveness of a given military force. In the field of economics, it's described as the effect that occurs when a change in spending causes a disproportionate change in aggregate demand. Whether you apply this concept to the military, engineering, macroeconomics, or mathematics, you get the idea. In marketing, it's about multiplying media exposures, customer experiences, and brand value, to ultimately cause a disproportionate impact on business results. Building a brand, protecting it, strengthening it so it favorably differentiates a company's offering and decisively influences consumer preferences at those moments of "truth," requires the type of expertise that only top-notch agencies offer.

CLIENT VIEWPOINT

"At Taco Bell, we look at three approaches to content: Create, Co-Create, and Curate. Create is our own content, Co-Create is content created in partnership with consumers, and Curate is taking the user generated content we like and showing it to more people." [16]

—CHRIS BRANDT, FORMER CMO, TACO BELL CORP, EVP AND CHIEF BRAND OFFICER, BLOOMIN' BRANDS, INC.

FORMULA FOR
OPERATIONALIZING SUCCESS

THE RIGHT PRIORITIES + **THE RIGHT TALENT** Internal & External + **THE RIGHT PROCESS** + **THE RIGHT TOOLS** = **SUCCESSFUL MARKETING**

INVESTMENT

The formula for operationalizing success is to combine the necessary priorities, processes, tools, and talent to make advertiser teams better clients that produce better work. Talent comes in two primary flavors: internal and external, i.e., agencies. Without this crucial ingredient, they are unlikely to succeed. Therefore, a company's potential to successfully tackle its challenges and win in the marketplace is directly correlated with its ability to partner and work in tandem with the right agency. As we saw previously, agencies have many benefits that make them priceless resources. The best agency/client relationships will be based on a sound assessment of the capabilities and resources most valued by the client. Brand advertisers need agencies because they provide something to them that is unique and critical to their marketing success and has a multiplying effect on their bottom line.

TOP 3
BEST PRACTICES
for Advertisers

① Learn to appreciate the nuances and unique qualities of the agency world.

② Identify the agency qualities most relevant to your business needs.

③ Combine priorities, talent, process, and tools, to operationalize success.

2

GOLDEN EGGS

Understanding the mysterious
world of Madison Avenue

"There are very few men of genius in advertising agencies. But we need all we can find. Almost without exception they are disagreeable. Don't destroy them. They lay golden eggs."

—DAVID MACKENZIE OGILVY, ADMAN LEGEND

For most people, Madison Avenue is a north-south avenue in busy Manhattan, characteristic of a crowded and noisy New York City neighborhood with tall, grey, imposing buildings. In the world of advertising and communications, Madison Avenue has a much different connotation. For years, it symbolized the explosive growth of the advertising industry of the 20th century as it saw famous agencies like BBDO open shop there and grow insanely rapidly. Madison Avenue became the gold rush of advertising as companies poured substantial budgets into the capable hands of agencies to build iconic brands, to gain market share, and lay their clients' golden eggs. Although

Madison Avenue saw its fair share of agency success stories and rising stars, more than anything it represented the birth of a respectable profession and, in many ways, institutionalized it. Madison Avenue became synonymous with an entire industry. At the heart of the relationship between agencies and advertisers is the marriage of innovation and creativity. The proliferation of media channels, including the rapid development and integration of digital platforms, technologies, and mediums, has increasingly fragmented consumer audiences, making it more complex for brand advertisers to reach their target audiences in a cost-effective way.

FROM MAD MEN TO SMART PLAYERS

The advertising industry has always been grounded in the business of generating compelling ideas and engaging consumer experiences from the relentless, creative minds that walk the halls of agencies. Despite its glorious past, the agency industry has not always benefited from a solid reputation. Madison Avenue has also often been stereotyped as a business that is more reckless and more ruthless, arrogant, egocentric, and competitive than other professions. Because the benefits agencies provide to clients have historically been difficult to demonstrate with quantifiable precision, it often led to high profile agency reviews as incumbent agencies attempted to defend themselves. To add shame to injury, the industry's image has often been tarnished by scandals and lawsuits due to improper billings, accounting irregularities, claims of fraud such as kickbacks and rebates, and other types of illegal practices investigated by the DOJ. The reputation of globe-trotting agency executives with larger-than-life personalities and lavish, glamorous lifestyles has fueled growing concerns among advertisers and forced them to scrutinize agency billings and conduct regular audits. Thankfully, legislation such as Sarbanes-Oxley significantly improved client confidence because of greater transparency in agency financial and accounting practices.

AGENCY VIEWPOINT

"Agencies have to constantly be moving, and you can't just be content with where you are. When you see all of the new threats that we have as an industry and new companies and startups, it's about how you attract the right talent, because that's where the ideas come from." [17]

—CHRIS WALLRAPP, PRESIDENT, HILL HOLLIDAY

Recent AMC Originals' hit television show *Mad Men* exemplifies the fact that for decades agencies have been synonymous with sexy 30-second TV commercials, interruptive one-way communications, clever taglines, and three-martini lunches with glamorous women. The Golden Globe-winning TV drama series played on stereotypes and realistically captured the lives of ruthlessly competitive men and women of Madison Avenue in the ego-driven 1960s advertising world. After all, unflattering events such as the Julie Roehm-Wal-Mart Stores, Inc.-Draftfcb saga, the Shona Seifert ONDCP conviction, and the Dentsu sexual-harassment and discrimination scandal have given prosecutors and the public something to chew on, blurring the line between 1960s fiction and 21st century reality.

These scandals that involved massive timesheet inflation schemes and accounting fraud woes have given a black eye to the whole industry. The media rebate issue and the lack of transparency about media and production practices from the past few years, especially when agencies are acting as agents and principals on behalf of their clients, have led to clients scrutinizing every aspect of their financial and contractual relationships. But the insular post-World War II Madison Avenue and today's communication industry arguably have less and less in common every year. The principles of how agencies produce their art form might not have changed much, but the acceleration of technology and changes in consumer behavior and media outlets have changed the game. The industry has grown up, and it made changes of cataclysmic nature to deeply alter its course, from Madison Avenue to its new centers of gravity in Paris, Tokyo, London, and soon New Delhi and Beijing.

Today, despite the hiccups of the past, the agency world still enjoys the solid reputation established by industry pioneers and legends such as Marcel Bleustein, David Ogilvy, Leo Burnett, Bill Bernbach, and Jay Chiat. Most of these charismatic founders proudly named their agencies after themselves, extending their creative vision, business philosophy, and wisdom for many years to come. These respectable business leaders also helped put the business of marketing and communication services on the map, bringing together marketers, agencies, and media companies. More importantly, they built a reputation for hard work, break-through ideas, and an undivided passion for their profession. They were and remain the soul and the spiritual stone on which this industry has been built and the source of its integrity and ethics code. They shared many characteristics, but it is worth noting that today, they are all deceased. They belong to a glorified past. Today, the world of agencies looks more like an offshoot of the Silicon Valley, with techies walking the halls of their offices.

Their footsteps have been followed by a new era of talented agency entrepreneurs such as Jeff Goodby, Irwin Gotlieb, Dan Wieden, Linda Kaplan Thaler, Jean-Marie Dru, Bob Greenberg, Shelly Lazarus and Lee Clow, to name a few, as well as the infamous financial moguls and industry captains Sir Martin Sorrell (former CEO of WPP), John Wren (Omnicom Group), and Michael Roth (Interpublic Group). A new era of leaders is emerging: Moroccan French businessman Maurice Levy remained the CEO of Publicis from 1987 to 2017 and has now been replaced by Arthur Sadoun. Mark Reed is now CEO of WPP, replacing the legendary Sir Martin Sorrell. By the time this book is published, we may see other thought-leaders, movers, and shakers in this vibrant industry come into the spotlight. This industry has profoundly reinvented itself over the years, adapting to rapidly changing market conditions, a transformed media landscape, evolving consumer habits, and high client demands. If there is one thing constant in the agency business, it's change itself. Agencies feel squeezed as clients build in-house agency capabilities, and they see the continued decline of stable, long-term retained-based accounts. The competition is also multiplying with the entry of consultancies, tech firms, and publishers creating their own offerings, like the *New York Times'* T-Brand Studio, which offers a unique combination of creative content services and distribution.

OVERCOMING THE "WE DO IT TOO" SYNDROME

Although slogans like Nike's "Just Do It," Avis's "We Try Harder," or De Beers' "A Diamond Is Forever" are memorable, and icons like The Marlboro Man, The Energizer Bunny, and Ronald McDonald stick with us as avid consumers, they are the tip of the iceberg and a gross under-estimation of what agencies do today for their clients. Agencies now go much further and deeper into their clients' marketing communications layers than what may have in the past been seen as simply delivering clever messaging: They now tell compelling stories, create brand experiences while educating and entertaining, and eventually turn customers into fervent brand advocates. Agencies are no longer in the business of disrupting but are instead adding value to the brand through relevant storytelling along with data mining and consumer engagements.

CLIENT VIEWPOINT

"For agencies, the critical thing is to find what they're really good at and where they can really add value. An agency can't be all things to all men, particularly because marketing now is such a diverse range of disciplines, from highly creative to data-focused. It would be ideal [to find an agency that can do that] but I don't think it's possible." [19]

—JENNELLE TILLING, FORMER GLOBAL CHIEF MARKETING OFFICER, KFC, FOUNDER AND CHIEF BRAND STRATEGIST AT MARKETING WITH INSIGHT

Consumer consumption of media has evolved significantly in the past two decades. The number of media vehicles has never been greater, leaving consumers with more options to choose from, but with the same amount of time to make choices. Inevitably, each of these channels is getting less reach, and media fragmentation is forcing advertisers to rethink their marketing investments. Emerging technologies have opened the door for ongoing media innovations while creating new challenges. Today you can't leave an agency meeting without hearing about the next big thing on mobile, AR, VR, Voice-activation, or AI—new media opportunities and new exciting consumer applications that, yet unproven, have great upside potential. Are agencies prepared for this unprecedented demand for innovation? Did agencies overestimate their importance to advertisers? Do they have the skills to tap into these opportunities? Clients want to shift their spending to reach consumers where they are, and that means while playing games, or on their smartphone and iPad, in their instant messengers, their Xbox game console, their blogs or social media accounts, so be it. They want to speak to the diversity in their customer audiences (Hispanic, Asian, African-American, Gay/Lesbian, and other consumer segments).

Media fragmentation is not likely to slow down. Advertisers will need to weigh the benefits of having increasingly fewer mainstream, large-scale media options, or the highly targeted, small-reach, innovative, but more expensive channels that are offered to them. Advertisers continue to hire top talent in this area to identify and harness new opportunities. This is changing the balance of power, and agencies are challenged to deliver incremental value from client engagements. Companies are putting a premium on understanding customer behavior and how they respond to various media exposures. These new communication and distribution channels inevitably demand specialized skills. Thankfully, agencies have responded to the demand by introducing a wide array of specialized offerings that take full advantage of these new consumer trends. They have built in-house capabilities or forged relationships with technology players. They want to remain clients' trusted advisors beyond the traditional world that Madison Avenue has been known for. They are also eager to cash in on faster-growing, higher-margin opportunities. For clients, relying on one agency to cover such a wide spectrum of media and audience segments is more difficult than ever, and few agencies are in a position to do so seamlessly for their clients. The need for specialization, segmentation, and innovation often requires them to hire specialized firms to access resources that wouldn't otherwise be available to them.

AGENCY VIEWPOINT

"Technology is too fast, but the success of R/GA is that it's a business that's based on an idea rather than a craft. The problem with the advertising agency model is that it's based on a craft." [20]

—BARRY WACKSMAN, EVP, GLOBAL CHIEF STRATEGY OFFICER,

R/GA

The agency business is no longer what it used to be. The landscape is changing so quickly, it's hard to keep track of who's who, between the new guys on the block and this year's top players. There is always a new competency being developed, a major shake-up on the way, another game-changing merger or acquisition. It's quite easy to get lost these days in the maze of the complicated world of Madison Avenue. However, to make informed decisions, clients must fully understand its dynamic and complex nature. Unfortunately, there are no definite ways to organize the vast, rapidly changing, and unpredictable world of advertising and marketing communications services. I wish there were, for the marketer's sake. Anyone looking up the extensive and diverse list of services provided by agencies on their websites could understandably ask, *"What is it that they do again?"* Agencies certainly know how to spin, sometimes promising capabilities they are unable to truly deliver. And no agency wants to be put in a box. Agencies have mastered the art of talking about themselves in ways that make you wonder what they actually *don't* do (what I like to fondly call the *"we do it too"* syndrome). It's apparent that no agency wants to miss the phone call from a prospective client simply because the agency didn't list everything they "could do" in their presentation materials.

Over the years, I've met with all kind of agencies all praising their unique proposition, from the boutique shop, proudly raving about its independent spirit, speed, and low overhead, to the proud network-affiliated agencies singing the praises of end-to-end integrated offerings and the benefits of economies of scale and global reach. For most of them, having a value proposition that was truly authentic and differentiated was half the battle. The other half was convincing clients that they were uniquely qualified to do the job. To add to the confusion, publishers and digital advertisers are offering creative services to advertisers, cutting out the middlemen in the process at times, or inserting themselves into the agency supply chain. For example, Facebook built its in-house capability through its Creative Shop which helps brands like Budweiser, Ford, Sprint, Toyota, and agencies like Droga5, 360i, and DigitasLBi understand how to effectively use Facebook and Instagram as well as new formats in their campaigns.

TYPES OF ADVERTISING, MARKETING, AND COMMUNICATION AGENCIES

Although there are no industry standards per se, there are some fundamental principles on how to logically group agencies. First, agencies range in size and scope. From the large full-service agencies headquartered in major cosmopolitan cities with satellite offices in every corner of the continent, to the small agencies operated out of a single office space, there is an agency offering for every client. Large agency networks have big clients, domestically and internationally, with thousands of employees and billings in the billions of dollars. Their organizational structure, whether small or large, is for the most part identical, with functions like strategic planning, account management, creative, production, data, and media. It's likely to vary slightly based on scale and specialized areas. The proliferation of digital that can now be found in most marketing disciplines has blurred the line, making the distinction between "above and below the line" (a now dated term) now virtually obsolete. It's much more difficult to tell who does what. "How" the work is produced or distributed is no longer a meaningful way to distinguish advertising and marketing communications disciplines. Rather, it's identifying the "role" they serve in the marketing funnel that is most helpful in understanding how they contribute to the mix.

AGENCY VIEWPOINT

"We haven't adapted. When people talk about creativity in our industry, they're talking about Don Draper. They're not talking about the new definitions. Believe it or not, people inside media agencies are creative. Software engineers are creative . . . It's the definition of it—we haven't contextualized it correctly yet." [21]

—**SIR MARTIN SORRELL**, FORMER CHIEF EXECUTIVE OFFICER, WPP AND EXECUTIVE CHAIRMAN, S4 CAPITAL

No discipline can operate in a silo today; it requires partnerships and alliances among independent agencies, integrated or combined offerings by large agencies, or internal client coordination to turn these aggregate resources into more effectively channeled and unified efforts. Social media, for example, have profoundly changed how we define the PR discipline today. PR is now increasingly about engaging and monitoring influential audiences through social networks and earned media. Although most agencies would rightfully argue that being labeled as either a "creative" or a "PR" firm in a multifaceted marketing world is no longer that distinctive, it remains a practical way of categorizing agency services and making sense out of today's cacophony. Although there are no agreed upon standards for how to organize the vast range of services available to advertisers, thankfully holding companies and industry awards like Clio Awards, Cannes Lions, and Effie Awards, all contributed to a somewhat logical grouping that can be used by advertisers to make sense of what they do, as summarized below. Please note that agencies are rarely falling into a single category of service, so expect them to go across multiple categories.

TYPES OF SERVICES

CORE SERVICES:

Full service	Branding
Creative	Social media
Digital	Search
Media	Promotional and activation
Direct /CRM	Experiential/Event
PR/PA	Multi-cultural

OTHER SPECIALTIES :

Market Research	Brand Strategy and Consultancy
Production	Design (brand, packaging, environmental, etc.)
Video	Shopper Marketing and Point of Sales/Merchandising
DRTV	
Content Marketing	Email Marketing
Visual/Sound Identity	Entertainment/Event Marketing
Product Placement	Loyalty
Customer Analytics and Measurement	Data Management
Customer & Data Intelligence	Corporate Communications and Employer Branding
	Custom and Media/Publishing
Mobile Marketing	B2B, etc...

CATEGORIES OF ADVERTISING AND MARKETING COMMUNICATION AGENCIES

TYPE	DESCRIPTION OF SERVICES PROVIDED	AGENCY EXAMPLES
FULL SERVICE	These agencies offer an integrated approach to advertising and marketing communications, providing end-to-end services to clients looking for a single one-stop shop to handle the various elements of their marketing mix.	Ogilvy, Leo Burnett Worldwide, Saatchi & Saatchi Fallon, McCann Worldgroup, Young & Rubicam Group, Publicis Worldwide, TBWA Worldwide, BBDO Worldwide, DDB Worldwide Communications Group, Denstu Aegis Network, and more.
CREATIVE	These agencies are primarily focused on advertising services with strategy and creativity at their core. They range in size from small independent boutiques to large creative agencies (e.g., McCann) which are part of a full-service network (e.g., McCann Worldgroup). They offer great creative thinking and breakthrough ideas. This type of agency is particularly tailored to clients looking for creative services to complement a roster of specialized agencies or for clients looking for highly creative work and big ideas that can brought to life across many channels.	McCann, MullenLowe, VMLY&R, mcgarrybowen, Droga5, 72andSunny, Goodby, Silverstein & Partners, Venables Bell & Partners, Martin Agency, Anomaly, and more.
MEDIA	These agencies handle full service media planning and media buying on their clients' behalf. Decoupled from advertising services as the media landscape became more complex to maneuver, media planning and buying across media channels requires economies of scale to secure competitive buys and deep subject-matter expertise to provide insightful planning recommendations. Some of these media companies have built specialties, such as print advertising, insert media, outdoor advertising, paid and organic search, branded entertainment, asset barter, and so forth. Others combine multiple media agencies to form powerful and diverse media agency networks.	MEC, Starcom, Denstu Aegis, MediaCom, PHD, Havas Media, Maxus, Zenith, Mindshare, Vizeum, UM, Carat, Mediavest/Spark, Initiative, OMD, Heart & Science, Horizon Media, and more.

TYPE	DESCRIPTION OF SERVICES PROVIDED	AGENCY EXAMPLES
DIRECT / CRM	These agencies provide direct response, direct mail, database marketing, and customer relationship services. Unlike advertising and media services that have historically been focused on driving awareness and perception change, direct marketing/relationship marketing aims at triggering a response that can be acted upon. These services are typically used by clients looking to build relationship programs, increase customer loyalty and advocacy, run direct sales and demand generation, and lead qualification/maturation campaigns in traditional media, and increasingly more in digital media.	Epsilon, Wunderman, Acxiom, Rapp, Experian Marketing Services, Merkle, Harte Hanks, and more.
PUBLIC RELATIONS & PUBLIC AFFAIRS	These agencies help clients handle their PR and PA activities and tend to focus on traditional activities such as corporate image, media relations, media training/events, press releases and media materials, issues management, speech writing and speaker placement, as well as innovative PR competencies such as blogging, social media, crisis communications, and reputation management.	Edelman, Weber Shandwick, FleishmanHillard, Ketchum, Burson-Marsteller, Hill+Knowlton Strategies, and more.
BRANDING	These agencies help clients with their brand strategy and provide services that include brand assessment and audits, brand portfolio strategy, value proposition development, brand architecture and positioning, brand valuations, naming and messaging, graphics, and identity and packaging design, just to name a few.	FutureBrand, Landor, Fitch, Hall & Partners, Interbrand, and more.
SOCIAL MEDIA	These agencies focus on a wide variety of social media services including strategy, influencer marketing, engagement, word of mouth marketing, sentiment, and social media reporting.	We Are Social, Big Spaceship, Social Control, Influencer Marketing Agency, Renegade, Campfire, Social2B, Chatterblast, Social Distillery, Liveworld, Powerhouse Factories, and more.
SEARCH	These agencies provide clients with Search Engine Marketing services (SEM) which often include both SEO (optimization) and SEA (advertising).	Performics, iCrossing, GroupM Search, Resolution Media, 360i, SapientRazorfish, Acronym, and more.

TYPE	DESCRIPTION OF SERVICES PROVIDED	AGENCY EXAMPLES
PROMOTIONAL & ACTIVATION	These agencies provide clients with promotional services that range from marketing incentives, sales promotions, product sampling, consumer promotions, fulfillment services such as sweepstakes, contests, and games, sponsorship activities, and more.	Advantage Marketing Partners, Mosaic, Freeman, Momentum Worldwide, Marketing Arm, Integer Group, Octagon, TracyLocke, and more.
EXPERIENTIAL/ EVENT	The agencies focus on experiential marketing and events.	Advantage Marketing Partners, Mosaic, Freeman, Momentum Worldwide, GMR Marketing, Jack Morton Worldwide, and more.
MULTICULTURAL	These agencies focus on speaking to minorities, taking into consideration their purchasing patterns and media preferences, whether ethnic or cultural. Agencies can be specialized in one or multiple specialties such as Hispanic/Latin American, African-American, Native American, and Gay/Lesbian.	Alma, The Community, Lopez Negrete Communications, Latin World Entertainment (LWE), Republica, Bravo Group, Burrell Communications, UniWorld Group, Fuse, AdAsia Communications, IW Group, Intertrend Communications, and more.

Other Specialties: Equally important to both clients with specific, specialized needs and those with generally smaller overall marketing expenditures, these marketing agencies can add to advertisers' marketing arsenal. Some agencies have developed deep subject matter expertise in various specialized forms of marketing or communication, such as Market Research, Production, Customer Analytics and Measurement, Customer & Data Intelligence, Mobile Marketing, Brand Strategy and Consultancy, Design (brand, packaging, environmental, etc.), Video, DRTV, Content Marketing, Visual/ Sound Identity, Product Placement, Shopper Marketing and Point of Sales/Merchandising, Email Marketing, Entertainment/ Event Marketing, Loyalty, Data Management, Corporate

Communications and Employer Branding, B2B, and Media/ Publishing. New emerging digital capabilities such as word of mouth marketing and SEO/SEM can be found here as well as in end-to-end integrated digital agencies.

This category of agencies also includes firms with deep segment-specific expertise like Wellness and Healthcare Communication agencies that have a very intimate knowledge of practices in this highly regulated industry sector. Other agency vertical segments include (just to name a few) Travel and Hospitality, Industrial Advertising, Luxury Marketing, Youth Marketing, Real Estate, Nonprofit, Sports, B2B, and more. They sometimes specialize in specific platforms. For example, Dentsu Aegis Network's 360i launched a new, dedicated unit devoted to developing brand strategies, discovery, and "e-commerce optimization" around Amazon's growing marketing platform.

INDUSTRY VIEWPOINT

"Individual agencies are partially to blame for adding to client confusion by not providing a clear point of difference vs. their competitor agencies. There are over ten thousand marketing agencies. Just imagine how difficult it is to pick the right one. That's why clients get lost." [22]

—PETER LEVITAN, CEO, PETER LEVITAN & CO.

When it's all said and done, because there is no right or wrong way to cluster agencies, don't expect all your agencies to naturally fall into these categories. Some standards have emerged as agencies establish new capabilities like social media,

SEM, or mobile advertising, once backed up by fast-growing client billings. We should expect to see changes in the way the agency industry organizes itself over time. Organizations like AdForum provide advertising agencies and production companies a digital space to search by type of service, but also showcase their creative work (over 170,000 campaigns) and talents (with over 36,000 agency profiles). Certainly, there are many other ways, besides core competencies, to divide up agencies: client wins, awards won, revenue ranking (from top to bottom), agency affiliations (e.g., BBDO Worldwide Network); public vs. independent; geographic location (international vs. domestic, by city); generalists vs. specialized. These criteria can prove to be most helpful for clients seeking to filter down the list of agencies.

The agency supply chain is often richer than what meets the eye. Agencies typically subcontract with other specialty vendors for skills that they do not readily have in-house such as printing, production, material fulfillment, premiums, studios, and many others in various complementary industries and professions. They do so to provide clients with a one-stop solution for all their needs. These vendors tend to be either highly specialized or too infrequently used by advertisers to economically justify the agency having these services available in-house. They also add on to their scope, making it confusing for clients trying to understand their core competencies. For example, creative shops like Wieden+Kennedy, Droga5, and Walrus also offer media strategy, buying, and planning to service clients looking for the convenience and added benefits of integrated creative and media strategy and execution. Agencies also acquire new capabilities: Sponsorship agency Lagardère Sports and Entertainment launched a full-service global agency, Lagardère Plus, following its acquisition of London-based creative shop Brave.

THE EPOCHAL BATTLE OF INDUSTRY TITANS

Perhaps one of the greatest challenges faced by any company is to understand the complex and evolving nature of an industry consistently innovating and reinventing itself. We've all heard of the glamorous agency names like BBDO, Young & Rubicam, Ogilvy, and JWT that made Madison Avenue a name for itself. How about all the others? Unless you analyze this industry for a living or understand it for some circumstantial reasons, it's unlikely that you have much visibility of the intricate make-up of large agencies or to the number of boutique agencies with catchy names like Laundry Service, Carrot Creative, Mother, Anomaly, Redscout, Firstborn, Barbarian Group, 72andSunny, Big Spaceship, Hearts & Science, or Strawberry Frog. You are not to blame. And you are not alone. Yet many of these remarkable agencies are now working with marquee clients and have been widely acknowledged by industry peers. So why is it so hard to keep a pulse on newcomers and the industry at large? Well, because there are so many of them bringing various skills and credentials. This is a highly fragmented industry with agencies renaming themselves regularly, being acquired, being merged, or, for the few unfortunate, going out of business. Without industry resources such as the Association of American Advertising Agencies (4As), AdForum, AdWeek, and Advertising Age's infamous annual list of top agencies, we would be hard pressed to keep a tally. Now it's time we put some of these agencies under a microscope.

INDUSTRY VIEWPOINT

"I observe that small brands that have one decision-maker are far better able to integrate communications disciplines, assuming they have access to the resources to invest in. The biggest marketers [have resources], but they can't integrate. Smaller brands can integrate but they don't have the resources. Somewhere in the middle of that is the opportunity for a PR agency to do more than just PR." [23]

—**BRIAN WIESER**, SENIOR ANALYST, PIVOTAL RESEARCH

So, what do we know about them? As in any other industry, the agency business has a few dominant players, and a small number of holding and parent companies, which are all publicly traded and account for a disproportionate share of the spend worldwide. The holding companies represent a federation of companies, together yet independent, giving them the flexibility to adapt to diverse and ever-changing client scenarios, and the ability to come as one to meet the requirements of the largest advertisers. These holding companies were initially formed by a few large agencies merging to create greater economies of scale and stronger, more complete offerings and synergies while working around client conflicts. The four largest holding companies are WPP Group, Omnicom Group, Publicis Groupe, and Interpublic Group of Companies (IPG). They are closely followed by a few other agencies that are of material size (based on 2017 worldwide revenue): Dentsu Inc., Havas, Hakuhodo DY Holdings, Epsilon, BlueFocus Comm. Group, and MDC Partners. Competition is intensifying as large consulting firms are entering the digital marketing space. According to Ad Age, with combined revenue of $13.2 billion, the marketing services units of Accenture (Accenture's Accenture Interactive), PwC (PwC's PwC Digital Services), IBM (IBM Corp's IBM iX), and Deloitte (Deloitte's Deloitte Digital) sit just below WPP, Omnicom, Publicis Groupe, Interpublic, and Dentsu.

MAJOR HOLDING COMPANIES
IN ADVERTISING AND MARKETING COMMUNICATION

| WPP GROUP | OMNICOM GROUP | PUBLICIS GROUPE | INTERPUBLIC GROUP OF COMPANIES | DENTSU | HAVAS | MDC PARTNERS |

INDUSTRY VIEWPOINT

"The presence and influence of consultants on Adland-related businesses is big—and will only get bigger. Accenture Interactive reported it had $4.4 billion in revenue last year, which is about the size of a small Adland holding company . . . At this point, they're not 'encroaching' on the ad biz. They are a big part of it."[24]

—RICHARD WHITMAN, COLUMNIST, MEDIAPOST

CLIENT VIEWPOINT

"The advertising industry is highly fragmented. Now we have experts in media, CRM, etc. Everyone is struggling on how to make agencies work together. But we clients want integrated solutions. I don't want my agencies to compete for land grab. Give me an agency with a 360-degree solution on how to best reach my customer. Clients are looking for agencies with these capabilities, so they don't have 10 agencies calling them to get an assignment. I want one agency which has full accountability." [25]

—**SUSAN MARKOWICZ,** GLOBAL ADVERTISING AGENCY
MANAGER, FORD MOTOR COMPANY

Holding companies organize their professional services around clients and provide those in all industry segments through multiple agencies around the world on a global, pan-regional, and local basis, across multiple communication disciplines. They promote the value of independence to better foster agility, creativity, and innovation among their members. Holding companies were created in response to the globalization of the marketplace as well as to resolve client conflicts that previously prevented them from taking on many clients in the same business category. They responded to the need of global brand advertisers looking to build global brands and speak as one voice. As advertisers increase their demands for effectiveness and efficiency, they need to consolidate their business with larger, multi-disciplinary agencies or integrated groups of agencies. Multiple agencies came together to collaborate in formal and informal virtual client networks that cut across organizational structures to meet their marketing needs. As a result, holding companies are now able to take on competitive clients within a vertical by aligning them to different in-network agencies, therefore avoiding loss of new business opportunities.

DEMYSTIFYING HOLDING COMPANIES

Although all holding companies share common characteristics, these global leaders in marketing communications are often run very differently. The operating units under each network collaborate in a formal or informal virtual network, aligned around unique client marketing needs, typically in modular fashion. IPG pioneered the concept of the holding company approach. They act as a "virtual network" giving them the ability to integrate services across all disciplines and delivering those across inter-connected families of agencies and geographic regions simultaneously. Their network strategy is believed to facilitate better integration of services to meet the demands of the marketplace by pulling the resources best suited to meet the needs of a client. A holding company allows local markets to take advantage of the strong creativity, strategic resources, know-how, tools, and new technologies that they might not otherwise be able to access. They can deliver integrated services via a web of interconnected yet autonomous companies, balancing global and local client needs.

AGENCY VIEWPOINT

"Organic growth is the key metric of the industry; it is the demonstration of our attractiveness in the market; it is the demonstration that we are competitive and that our model is both built on our clients' needs and sustainable." [26]
—ARTHUR SADOUN, CHAIRMAN AND CEO, PUBLICIS GROUPE

On principle, the critical mass generated by the holding company model allows them to focus their efforts on attracting, retaining, and developing the best talent pool possible. Their operating units may be asked at times to come together and partner to serve a particular client. Or they may end up competing with each other. They can play on the strengths of the network and minimize its potential weaknesses. Clients and employees, for example, can be moved from one agency to another that might be a better fit. The holding company sets company-wide financial targets and defines corporate strategy, directs collaborative inter-agency programs, establishes common financial and operational controls, guides compensation policies, handles investor relations, and handles mergers and acquisitions. In addition, it supposedly lessens the administrative burden of operating agencies by centralizing basic functional services such as real estate, legal, accounting and finance, travel, recruitment, compensation, investor relations, procurement, insurance, tax and legal affairs, information systems, and technology. Those benefits come at a cost as some overhead is charged back to the operating units, a cost ultimately paid by clients.

It wouldn't be fair to assume that all holding companies are structured the same or pursue similar goals. For example, WPP Group has clearly shown its commitment to the parent company approach, beyond the financial purpose served by holding companies. WPP Group acts as a sort of central nervous system, a single point of accountability to leverage all group assets, as does any other holding company, but does so in the pursuit of new business—an approach it took with HSBC, Intel, Samsung, Nestlé, and many others over the years. WPP Group is not singular. Omnicom Group, Interpublic Group, and Publicis Groupe have their own version of this "team" approach to servicing big advertisers.

At the core of holding company pitches is the client's desire to reduce the conflicts and territorial issues that prevent them from pursuing media-neutral approaches with multiple agencies when those services are not available from a single full-service integrated agency. The concept is not new, of course. Agency networks fulfill a similar role on a smaller scale. Getting better coordination from multiple agencies with individual P&L is not always easy, but it certainly hasn't stopped the proliferation of combined entities hoping to appeal to clients looking for integrated offerings. The four giant holding companies are responsible for a disproportionate share of the spend, working for a much-diversified client portfolio, both in size and industry type. The holding companies play a large influential role in the combined successes of all their operating units. They each employ thousands of employees working all around the world, in hundreds of individual companies in various disciplines. Let's take a closer look at the top four holding companies.

WPP GROUP

Wire and Plastic Products was originally a UK manufacturer of wire baskets, an investment through which Sir Martin Sorrell started to build his worldwide marketing services company through massive and highly publicized acquisitions such as JWT Group, Ogilvy Group, Young & Rubicam, Grey Global Group, 24/7 Real Media, Taylor Nelson Sofres, and others. Formed in 1985 and headquartered in London, WPP Group's (WPP) mission is *"To develop and manage talent; to apply that talent throughout the world for the benefit of clients; to do so in partnership; to do so with profit."* Today, the group employs over 200,000 employees in over 3,000 offices, focused on three major key areas: technology, data, and content. WPP Group is comprised of many large groups and individual sub-agency brands—Young & Rubicam Group (VMLY&R, Wunderman, Landor, Iconmobile, Cohn & Wolfe, and others), Group M (Mindshare Worldwide, MediaCom, Xaxis, MEC, Maxus, etc.) as well as Ogilvy, J. Walter Thompson Co, Kantar, Grey Group, WPP Digital, tenthavenue, and other holdings (AKQA, Flitch, Cole & Weber, etc.).

As a parent company, the group's mission is to develop, manage, motivate, support, and ultimately apply talent for its operating units, releasing them of the majority of their administrative and financial responsibilities by achieving efficiencies in information technology, procurement, professional development, and client coordination that no individual company would be able to achieve on its own. In return, operating units can focus their energy and resources on achieving their strategic and operational goals. WPP Group encourages its operating companies to work together, bringing their own disciplines to benefit clients in need of a more holistic service offering. WPP has appointed Global Client Leads responsible for coordinating efforts on the client's behalf to leverage the full extent of what the group has to offer through its many operating units. WPP Group ensures there is a single ownership where specific client business most logically resides. As of 2017, they reported having 48 account teams with over 38,000 employees working on client accounts.

OMNICOM GROUP INC.

Omnicom (OMC) was born in 1986 out of the merger of three advertising giants who played a predominant role in building the advertising industry as we know it today: BBDO as well as Doyle Dane Bernbach and Needham Harper Worldwide. Like WPP, OMC is a globally diversified conglomerate with thousands of clients from around the world in a broad variety of industries. It has been led by John Wren, President CEO, since 1997. Built for the omnichannel world, OMC operates as the parent company for over 1,500 agencies in over 30 marketing disciplines and over 100 countries. OMC is organized around three separate and prestigious global agency networks—BBDO, DDB and TBWA. Its agency portfolio also includes two of the world's largest providers of media services with OMD and PHD, both part of the Omnicom Media Group. Omnicom Media Group also includes the leading global data and analytics company, Annalect, as well as several media specialist companies—search specialist Resolution, digital trading platform Accuen, Novus, Optimum Sports/Fuse, Outdoor Media Group, Content Collective, and direct response agency Pathway. DAS Group of Companies complement, the services from the media and agency groups through a combination of networks and regional organizations. DAS is comprised of a diversified group of over 200 agencies across various marketing disciplines, ranging from public relations to CRM, shopper branding, promotional marketing, branding and research, and healthcare. With hundreds of offices around the world, BBDO Worldwide and DDB Worldwide are considered two of the most creative and influential advertising and marketing networks in the world. TBWA Worldwide, aka The Disruption® Company, includes brands such as AUDITOIRE, BEING, Digital Arts Network (DAN), eg+ worldwide, The Integer Group®, TBWA\Media Arts Lab, and TBWA\WorldHealth.

CLIENT VIEWPOINT

"The agency business is reinventing itself and we're a part of that transformation." [27]

—JAMES R. ZAMBITO, SENIOR DIRECTOR, GLOBAL CORPORATE AFFAIRS, JOHNSON & JOHNSON

INTERPUBLIC GROUP OF COS

Headquartered in New York City, the Interpublic Group of Companies, Inc. (IPG) is considered the grandfather of global marketing communications companies. First incorporated in 1930 under the name of McCann-Erickson Incorporated, succeeding the advertising agency founded in 1911 by A.W. Erikson, and Harrison K. McCann, IPG was born in the early 1960s with a network of two agencies, McCann Erikson Worldwide and McCann-Markschalk. Today, major IPG brands include Craft, FCB (Foote, Cone & Belding), FutureBrand, Golin, Huge, Initiative, Jack Morton Worldwide, MAGNA, McCann, Momentum, MRM//McCann, MullenLowe Group, Octagon, R/GA, UM, and Weber Shandwick. Other leading brands include

Avrett Free Ginsberg, Campbell Ewald, Carmichael Lynch, Deutsch, Hill Holliday, ID Media, and The Martin Agency.

IPG is organized around three global networks: McCann Worldgroup, FCB (Foote Cone & Belding), and MullenLowe Group, which provide integrated, large-scale advertising and marketing solutions. McCann Worldgroup is comprised of leading creative agencies like McCann Erickson, digital marketing, relationship management MRM//McCann, event marketing and promotion with Momentum, consumer healthcare communications with McCann Health, and the network's global adaptation and production arm, Craft Worldwide. UM (media), Weber Shandwick (public relations), and FutureBrand (brand consulting) also align with McCann Worldgroup to deliver fully-integrated solutions to advertisers.

Global media services companies include the legendary UM and Initiative, which operate under the IPG Mediabrands umbrella. IPG also offers a range of specialized communication agencies across a range of disciplines: Weber Shandwick and Golin for public relations, Jack Morton for brand experience, FutureBrand for brand consultancy, Octagon for sports, entertainment, and lifestyle marketing, R/GA, Huge and MRM// McCann for digital. In addition to its global portfolio of agencies, IPG also offers advertisers a range of US-based integrated independent agencies like Avrett Free Ginsberg, Carmichael Lynch, Deutsch, Hill Holliday, ID Media, and The Martin Agency.

AGENCY VIEWPOINT

"Our agencies have to have the capabilities or partner with standalone digital shops. McCann has its own digital capabilities; Mullen Lowe has Propero as well as its own—and the whole point of our open architecture is allowing them to reach out to R/GA, Huge, and other digital units." [28]

—MICHAEL ROTH, CHAIRMAN AND CEO, INTERPUBLIC GROUP

PUBLICIS GROUPE

Publicis ("publi," the abbreviation of "publicité," or "advertising" in French and "cis" for the number six ["6" was his favorite number]) was founded in 1926 in a poor neighborhood of Paris by a 20-year-old French advertising pioneer, Marcel Bleustein-Blanchet. Publicis opened a New York office in 1957 but truly entered the vast and prosperous United States market in 1988 through a merger and strategic alliance with Foote, Cone and Belding. The venture ended in 1996. Publicis Groupe was created in 2000 when Publicis, the Paris-based agency, acquired Saatchi & Saatchi for $1.7 billion. It gained a solid foothold in the US and became the fourth largest marketing communications company in the world only after merging with Bcom3 Group under the leadership of CEO Maurice Lévy. Today, Publicis Groupe is one of the world's largest communications groups. Publicis Groupe's slogan is *"Viva La Difference!"* cultivating and celebrating how they are different from the competition based on culture, methods, and approach to communication.

AGENCY VIEWPOINT

"A driving force in the market, Publicis Groupe believes in the power of creativity, intelligence, and technology to pioneer change, just as it has done for the last 91 years." [29]

—ARTHUR SADOUN, CHAIRMAN AND CEO, PUBLICIS GROUPE

Publicis Groupe is organized into four Solutions Hubs in over 100 countries: Publicis Communications, Publicis. Sapient, Publicis Media, and Publicis Health. With Publicis One, Publicis Groupe offers a plug and play solution for advertisers looking for a fully integrated group of agencies to serve their business under one roof and one leader. Publicis One combines all of the Groupe's services from creative, to media, digital, and health in each country outside of the Groupe's top 20 markets. Publicis Communications is the creative communications hub of Publicis Groupe, bringing together the Leo Burnett, Saatchi & Saatchi, Publicis Worldwide, BBH, Marcel, Fallon, MSLGROUP, and Prodigious networks. Considered the "founding pillar," Publicis Worldwide has been the largest agency network within Publicis Groupe, with a particularly strong footing in Europe. Publicis.Sapient is the digital platform combining the digital creativity from SapientRazorfish with the deep industry expertise of consultants and technologists from Sapient Consulting. Publicis is constantly looking for innovative ways to serve its clients. The Groupe launched "Sapient Inside," a new division to bring tech and creativity closer by "embedding" digital specialists (digital consulting and technology experts) within its traditional creative shops and providing a seamless link to the Publicis.Sapient platform's expertise. Publicis Media provides strategy, insights and analytics, data and technology, and performance marketing services operating under six major brands: Starcom, Zenith, DigitasLBi, Performics, Spark Foundry, and Blue 449. Publicis Groupe has been aggressively building its digital offering. Its acquisition of Boston-based Digitas (founded in 1980), Razorfish (from Microsoft's prior acquisition of aQuantive), and Boston-based digital network Sapient for $3.7 billion were strong confirmations that it intends to be a major player.

AGENCY VIEWPOINT

"This is a unique model. No one else can do it for the unique reason no one can be credible on both sides. You have WPP, Omnicom, IPG that could work on the marketing side. Sometimes we're better, sometimes not. You have the Accentures of the world working on the digital business transformation part. But none can link both." [30]

—ARTHUR SADOUN, CHAIRMAN AND CEO, PUBLICIS GROUPE

Outside of WPP, Omnicom, IPG and Publicis, there are a few other network organizations worth mentioning, given their size, reputation, and influence: Dentsu, Havas, and MDC Partners.

- Dentsu: Dentsu bought Aegis in 2012 and formed Dentsu Aegis Network. Dentsu Aegis Network is made up of 10 global network brands: Carat, Dentsu, Dentsu Media, iProspect, Isobar, mcgarrybowen, Merkle, MKTG, Posterscope, and Vizeum, supported by its specialist/multi-market brands.

- Havas: Originating from the family name of Charles-Louis Havas who created the first French press agency in 1835, today's French multinational group by the name Havas is one of the largest global advertising communications groups in the world. The group is organized around two main divisions: Havas Creative Group (including Havas Worldwide, Arnold Worldwide, and a range of other agencies) and Havas Media Group (including Havas Media, Havas Sports & Entertainment, and Arena Media).

- MDC Partners: Founded in 1980 in Toronto, the company held its IPO in 1987. MDC Partners has over 50 partner firms around the world in Advertising/Branding/Design, Digital/Social, Experiential Marketing, Media Planning and Buying, and CRM, as well as PR/IR and Crisis Management. Many of those are high-profile, award-winning agencies including 72&Sunny, Anomaly, and CP&B. The group is structured as a partnership model, in which it acquires a majority stake in its partner agency, leaving a percentage of ownership with the founder and expecting them to operate with limited support.

Agencies reinvent themselves continuously. Don't be surprised that by the time you read this, these holding companies have already reorganized, restructured, or consolidated their operations, sold assets, diversified their agency portfolio, changed names, merged agencies, or simply acquired new ones that make this overview obsolete. It's the nature of the business of advertising. If this is where your passion lies and the profession you chose, then you might simply need to get used to this constant change. Agencies can grow by winning new business, organically or through acquisitions. The industry consolidation experienced with the big four holding companies has been the undeniable trend of the past decade as they realized that the globalization of the marketplace required them to evolve their offering and meet the needs of even more demanding global clients. Client consolidations became prevalent in many industries. How do agencies keep up? They consolidate to stay in the game, mostly in digital where budgets are migrating and in media where economies of scale translate into a competitive edge as advertisers look for greater media buying efficiencies. Although it's easier to think about the agency offering in terms of the big players, brand advertisers are also tapping into the wider marketplace of agencies, including indie shops and small- to medium-size independent specialized firms.

AGENCY VIEWPOINT

"Agencies need to get back to what they do best. They have always built fantastic impactful work when they have based it on great human insight. But they have been focusing too much on digital for digital's sake. Great work is based on human truths and powerful ideas, then think about execution and the relevant way to produce the work." [31]

—**ROB NEWLAN,** CEO, VIRTUE WORLDWIDE-THE CREATIVE AGENCY BY VICE, FORMER REGIONAL DIRECTOR, EMEA, FACEBOOK'S CREATIVE SHOP

DAVID VS. GOLIATH

The remaining share of the business is divided up between smaller agency networks, large and medium-size independent agencies, and small (and "want-to-be-and-want-to-remain small") advertising boutiques. The continued industry consolidation, accelerated by the race for digital marketing supremacy, has energized the industry and encouraged the emergence of new, small agencies hoping to get on the bandwagon and either find a niche or get acquired by traditional agencies anxious to stay in the competition. Not unlike the epic battle of the young David and the Philistine warrior Goliath, the big guy is not always the one standing up. Independent agencies such as iconic Wieden+Kennedy, Richards Group, or Venables Bell + Partners continue to show up as nimble contenders to large agencies for client assignments. These agencies have built robust approaches to solving client problems combined with creativity, agile organizational structures, reduced overhead, and a culture of collaboration and partnership that translates for clients into lower cost delivery, fast turnaround, and highly impactful solutions that can come from anywhere in the agency.

Ask them to scale or operate globally, however, and things can get a bit more complicated. Will they remain independent? It's hard to predict. These independent shops end up being acquired by ambitious holding companies or private equity investors. Many small boutique agencies are making themselves powerful adversaries, finding the big firms' "Achilles' heel" and building direct relationships with big brand advertisers, many of which discreetly outsource complex digital assignments to these shops. It's cyclical in the end. Boutique agencies are acquired or grow to become large ones, opening room for the small shops to promote less cookie-cutter work and more nimble, personalized, agile services. For example, award-winning creative shop Crispin Porter + Bogusky (CP+G) was acquired by MDC Partners in 2008. Previously independent firms Digitas and Razorfish were acquired by Publicis Groupe, leaving a few rare and truly independent, privately-held shops especially in digital, which has seen a rapid acceleration of mergers and acquisitions. Many of these agencies vividly proclaim their desire to remain fully independent, hoping to avoid the financial pressure of a group P&L that may require them to be less selective about the clients they bring on to meet revenue or profit targets.

AGENCY VIEWPOINT

"In short, we sit at the intersection of creative brand innovation, digital transformation, and business strategy. Like a traditional advertising agency, we have the creative capabilities that help companies thrive, but we also offer the business acumen, technological capabilities, and industry insights needed to truly transform businesses and spur long-term growth." [32]

—ALICIA HATCH, CMO, DELOITTE DIGITAL

They also want to maintain their creative freedom that is particularly important to their founders and creative leadership. Few are those who resist the temptation of a financially sound business arrangement that could reward its owners and provide access to capital that could be invested in the agency's growth. Although we are likely to see clients continue to experiment with small, agile, innovative, independent boutique agencies to challenge themselves, it is clear that most small independent shops do not have the backbone and muscles to support a large, demanding global client. Smaller, nimbler boutique agencies, however, will continue to emerge and blossom. The David and Goliath battle has been going on for a while, and it is of epic proportions.

The big holding companies will continue to furiously battle for supremacy, aggressively pursuing new clients, protecting existing ones, and acquiring new assets and competencies that complement their integrated client offering. What is most certain is that tomorrow's agencies, regardless of their size, will be increasingly versatile, innovative, and "customer-centric." Ironically, the holding companies may no longer be the Goliath we thought they were with the entry of the big consultancies, namely Accenture, PwC, Deloitte, and IBM. These consultancies present new opportunities for advertisers looking for ways to digitalize the many facets of their business, including all consumer-facing ecommerce activities and, as a result, many of the related marketing and communications. These four consultancies (the marketing services units of Accenture, PwC, IBM, and Deloitte) now rank among the 10 largest agency companies in the world with combined revenue of $13.2 billion, mostly through a mix of acquisitions, organic growth, building out new practices, geographic expansion, and consolidation of marketing-related services. Advertisers are responding positively to this new offering, considering consultancies for digital work as agencies are fighting for their turf. In 2017, McDonald's hired Publicis.Sapient, in partnership with global consulting and technology services company Capgemini, reportedly to create the restaurant experience of the future, including kiosk ordering, web applications, mobile applications, and more.

Consultancies are building or acquiring creative and digital solutions to be viable alternatives for advertisers to consider. Accenture Interactive launched a content studio to deliver innovative and engaging content to clients, including a state-of-the-art TV and video post-production facility, and supports new, collaborative models for delivering branded content. What will tomorrow look like? The balance of power is likely to shift because of these new market dynamics. We will continue to see increased M&A activity as well, changing the landscape as we know it today. The agency community is often a maze that is difficult to navigate without getting lost in its complex web of partnerships and affiliations. Although further consolidation is likely, Madison Avenue will remain a puzzling world in constant flux and transformation. The agency landscape is now permanently altered as a result of lasting changes in technology, digital, media, and consumer habits. Having a basic understanding of major types of agency services and of the major agency industry players is a requirement for anyone in advertising, marketing, or communications. Congratulations are in order. Hopefully, after this chapter, you know more about the agency industry than anyone else in your entourage. And you now realize that the world of Madison Avenue is not so mysterious after all.

TOP 3
BEST PRACTICES
for Advertisers

1 Stay up to date on new industry developments (newly formed agencies, mergers and acquisitions, reorganizations) in the agency industry by reading trade magazines, blogs and industry reports.

2 Continuously research best performing agencies using criteria like YOY revenue growth, major client wins, industry awards, new key hires to keep on pulse on top talent.

3 Regularly read earnings reports from publicly traded companies like WPP, Omnicom, Publicis, IPG, Havas and others to understand their primary business drivers and priority areas.

3

"THE BUCK STOPS HERE"

Mastering the discipline of
managing agency partners

"Each problem that I solved became a rule, which served afterwards to solve other problems."
—RENE DESCARTES, PHILOSOPHER, MATHEMATICIAN, SCIENTIST, AND WRITER

It's late Sunday evening, and you just received a phone call from Mark, your company's Chief Marketing Officer (CMO), in a state of panic. The latest creative concepts produced by the agency are still not hitting the mark and time is running out. Mark is growing concerned about the competition's recent gains in brand awareness and favorability as well as the aggressive fourth quarter revenue targets. After numerous rounds, the concepts are still off-strategy despite everyone's efforts to come up with strong work. The relationship with the agency is also worrisome. Wendy, the agency's Group Account Director, alerted you that the team's run rate is dangerously high, burning staff resources well in excess of what was originally budgeted. There are also growing concerns about the account's shrinking profitability and you fear that the agency may pull their best talent off the account. The agency's CEO is on Mark's case and she's now asking for a budget increase to finish the second half of the year. This is coupled with the fact that the agency raised concerns in the last QBR about the lack of input, clarity, and guidance in the annual scope management and project briefing process.

The agency seems confused about who the decision-maker is. There were too many reviewers to please, diluting the initial concepts presented. The agency staff is burned out and is becoming de-motivated. Collaboration with other roster agencies seems suboptimal and territorial issues surface constantly, distracting everyone. The agency recently hired a new hotshot Creative Director after the agency's creative product was identified as weak in the last agency performance evaluation. The situation is tense. The contract is up for review. Budgets are firmly locked. Time is of the essence. Mark is asking you to either turn the situation around or move the work to another agency within weeks. Sound familiar?

WELCOME TO AGENCY MANAGEMENT 101
Suddenly you wish you had taken Agency Management 101 back in business school. You aren't to blame . . . it simply didn't exist. C-level executives haven't typically thought about actively managing agencies as a formal role within their organization to improve both the effectiveness and efficiency of their client/agency engagements. Although they appreciate that unique skills may be required, they don't often think about it as a distinct business function or professional discipline they need to build in their organization. Then again, "Why should we?" some wonder.

The most skeptical would ask:

I'M SEEING THE AGENCY ON MONDAY - CAN'T WE JUST COVER THIS OVER COCKTAILS AT HAPPY HOUR? IF THINGS DON'T WORK OUT IMMEDIATELY, CAN'T WE SIMPLY GET ANOTHER AGENCY?

HOW HARD COULD IT BE? SHOULDN'T AGENCIES MANAGE THEMSELVES ANYWAY TO SERVE OUR BUSINESS? AREN'T WE ALREADY PAYING THEM ENOUGH TO BE SELF-RELIANT AND SELF-MOTIVATED?

SHOULDN'T THE PURCHASING DEPARTMENT HANDLE THEM, ALONG WITH INK CARTRIDGES AND SHIPPING VENDORS?

Reality is far different. Agencies are not commodities (at least not the ones you want to work with). To the contrary. It's insane to see so many brand advertisers treat them as such, ignorant of the golden egg potential at their fingertips. However, agencies do require active client management and consistent oversight to deliver business performance, cost efficiencies, and top value to the bottom line. Thankfully, most advertisers have come to realize that these strategic partnerships require a higher level of direct, ongoing engagement than traditional vendor relationships.

CLIENT VIEWPOINT

"We have used a number of agencies in the past, but we're looking to build stronger relationships with key strategic partners, so we're streamlining our agency relationships and looking to really leverage their expertise." [34]

—ANDRÉ BRANCH, FORMER CHIEF MARKETING OFFICER, NBTY

For advertisers wise enough to consider agencies a strategic extension of their marketing organization, it's no less important or demanding than getting top performance from internal staff. A CMO is accountable for having the right mix of marketing skills on his or her team, setting clear goals and metrics to measure team performance, continually recruiting, developing, and retaining key talent, and ensuring that these critical human resources are trained, managed, engaged, motivated, accountable, and rewarded. Common-sense principles of managing an internal department apply to external talent agencies as well. Whether in good or tough economic times, Wall Street rewards companies that manage their talent and investments wisely. Wall Street also rewards companies that use their marketing and media budgets as aggressive growth engines for their company. Companies no longer award their trimmed-down budgets to agencies tasked to handle company-critical marketing efforts then cross their fingers and hope for the best. Not if they need to deliver market results to the CEO, the board, and shareholders—and certainly not if they intend to stay on the company's payroll. There is way too much at stake these days. Marketing expenditures are one of the largest non-payroll expenses any company has. And marketing is too critical to a company's ability to compete and sustain continued growth not to strategically manage this investment. Advertising and communications agencies are simply too instrumental to a company's ability to build great brands, grow revenue, and gain market share.

FROM ART TO, WELL, . . . SCIENCE

Like an orchestra, you need more than talented, well-trained musicians to perform a concerto. You also need a conductor with an intimate knowledge of resources at hand, and the right sheet music—the equivalent of a blueprint for how to get the most from your agency—to get to the right outcome. Even the most skeptical companies have come to realize that wisely assigning experts time and resources in managing agency relationships yields stronger dividends than a portfolio of unmanaged investments. Expectations are often non-linear in a business environment where external and internal conditions are dynamic and hard to predict. Luckily, in this instance, there is a clear relationship between cause and effect—over both the short and long term. The performance of an agency is a direct function of the energy invested by the client in making sure the relationship is properly set up and the partnership is adequately supported on an on-going basis. Garbage in, garbage out:

AGENCY VIEWPOINT

"If you don't know how to partner, you might as well get out of the way. Because partnership is everything in this business today." [35]

—JOHN OSBORN, CEO, OMD USA (FORMER PRESIDENT/CEO OF BBDO NEW YORK)

Clients get out what they put in. The reverse is true as well. A well-orchestrated yet flexible approach to working and managing agency partners is the key to marketing success. Working with an agency partner is far more complex, and vastly more demanding than most vendor relationships a typical busy purchasing department is accustomed to. The role of agency management or agency relations still suffers from a lack of consideration in some marketing and procurement organizations, even though it is far more rewarding and strategically beneficial to companies if the agency is managed properly. This means that the right agency roster has been picked, the metrics for success are clearly understood, the agencies have been thoroughly briefed, the teams are partnering effectively, the right agency resources are working on the right assignments, and so on. Marketing professionals who rely on their agencies to deliver high-performing work at the right value must learn, adopt, and apply agency management industry best practices to get outstanding work from their agency partners while maintaining a healthy relationship with them. The complexity of the agency world comes from its large number of connected elements that draw from many corporate functions within a company, including strategy and planning, scope of work management, contract and fee negotiations, financial reconciliations, agency onboarding and training, and performance evaluations.

Every organization is somewhat different, but it typically involves the collaboration and support from the following departments: marketing, legal, procurement, finance, and IT. No matter how much rigor and thoughtfulness advertisers put into it, the discipline of managing agency partners remains a careful blend of art and science. The concept of "science" is introduced when results are not only verifiable but also predictable and reproducible. Although fitting that litmus test at times, the up-and-coming nature of agency management, combined with the ever-changing marketing function, requires finding new ways to creatively solve business challenges. The discipline is arguably still immature in some companies and prone to experimentation for the years to come. I've had the privilege to see and contribute to the establishment of sophisticated practices in agency management among the world's largest brands. It's quite exciting to see marketing leadership staff up for this important specialty in marketing. Best practices, professional standards, and tools are beginning to emerge in this area, giving advertisers what they need to make the most effective use of their agencies.

FINDING THE FULCRUM OF EFFICIENCY AND EFFECTIVENESS

The 15 percent commission system that influenced large media buys is long gone, but not the important role media plays as a discipline. Savvy media planners and buyers now have a shot at trading their cubicle for a window office next to their creative counterparts who have always enjoyed this brass ring, something not envisioned even a few years ago. Their star is rising. After all, media buyers and marketing procurement professionals speak a common language: they know how to save money and efficiently leverage limited budgets. Agency compensation agreements are now usually based on "cost plus" labor agreements where profit is negotiated separately on top of labor costs; these have for the most part completely replaced the commission-based contracts. Agency fees have been fiscally "commoditized" by procurement's forceful entry into the marketing spend category. New agency CEOs, skilled in finance and operations, are set to reinvent their agencies into highly successful profit-driving businesses. This is a challenging undertaking for these industry captains who face pressure from higher client expectations at the same time as increased cost pressure from their clients' number crunchers and from their finance and procurement departments.

AGENCY VIEWPOINT

"Too many marketing managers are not properly trained to manage agencies. They are often promoted to marketing from finance, operations, or sales functions. As for procurement, I wish they would understand the art and science of advertising and creating ideas, and not view it as a commodity. Procurement is killing great thinking, and clients are going to get mediocre results, since they cannot afford to put the best talent on accounts that are under-paying their agencies. Successful relations are born when clients provide access to agencies, and the agencies behave and communicate and advise in a candid and transparent manner." [36]

—**MARC A. BROWNSTEIN,** PRESIDENT AND CEO, BROWNSTEIN GROUP

Whether the function is called Purchasing, Procurement, or Strategic Sourcing, the sudden emergence of this expense-management role in the corporate world is highly debated as it relates to the management of agency services. Yet procurement's growing influence in the industry in recent decades is undeniable. The result is acute pressure on agency pricing based on competitive benchmarks, and on audits and procurement-led financial negotiations. These tactics can squeeze agency profits and potentially threaten their ability to sustain the very business that is helping clients drive their own growth and profitability. Compensation was certainly easier for agencies twenty to thirty years ago! To the agency's despair, the client's procurement department is historically known for purchasing manufacturing parts and other highly commoditized "buy it anywhere" products, and negotiating materials and shipping costs rather than breakthrough creative thinking and strategic counsel. This tension is touching a sensitive nerve in marketing and agency executives who have historically handled this by using a broad palette of buying criteria.

Today there is a very apparent shift in roles played out in different corporate functions relating to working with agencies. Not so long ago, agencies would often conduct business over cocktails, on a golf course, between speeches at an awards ceremony, or at a nonprofit auction event with a CMO with whom they had a strong years-long personal relationship. Today, agency executives are increasingly dealing solely with tough procurement professionals in their business transactions. The same procurement professional they are negotiating with might be responsible for budgets for PCs, travel, and office furniture, and want a bottom-dollar deal. They might be willing to trade a long-time agency partner for another to save a buck. This may be slightly exaggerated, but you get the point. Not everyone in finance or procurement is sensitive to the powerful social media buzz of a compelling new online community; the insight and value brought to bear by a top-notch Account Planner just hired away from a competitive agency; or the agency's breakthrough use of an emerging media campaign that exceeded revenue objectives. "What did you say your overhead was again?" is painfully echoing through the halls of Madison Avenue, instilling fear of e-sourcing, or "Online Reverse Auctions," or other techniques used to further drive down prices.

INDUSTRY VIEWPOINT

"Marketing needs procurement, but it may be more appropriate in some cases for marketing procurement to report to the CMO not the CPO. As the approach required in procuring marketing services is so nuanced, so it follows that specialist skills are required of those in procurement to understand the complex value equation." [37]

—TOM DENFORD, CO-FOUNDER & CHIEF STRATEGY OFFICER,

ID COMMS LTD.

Agency expenses represent a sizeable portion of a company's marketing budget, so it hasn't gone unnoticed by CFOs and procurement executives seeking to get all vendors to re-examine and justify the pricing of their services. Procurement's primary objective is typically to maximize shareholder value by pursuing maximum productivity from a company's external spend, consolidating the supplier base whenever appropriate, and handling common transactions such as requisitions and purchase order processing. To fulfill their efficiency agenda, they are increasingly partnering with their business counterparts to source agency services at the right cost. Appropriately, they foster a culture of fiscal accountability, setting spend control targets. The concept of "Marketing Procurement" has emerged as its own discipline, led by savvy professionals, providing marketing departments and senior leadership a valuable and well-informed internal partner to frame and support well-crafted agency relationships. Unfortunately, the agency business is not often well understood outside of the company's marketing department. It is frequently associated with the outdated stereotype of charismatic entrepreneurs with large expense accounts and excessive overhead at the cost of large, sluggish clients. The world has changed, even though perceptions have not, and the continuing cost pressures inflicted by CFOs on their organizations have not spared the marketing function—as evidenced by the preeminent interest of this topic at industry events. As the growth in digital media has made this sector of marketing spend more accountable, expectations for tight cost controls and rigorous marketing budget management across all agency functions has only accentuated procurement's role.

CLIENT VIEWPOINT

"I think some of the procurement comments are a little bit much ado about nothing. ... We call them purchase professionals. They are absolutely a valued part of our partnership team. And they work together with us. If procurement is leading, taking over, then that means somebody on the brand is derelict in their duty. And we just don't see that." [38]

—MARC S. PRITCHARD, CHIEF BRAND OFFICER,

PROCTOR & GAMBLE

However, simplistic approaches such as indiscriminately reducing agency-related expenses and fees may unintentionally result in reduced work quality and second-tier talent, and therefore lower marketing effectiveness and business impact. Former WPP CEO Martin Sorrell coined the term "short-termism" as advertisers focus on short term decisions that range from the way they manage marketing priorities and budgets to agency relationships. Procurement-driven fee pressure continues to be a frequently cited secular concern among advertising agency executives. Like any business, agencies assign their best resources to profitable clients with long-term potential and those who know how to fairly compensate them for their services.

In a surprising move, PepsiCo eliminated its global marketing procurement department in late 2015, shifting oversight of agency relationships, agency compensation, and other activities like media to PepsiCo's individual brands to be under brand executives now responsible for contractual compliance and financial due diligence. The move sparked mixed reactions across the industry about the impact and value of corporate procurement departments to client organizations. Procurement must go beyond the efficiency agenda or experience more change. Marketing Procurement is without a doubt an important sister organization. Their value is in acting as a neutral third party. And marketing teams do not have the skill sets required—such as negotiation, contracting, supplier and risk management—to play that role.

AGENCY VIEWPOINT

"Procurement and agency management are useful endeavors. A lot of money and effort is wasted by ignoring these things. However, clients have gone far overboard with this stuff, and they are now in the process of costing themselves big money, even as they think they're saving it. Cost consultants often don't know that their criticisms compromise creative product, make it less effective, and thus cost companies millions in future benefits." [39]
—**JEFF GOODBY,** CO-CHAIRMAN AND PARTNER, GOODBY, SILVERSTEIN & PARTNERS

In other words, as in any other industry, agencies will pursue, invest in, and protect their higher-profit clients. Advertisers cannot viably compromise the quality of their market presence and long-term business value for short-term cost savings over the long haul. Marketing leaders and traditional procurement professionals don't always see eye-to-eye on how to set the right compensation balance point or how to measure agency value. Their agendas are often aligned, but their priorities might not be, occasionally creating healthy tension. However, in economically challenging times, enthusiasm often concedes to pragmatism. Spend-control becomes a necessity that even talented agency executives and marketing leaders can't argue with. A more rigorous process, involving formal requests for information (RFIs) and requests for proposals (RFPs), overtakes informal courting, previously handled over dinner by marketing and agency executives. Adept advertisers can apply healthy cost-pressure without negatively impacting the agency's work or damaging valuable business and personal relationships.

Under pressure, it's not surprising that agencies are resetting the dialogue to focus on value-add, creativity, and ideas they bring to clients, and less on the material nature of time and resources needed to accomplish client goals. Agencies have figured out that what applies to their clients also applies to them: Differentiation is the key to unlock the potential of a brand. To overcome procurement's mechanistic decoupling of services as commodities, agencies are investing in differentiating themselves and their services from the competition and building value to justify higher pricing. They feel strongly that they are in the business of building top-line growth, not solely to help advertisers reduce cost. This is the balancing act of driving marketing efficacy, not driving your relationship to the edge of a rocky cliff. This is where the Agency Management function comes in.

CLIENT VIEWPOINT

"P&G views agencies as partners, not suppliers, because partnerships produce better results. Partners share a common purpose, share value, and share pain." [40]

—MARC S. PRITCHARD, CHIEF BRAND OFFICER,
PROCTOR & GAMBLE

THE EVOLVING ROLE OF AGENCY MANAGEMENT

The Agency Management discipline provides a much-needed balance to a cost-driven approach to buying marketing services or a more casual "fair exchange value" approach to deal-making with agencies. Agency management professionals can shift the conversation from purely cost management to an opportunity growth discussion, leading to better decisions and collaborative trade-offs with agency partners. In the world of advertising, judgment calls based on the price-value equation are arguably better made by the business function ultimately responsible for its business outcome. After all, agency-spend is an investment. It doesn't mean, however, that these decisions shouldn't be informed by, and made in concert with, finance and procurement departments. To drive business results that clients can take to the bank, advertisers must treat agencies as strategic business partners, not merely suppliers. Agency Management is therefore a business discipline focused on the development, management, and nurturing of a company's partnership with its agency partners with the explicit goal of consistently improving its work output, investment value, and tangible business impact. It applies to the few who oversee the functional discipline for their company as well as all of the marketing professionals who rely on agencies to get their work done on a daily basis.

Broadly stated, the agency management function is responsible for the effective allocation and optimal use of agency talent to support the company's marketing objectives and priorities. Simply stated, it's about making sure that the company has the right agency, doing the right type of work at the right investment level, and in the most efficient ways.

It's insane to think that under-informed advertisers are not investing in effective agency management practices, often shooting from the hip, aiming with all the precision of a shotgun, and hoping for the best. They glaringly fail to realize the full benefits of a well-managed partnership. The role of agency management as a corporate discipline is about getting better work and greater value from these partnerships. It's the ultimate marketing enabling function. The right agency management competencies enable CMOs to accomplish more with their agencies and improve agency performance. It's an important marketing muscle marketers are now learning to build and flex in support of their many roles and responsibilities. It leads to key decisions about talent, team collaboration, budgets, process optimization, and work performance.

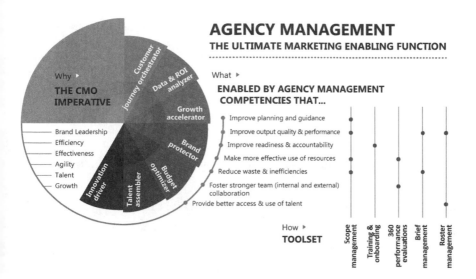

To reap the benefits of this function, advertisers must master both the practice of astutely managing agency relationships (aka agency strategy and operations) and getting work done through agencies (aka client/agency engagement):

- **Client/agency engagement:** It refers to all activities between marketers and agency personnel, ranging from scoping the work, reviewing proposals from the agencies, briefing agencies on assignments, reviewing and approving the creative or agency output (based on the type of work required), approving work or invoices, reviewing status reports and project results, providing feedback to agencies, and participating in post-mortem discussions. These engagement activities also include daily project-level interactions with various agency staff (e.g., account management, creative, production, etc.) to get the work done. These important assignment-based activities are fulfilled by project and budget owners throughout the marketing organization in partnership with agencies.

- **Agency strategy and operations**: It refers to the disciplined handling of all contractual, economical, and operational aspects of the partnership. These management activities are typically fulfilled by a few select individuals within the company, either in marketing procurement with a dotted line to marketing, or as marketing operations, agency relations, or an agency management function within the marketing organization. These activities are handled centrally by one or multiple subject matter experts. Ideally, the individual or team have relevant agency and client experience, sound planning skills, and a solid track record of partnering with other company departments such as legal and finance.

It's important to note that although all activities related to agency strategy and operations are typically centralized, everyone in marketing or procurement—whether they directly or indirectly interface with the agencies—must have a basic understanding of the company's core operating and partnership principles. In the following chapters, we will discuss aspects of client/agency relationships that are specific to "agency strategy and operations," like agency compensation or agency models, as well as those specific to "client/agency engagement," like input briefing. What are the core expectations and activities involved in this function? Those fall into four primary categories: talent, relationship, work/outcomes, and performance.

KEY AGENCY RELATIONS / MANAGEMENT RESPONSIBILITIES

STRATEGY & GOVERNANCE	PARTNERSHIP MANAGEMENT	ENGAGEMENT & DELIVERY	MEASUREMENT & OPTIMIZATION
DEFINE	NEGOTIATE	EVALUATE	MEASURE
SEARCH	ASSIGN	SCOPE	MOTIVATE
ORGANIZE	GUIDE	BRIEF	TRAIN
ENABLE	COORDINATE	MANAGE	TROUBLESHOOT
SOCIALIZE	NURTURE	APPROVE	IMPROVE
TALENT	RELATIONSHIP	WORK / OUTCOMES	PERFORMANCE

- **Talent**: These activities are primarily centered around strategy and governance. It starts with a clear definition of the chosen agency strategy and underlying roster agency model (define); the alignment of company needs with the right partners and the process of sourcing, finding, selecting, and hiring agencies (search); the management of the roster of agencies so those can be organized by relevant criteria and easily accessed by the marketing team (organize); and the articulation of the strategy, policies, annual plans, and overall corporate governance related to agency partnerships (socialize).

- **Relationship**: These activities are primarily centered around partnership management. They include the negotiation of favorable business and compensation terms (negotiate); the organizational alignment of agencies to the business, e.g., either geographically, by business unit, brand, project, etc. (assign); the partnership principles and service level agreements that guide internal teams and external partners on how to best collaborate and be mutually accountable (guide); and the oversight of these business partnerships in order to build healthy and long-term partnerships (nurture).

- **Work/Outcomes**: These activities are primarily centered around engagement and delivery. They include the campaign process design, roles definition and set up of annual programs (enable); the implementation of tools and processes to enable an effective work engagement between agency and marketing teams (coordinate); the overall planning and scope of work development and alignment process (scope); the orchestration of the agency reporting, effective reconciliation of staffing, financials, and deliverables, as well as oversight or management of QBR activities (manage); and quality measures and various KPIs, including process controls and approvals (approve).

- **Performance:** These activities are primarily centered around measurement and optimization. They include the data capture and development of actionable insights based on the work performance and/or relationship (measure); the management of incentive-based compensation or bonuses as well as other rewards and acknowledgments (motivate); the onboarding and training of agency talent and internal marketing teams (train); the risk mitigation and support provided to handle difficult or unwanted situations or escalations (troubleshoot); and continuous improvement and program enhancements and refinements (improve).

Although they may vary in scope and in complexity, typical agency management includes the objectives, priorities, and primary purposes shown in the following chart:

PRIMARY OBJECTIVES	KEY RESPONSIBILITIES	PRIMARY FUNCTIONAL AREAS	PRIMARY PURPOSE
Development, management, and nurturing of a company's partnership with its agency partners with the explicit goal of consistently improving its work output, investment value, and tangible business impact.	TALENT	STRATEGY	Determine client needs, lock on the best agency resource model and roster.
		SEARCH	Identify, review, and select a new agency.
	RELATIONSHIP	CONTRACT	Determine contract T&Cs and ensure full compliance.
		COMPENSATION	Determine best approach to fair and equitable compensation.
	WORK / OUTCOME	SCOPE / BRIEFING	Define scope of work and workload. Input brief development and delivery.
		EVALUATION	Conduct performance evaluations and implement improvement plans.
	PERFORMANCE	TRAINING	Implement agency onboarding and client/agency training.
		MEASUREMENT	Measure and continuously improve all aspects of the client/agency relationship.

CORE RESPONSIBILITY: AGENCY STRATEGY

This is the operating model by which an advertiser determines the number and type of agency partnerships it will require to support its marketing strategy and how those will interface with each other and within the marketing organization. This is by far one of the most high-stakes agency management responsibilities and yet is often absent or handled informally. It first ensures the advertiser needs are well-defined and regularly vetted with internal stakeholders. It then helps determine which type of agency organizational model and portfolio of agencies are best suited to address its most immediate but also long-term priorities. In Chapter 4, we will help answer the following questions:

- What agency skills are most needed today to meet our marketing needs?

- What agency competencies will we require in the next two to three years?

- Should we build some in-house capabilities to augment or replace the work we typically outsource?

- Which agency should be assigned to what brand or line of business or geography?

- What type of specialty agencies do we need to produce best-in-class work?

- Should digital be handled differently than other creative work?

- How often should we re-evaluate our approach? Against what criteria?

- What level of integration and collaboration is expected between our roster agencies?

- Who will be responsible for the integration of the many moving parts of our marketing mix?

- Should digital and traditional media be handled by the same agency?

- Should production activities be decoupled from creative?

- Will the same agency approach for PR work for social media?

- Should we consolidate all activities under one full service agency?

- Should we concentrate our work with agencies from the same holding companies?

- Should all or some of the work be handled as a retainer or as project assignments?

- How do we best support global requirements and ensure brand consistency worldwide?

- Should we emphasize flexibility or efficiency in the agency model?

There are many variables that might influence what agency strategy is selected and implemented. Some advertisers may even require multiple models and a unique portfolio of agencies to serve the many, diverse needs of their organization. Answers to these questions will provide insight into the type of agency model(s) best suited. Agency management is responsible for establishing clear objectives, and for selecting and implementing the best agency strategy for the company. For more information, see Chapter 4.

CLIENT VIEWPOINT

"Clients must be as integrated as they expect their agencies to be. There are too many silos today on either side. Everything must be integrated. Agencies tend to mirror their clients, but if the client doesn't lead in this area, then agencies won't follow." [41]

—SUSAN MARKOWICZ, GLOBAL ADVERTISING AGENCY MANAGER, FORD MOTOR COMPANY

CORE RESPONSIBILITY: AGENCY SEARCH

This is the set of activities by which an advertiser matches the needs of the organization with the best agency partner. Searching for and selecting the best mix of agencies on your roster is another critical agency management responsibility. It requires a solid understanding of what the company needs from its agencies. It also requires a rigorous, effective, collaborative process that gets to the right outcome: an agency partner with the best competencies, experience, talent, and resources to meet or exceed their expectations. In Chapter 5, we will help answer the following questions:

- What talent gap do we have in our current agency roster?

- How do we identify the initial list of potential agency partners for our search?

- How will agencies be vetted?

- Will we conduct a full RFI and RFP or follow a more expedient approach?

- How do we keep the search process as efficient as possible for all involved?

- Who will be responsible for managing this process end to end?

- How will we conduct in-person chemistry checks?

- What best practices should we follow to make effective use of our time and resources?

- What criteria will we use to decide which agency partner is best suited for our needs?

- How should we handle spec work?

- Will we ask the incumbent agency to participate in this pitch?

- Will we need the assistance and support from an external search consultant?

- Who will be involved in the decision-making process? Who will make the final call?

For companies with high agency turnover or expanding needs, having well-honed skills in agency search proves to be especially handy. Agency reviews and searches have become so frequent in today's dynamic environment that some best practices have emerged, setting up standards to which both clients and agencies can and should adhere. Clients may decide to hire an agency search consultant with an intimate knowledge of the marketplace or rely on the support of their marketing procurement organization for some aspects of the search process. Doing so can speed up the search process, introduce efficiency, and increase the client's likelihood of finding the best agency match. For more information, see Chapter 5.

CORE RESPONSIBILITY: AGENCY CONTRACT

Any sound business relationship is governed by a set of contract terms that provide important guardrails and set clear expectations for both parties to adhere to. Often negotiated as multi-year contracts, they provide useful information requiring careful business and legal consideration. The master service agreement is typically supported by contract addendums which flesh out even greater details such as scope of work, staffing plans, rate cards, and other relevant documentation. Taking time up front to establish clear, shared expectations and legal parameters for the newly formed relationship ensures that the partnership can quickly move into execution mode with confidence that both parties' interests are protected. It may also prevent both parties from falling into potentially costly litigation proceedings over misunderstandings that could have been prevented from the start. In Chapter 6, we will help answer the following questions:

- What are the negotiable business terms in agency contracts?

- What are contract best practices today, and how will those impact past agreements?

- How will audits be conducted to ensure full compliance?

- How do we best prepare for these contract discussions?

- How do we ensure contract terms are being well understood and followed internally?

- What are the common pitfalls or mistakes made while putting together agency contracts?

- What are the most contentious parts of the contract? What feedback should we expect?

- What aspects of the contract should we consider auditing and how frequently?

- How do we establish an audit plan that is reasonable and effective?

AGENCY VIEWPOINT

"The biggest challenge we face as an industry is convincing clients to focus on the top line rather than reducing costs, and to realize that ad spending is "an investment, not a cost." [42]
—**SIR MARTIN SORRELL**, FORMER CHIEF EXECUTIVE OFFICER, WPP AND EXECUTIVE CHAIRMAN, S4 CAPITAL

The individual or team responsible for agency management directly interfaces with the company's legal department and facilitates the back and forth process between the respective legal teams and the relationship owners. If there are disagreements about the business terms, they intervene to guide internal discussions. Some contract terms are more negotiable than others and may require further input or decisions from the company's stakeholders. Although finalizing a contract can require the active involvement and support of other internal departments, having the right business terms to address marketing needs ultimately falls under the agency management team's responsibility. For more information, see Chapter 6.

CORE RESPONSIBILITY: AGENCY COMPENSATION

There are numerous ways to structure agency compensation agreements. Why is it so challenging for advertisers and agencies to come up with the perfect answer? There are many permutations of compensation methods, all with distinct advantages and potential trade-offs that must be carefully evaluated. Advertisers must model and evaluate a range of scenarios to decide which path will yield the best short- and long-term outcomes for the relationship. In doing so, the agency management team must reconcile the needs of different parts of the company, such as marketing and finance, in order to derive the most value. In the end, both parties must feel that the agreed compensation is fair, competitive, and motivating. Clearly, what's fair to the client and to the agency can be diametrically different. Similarly, what seems reasonable to finance might be at odds with the viewpoint in marketing: Marketing wants a Lamborghini V10-powered coupé to win the competitive race, but finance would rather deploy a fuel-efficient Toyota Prius. These can be controversial topics and subject to endless internal and external negotiations. In the end, no two contracts are alike. In Chapter 7, we will help answer the following questions:

- Which compensation method is most beneficial to both parties?

- What are the current compensation trends, and how will those affect our decisions?

- Who should be involved in these compensation decisions internally?

- What is a reasonable level of profitability on our account?

- How do we keep the marketing organization up to date on changes to compensation terms?

- Should we set up a performance incentive bonus, and how will this be set and managed?

- What terms will encourage both parties to behave in the best interest of the relationship?

- How do we ensure the terms will motivate the agency to perform at its best?

- What are reasonable payment terms for this type of work?

- How often should we re-evaluate our compensation agreements?

- How will differences of opinion or disconnects about compensation be handled?

- How do we compare and benchmark our terms, so we know we pay fairly?

- What data should we ask for to monitor the financial health of our agency relationships?

CLIENT VIEWPOINT

"Having unprofitable agencies is not good business, and can lead to practices we don't want, so we're taking a closer look at matching fees to services." [43]

—MARC S. PRITCHARD, CHIEF BRAND OFFICER,
PROCTER & GAMBLE CO.

As new practices emerge, the agency management function must assess alternatives and find the best compensation methods to get to the right outcome for the partnership. Agency compensation is also about how clients manage agency-related expenses, a responsibility shared with the finance organization. Because cash flow is a vital bloodstream for agencies, the flow and timing of payment significantly influences the relationship. Small client relationships may only require tracking agency expenses and ensuring prompt payment. For large, multi-national relationships, agency-related expenses require additional management supervision to handle a sizeable number of transactions efficiently and in a timely manner. They also require oversight in multiple worldwide locations and dealing with financial concerns such as foreign exchange rates, VAT, hedging, AVBs, media credits, and pre-payments. For more information, see Chapter 7.

CORE RESPONSIBILITY: AGENCY SCOPE/ BRIEFING

Scope of work planning is the essential process of identifying and cataloging the work to be done by the agency roster, articulating expectations as precisely as possible through the client input briefing process and ensuring that the agency can assign resources where they are most needed to carry out the mission at hand. It also happens to be one of the most challenging tasks faced by clients today. Clients are 100% obligated to accurately define their objectives, spell out their marketing plans, and scope the work asked of the agency. If they don't, clients will end up with unnecessary levels of re-briefings and creative rework that will burn through the budget and cost them dearly. In Chapter 8, we will help answer the following questions:

- How are marketing priorities defined and communicated to the agency(ies)?

- Is there a common framework and taxonomy to ensure scope consistency?

- What level of information is the agency requesting to adequately staff and prepare?

- What workflow process is required to get internal alignment on key priorities?

- Should agency cost per staff or deliverables be benchmarked regularly?

- What level of scope or budget information do agencies require to align their own resources?

- How are agency reconciliations conducted? What decisions are expected as a result?

- How are input brief documents created and shared with agencies?

- How do we measure the quality of the input provided to the agencies by marketers?

- What are the essential elements of a client input brief?

- Are input briefs consistently providing success metrics or clear objectives?

- What best practices should advertisers consider and apply to get better results?

- How many revisions of the briefs are considered reasonable?

- How should advertisers provide actionable feedback during creative reviews?

- What are the most common mistakes made by advertisers when providing feedback?

CLIENT VIEWPOINT

"Marketing has fundamentally changed from marketing to publishing, and the pace and turnaround is so much faster. What we're asking for is ideas, but in a different shape and form... We need quick pulses. We're looking for a great idea that connects and has a little story that we can tell. Our brands need to tell stories every day and that is what we're briefing for." [44]

—**JENNELLE TILLING,** FOUNDER AND CHIEF BRAND
STRATEGIST, MARKETING WITH INSIGHT (FORMER GLOBAL
CHIEF MARKETING OFFICER, KFC)

Agencies must translate the client's scope of work into a well-tuned staffing plan and must factor in several variables when determining the right mix of resources. Many of them are subjective at best, such as how efficient or inefficient the client is at approving work or the degree of clarity about the scope. In turn, reviewing and approving the way the account is staffed and trained, making sure its people have been carefully prepared, and monitoring the effective use of these resources, is the client's responsibility. A company's ability to ramp up agency personnel quickly and effectively will directly impact the quality of the agency work and client/agency productivity. A poorly orchestrated scope of work or client input brief process will inevitably result in significant inefficiencies, higher agency fees, and budget waste. Why is the potentially most impactful thing an advertiser can do to gain the most value from its agency relationships also the most difficult to do at the core of this important agency management responsibility? Many companies have a very difficult time planning, prioritizing, scoping, and briefing what they want their agency to do. Unclear strategy, ever-changing competitive threats, or unexpected budget cuts all get in the way of providing clear guidance to agencies. However, without it, agencies cannot staff effectively and prepare themselves to take on the work. Effective client input briefing is equally critical. A successful agency/client engagement hinges on a clear definition of what is expected, when it is to be delivered, and how the work will get done. This is the essence of a solid engagement, and why agency management is instrumental in establishing an efficient process to enable the exchange of information between marketing project owners and agencies. For more information, see Chapter 8.

CORE RESPONSIBILITY: PERFORMANCE EVALUATION AND TRAINING

Is the relationship living up to its promises? As in any relationship, it is expected that issues will arise from time to time; a few things will need to be tweaked to run more efficiently. Since we're dealing with human beings interacting with each other, the intangibles are a very real part of what we consider when evaluating the quality and effectiveness of a relationship. In Chapter 9, we will help answer the following questions:

- What are the most important attributes for agencies to exhibit in this relationship?

- What are the most important attributes for clients to exhibit in this relationship?

- How often should we evaluate the client/agency relationship and its overall performance?

- What is "meeting" or "exceeding" expectations in this relationship?

- How often should this type of performance evaluation be conducted?

- How do we spot potential disconnects in the relationship? How do we reset expectations?

- Who should be involved in providing feedback? Should this feedback be anonymous?

- Will these results be used to determine some type of incentive-based compensation?

- How will this information be used to inform improvement plans?

- How will significantly underperforming relationships be handled?

- Are all attributes or criteria of equal value to the advertiser or agencies?

- What type of training would enhance the ability of the agency to deliver better work?

- What do advertisers need to know to be better clients to their agencies?

AGENCY VIEWPOINT

"There must be an understanding of the right alchemy that could potentially deliver that level of creativity. Ultimately, it takes a strong client-agency partnership, a clear brief articulating the challenge, and an appetite from the client to embrace risk (rather than focusing on how to mitigate it) and to lean into that uncomfortable feeling that often comes with a bold move." [45]

—MARLA KAPLOWITZ, PRESIDENT AND CEO, 4AS

It is the responsibility of agency management to monitor the overall agency/client performance and relationship health by instituting a standard and regular performance review process with the agencies, based on key performance indicators (KPIs) that have been agreed upon by both parties. Based on these results, improvement areas can be identified on both sides and action plans put forward and monitored to ensure continual improvement and healthy, productive relationships. It's also important to provide onboarding and training information to agencies and marketing teams so they are ready to engage and are informed of the many aspects of the relationship they must be aware of or even comply with. Agency staff need frequent and unfettered access to information relevant to the work they are doing on the client's behalf—guidelines, policies, brand assets, product briefings and research, internal tools, and any information that can facilitate a seamless and productive engagement. Providing training to new and existing agency staff must be paramount to keep all staff refreshed and updated on potential changes to the company's business, competitive environment, strategic initiatives, standards, and policies. Please note that training and performance evaluation are combined in the same chapter, given the importance of training in helping advertisers and agencies perform at their best. For more information, see Chapter 9.

ESTABLISHING A FRAMEWORK FOR SUCCESS

Although these functions outlined on the previous pages are the most common responsibilities held by the agency management discipline, its role does not end here. Agency management has direct and structured accountability to the company's senior management internally and to leadership at the agencies. The client's agency management team may conduct regular meetings with senior management on either side of the fence to discuss the health of the whole relationship—what's working well, what could be working better, the overall quality and business impact of the work, key financial data points, key hires and departures, and other operational details. It is an ideal time to discuss business priorities, any shifts happening internally or externally, and to check in on long-term goals for the partnership.

The agency business is primarily a talent business. Advertisers must pay close attention to the experience, seniority, and skills of the staff that the agency assigns to the relationship. Hiring and retaining key talent is what makes or breaks agencies and their ability to keep accounts. For the most part, as with most businesses, agencies are only as good as each of their people. Clients want minimal disruption or personnel turnover in their business. Is the account fully staffed? Are the account resources too junior, too senior, or too distracted to carry out the work? Do we have the right mix of talent? Weak or frequently changing agency staff results in poor outcomes for the client and loss of institutional knowledge. It causes inefficiencies with sizeable financial impact (severance and legal expenses, on-boarding costs, learned lessons forgotten, and so forth).

CLIENT VIEWPOINT

"We're asking [our partners] for a very big part of themselves. How we encourage that and nurture that has a lot to do with the quality of work we get and the people willing to work on our account. You want the best people on your business." [46]
—**DANA ANDERSON,** FORMER SENIOR VICE PRESIDENT AND CHIEF MARKETING OFFICER, MONDELEZ INTERNATIONAL, CMO, MEDIALINK

President Harry S. Truman's desk in the Oval Office of the White House bore a sign with the phrase "The Buck Stops Here." Originating from a phrase used in the game of poker and made in 1945 in the Federal Reformatory at El Reno, Oklahoma, the sign mounted on its walnut base left no doubt as to who was in charge and who had ultimate responsibility for making and dealing with the consequences of important decisions. As it relates to the management of agencies, the accountability question remains: Who has "the buck stops here" responsibility within a client organization for the vibrancy and efficacy of business-critical partnerships? All too often, the lack of ownership and accountability for agency performance is itself responsible for the failure of an agency relationship. Either no one seems to be on point, or too many people have conflicting agendas, leaving agencies wondering which decision maker to turn to. Designating one individual or an agency management team to coordinate and facilitate the effective management of the relationship will minimize confusion and increase ownership for success, which in turn will significantly strengthen the partnership.

CLIENT VIEWPOINT

"The marketing procurement role is to act as a strategic buffer between the agencies and the needs of the company, answering to both. We like to think about ourselves as another informational point for the agencies and for the business." [47]

—JEFF DEVON, FORMER SENIOR DIRECTOR, INDIRECT PROCUREMENT, HP/HPE

The discipline of agency management is based on a set of fundamental concepts and best practices that anyone in the company who is involved in marketing should become familiar with, regardless of company size. Each of them has some responsibility for fully leveraging the investment made in its agency partnerships. This is an opportunity every marketer must take seriously to make the best use of company resources. Agency management must therefore be treated as an essential discipline, regardless of whether a company feels it can afford to dedicate resources to it or chooses instead to add that role to someone strategically placed within the company. Important agency-related decisions are often vetted and approved by a senior leadership team or by a virtual team of key stakeholders from multiple client organizations and corporate functions. From hiring a new firm, negotiating a contract, to effectively briefing the agency on a new project and getting the best possible work from them, agency management responsibilities require a mix of fundamental skills in business, marketing, people management, and finance. The agency management function has often historically lacked proper structure, planning, and operational rigor, leading to time-wasting reviews, disappointing results, and a host of other inefficiencies that can end up costing companies as much as a third more of their total agency spend.

The ideal resources for this agency management function will have both client and agency background. Having worked for an agency at some point in their career will provide them with a unique perspective that is difficult to obtain otherwise. It also reassures agencies to know that they are interacting with someone who understands their perspective. The agency management role also requires a diverse set of business skills and professional experience, on both the client and agency side, to enable smooth, streamlined operations between the two organizations. The last thing any advertiser needs is an agency distracted from doing its best work because of inattentive briefings, personnel clashes, or payment delays due to lack of thoughtful planning and anticipatory internal coordination.

Agency management is also about governance and change management, constantly aligning organization needs and measuring the performance of agency management programs in impacting business drivers. As such, the role requires people of well-rounded experience, with a solid reputation for building strong partnerships and a passion for adopting emerging industry best practices and testing new concepts that drive business and financial performance and improve operational effectiveness. In Chapter 10, we will address what drives clients mad and agencies crazy, and what constitutes the DNA of a successful partnership.

EMPOWERED AND ENABLED BY TECHNOLOGY

The emergence of discipline-specific technologies in the field of agency management is hugely promising and is likely to see accelerated adoption in businesses of all sizes, harmonizing processes and streamlining and automating tasks that were previously manual, labor-intensive, and prone to error. These include annual planning/scoping, assignment/project briefing, relationship and performance evaluations, agency roster management, and readiness training/on boarding for agencies and internal marketing teams.

INTEGRATED APPROACH
TO MANAGING AGENCY PARTNERSHIPS

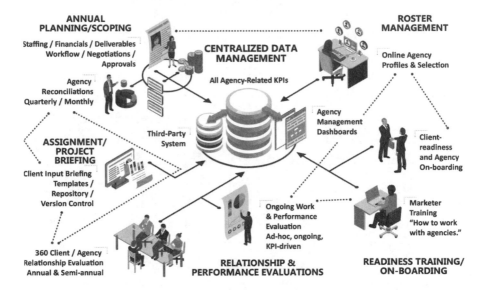

These powerful tools and solutions are now coming of age, fueled by innovation in the field of cloud computing, system integration, software-as-service marketing automation, and business re-engineering and productivity improvement. As they evolve they have the potential to dramatically reduce the time and effort required to administer these activities. By reducing administration costs, improving controls and trace-ability, increasing productivity, and enhancing transparency and executive decision-making capability, they can free you to focus on strategic priorities and outcomes. They can also increase data accessibility to a wider number of stakeholders within the company, further advancing the understanding and practice of responsible agency management inside client organizations. This data—whether supplied by agencies like financial reconciliation or sourced internally like cost per deliverable—can then inform and improve decision making. However, simple access to these solutions is no substitute for common-sense practices and sound business judgment. As in any relationship, agency management is more a journey than a destination. Companies are encouraged to take a "crawl, walk, run" approach to building their own agency management function to avoid any missteps and to ensure a balanced investment of time and resources. The function is inherently deeply influenced and shaped by the work of other departments. It requires cross-group collaboration and aligned commitments. In the end, realizing the greatest value from agency partnerships is not only about agency management, but about leadership. Leadership, and what the company organizes itself to ask of agencies, is about inspiring and motivating talent. It's about pushing the limits, focusing on what truly matters, taking occasional risks, and creating an environment that makes smart people want to go the extra mile to fulfill a shared vision. Leadership in agency management is what drives greatness and delivers meaningful results that both the client and agency can be proud of.

TOP 3
BEST PRACTICES
for Advertisers

1 Formalize the role of driving optimal value from agency partnerships within your organization and institutionalize this Agency Management/Relations function and relevant key competencies.

2 Clarify roles and responsibilities for all stakeholders and enable marketers with daily interactions with agencies to work effectively by providing them with the right tools and resources to do so.

3 Leverage technology, software solutions, and automation whenever possible to streamline agency-related activities, reduce labor-intensive and error-prone activities, and improve decision-making.

4

WHERE IS YOUR MOUNTAIN AND ARE YOU CLIMBING IT?

"Strategy is the art of making use of time and space. I am less concerned about the latter than the former. Space we can recover, lost time never."
—**NAPOLEON BONAPARTE,** POLITICAL LEADER AND MILITARY STRATEGIST

The average client-agency relationship is in sharp decline, creating much tension and uncertainty for both advertisers and agencies. The need for a robust agency model has never been timelier. It establishes a collaborative framework for success and a necessary operating model for existing and new agencies. The essence of strategy is clarity of purpose and designing a clear path to achieve that purpose. Advertisers must choose a strategy that has been designed to support their most pressing organizational needs, but also supports their long-term goals. The agency model, the company's blueprint to organize its agency roster most effectively, must also be implemented flawlessly. Stated differently: Advertisers must find their mountain and start climbing it. It's insane to think that billions of marketing dollars are still channeled through randomly selected agencies by clients of all sizes without a clear agency strategy or model and with no clear path to turn these agencies into higher-value partnerships. Surprisingly, most advertisers still make ill-informed, on-the-fly decisions. They lack a sound operating model, organized around internal competencies, organizational big bets, or a more holistic and integrated approach to marketing. Companies rarely invest the time and effort needed to design and align on an overarching strategy before making important decisions such as kicking off a new agency search or assigning work to roster agencies. They don't look at themselves in the mirror and ask difficult questions. As a result, they end up losing time and resources they can never recover.

AGENCY VIEWPOINT

"Hold a mirror up to your organization, inclusive of external partners, and ask yourself whether you're structured for success. There's no single right way to organize, but there are questions that can help determine the best approach. Do you have the expertise you need to plan and execute superbly? Are teams or incentive structures aligned toward outcomes, rather than budget allocations that encourage fiefdoms based on specialty areas? Can you afford to attract and retain specialized talent to your organization, or is it more effective to use partners?" [48]

—BRYAN WIENER, EXECUTIVE CHAIRMAN, 360I

A successfully-implemented model ensures that advertisers get the most from their agencies: the right agencies, with the right competencies, working on the right assignments, and producing great work at competitive pricing. The fanatical Chief Marketing Officer high turnover phenomenon has led to short-term strategy which, in turn, often results in short-sighted agency decisions. The absence of a clear agency strategy and action plan can add confusion and uncertainty, internally and externally. Strategy always provides clarity and focus and aligns people and resources behind a common goal. Once the strategy is set and a plan has been developed, it's about ensuring executive buy-in and support across the entire organization. Strategy is always a continuous process. Periodical reviews of the agency model and operating plan allow for course-correction and improvements.

UNDERSTANDING ORGANIZATIONAL NEEDS

Advertisers want to capitalize on the value of a consistent, well-coordinated agency model that contributes to marketing performance. Designing such a model requires a minimum level of research and investigation. We must first conduct a thorough assessment of the organizational needs and priorities. How do we get started? Interview important stakeholders, i.e., marketing leaders, budget owners, and those who directly interface with the agencies. Interview agency leaders as well to get their perspective and input. Find out what agency competencies are most needed, and which skills and resources are most valued. Draw upon insights gained from past agency relationship successes and failures. Evaluate current talent gaps and opportunities. Assess the health of current agency relationships. Find out their strengths and areas for improvement. Consider organizational, financial, and cultural roadblocks. Study the competition. Explore the agency models they implemented and why. The needs of the organization are likely changing. Anticipate what's needed to deliver against marketing budgets and priorities.

CLIENT VIEWPOINT

"The model is built around four pieces of content that take four months to develop and cost $2 million each. It's not a sustainable model. . . .The big issue is: are we as an industry, on both the agency- and client-side, structured to be able to deliver this? This is a disruption that's happened around us, and we're still talking about 30-second television ads." [49]

—BRAD JAKEMAN, FORMER PRESIDENT, GLOBAL BEVERAGE GROUP, SENIOR ADVISOR & CONSULTANT, PEPSICO

The result of your analysis is the initial development of a sound strategy and the resulting agency model—a strategic framework that establishes the mix of agency talent needed and how these agency resources will be seamlessly organized to deliver the most value to the organization. Often easier said than done, developing such strategy requires answering these fundamental questions:

- What operating model has the company used in the past and how well did it work? What lessons did we learn? What business or marketing objectives will the agency model be supporting? How central are marketing strategy, experience delivery, and performance to the model considerations?

- What professional or specialty skills should be outsourced to agencies and marketing service providers? What skills are most needed to augment and complement internal talent and resources? Should the company consider doing some of its work in-house? Should some of the work be fully automated or enabled by technology?

- Which marketing services should be integrated or decoupled (creative, media, production, digital, analytics, etc.)? Should the company assign a "lead creative agency" for the other disciplines to rally behind and execute on the one idea? Who will be responsible for the work integration and the holistic view of the customer? What type of marketing content creation and distribution should the model enable?

- What type of agency will best support the company's current and future priorities? Should the company seek to work with a large network-affiliated agency or a small independent boutique agency?

- If the operating model invites for multiple agency relationships, what criteria should be used to align an agency to a given product, brand, audience/segment or geography? Who will be the ultimate decision-maker? How do we avoid having these agencies operate in unwanted silos? Will the agencies be expected to collaborate and if so, how? What common engagement rules and cross-channel performance metrics should they be operating with to ensure full alignment of resources and efforts?

- Is there adequate endorsement for the agency strategy and selected agencies at the executive level as well as a relatively consistent level of investment to support it? Is the operating model organized to run cost-effectively?

- How will the company measure the success of its agency strategy and operating model?

Clear, well-supported answers to these questions are essential to develop an agency plan for long-term success and to assemble a roster of agencies that will become the in-market firepower the company can rely on. The upfront time invested will always prove to save time and money and will be hugely beneficial in the end. It becomes the company roadmap to a shared definition of success with the agency/ies, no matter how big or small your company. Aligning the company around a single agency strategy is not only a sound logical approach; it will prove to be vital to mutual success. It will become a priceless reference point when tough decisions will undoubtedly have to be made. It may lead to actions designed to strengthen the quality of the work, improve the client/agency engagement, drive greater cost-efficiencies, and build new agency and client team skills and capabilities. However, if the chosen agency strategy doesn't address and deliver on genuine business challenges faced by the company, it will not receive the level of executive and staff attention and support it needs to flourish. Ideally, measurable objectives are established at the beginning of the fiscal year based on the business priorities required to achieve market, investor, or business expectations.

Objectives focus on what needs to be done, when it needs to be done, and how much needs to be invested in getting it done. They should also outline how to enforce accountabilities, increase transparency, and inform partnership opportunities. The annual agency plan—often a subset of the overall marketing communications plan—articulates how the company proposes to achieve its objectives, what agency model it will implement, and how to highlight specific activities that will be needed to carry out the mission. It's about making sure the right agency(ies) are doing the right assignments, effectively and efficiently. It also provides actionable insight into the challenges faced by either the client or the agency. Advertisers must give themselves enough time see the results of their agency investments before deciding if further agency adjustments are necessary. Any timeframe shorter than a year is likely to be premature and wasteful. A lot can happen in a year. However, if you do not set your sights on a spot on the horizon, you may never effectively leave port. The purpose of a sound agency strategy is to equip the company with an understanding of its top priorities that require external talent and a clear plan for how the company will align itself to focus the energies of its agencies to achieve those goals.

CHOOSING THE RIGHT MODEL FOR YOUR BUSINESS

Building a sound agency strategy is a matter of setting a clear direction for the way a company will realize the most value from its agency partnerships and making sure those partners meet their objectives.

CLIENT VIEWPOINT

"In the last two years, we've created approximately 2,500 pieces of marketing content a year. This year, we will create roughly 5,000 pieces of marketing content, so we're making more content, but we're also challenging ourselves to make our content much more valuable to our customers." [50]

—DEBORAH WAHL, FORMER CMO, MCDONALD'S

These decisions will typically be based on two dimensions: the options desired (both in breadth and depth) according to flexibility necessary in the agency roster and the type of cross-agency coordination desired, and whether this will be handled by the client internally or by the agency externally. To determine the right agency model, clients will want to evaluate the breadth of options available and the implications each scenario may have for the company's marketing effectiveness, integration, costs, speed to market, agility, process efficiencies, brand/message control, and internal resourcing. Over the years, a few agency models have emerged to answer the most common requirements of advertisers who naturally have varying degrees of complexity, scope, and organizational needs. There are important drivers that advertisers must consider and prioritize to determine which model is best suited to satisfy their company needs:

TALENT

Breadth of competencies and skillsets. Overall quality of resources. Ability to attract, hire, retain, train and grow best in class talent.

INTEGRATION

Ability to strategically and tactically plan and execute fully integrated campaigns across all touch points and marketing disciplines. Ability to coordinate all activities in seamless manner.

EFFICIENCIES

Ability to realize cost efficiencies through economies of scale, streamlined processes, reduced waste and improved rates.

FLEXIBILITY

Ability to make roster changes, scout marketplace and access broad range of agency resources. Agility and flexibility in handling agency resources.

GLOBAL

Ability to address regional and local staff requirements. Ability to plan and execute work in multiple geographic locations. Access to global resources.

SPECIALTY

Depth of competencies and skillsets. Ability to provide, access or manage specialty skills and competencies.

SIMPLICITY

Simplicity of operating model, reducing moving parts and concentrating on the work vs. management of agency resources.

KEY CONSIDERATIONS TO SELECT THE RIGHT AGENCY MODEL

No matter how good each individual musician is in any given orchestra, if their instruments are not working together in a harmonious way, you inevitably end up with cacophony and noise. This might be a tired analogy to some, but it's hard to ignore such a powerful and simple concept when it applies to agency management. All companies understand the strategic importance of aligning and organizing talent in a synergistic way. What applies internally also applies to external resources like agencies, yet too few apply the rigor and discipline required. To perhaps oversimplify, choosing the right agency model often comes down to the following two considerations as illustrated below: depth and breadth of agency services offered and whether integration is agency- or client-led. Agency models centered around holding companies offer greater scalability (size of offering and global scale) and agency-led integration across the various disciplines of services needed. Whether the scope is domestic or global in nature may also have a significant impact on deciding which agency model is best-suited for a given advertiser. On the opposite side of the spectrum, some advertisers may favor hyper-specialization and take ownership of the orchestration and integration of these agency services, which is easier when the scope is domestic in nature. Stated differently: Are you favoring simplicity, seamless agency-led integration, and economies of scale; or are you choosing to emphasize choice and flexibility, i.e., client-led integration?

CLIENT VIEWPOINT

"We are not only reviewing our agencies but also our agency model." [51]

—**IVAN POLLARD,** FORMERLY SENIOR-VP FOR CONNECTIONS, INVESTMENTS AND ASSETS, COCA-COLA NORTH AMERICA

Advertisers may choose to establish a relationship with a holding company, a network, a full-service agency, a lead agency, and/or a roster of independent agencies in a sort of open source model. They may build an in-house agency or implement a combination of all or some of the above. Bundled services include holding company- or network-led models as well as integrated agency models where multiple expert services can be accessed through a single umbrella relationship. They are often referred to as one-stop shops and are popular among global brands. These centralized resources "under one roof" tend to organize themselves around streamlined client coordination and integration. Essentially, the holding company, agency network, and full-service models rely heavily on the agency coordinating across the agency roster and integrating the work on the client's behalf. These types of agency models favor retained staff agreements. On the opposite end of the spectrum, the so-called "open source" model allows marketers to cherry-pick agencies from an approved list, but the client is on point to ensure the integration and coordination of these services, as well as the collaboration, often between competing agencies.

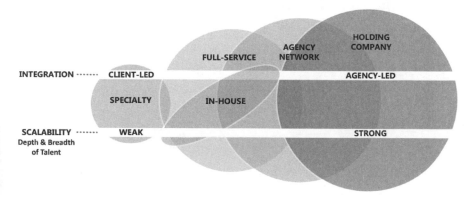

TWO MAJOR PIVOT POINTS: CLIENT OR AGENCY-LED
INTEGRATION AND TALENT SCALABILITY

This à la carte approach offers maximum flexibility to the client and favors project-based engagements through which advertisers like Kimberly-Clark are no longer guaranteeing business for their agencies. In-house agencies are also on the rise. Most advertisers have now in-sourced some small aspects of their marketing activities like social, production, content, etc.; work that was previously handled by specialized agencies. Unbundled services provide more flexibility and best-in-class functional specializations. Large agencies are built on economies of scale which can be critically important to clients with a global footprint or ambition. They can cross cultural lines; balancing client needs for global strategy with requirements for local relevancy and flexibility.

But is flatter and leaner better? Large companies have matrixed businesses with diverse needs. They cannot put all their eggs in the same agency basket. As a result, they use several agencies to support various business groups, either in or out of the network. They may occasionally diversify their agency roster to test new capabilities or try new relationships. However, whenever possible, they centralize their media planning and buying needs through one media agency of record (AOR) to capitalize on economies of scale.

CLIENT VIEWPOINT

"We have the responsibility to do strategic category reviews every 12 to 18 months. We are constantly looking at the quality and performance of our agency, the changes in our business needs, and changes in the marketplace, to evaluate whether or not we have the right number and the right type of agencies on our roster." [52]

—**MICHAEL E. THYEN,** DIRECTOR OF PROCUREMENT, INTERNATIONAL BUSINESS UNIT, ELI LILLY AND COMPANY

EMBRACING THE "GLOCAL" CHALLENGE

As companies expand internationally, they must also consider the best agency model to support their global ambitions. Brand uniformity, campaign synchronicity, efficient global deployment, and speed to market are vital considerations. As companies have expanded their businesses abroad, so have the agencies to support them. Many agencies have built or acquired offices in all countries and regions where clients have a need for their services, as an alternative to clients disseminating brand/campaign guidelines and letting their subsidiaries work with uncoordinated, disparate, local agencies. Today these agencies land global campaigns that carry one voice globally but are adapted locally to resonate with local audiences—a concept often referred as "glocal." A much better outcome is achieved than the cacophony and brand devaluation that could result from messaging inconsistencies. In optimal cases, clients use these local offices not only to land the work in the field, but also to check for local cultural sensitivity during the idea and concept development stage so there are no surprises when the campaign breaks. Often ideas are generated from the global teams working with corporate headquarters, but the most sophisticated agencies embrace ideas and best practices coming from anywhere around the world and share them with all the offices. Advertisers often use specialized global production vendors that work with their creative agencies to create, translate, localize, adapt, manage, and deliver campaigns in local markets through more efficient in-market resources or a "hub and spoke" model.

Rather than building their own network, some agencies are partnering directly with lower-overhead, streamlined, global production and transcreation companies to bundle services and bring a one-stop competitive solution to their clients. Whether advertisers are relying on their global agency network or specialized production and deployment resources to go to market, they realize that to achieve business goals, global campaigns must go beyond "take and translate" models that simply speak the local language. Having copywriters and art directors that are fluent in multiple languages might be a plus, but it's about understanding the cultural and local nuances of each individual market to land work that makes campaign investments credible, affordable, and effective. And finally, global advertisers need agency partners that can manage asset trafficking, distribution, tracking, and using the latest Digital Asset Management (DAM) solutions.

OVERCOMING THE COST OF COMPLEXITY

The much-greater complexity of marketing as a discipline combined with the increased media fragmentation naturally contributed to a rise in the number of subject matter experts and specialized agencies.

CLIENT VIEWPOINT

"We had too many agencies—3,000. We are halving the number of agencies we work with and investing more with our strategic agencies. We'll still be working with locally relevant agencies—that mobile specialist in Jakarta—but that group in the middle didn't offer any differentiation. It will save time, but also means we can negotiate better, more complex agreements with fewer agencies." [53]

—**KEITH WEED,** CHIEF MARKETING AND COMMUNICATIONS OFFICER, UNILEVER

As agency rosters doubled or even tripled in size, so did the operational costs involved with the management of these partnerships. The so called "cost of complexity" became a growing concern that ultimately led advertisers to consolidate whenever possible. That was the case for Swedish furniture retailer Ikea, which consolidated its $444 million global media business into two holding companies, WPP and Dentsu Aegis Group, for work that was previously spread across five holding companies. AT&T consolidated its creative, digital, and media accounts with Omnicom, allowing the brand to have a single integrated team to move quickly, innovate at scale, and take a data-driven, holistic approach to consumer engagement, melding data and analytics with the creative. Under the new agency model, Omnicom became responsible for creative, media, digital, data, and analytics. BBDO took the lead on creative, while Hearts & Science handled new media.

AGENCY VIEWPOINT

"During the last 30 years, we have grown through the silo approach [with] disciplines. The system has shown some limits in how the client can benefit from it. It shows clients are not ready to pay for duplication of services or people. They want something which is seamless, and fully integrated in one single platform." [54]

—**MAURICE LÉVY,** CHAIRMAN OF THE SUPERVISORY BOARD AND FORMER CHAIRMAN, PUBLICIS GROUPE

MOST COMMON AGENCY MODELS

Ready to deep dive to better understand the options available? Let's take a closer look at the most common agency models advertisers are deploying, including holding company, network-led, full-service, lead, open source, in-house, and hybrid or other innovative models. We will then examine the pros and cons of each:

AGENCY MODELS

 = ADVERTISER

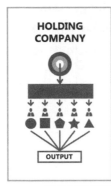

HOLDING COMPANY

NETWORK-LED

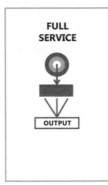

FULL SERVICE

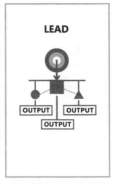

LEAD

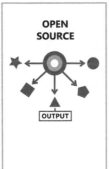

OPEN SOURCE

IN-HOUSE

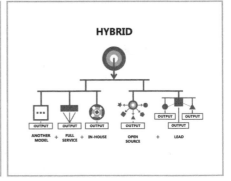

HYBRID

DEEP DIVE: "HOLDING-COMPANY" MODEL

The holding company acts as a parent company, overseeing a portfolio of best-in-class agency talent. Holding companies historically served as financial shells, designed to avoid competitive conflicts. Today, the holding company takes an active managerial role, bringing together the perfect mix of talent to meet the unique needs of an advertiser. The holding company handles the complexity of coordinating multiple agencies, networks, and disciplines across multiple geographic areas. Under this model, an integrated agency team is assembled across a range of disciplines and their many operating units. Omnicom built a dedicated McDonald's agency called "We Are Unlimited" to handle the McDonald's US creative business, marking the end of the 35-year relationship with Publicis' Leo Burnett. The multidisciplinary shop was initially composed of 200 staffers, including individuals from Facebook, Google, Twitter, Adobe, and The New York Times' T Brand Studio, in addition to people from other Omnicom agencies.

CLIENT VIEWPOINT

"Ford Motor Company has a network-holding based approach to its agency roster. The consolidation of agencies under the WPP virtual umbrella gives us single accountability, a single P&L to worry about, economies of scale, and a single point of coordination." [55]

—SUSAN MARKOWICZ, GLOBAL ADVERTISING AGENCY MANAGER, FORD MOTOR COMPANY

This model is best tailored for global companies with large spend. WPP has considerable experience setting up seamless cross-group client teams. Examples include Team Pfizer, Team BP, Team Vodafone, and many others. Considered one of the largest of 45+ WPP global client teams, automotive giant Ford is another example with WPP's dedicated unit GTB (or Global Team Blue). GTB is a single global entity that includes agencies Team Detroit, created in 2007 to combine JWT, Ogilvy, Mindshare, Y&R and Wunderman; Blue Hive, the WPP units that serve Ford outside the US, and Retail First. Staff are dedicated 100% to the client's business and are not distracted by other client opportunities. Because they are free from chasing new clients, they are focused on driving results for their client.

CLIENT VIEWPOINT

"Agencies must embrace cross-agency collaboration. At the holding company level, it means tapping into the best possible talent to serve the needs of the client. Motivating the best talent to not just work our business but really drive our business is what we're interested in at J&J." [56]

—JAMES R. ZAMBITO, SENIOR DIRECTOR GLOBAL CORPORATE AFFAIRS, JOHNSON & JOHNSON

The primary benefits of this model are: dedicated client leadership, integration of ideas across all media, access to best-in-class talent (functionally and geographically, across all the parent company agency brands), simplified relationship management (one contract, one P&L), talent breadth and depth, economies of scale, operational synergies, and cost efficiencies through process standardization and integration. Although it can be a powerful solution to clients requiring a vast and rich set of capabilities, the model's efficiencies must outweigh the cost of managing the inherent risk and complexity of this operating model. Typically a massive and complex undertaking, highly publicized and scrutinized, adopting a holding company model can be quite difficult to execute without hiccups. Look at Bank of America selecting Omnicom in 2005 to handle its marketing and media services business based on a Core Team of Omnicom agencies, including Live Technology, Organic, BBDO Worldwide, Javelin, OMD Worldwide, and others. Two years later, Bank of America decided to end its exclusive relationship with the network holding company and put its media planning and buying duties into review, signaling that advertisers may occasionally break the model and instead seek best-in-class agencies. The approach has inherent talent limitations and less flexibility once a client commits to a given holding company. This model requires long-term commitments on both sides.

DEEP DIVE: "NETWORK-LED" MODEL
The network-led model is appealing to large clients looking to establish a long-term partnership with an agency network such as Young & Rubicam Group, DDB Worldwide Communications Group, BBDO Worldwide, Ogilvy & Mather, McCann Worldgroup, or TBWA Worldwide. Although these agency networks are part of holding companies, they operate independently as well. Each network is typically composed of multiple, unified, specialized operating units that advertisers can easily access. The relationship with the advertiser can be set under one contract. One agency (the creative one) typically acts

as the lead on the account and coordinates behind the scenes how to leverage other agency network resources as needed. For example, Ogilvy & Mather became IBM's sole agency for all the company's marketing and branding efforts in 1994. As a result of this relationship, IBM also has access to many of the group resources including OgilvyOne, Ogilvy Public Relations, Neo@Ogilvy, and others. McCann Worldgroup also operates as a global network of integrated advertising agencies. McCann Worldgroup clients partner with McCann and can leverage other specialty marketing agencies inside the network like FutureBrand, UM, Momentum, MRM//McCann, Weber Shandwick, and more. Similarly, Omnicom's DDB introduced "DDB Flex"—an operating model that creates bespoke, cross-agency, integrated teams based on clients' businesses.

The holding company and network-led models both present similar benefits to large advertisers: a one-stop shop and an integrated approach, economies of scale, and access to a wide set of competencies and talent. Both models can reduce the coordination and orchestration role played by the client in other more decentralized models . . . at a cost, of course. For brand advertisers concerned about the holding company's ability to bring disparate agency resources together and operate the new combined entities under one team, a network-led model is a viable integrated agency solution.

CLIENT VIEWPOINT

"The goal of this latest wave of agency streamlining we're seeing right now is obviously greater integration. ... It's supposed to make it easier for those of us hiring the agencies. But the reality is that we get greater uniformity and more risk-averse middle managers, fewer new ideas, and more redrafts. The voices and perspectives of true experts and innovative thinkers are buried deeper in the bowels of corporate giants, shielded from the light and sanded down before they ever reach our customers. And all because the agencies think that their clients are just too lazy to handle the best talent. I see some of our competitors going all in on single agencies, and I find it very hard to believe they are getting high quality work out of that." [57]

—**DIEGO SCOTTI**, EXECUTIVE VICE PRESIDENT AND CHIEF
MARKETING OFFICER, VERIZON

DEEP DIVE: "FULL-SERVICE" MODEL

The full-service model remains a popular model among advertisers looking to better orchestrate their marketing and communication activities with a single agency. The advertiser relies on one full-service integrated agency of record to service all of its needs. Contrary to the holding-company or network-led models (which are also one-stop shops), all the services are sourced from within one single multi-disciplined agency. Integrated agencies (for example, Saatchi & Saatchi or Wieden+Kennedy) bring cross-functional disciplines—creative, media, digital, direct, PR, promotions, and so forth—together under one branded offering and within a single entity. Full-service integrated agencies may occasionally outsource work or partner with specialized firms, but they are coordinating these efforts on the advertiser's behalf. This sort of command-and-control approach allows clients to manage all agency activities centrally with greater brand consistency. The primary benefit is to bring brand consistency to marketing efforts, speaking as one unified voice in the marketplace. Dealing with a single agency allows advertisers to invest less time on coordination and vendor management. A single agency partner provides better economies of scale and increased cost efficiencies. Having one single point of contact at the agency can sizably reduce complexity and administrative efforts (fewer moving parts, fewer relationships to take on directly) and improve productivity for the client. This type of model is appealing to medium-size advertisers under constant pressure to better coordinate and integrate all their marketing efforts. However, with this approach, an advertiser is effectively putting all its eggs in one basket, which is a higher-risk strategy. It's also uncommon to find full-service integrated agencies that meet or exceed expectations at everything they do.

AGENCY VIEWPOINT

"The Adland 'Agency of Record' model, which has been around for decades, is losing relevance at an accelerated pace in today's world... it's a struggle and no one agency can do it alone. It takes a village to make the magic happen. And it requires collaboration and multiple partners to drive [clients'] business forward." [58]

—**BILL KOENIGSBERG**, FORMER 4AS CHAIRMAN AND FOUNDER, PRESIDENT AND CEO OF HORIZON MEDIA

DEEP DIVE: "LEAD" MODELS

Often called the "unbundled" agency model, advertisers may consider partnering with multiple agencies if the business is large enough to justify it and if the client wants to maintain a healthy level of competition among its agencies. Clients are increasingly exploring multiple agency relationships vs. the single end-to-end full-service, lead-agency approach of prior decades. Some advertisers are willing to trade off the ease of one-stop shopping for multiple "best-in-class" specialized agencies. Advertisers want to have the ability to load-balance the work, pick the right agency with the right skills for a given assignment, and keep the agencies on their toes so no one takes their business for granted. Under this model, the client has already selected several agencies in complementary disciplines. They may rely on a lead agency to act as a general contractor and coordinate with various approved agencies. The lead agency (typically a "creative" agency) acts as the brand steward and handles all aspects of the campaign in collaboration with other agencies. As general contractor, they are expected to work with the plumbers and electricians to get the house built, but the contractual and financial relationship with these specialty shops is owned by the client directly.

There have been many examples of this model over the years. For example, P&G's Brand Agency Leader (BAL) approach was designed to encourage agency collaboration and accountability. To avoid talent duplication, overlapping capabilities, operational inefficiencies, and poor cross-team collaboration, P&G introduced a new approach to working with its agencies. P&G's BAL model ensured one agency was assigned a "lead" role on each brand and was on point to coordinate all other agency efforts with a single master plan, a single fee, and an incentive compensation adjustment that tied to brand sales, share, and qualitative metrics. Although P&G selected and approved all agencies involved, the "lead" agency (BAL) was managing the team of agencies. A sort of bill of rights, a set of principles that agencies agree to (for example, share ownership of the work, work as a team, ideas can come from anywhere, consumer at the center) ensures complete alignment.

CLIENT VIEWPOINT

"The Brand Agency Leader Approach is working very well for P&G against our primary objective to deliver more integrated brand building to our consumers and to do that with less time and touches for all involved. This has been a very positive change for us that could not have been accomplished without the support and long-standing relationships of our agencies." [59]

—RICHARD C. DELCORE, SENIOR ADVISOR, THE BOSTON CONSULTING GROUP—FORMER DIRECTOR, GLOBAL BRAND ENTERTAINMENT & VP P&G PRODUCTIONS

DEEP DIVE: "OPEN SOURCE" MODEL

Under this model, an advertiser chooses to work with a pre-approved pool of agencies. This is the antithesis of the popular AOR model which is engineered for long lasting and exclusive partnerships. This open source model requires governance, internal coordination, extensive vendor management, and operational oversight. Quality control is harder to maintain in a more distributed model. This model also often makes cross-agency collaboration, and therefore work integration, significantly harder to achieve as territorial issues are likely to emerge between roster agencies. The primary benefit of this model is flexibility and choice. This model tends to be short-term focused and transactional in nature. This approach emphasizes one-time engagements and project pricing. Agencies are often asked to pitch for assignments or bid for work. The limited line of sight agencies have about future client work makes it challenging for them to commit resources and secure and retain top agency talent. Agencies often have to rely on a pool of freelancers to deal with the unexpected activity burst. Additionally, in this model, the advertiser is solely responsible for ensuring work integration, encouraging cross-team collaboration, and handling territorial issues while avoiding process inefficiencies. The advertiser must often act as a referee when issues arise.

CLIENT VIEWPOINT

"We go project-by-project, brand-by-brand. We don't restrict ourselves to … one agency. I hate to say one brand is with one agency for eternity... The way we look at it is: Who is the best-suited for what we are trying to do with the consumer and the message?" [60]
—RAM KRISHNAN, CHIEF EXECUTIVE OFFICER AND CHIEF MARKETING OFFICER, PEPSICO—FORMER CMO, FRITO LAY NORTH AMERICA

Best Buy and Frito-Lay are recent examples of advertisers that decided to ditch the agency-of-record model and go project to project, brand by brand, with no specific AOR. Under this scenario, longtime agencies must pitch for work alongside other shops. In 2014, Mondelez International launched an experiment called "Project Sprout" which involved working with multiple agencies on the Trident and Dentyne brands, using smaller client-agency teams, accelerated timelines, and decision making with a sharp focus on performance. In past years, Fiat Chrysler Automobiles added new agencies like Interpublic's FCB and Omnicom's DDB to its roster of agencies that included Wieden+Kennedy, mcgarrybowen, Doner, Armando Testa, Richards Group, Huge, and UM, moving away from the agency-of-record model in favor of having a roster of agencies that compete for assignments.

CLIENT VIEWPOINT

"In a fast-changing media landscape, we need to continually find powerful ways to emotionally engage our consumers. We believe that a robust, multi-agency structure is the best way to serve our brands. It allows us to align the needs of each brand to the unique capabilities of each agency." [61]

—**PETER HORST**, FOUNDER, CMO INC., FORMER CMO,

HERSHEY

DEEP DIVE: "IN-HOUSE" MODEL

Under the in-house agency model, a client decides to bring in-house some of the work that would otherwise be conducted by agencies. Some advertisers have the resources and have built the operational rigor required of an in-house agency. Others do not want to deal with the complications, time, and effort required to coordinate and bring together the various agencies within the roster. Fundamental questions about the value that agencies deliver to clients have been the source of heated discussions and industry debate for years, and especially in recent years as advertisers felt the need to own some competencies internally due to transparency concerns, costs, speed, and other strategic considerations.

CLIENT VIEWPOINT

"Our success with [our in-house agency] ECS proves that when done right, you can have the best of both worlds—an in-house agency that provides a cost-effective, nimble, deep understanding of your brand, and the right level of talent, creativity, and outside perspective." [62]

—MEREDITH VERDONE, CHIEF MARKETING OFFICER,

BANK OF AMERICA

One of these highly debated topics is: What do agencies do that clients truly can't do themselves? There isn't a client in the world that hasn't at least once had this thought: Why don't I do this myself and save all those agency fees? Why don't I do it in-house, and have more control over deadlines, quality, and brand compliance? Should I create an internal team to handle some aspects of what our external agencies typically take on? And yes, this idea extends across industries and the general population as well. In this self-empowerment, auto dictate, and "XX for Dummies" culture, people try to sell their houses themselves, do their own taxes, fix their own plumbing, or even defend themselves in court. It can't be that hard, right? Wrong. Forming an in-house department for handling all or some agency duties is an important consideration for any advertiser, and is a delicate, often complex, undertaking. Many advertisers have taken on that challenge and built or experimented with such in-house capabilities. Companies such as Intel, Wells Fargo, AT&T, State Farm Insurance, Hilton Worldwide, Bank of America, Sprint, Disney, and Discover Financial Services have built in-house agency teams to take on a growing volume of assignments. Marta Stiglin, Board Director, In-House Agency Forum summarized it well: "One of the biggest advantages an in-house agency has is its unlimited opportunity to learn from within—something external agencies are hard-pressed to do. Being part of the same company, you live and breathe the culture and the brand. The client's products are your products." For example. Bank of America's in-house agency, Enterprise Creative Solutions (ECS), was built as a low-cost, single-service cost-efficient brand champion years ago, and evolved to become a traditional agency with account, creative, and production working for every line of business in nearly every channel. ECS handles a steady annual job volume of more than 19,000 projects according to its CMO, Meredith Verdone. In-house agencies are known to be nimble, cost-effective, and well aligned to the brand and the strategic imperatives of the business.

CLIENT VIEWPOINT

"The more you outsource, the less of a creative culture you have. It's funny coming from a guy who ran agencies, but it's one thing to brief an agency and to give feedback to an agency on their work. And it's another to create it. Creating is believing, creating is seeing, and creating is contagious." [63]

—**PETER MCGUINNESS,** CHIEF MARKETING, COMMERCIAL AND DEMAND OFFICER, CHOBANI

Let's be honest: agency structures, processes, and pace of delivery are not evolving as quickly as advertisers want. The trigger to move to an in-house structure is also the result of bottom-line pressure and focus on cost-savings. The spirits maker Pernod Ricard saved $71.5 million by purchasing 25% of its media in-house during the first half of 2017, buying inventory directly from demand-side platforms. Although their primary motivation is often to realize cost efficiencies or to reduce external marketing costs, they sometimes wish to build a permanent skill set internally or have unique needs that might be challenging to secure externally due to the specialized nature of the company's business. The In-House Agency Forum (IHAF) was created in 2005 and provides its members tools, benchmarks, and insight in support of every function within an advertiser in-house agency model. Despite being one of the largest advertisers in the US, telco giant AT&T built a 150-person in-house team to support over 30 diverse lines of business with many of its resources embedded within client teams. According to IHAF, they produce over 7,000 unique pieces annually.

CLIENT VIEWPOINT

"We are embedding creative thinking into the business by hiring creative people from outside the company to come and work directly for us." [64]

—BRYNN BARDACKE, VICE PRESIDENT CONTENT AND CREATIVE EXCELLENCE, THE COCA-COLA COMPANY

Sprint created an in-house agency called YellowFan Studios, with creative responsibility for providing film and print production, design, and creative services, as the company worked to cut $2.5 billion in costs. Deutsch remained the agency of record for general market advertising, and Alma the agency of record for Hispanic advertising. The in-house agency doesn't have to compete with external agency resources, which they can often complement. To the contrary. They are often expected to collaborate. It is structured similarly to any other service agency, but accounting is typically handled as a cross-charge from another department to the in-house team or a cost center billing method. In-house agency departments do not need to be limited to creative services for collateral or promotional materials, but these are the most commonly handled services. The in-house department might also be set up as an internal media buying team, instead of relying on the services of a media company. In recent years, advertisers have diversified the type of in-house agency services they provide to also include social media and programmatic planning and buying, due to their strategic nature.

CLIENT VIEWPOINT

"We used to outsource all our execution to agencies, which did not work well because we did not have the agility to work quickly. We've now insourced a lot of execution; we still have major agency relationships, but they are much more strategic and long term in nature. All the areas around email, search, and programmatic advertising were in-sourced." [65]

—SIMON MORRIS, SENIOR DIRECTOR, CAMPAIGN MARKETING, CONSUMER, AND SMB, ADOBE

Allstate, StubHub, Unilever, and Netflix have all taken some digital ad buying in-house. To move faster, cut budget, streamline internal communications, better leverage data, and drive business results, Sprint also created its own digital ad agency, now handling digital ad buying and advertising creative, as well as "programmatic" ad buying, search advertising, and even traditional media buying, which have typically been handled by outside ad agencies. How much of the work can advertisers take on and in-source? Two years prior to setting up its own in-house agency, 96% of Intel's work was done with external agencies. Then Intel moved work in-house to gain quality, better brand alignment, and cost efficiencies, through its in-house agency it calls Agency Inside. Intel even opened an office in San Francisco to attract key talent.

CLIENT VIEWPOINT

"Over the course of the past year and a half, after I developed the structure of the agency, I've been bringing different parts of the work in-house. We started with social and digital, as well as a lot of the actual brand work that we do. I'd say today, probably 65 to 70 percent of the work is done in-house, and the rest we continue to use external agencies to divide it up." [66]

—**TERESA HERD**, VICE PRESIDENT, GLOBAL CREATIVE DIRECTOR, INTEL

An in-house agency model might make sense for some activities, but clients must objectively evaluate their options and decide whether building an in-house agency or hiring an external one is the way to best support their business needs in the long run. Many in-house agencies have limited scope and fulfill a very specific purpose. PepsiCo decided to handle more social in-house, leveraging internal resources and its 4,000-square-foot content creation studio in the heart of SoHo. Taco Bell created a dedicated in-house team of millennials who craft content specifically to talk to Taco Bell's millennial fans in the language they understand.

Although there might be some benefits in having some of these services in-house, advertisers often prefer to get greater value from a talent base that is constantly sourced, upgraded, and trained to far exceed what a client could do on its own. Why is that? The answer is threefold: (1) we're not an expert in everything (no matter what we think), and it's hard to keep on top of key trends; (2) it would be too costly to set up and maintain an in-house agency (yes, some might disagree); and (3) we miss out on having access to outside talent and perspective, especially in creative innovation. In some instances, advertisers have closed their in-house agencies because they lacked the marketing skills required to consistently produce top quality work. Second, the overhead of having a fully dedicated copywriter, art director, media director, planner, strategist, and a host of other talents would probably be highly cost-prohibitive at first. You may not need all of these resources at all times. Why keep them on payroll? Using a freelance pool presents some challenges as well. Agencies can spread these expenses across multiple clients and provide access to more dedicated resources. Clearly, outside agencies service a range of unique, value-add competencies that make them a valuable and irreplaceable resource. Pepsi's Kendall Jenner ad was pulled amid criticism and brought forward much debate about the use of in-house agencies. Pepsi's ad was created by PepsiCo's in-house content creation arm, Creators League Studio, which brings in writers, art directors, cinematographers, and other talent on an as-needed basis. Critics were quick to point out the potential risks and short-comings of using in-house agencies for high profile campaigns, suggesting that outside agencies are better equipped to avoid the type of backlash that ultimately unfolded in the media. The last point is perhaps the most cogent. Rigid client methodologies and internal procedures often minimize creativity and therefore are not grounds for innovation or freedom of creative expression. Therefore, the most common scenario still involves the use of an outside agency or even multiple ones based on the type and scale of services needed.

CLIENT VIEWPOINT

"Five years ago, we would have expected the agency to do everything, soup to nuts—figure out strategic partnerships, social strategies and digital initiatives—but now we go to other partners. In the past, we would have maybe worked with one or two agencies; now there are four or five creative partners and our own content studios." [67]

—SIMON LOWDEN, PRESIDENT AND CMO, GLOBAL SNACKS AND GLOBAL INSIGHTS, PEPSICO

DEEP DIVE: HYBRID MODELS AND OTHER INNOVATIVE CONCEPTS

No single agency model can satisfy all these requirements. Brand advertisers must consider the pros and cons of each scenario before deciding on the most effective model for their business. While these model scenarios are helpful to understand the nuances of different approaches, the reality is often more complex as multi-brand, global companies must often satisfy a wide range of organizational needs. It means that they might need to contemplate more than one agency model, an approach particularly appealing to the multi-brand global companies unwilling, or simply unable, to default to the convenience of an all-encompassing holding company model for a given business unit or geography. These companies might choose to combine multiple agency models to get to their desired results across all their brands and geographies.

CLIENT VIEWPOINT

"My concept of AORs is a little bit more flexible, but we still have AORs. What we do is we give a brief to our AOR of the brand. In 99.9 percent of the cases they come back with something we don't like. But then we keep going back and forth. It's a shared creative process. We love bouncing with ideas. They have a period of time to deliver something we are all convinced with. If this doesn't happen, then we open the brief to any other AOR. All of them have generally 70 percent of the brand they own, and 30 percent of conquest on something else. This is very interesting. They don't really like it, obviously. But the smartest ones like it. It's conquest. Like it or not, it introduces some tension and some competition in the system." [68]

—OLIVIER FRANCOIS, GLOBAL CHIEF MARKETING OFFICER,

FCA

An advertiser might want to rely on a full-service agency model for one of its brands, leverage the flexibility of an open source model for specialized digital services, and realize some efficiencies by building an in-house agency to handle its creative services. In his speech "We are Stronger Together than we are Apart" at ANA Master of Marketing, Verizon's CMO Diego Scotti challenged these brands, including competitor AT&T, which also consolidated its agency roster with Omnicom, to get better-quality work from a group of best-in-class agencies that collaborate effectively together. Consider a hybrid model if you want to minimize trade-offs and unlock the benefits of complementary agency models strategically applied to diverse needs in your organization. Although the models introduced previously are the most common, we are likely to see many alternative innovative models emerge.

That was the case when Spark44, "the first global client/agency joint venture model" was launched as a joint venture between Jaguar Land Rover and Spark44 management. The model offers a single shared P&L across all locations or specialties, 60 individual agency reps aggregated into one dedicated and high-performance client team. The results: an independent structure, culture, and team with shared goals, a shared investment, and absolute transparency. Spark44 also achieved significant aggregate savings—in both agency fees and production—for Jaguar Land Rover.

CLIENT VIEWPOINT

"This is not about 'we' and 'they.' This is about 'us'!" [69]

—HANS RIEDEL, CHAIRMAN EMERITUS, SPARK44

New agency solutions are also emerging to offer hybrid services. That's the case of OLIVER, which builds dedicated agencies inside their client organizations to deliver better work more efficiently with the benefits of having these resources embedded. The London-based entity refers to it as "Better Inside" and covers a wide of range of services. With global hubs and over 70 in-house agencies placed within some of the largest brands, solutions like OLIVER are ideal for clients looking for an outsourced in-house agency solution with fully brand-immersed teams.

BRINGING THE AGENCY MODEL TO LIFE

A strategy has been defined and agreed upon. Everyone is clear about what the company is trying to accomplish and what the priorities are. It's still too premature to declare victory. A strategy is only as good as one's ability to execute it. The company must develop a robust operational plan that spells out the actions it will take to bring the strategy to life. It must define clear roles and responsibilities for all agencies, and articulate key operating principles and requirements that the agency (and employees) must adhere to. It must state expected client/agency engagement practices and the operating budget required, aligning scope of work to staffing plans, and encouraging effective team collaboration and management of resources.

CLIENT VIEWPOINT

"You need very clear rules of the road for who can use what agencies at what time. What we don't want is people saying, 'I worked with this agency at my old job, and I want to work with them now.' Only if it adds value. It's very expensive to onboard a new agency and takes away from the strategic relationship with the other agencies." [70]

—**EVE REITER,** FORMER FORMER STRATEGIC SOURCING AND PROCUREMENT EXECUTIVE, AMERICAN EXPRESS

AGENCY MODEL OPERATIONAL PLAN

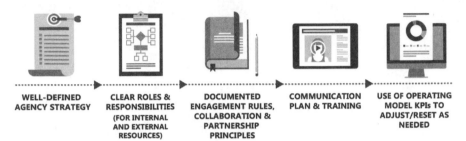

| WELL-DEFINED AGENCY STRATEGY | CLEAR ROLES & RESPONSIBILITIES (FOR INTERNAL AND EXTERNAL RESOURCES) | DOCUMENTED ENGAGEMENT RULES, COLLABORATION & PARTNERSHIP PRINCIPLES | COMMUNICATION PLAN & TRAINING | USE OF OPERATING MODEL KPIs TO ADJUST/RESET AS NEEDED |

Clients must determine the right escalation process for their company to facilitate valuable and timely conflict resolution. The most common operating process involves the end-to-end management of a project from strategy development and agency briefing to campaign measurement and optimization, documenting each step and the expected responsibilities of the different roles at the client and the agency, respectively.

Another important consideration is determining the resources and budget requirements. Some agency models require light operating support, while others require heavy support and funding. Having a sound agency strategy is imperative. But it's not enough. It also requires rolling up sleeves and making sure the strategy is well understood across the organization and fully supported internally. No strategy can be successfully implemented without a robust communication plan that aligns the entire company behind a common approach and communicates these benefits through the banner of a unified mission. Budget owners and marketers may be told to work with an agency they didn't choose. These same employees may have worked with other agencies in their past lives and are likely to push to continue to hire those at will. After all, this is a relationship business and relationships are what matter. Understandably, clients move from company to company and often hope to leverage their own, well-trusted agency partnerships rather than the ones mandated by the company. To complicate matters, these rogue agencies may not have to subject themselves to the demands and expectations imposed on larger ones, making themselves even more attractive to inexperienced marketers looking for shiny new deliverables and easy wins to propel their careers. A rogue agency may also appear to be more responsive and cost-effective than the company's agency of record, free of any centrally defined process and perhaps free of having to comply with what could be perceived as inconvenient and inflexible corporate standards. Small agencies are also willing to temporarily give up profits to secure a marquee client name on their roster that might help them secure other, more profitable business down the road. The combination of the two can be very appealing to marketers who frequently work in silos and are not overly committed to a model that might appear, at first glance, to predominantly benefit the corporation at large. The reality is that those can be highly inefficient, exposing the company to potential legal and PR risks, and may in turn suck a disproportionate share of corporate resources and prove to be counter-productive.

CLIENT VIEWPOINT

"We have no AOR for no one . . . The advertising landscape is now so fragmented, so the needs are fragmented, too. If you multiply this fragmentation with the number of brands that we have to serve, clearly, I think the worst answer would be one agency fits all. That doesn't work." [71]

—OLIVIER FRANCOIS, GLOBAL CHIEF MARKETING OFFICER,

FCA

Because agency decisions are often perceived as secretive if not subjective, it is important to educate the entire organization and encourage employees to support the company's overall agency strategy. Clients should consider the wide range of internal communication vehicles at their disposal to explain the company's approach and agency decisions, highlighting the excellent work done and results achieved in partnership with the agency(ies). Executing a carefully crafted communication plan doesn't mean going deep into every agency-related topic or over-selling the agency. By exaggerating the likely benefits of the agency model and ignoring potential pitfalls, advertisers can come short of meeting expectations and endanger the viability of the overall agency model. So, communications must be anchored into reality and must be backed up with demonstrable evidence of the value the model generates. To effectively communicate the benefits of an agency model, clients should consider partnering with their agency to implement a regular communication plan that includes a variety of "proof-points." This can be a combination of case studies, reports, sample portfolio, executive summaries, presentations, training, and speaking engagements.

Every marketer must also be reminded of the key role they play in making sure the company leverages these agency resources wisely and optimally. Accountability goes both ways. Similarly, marketers must be reminded of basic engagement principles and best practices and trained in effectively working with agencies: consistently providing thorough, clear direction to the agency, investing time and resources to drive great strategy and ideas, and aligning feedback internally so that the agency can efficiently do its best work. Celebrating joint successes will ensure that Client Project Leads and agency staff are acknowledged for their performance and set an example for others in the relationship to follow. Successfully managing the relationships also necessitates frequent and timely communications regarding important decisions about the company's strategic direction or key priorities. Agencies should communicate information to key clients on the account and announce important milestones, such as key new agency hires and staffing changes, acquisitions, and new client accounts. In the end, mindfully planning for communications is key to getting employees to care, become engaged, support the company's approach to agency management, and eventually turn them into active supporters and advocates of a streamlined agency strategy.

CLIENT VIEWPOINT

"We can make our dollars work harder for us by putting them toward growth initiatives rather than agency fees, and with an in-house agency, we can make sure the work is more coordinated. It's easier when everyone is in-house rather than working out of 12 different agencies." [72]

—LEE MASCHMEYER, CHOBANI CCO

CONTINUOUS IMPROVEMENT

The company's agency strategy cannot be set in stone. It must be based on the culmination of the insights, feedback, best practices, and dialogue that occur throughout the year. It is likely to evolve, adapting to changing market conditions. But we can't improve what we can't measure. As in any strategy, it must allow for input and on-going feedback. Employees on both sides of the fence should be encouraged to constructively and openly make recommendations on how to improve the partnership, improve the quality of communication between the parties, and effectively encourage ownership of accountability in the relationship. This is what Kaizen (the Japanese equivalent of "continuous improvement") is all about. There are several ways advertisers can fine-tune their agency strategy. These range from tightly-managed reviews informed by automated dashboards to informal 1:1 discussions to assess how well things are working. Regardless of the KPIs or measurement systems used, advertisers should ensure that these metrics are part of the company's regular rhythm of business, and that they closely tie to other operating metrics the company relies on to determine the health of its business. It's not easy to do. It depends on the company having come to the realization that a solid client/agency relationship will yield good work and a weak one won't, and therefore choosing to pay close attention to the health and quality of that relationship. Business reviews with the agencies, whether semi-annually, quarterly, or monthly, are golden opportunities for the client and agency leadership to review the work, identify roadblocks and partnership improvement opportunities, and stay closely aligned and focused on key priorities.

CLIENT VIEWPOINT

"We have a single leader who is responsible principally for each of the agency relationships on a day-to-day basis, and then we also have a quarterly process where we provide formal feedback in writing to each of the agencies and the leaders that manage our agencies. If either one of us sees some sort of issue, we quickly bring it up and discuss it in a very fact-based way. It's a collaborative problem-solving approach." [73]

—**MICHAEL LACORAZZA**, EXECUTIVE VICE PRESIDENT AND
HEAD OF INTEGRATED MARKETING, WELLS FARGO

These business reviews can be facilitated by drawing upon agency management dashboards. Like an automobile dashboard, agency management dashboards contain visual gauges and data pertaining to the successful operation of the agency model. They may include critical data points based on the nature of the relationship. These activity-based, performance-based or relationship health-related metrics may include business and campaign results, the number of projects handled, or assets created by the agency and the manpower required to bring them to market. Agency attrition, new hires, burn rate, and qualitative metrics such as satisfaction and team morale can also be addressed. These management tools for clients and agencies keep an objective pulse on the relationship. They can encourage fact-based discussions between clients and agencies by analyzing purposeful and actionable metrics that, ideally, have been jointly defined and agreed upon. As a result, action plans for continuous improvement can be initiated and progress can be made in key relationship areas over time. Clients should conduct these business reviews at least twice a year, or even quarterly, with their agencies. The type and size of the relationship may not justify a higher frequency, so every advertiser must determine what makes sense. At the very least, the agenda must allow for ample discussion and ideas exchange as well as a thorough review of scorecards and key performance indicators. A business review is the perfect occasion for an agency to shine and demonstrate their value to the client's business. It is also a perfect opportunity for clients to evaluate how effectively the chosen agency model is playing out. Advertisers should also consider conducting internal business reviews without agency participation to candidly discuss the status of these pivotal relationships.

Building a sound agency strategy and agency portfolio is paramount to any company's ability to compete successfully and make strategic use of agency partnerships. Agency models are dynamic in nature. Your company's agency model will inevitably change over time to stay aligned to your evolving priorities and organizational needs. What worked a year or two ago may no longer be the answer. Is your model now obsolete? Have you carefully considered all scenarios and picked the right strategy? Hiring a top-notch agency won't fill that gap either. The right agency model will. Having the best agency resources in the world might be simply a waste of talent if you cannot get them to work together synergistically.

TOP 3
BEST PRACTICES
for Advertisers

1 Understand and document your organizational needs to build an agency model that best serves marketing teams and support their objectives while evaluating available scenarios.

2 Select the best suited agency strategy, governance and operating model to support current marketing needs while anticipating future ones and secure executive buy-in and support.

3 Bring the selected agency model to life by clearly communicating expectations, rules of engagements to internal and external stakeholders while continuously evaluating its performance.

5

ASSORTATIVE MATING AND THE SWEATY T-SHIRT THEORY

Conducting a successful agency search

"He who would search for pearls must dive below."

—**JOHN DRYDEN,** WRITER AND POET

As in everyday life, individuals and companies can sometimes jump quickly into a relationship, without having a true sense of self, or without thoughtful consideration. Tabloids made fortunes telling the stories of celebrities like Jennifer Lopez, Colin Farrell, and Pamela Anderson, whose marriages didn't last more than four months. And when you thought you'd seen it all, celebrities Dennis Rodman and Carmen Electra's highly publicized marriage ended after only nine days in November 1998. In this culture of "speed-dating" or even "speed-marriage" how can we be expected to act any differently with business partners? A privileged society, deeply rooted in a pervasive atmosphere of speed, convenience, and instant gratification, has made it easy for companies and the people that lead them to embrace this growing cultural phenomenon.

Yet it is common knowledge that selecting the ideal agency partner is by far one of the most impactful decision advertisers make. It's insanely easy to pick up the phone and, on the spot, hire a new agency. It's insanely more demanding to find the right strategic partner to reshape the company's marketing approach and propel the business forward. Finding compatible agencies is no longer good enough in the highly competitive environment of the 21st century. Perhaps the dating and marriage metaphors have been over-used when describing the "do and don'ts" of finding the ideal business partner. Countless cultural anthropologists and experts in human psychology counsel us on how to find the right partner. It usually involves a series of somewhat logical steps, from assessing personal needs, matching candidates based on key criteria, conducting chemistry and reference checks, to the actual dating. Then if you plan to turn your date into something more, you can get terrific advice from marital experts and couples counselors on how to preserve, grow, and nurture this relationship over time. When applying these same kinds of strategies to the business world, the complexity is exponentially greater. Clearly, it's a more involved process than the one of a fish who uses electric signals to find the right mate. We wouldn't be so lucky. Regardless of the type of services sought, most clients don't look for a "brand" agency or a "PR" firm for their next assignment. What they look for is a strategic partner that can drive measurable business results and give them a competitive edge. When searching for a true marketing partner, how do we know we are looking in the right places? If birds of a feather flock together, aren't we searching for agencies that mirror our companies?

EVERYTHING I KNOW ABOUT AGENCIES I LEARNED FROM BIOLOGY

In a study known as the "Sweaty T-Shirt Study,"[74] conducted by biological researcher Claus Wedekind at Bern University in Switzerland in 1995, men were asked to wear the same cotton t-shirt for 48 hours.

They were not to wear any deodorant, cologne, or use scented soap. They were asked to avoid smelly environments, products, and activities. After the two days of wear, the t-shirts were to be placed into a plastic bag. Once returned to the scientists, the t-shirts were then placed into boxes equipped with a hole through which one could sniff the shirts. Women were invited one at a time to smell them, describe each odor and indicate which one they were most attracted to. Half of the boxes included t-shirts from men with Major Histocompatibility Complex (known as MHC) genes that were most similar to female MHC. The other half included t-shirts from men with dissimilar MHC genes. The women who volunteered to participate in this study did not know which t-shirts where which. Surprisingly enough, Claus Wedekind concluded that women were most attracted to men with MHC that was the most dissimilar from their own. The preference was stronger as the likelihood of fertility increased (women taking oral contraceptives were more likely to prefer the odor of men with MHC similar to their own). The rationale? The more diverse the genes, the stronger the immune system to fight potential diseases.

The key take-away here is that advertisers should consider agencies that are compatible, whose values match their own, but that are intrinsically different enough to spawn amazing results together. They should look for a trusted partner with the required skills and complementary capabilities to meet their needs, but that may also exhibit diametrically different core competencies than their own company. It's another way to say something we've known all along: opposites attract. Just like in real life, it's often for the best. But why are relationships so hard to maintain?

It's nonsensical that so many advertisers have been getting into the sad habit of hiring and firing agencies as they would commodity suppliers. Perhaps it's because, sadly enough, some agencies are behaving like this type of vendor. It's insane that so many agencies are missing the opportunity to establish themselves as inseparable allies and vital assets to their clients. Advertisers must also resist the temptation to launch into search after search looking for a bright, new, shiny pearl. They must resist RFP scope creep, or what some agencies call "RFPs from hell," inviting too many agencies to participate in poorly orchestrated, months-long discussions during which agencies are asked to fill out insanely long questionnaires and share their ideas for free. RFP stands for Request for Proposal. Rather, it should stand for Request for Partnership as a partnership is likely to yield greater value over time than a supplier-like relationship. Advertisers with long-term agency relationships may be naively criticized internally for looking like they are sleeping at the wheel or resisting change, having had the same agency partner for years. However, they must be increasingly discerning, and not jump quickly to change their agency, if they are to build a reputation of integrity and partnership that attracts the best agency talent to their company.

AGENCY VIEWPOINT

"The pitch process is out of control and about to experience a big backlash by conscientious agencies. It's going to be ugly." [75]
—**JEFF GOODBY**, CO-CHAIRMAN AND PARTNER, GOODBY, SILVERSTEIN & PARTNERS

Savvy clients must make sure they are judged internally on what truly matters to the business. It can prove to be quite challenging to launch a comprehensive agency search and find that new agency partner. Or to add a new strategic agency partner to an existing roster. Or simply to add a specialty agency where there is a gap in capabilities. Clients should carefully consider all their options before deciding to put an account in review. They may end up wasting precious time and resources on-boarding new agencies and going through learning curves. Only when they have decided that this is the best course of action should they move forward with a review. Data indicates that brand advertisers that launch reviews increasingly do so with the intention of switching agencies, so few incumbents will successfully retain the business once a review is under way. Ask Visa. They had been working with their agency BBDO Worldwide for 25 years before moving its global account to sister agency TBWA Worldwide. Unfortunately for agencies, most clients are no longer committing themselves to such long partnerships. The world of marketing is changing too fast. So are advertisers' needs. Yet too many clients are focused on the short term, conducting excessive agency reviews that end up undermining their long-term efforts and their ability to attract top talent. Bold agencies like Crispin Porter + Bogusky are now taking strong positions, as in the case of Volkswagen, by turning down invitations to participate in existing account reviews. Although history proves them right—chances to retain an account once in review are lean—few can realistically afford to take a "no defense approach" by letting a client go to the competition without a good fight. Clients must also follow industry best practices if they are to conduct an effective and efficient search.

CLIENT VIEWPOINT

"I am a big believer in building long-standing partnerships with agencies. You are seeing a lot of annual shifts right now by some of our key competitors, which I fundamentally believe is unhealthy to building meaningful brands." [76]

—DAVID KROLL, CMO, MILLERCOORS

COMMON REASONS FOR STARTING AN AGENCY SEARCH

A successful search is never guaranteed. Like you, I've seen my fair share of questionable searches with questionable results. Read the press and you will realize that, despite the number of agency reviews constantly under way, and the years of experience on both the client and the agency side, no process is ever bulletproof. Arguably the most crucial step in this process is the one that ends up receiving the least attention: It is "self-discovery." It is common sense: Clients must have a clear understanding of what business problem they are solving. What sparked this agency review? What are the business circumstances that led to this search? It forces clients to look deep inside and answer questions truthfully. It requires a comprehensive, honest self-assessment of the company's marketing strengths and weaknesses. For instance, is the brand strategy hitting the mark? Are we innovating enough with the current agency? Are we confident in the lead agency to successfully launch the new brand campaign? There are many valid reasons for a company to seek a (new) agency relationship. However, contrary to widespread belief, an agency search is not always rooted in performance issues or client leadership changes. Based on my experience, here are the most common reasons to start a search:

COMMON REASONS FOR STARTING AN AGENCY SEARCH

Reason #1: Change in Business. An advertiser may require new or incremental agency resources because of a new business, brand, or product line being launched, or organizational changes like business divisions being split or reorganized. Having a new agency partner is a positive change by some companies if there is a material departure from the prior brand positioning, execution, and work style, as Sprint concluded when moving its $1.2 billion account to Goodby Silverstein & Partners in 2007. It could also result from a decision to dismantle an in-house creative team like Best Buy did after 20 years handling its advertising budget in-house. It could result from clients being merged or acquired, such as Procter & Gamble's 2005 acquisition of Gillette, which forced multiple incumbent agencies (Publicis, Omnicom and WPP agencies such as BBDO, TBWA, Grey, Saatchi & Saatchi) to defend their share of the estimated $6 billion advertising account.

INDUSTRY VIEWPOINT

"Usually a new CEO comes in. Within six months, the CMO is held to scrutiny or leaves. Six months later, a new CMO comes in and puts the agency in review. We see this over and over." [77]

—**LYNNE SEID,** PARTNER GLOBAL MARKETING OFFICERS PRACTICE, HEIDRICK & STRUGGLES EXECUTIVE SEARCH FIRM, RETIRED

Reason #2: Leadership Turnover. Many reviews are initiated because of marketing organization overhaul and high turnover among Chief Marketing Officers (CMOs). The appointment of a new CMO often triggers an agency review, within weeks or months. In the case of Chevy, newly hired marketing chief Joel Ewanick shifted the entire $600 million account to Goodby Silverstein & Partners from Publicis only a month after Publicis won the account and without meeting with the incumbent agency. The pressure of increased marketing accountability and higher returns on marketing investment has significantly reduced the average tenure of CMOs. The next CMO has very limited time to prove himself/herself to the CEO and board of directors. Working with an agency the CMO is unfamiliar with and with whom the company may have had questionable results under the prior leadership, is undesirable. This is the opportunity to get a fresh start, either working with agencies that the CMO built a strong work partnership with over the years in a prior role, or simply to turning up the heat on the incumbent agency. Clients should certainly refrain from doing reviews to keep the agency on its toes. There are many effective and less costly ways to keep agencies motivated.

Reason #3: Competitive Conflicts. This is a common issue for clients. A conflict may come up because of a new multidisciplinary account win by an agency pitching an integrated offering, forcing a client to reconsider its relationships with agencies now in direct conflict with their competitors. An agency may wish to pursue a significantly more attractive (either larger or more profitable) client opportunity and deliberately resign its current account to pursue it. Discover Financial Services selected WPP Group's MediaCom to handle its planning and buying duties after Publicis Groupe's Starcom, the incumbent agency, decided not to defend the account because of a conflict with its new Bank of America account. Agency mergers also tend to create account conflicts. In the case of the IPG Lowe New York and sibling Deutsch merger in 2009, it created a conflict for Johnson & Johnson's Tylenol business, a key account for Deutsch. Lowe's clients Matrixx Initiatives' Zicam cold remedy and Separators' Lunesta sleep aid put their business up for review.

Reason #4: Performance Issues. Perhaps the most commonly stated reason for a review is poor agency performance. The client decides that the agency has repetitively failed to meet expectations (missing deadlines, quality of the work, staffing, costs, etc.), and attempts to improve the performance have been unsuccessful. Either inadequate party may conclude that the relationship is no longer performing at acceptable levels. It's time to move on. No advertiser has the luxury to waste time and resources with under-performing agencies. Under this type of scenario, the incumbent agency is unlikely to be invited to participate in the review. Transparency is the key here. There is no point inviting them if they do not have a chance of winning. If every attempt has been made to fix problems and save the relationship, why waste further efforts and resources on either side with an agency review? Clients should be transparent about the status of the relationship with the incumbent agency before the search/review is initiated. Remember that performance is a two-way street. Some of us may remember Dentsu Aegis's mcgarrybowen resigning the Sears account, which had a reputation for cutting fees and being demanding amid a much-delayed procurement-led review. A gentle wake-up call is an understanding that any partnership requires that both parties are mutually satisfied with the relationship, and that agencies, too, can choose to let go of under-performing clients.

Reason #5: Missing Competencies. Although reviews have historically been driven by cost pressure and the desire to revamp contract terms to be more competitive, advertisers may decide that new skills and competencies are needed but are not currently available through the current agency roster. This is often the case in digital marketing where new capabilities emerge frequently and agencies struggle to keep up on all fronts. The client may want to beef up their marketing muscle in social media, analytics, mobile, or search. Client needs change and evolve constantly based on market conditions and innovation. For example, recent media reviews seem less focused on cost efficiencies, but are instead focused on competencies in key areas such as digital media, programmatic buying, mobile/search, and media/creative integration. The incumbent agency (if there is one) might be invited to step up and build or acquire the missing expertise. Or they may lose to a new agency that can demonstrate they are a better fit. At the risk of stating the obvious, there is no "perfect" partnership. Even clients showing signs of obsessive–compulsive personality disorder with their agencies are unlikely to find the answer to their challenges by systematically jumping from agency to agency. I fondly refer to those clients as "Rocket Frogs," named after the Australia frog that can jump over two meters or up to 50 times its body length. Jumping is easy. Landing is harder. But working joint issues diligently is most rewarding. Most clients don't anticipate the significant opportunity cost associated with a search. If the incumbent agency is invited to participate and has a reasonable shot at keeping or expanding the account, it might still damage the relationship.

Although most agencies suggest that a change in management was the number one reason for being fired, studies indicate that price or value is a primary reason for contract termination. Other reasons for changing agencies include displeasure over the creative, mismatched agency size/ability, unhappy with project management/account management, unhappy with strategy, and understaffed/under-experienced staff. In the book *Adland*[79] James P. Othmer gives a humorous, provocative view into the incumbent agency psyche: "Being put up for review is akin to having your spouse announce in front of everyone you know that he or she no longer loves you and for the next several months he or she will be seeing other people—dozens of smarter, younger, cooler people, many of whom, by the way, you know quite well—and then having all sorts of experimental sex with the most interesting and promising of them, probably no more than six, often doing many of the things that you may have once suggested but were never allowed to."

INDUSTRY VIEWPOINT

"In our experience agency reviews are generally called for only a comparatively small number of reasons and, for the most part, many reviews could potentially be avoided if the underlying reasons were properly diagnosed and addressed in the early stages of their first symptoms. While that may sound a bit like a surgeon's health warning, the analogy isn't far off." [78]

—STEPHAN ARGENT, FOUNDING PARTNER,

THE ARGEDIA GROUP

Given typical switching costs, delays, and potential challenges associated with on-boarding a new agency, savvy advertisers carefully evaluate their options before making the decision to initiate a search. The investment in time and resources to conduct a search, to find, hire, and on-board a new agency is consequential. Not to mention what it takes to fully transition out the incumbent agency: Transitioning assets and doing financial reconciliations. In the event of competitive conflicts or continued, unsolvable performance issues, the decision to search for an agency partner doesn't leave much time for consideration. It is a critical mission and must be conducted swiftly. Any irreconcilable performance or relationship-related issues require much more careful consideration by both advertisers and agencies. Like a divorce, they must weigh the implications and often complications associated with parting from each other. Perhaps they can seek the assistance of a third party and give each other the opportunity to work on their differences before throwing down the towel and calling it a day. Although it may be that alternative agencies appear as shiny objects from a distance, inadequately working on the issues, or avoiding them until the point of no-return, is grounds for simply displacing problems from one relationship to another. Logically, one of the first questions any agency executive would ask during the preliminary stage of the search is how the relationship was with the previous agency. As they say, the grass is always greener on the other side of the fence. However, changing agencies will inevitably negatively impact current priorities and productivity during the review and potentially the transition time, so one must ensure that the problem is irreconcilable and that the client/agency relationship is beyond recovery.

THE VALUE OF SEARCH CONSULTANT

As part of its self-assessment, an advertiser must decide if the search/review will be handled internally or by a neutral third party. Companies should ask themselves: "Do we have the right skills and expertise on our team to conduct a comprehensive review and assess existing and prospective agencies? Do we have the time and resources to do so internally without disrupting the normal course of our business?" Often the answer is "no." Searching for the right agency is a demanding process that requires a good amount of experience and professional expertise. Therefore, it is widespread practice for brand advertisers to call for the help of an experienced client/agency matchmaker specialized in assisting companies to conduct a thorough agency review/search. Due to the hyper-specialization of the agency landscape leading to new shops opening their doors every day, it's increasingly harder for advertisers with limited time and bandwidth to invest much time in the search and selection process. Hiring an agency search consultant typically saves precious time for clients who don't have a deep knowledge of the agency industry, need help to narrow down the search to a few qualified candidates with the right credentials, and don't have the know-how to manage a search effectively. Clients tend to invest most of their time in the initial and final stage of the search process, leaving the bulk of the responsibilities and communications to the consultant.

It is equally difficult for procurement organizations that have incomplete visibility of the full breadth of the marketplace to step in and run the search. The Project Lead may not have the depth of knowledge, working experience, resources, objectivity, or even bandwidth necessary to successfully manage the search project from beginning to end. Beyond the expertise and best practices agency search consultants bring to the table, they can pre-screen agency candidates anonymously, a key benefit to brand advertisers who need confidentiality. Their objectivity can be of tremendous value to clients with very divergent opinions. Some of these consultants have built proprietary databases with proven quantitative and qualitative evaluation methodologies and systems to help brand advertisers find the perfect match based on client experience, competencies, talent, and overall cultural compatibility. These consultants keep themselves up to date on agency capabilities by conducting regular visits and keeping in constant contact with top agencies.

So, one might find it amusing to wonder: How do you search for a search consultant? Clients should leverage industry resources like the Association of National Advertisers (ANA), American Association of Advertising Agencies (4A's), and Adforum.com for a comprehensive list of search consultants. There are a few consulting firms with dedicated resources and vast expertise in this field, such as Pile and Company (Boston, MA) and Select Resources International (Santa Monica, CA). Clients will want to evaluate search consultants based on the following criteria: industry experience, client profile and affinity, recent assignments, seniority and experience, global resources, if relevant, and reputation. Some of these search consultants have international offices or partnerships overseas to handle global clients. To avoid any potential conflicts of interest, it's highly recommended that the contract with the search consultant should clearly state that they are not to accept financial incentives from agencies. Clients should seriously consider whether they are capable or willing to handle a search on their own or not. These talented match-makers are valuable resources to novice and sophisticated clients alike.

FOLLOWING A METHODOLOGICAL APPROACH

A well-conducted agency review/search is expected to result in the establishment of a highly productive, and hopefully long-term, partnership that translates into more effective work and better business outcomes. Some best practices are emerging based on years of experience and analysis initiated by clients, search consultants, and industry consortiums. Finding the right agency to support your business can turn out to be risky, time-consuming, frustrating, and daunting. But it is well worth the investment in time and effort if it is done properly. It requires a fair amount of research and preparation. The activities can be divided into two primary groups: internal and external. The internal phase (inward) consists of defining objectives and getting the project organized, and the initial research and filtering underway to identify potential agency candidates. The external phase (outward) consists of reaching out to the candidate agencies, exchanging information, and having them showcase their capabilities in credentials and/or creative presentations.

AGENCY SEARCH / REVIEW PROCESS

| NEEDS ASSESSMENT | ▶ | PROJECT PREPARATION | ▶ | RESEARCH & FILTERING | ▶ | RFI / RFP | ▶ | PRESENTATIONS | ▶ | SELECTION |

CLIENT VIEWPOINT

"Over the years, I've learned that clients must allow enough time to conduct an effective search. They need to have the right decision makers and get buy-off from management about the selection criteria before anyone gets into a room." [80]

—SUSAN MARKOWICZ, GLOBAL ADVERTISING AGENCY
MANAGER, FORD MOTOR COMPANY

In the last phase of this process, the client can finally reach his or her decision, select the agency, and initiate the on-boarding process. It's senseless to see clients initiate a search without having clear expectations about the process or the outcome and without the necessary experience to make this a productive exercise for all involved. A search demands discipline and absolute commitment to allow for a thorough probing and assessment of agency capabilities. Demonstrating basic knowledge and skills goes both ways. It's insane to see inexperienced agencies consistently fail at avoiding common pitfalls that systematically turn off clients. For example, many agencies still fail to adequately prepare or research the company or the client's category. Many agencies still fail to bring the staff that will be working on the account for client face-to-face meetings. Instead, they show up with their executive team knowing full well that none of them will be touching the business in a meaningful way. Too many agencies fail to listen and to ask questions to deepen their understanding of the client. It's "show and tell," and they lose sight of what matters to the client. Too many agencies over-commit in the spur of the moment, providing an unrealistic picture of the agency's true capabilities and resources back at the home base. Too many agencies present integrated offerings under false pretense, their multiple offices having little experience working together.

SEARCH PHASE I: NEEDS ASSESSMENT

Launching a new marketing campaign before finding out why the last one flopped is a bit like going into a second marriage without understanding why the first one failed. This phase of the agency search process is about coming up with a clear definition of services and competencies being sought by the client as well as the breadth and depth of resources required to carry out the work. What agency traits are most desired? If having breadth of services is an important client requirement, agency networks might be better suited than independent agencies. The selection criteria used to evaluate candidates can be determined only if the client is clear about its needs: Is the client looking for a full-service agency or for unbundled specialized marketing services? Is this an exclusive relationship? Is the client looking for one or multiple agencies? There is no magic silver bullet here. Investing the time early on to do this well will pay off and avoid wasted time and effort down the road.

CLIENT VIEWPOINT

"But if you do make the call for a pitch and eventually make the decision on a new partner, try to do the only thing that feels right for me at this moment: know there were other equally awesome alternatives, know there were other agencies that could've crushed it for your company, but throw your arms around the agency you've chosen, and hold on tight."[81]

—MICHAEL FANUELE, FOUNDER/CEO, TALK LIKE MUSIC— FORMER CHIEF CREATIVE OFFICER, GENERAL MILLS

The procurement and legal teams may provide a few criteria of their own to complement those developed by the marketing organization to address some fundamental requirements: credit rating, overall financial health such as balance sheets, income statement, and cash balance (for publicly traded companies), past and potential open litigation, and public records about the agency. Checking the financial health of prospective agencies is not only critical to ensure they stay in business while servicing your account, it also guarantees that the agency can invest in staffing rapidly enough to serve a new account. The answer to these questions will yield a "go/no-go" decision in the preliminary phase of the process. Once the initial filter has been applied, agency options will be determined based on a pre-determined set of criteria that are unique to each client. Some of the most common ones are shown in the figure below.

Core Competencies: Clients must articulate the strengths they are looking for to complement their marketing organization or their existing agency roster. Is this a search/review for creative or media duties? Is the client looking for a one-stop shop with full-service capabilities? Or is the client looking for a specialized agency to handle specific activities such as social media, sponsorships, or multi-cultural efforts? Advertisers must be transparent about what they are expecting the new agency to do as well as what they are not expecting it to do, which is sometimes equally important. If this is a review, the candidate agencies are likely to examine the incumbent agency to gain as much insight as possible on how they compare in terms of competencies.

Experience: Advertisers must determine the depth and breadth of experience they require on the account: Is the advertiser looking for an agency with experience in a specific industry segment or audience, or with relevant global experience? The work performed for past and current clients will speak credibly to their experience. The advertiser must decide whether that experience must originate from the agency's client portfolio (current and past) or from the staff's collective experience that might have been gained working for other agencies. Do they have the right experienced people on staff?

Client Portfolio Mix and Size: The makeup of the client portfolio of an agency is quite important for cross-polarization and best practices. For example, a packaged good company may want to select an agency with retail clients to leverage their understanding of packaging and merchandising. Is the client list synergistic? Another important criterion is the length of relationship within the existing client pool. Agencies can grow through acquisitions as well or organically through existing client relationships. It is indicative of the agency's aptitude to retain clients. Some agencies are in constant search of new business, speaking to their aggressive growth agenda or to their inability to keep clients. Agencies constantly participating in searches can be easily distracted. Clients should stay away from "hot-shot" agencies, eager to win new business but unable to build long-term partnerships. The size of client accounts is also an important consideration from a risk and critical mass standpoint. The agency must be big enough to handle the account but not too big that a relatively small client wouldn't get noticed. An agency with one predominantly large client might be concerning as well. Agencies have learned that over-dependence on a large client can be devastating when the client resigns the account. The sudden loss of a large account could seriously destabilize the agency and its ability to fulfill its other client commitments. The size of the prospective account in context of existing client accounts will directly impact the level of attention, and the quality and seniority of the talent assigned to the account. Large accounts (in revenue and profits) get "A" talent. Small accounts are likely to get "C" talent. It's common sense. Agencies invest their top resources in their best clients. It's always best for clients to be a massive fish in a small pond. And it's not just about revenue. Being a big fish means being one of the largest and most profitable clients in their portfolio. Being a small client can present some benefits as well. It means that a substantial portion of the agency overhead is picked up by large clients. And the smaller client has access to best practices that wouldn't otherwise be available.

Geographic Coverage: Is the scope domestic, regional, or international? Does the advertiser need agency resources in specific countries? Most agencies have international offices or partnerships, but there are few agencies with extensive international presence. Proximity to the client might be an important consideration as well for some clients. A client headquartered in San Francisco might be hesitant to hire an agency in New York City. Regardless of the advances made in telecommunications and video conferencing technology, regular face to face interactions are still highly valued by both parties. Being on opposite sides of the country, or even being separated by multiple states, might make travel too cost-prohibitive or simply too inconvenient (time difference, availability of resources, meeting style preferences, willingness to travel). The reality is that clients prefer to work with agencies that can be at their offices at very short notice. Long-distance client/agency relationships are rarely sustainable, pushing agencies to open offices within proximity of their clients. Agencies tend to gravitate toward large cosmopolitan cities such as New York, Chicago, San Francisco, Tokyo, Paris, and London that are known to attract and produce talent. So, agency proximity might require talent trade-offs. Unless a client is lucky enough to be based in New York, of course. That's the case for Heineken USA, which limited one of its prior creative account reviews to local shops specifically in Manhattan near their offices. It's common for agencies to separate the account management and business development functions by operating satellite offices close to clients, balancing the need for proximity and access to talent.

CLIENT VIEWPOINT

"Ikea is a mission-driven company. We have a series of values that are really core to who we are, and we ensure that everyone who works here understands and exhibits these values. We look for the same thing in our agency partners." [82]

—CHRISTINE WHITEHAWK, COMMUNICATIONS MANAGER,

IKEA

Culture and Personality: Although often overlooked at first, the culture and personality of an agency can be a determinant for the long-term fit of a relationship with an advertiser. Some clients will even conduct a cultural audit to identify and understand the nuances in corporate cultures and how they might impact the quality of an enduring client/agency relationship. Are you looking for an agency with a more traditional, conservative culture, or one that excels in creativity and innovation? Do you embrace a culture of entrepreneurship, or do you emphasize a culture of teamwork and collaboration? Are you willing to tolerate a high degree of creative freedom, or do you want an agency partner that plays by your brand playbook? Do you want an agency that prioritizes quality over speed? There are many facets of an agency's culture that can foster a very productive or antagonistic relationship if mismatched.

SEARCH PHASE II: PROJECT PREPARATION

Time has now come for the client to prepare internally and to assemble the resources required to carry out the search. Although there are industry best practices worth considering, most of which have been published by the Association of National Advertisers (ANA), American Association of Advertising Agencies (4A's), and World Federation of Advertisers (WFA), the way to approach this process should be tailored based on the unique requirements of a client. At the onset of the search, a team of hand-picked individuals is usually put together from multiple departments—marketing, procurement, and legal. Key stakeholders from the business units or subsidiaries may also be invited to give input and buy-in. It's important to make this a collaborative process from start to finish, especially if they are expected to actively embrace and evangelize the chosen agency.

Too often, client teams that weren't invited to participate end up rejecting the relationship afterward when issues arise, as they inevitably do. The more upfront the buy-in, the more likely the decision is to stick and support to be provided. The team is formed, composed of a Project Lead and a Core Team.

The Project Lead is first appointed by the Project Sponsor who oversees the entire project. The Project Sponsor is either the final decision maker or the arbitrator, should the Review Team be unable to reach a decision. Given the strategic importance of an agency search, the CMO or VP of Marketing is often the Project Sponsor, if not the Project Lead in smaller organizations. Once the "go-to" Project Lead has been assigned, he/she is responsible for assembling the Core Team, a virtual team typically composed of representatives from around the company and relevant business groups. The Core Team typically includes select clients—typically marketers—as well as key representatives from legal, procurement, and PR. The Core Team meets on a frequent basis to make sure the project objectives are met within the defined parameters, keeping the project on time and on budget. Having the right individuals on the team, with relevant experience and the right sphere of influence, is essential to both gathering meaningful feedback throughout and the credibility of the selection process. The Core Team will sign off on all documents produced, so everyone is working from the same sheet of music. The final decision may be reached unanimously or by most of the team. They may make their recommendation to the Project Sponsor who is the ultimate decision-maker.

Once all key individuals have been engaged, the search methodology and timeline must be defined and agreed upon. The project schedule is often a source of tension, since the need for an agency to take on work immediately must be tempered by the need to follow a well-orchestrated process that delivers a viable, long-term solution to the company. The duration of the project will vary significantly based on the nature of the review, its scope, and the client itself. A global agency search can take up to four to sixth months, in some cases even longer, especially if it involves many participants around the world. A domestic search can take up to two to three months, depending on the complexity and scope of the search, but most advertisers will target an eight-week window or shorter if they can.

Advertisers looking to hire a new agency for one assignment may need an accelerated search to get a new agency hired within weeks, not months. Clearly, the process for a much simpler project-based search wouldn't require nearly as much effort and due diligence as a search for a long-term partnership. The schedule must be vetted internally to ensure it provides sufficient time for all parties involved to contribute. No one wants to start over simply because the decision was rushed or there wasn't any internal buy-in. An agency search consultant can speed up the selection process and save the company precious time. Before the process is formally kicked off, members of the Core Team must commit the time to participate in all key milestone meetings and decisions or agree to delegate. Revisiting decisions that have already been made can be disastrous and demoralizing. If there is an incumbent agency, the agency leadership must be notified in a timely manner to allow them to handle PR and employee inquiries.

ADVERTISER SEARCH RESPONSIBILITIES

ROLES	TYPICAL RESPONSIBILITIES
PROJECT SPONSOR	Is accountable for the overall project Is the final decision maker or arbitrator in the event of a tie-breaker
PROJECT LEAD	Assembles the Review Team Defines the schedule and associated milestones Is responsible for the successful completion of the project Is the spokesperson for the project inside and outside the company Is the direct interface to other departments
CORE TEAM	Represents the interests of the company Screens potential agency candidates Participates in agency visits Reviews agency materials and responses to RFI and RFPs Participates in agency presentations Provides input to inform decision May be asked to cast a vote
CONSULTANT (OPTIONAL)	Provides project management and coordination support Shares knowledge of the agency market; identifies potential candidates Interfaces with agency candidates Facilitates agency fact-finding, pre-screening, reference checking Weighs in on the selection May be asked to handle post-selection activities, e.g., negotiations, on-boarding

A communication plan will need to be established that includes internal FAQs, email announcements, and press releases. Agency searches/reviews always generate buzz and press inquiries.

A PR plan ensures that any leakage to the press can be handled in the best interest of the company and the agencies (should those be publicly disclosed). Having clear expectations and objectives is of utmost importance to best prepare for a search.

SEARCH PHASE III: RESEARCH AND FILTERING

At first, the options may seem endless or somewhat over-whelming, with countless agencies to choose from. There are thousands of talented agencies around the world with unique credentials and competencies. Finding the ideal partner among those is a bit like finding a needle in a haystack. Where do you start? This is where a search consultant can be handy. He or she can quickly and objectively come up with a preliminary list of potential candidates based on his or her experience and knowledge of the industry alone. Clients can also leverage a variety of industry references, business journal listings, and other resources that provide robust, multiple-criteria, search-able agency directories, and services with in-depth agency profiles, such as the Advertising RedBooks™, Adforum.com, Agencyfinder.com, ANA, American Association of Advertising Agencies (4As), and other relevant organizations. Annual lists of top agencies are published by trade magazines such as *Ad Age*, *AdWeek*, and other specialized trade publications. It's senseless to see ill-informed clients invite large numbers of candidate agencies to the process without first attempting to reduce the list to a reasonable number, wasting their own time and valu-able resources and those of the agencies in the process. Clients are encouraged to identify no more than 10 to 15 agencies at this stage of the process. Although there is no magical number, common sense calls for a number that is large enough to provide sufficient choice but small enough to be manageable. Once RFI responses have been received and evaluated, no more than six to eight agencies should be invited to respond to the next-phase RFP. After that evaluation milestone, only three to four agencies should participate in face-to-face presentations. The 4As calls this the "15-8-4 rule."

To narrow down the list to qualified agency candidates, the Core Team should consider filtering out agencies with competitive conflicts that are unlikely to be resolved favorably (e.g., the competitor's account is significantly larger than yours, so there is no way the agency would jump ship). The agency will need to decide whether they would consider dropping their existing client(s) if/once awarded the business. The concept of "conflict" has evolved in recent years. Lack of industry standard definition has led clients to decide for themselves what is tolerable and what isn't. Holding companies have broadened their offering through multiple branded agencies under the same umbrella, in order to deal with those conflicts and give themselves an opportunity to pursue multiple clients in the same category. If you are Burger King, do you have all companies in the food industry on your list of competitors or only those in the fast food business? This is a subjective judgment call for brand advertisers to make. Clients would typically produce a list of their key competitors at the beginning of the project.

Once the preliminary list has been compiled, the selected agencies are asked to participate in the review process. At that point, the advertiser must provide some basic information about their search. The intent is to offer sufficient information for an agency to decide if they want to participate in the review. The agency packet might include an introduction to the company (vision and mission statement), a business and financial overview, an overview of key business objectives as well as marketing challenges, and a description of prior marketing service provider arrangements. It can include current agency rosters and tenure (including any recent additions and terminations), what is expected of the agency, scale and scope of the relationship, expected marketing expenditures/budgets, prior compensation methods, reasons for the review, timing and key milestones, number of agencies invited (is the incumbent agency invited?), selection criteria, decision making process, access to resources and key contacts, process for work approval, existing program and research measurement, and success metrics. If one of the agency candidates works for one of the client's competitors but is considering resigning the account, it becomes a much more delicate situation given the confidential nature of their involvement. This would need to be managed with the utmost level of confidentiality to avoid any leakage that would jeopardize the search and the agency's relationship with their client.

Once the agencies have received their packet of information, a phone conversation can be scheduled to answer any additional questions they may have. Thankfully, the 4A's published a paper on agency search agreements to provide agencies with best practices on how to obtain formal agreements between an agency and a prospective client or for handling a client's request for proposal. The paper provides some useful guidance on sensitive topics such as confidentiality, information disclosure, need for transparency, ownership of agency ideas and work, and reimbursement for agency activity and expenses. Questionnaires such as the "AAAA Standardized Marketer New Business Questionnaire" and the "AAAA Standardized Agency New Business Questionnaire" facilitate up-front discussions, putting agencies on a more equal footing and improving agencies' understanding of the client's needs.

SEARCH PHASE IV: RFI/RFP

The 4As recommends that advertisers and agencies enter into a formal agreement at the outset of every agency search, covering key topics such as confidentiality, ownership of agency ideas and work, and reimbursement for agency participation and expenses. Since clients and agencies are very likely to disclose proprietary information about how they do business (process, technology, approach/methodology), they recommend that access to and use of such confidential information should be protected by a mutually binding confidentiality agreement which protects both parties. The concept of ownership of agency ideas and work can be more controversial. The agency is likely to produce ideas and concepts and to share recommendations that have intrinsic value to the client. The 4A's therefore recommends that the agency preserve ownership of those ideas and any tangible work in a written agreement. Finally, the agency may expect to be compensated for its time participating in the review in addition to the costs associated with the review (travel expenses, etc.). The reimbursement of expenses is common but compensating agencies for their time participating in an agency search is less common and is sometimes debated by clients who expect agencies to absorb these costs as part of their new business development efforts. Some agencies may choose not to participate in a review based on these terms. Clients must weigh the pros and cons accordingly. Once agencies express interest in participating in the review, a more involved information-gathering process will start to validate and complement the information already collected about the agencies. The purpose here is to further reduce the list of qualified agencies to the final few candidates. To make an informed decision, the client will require participating agencies to fill out a Request for Information (RFI) document.

Clients need to be reasonable, however, and limit the number of questions to those that are most relevant and insightful. It's insane to see clients send very extensive RFI templates with every question imaginable that agencies must then fill out. Sadly enough, most of the answers will probably not be read in their entirety by the client. In some rare cases, the RFI is not restricted to a set of pre-determined agencies. The purpose of the RFI is to provide detailed information about the agency's profile, management team, organizational chart and operating structure, business approach, financials, credentials, client list, and potential conflicts (and more importantly, how they would be resolved), core and extended capabilities, and so on. It typically requests case studies and creative work samples that might help illustrate the agency capabilities. It is standard documentation that agencies are accustomed to providing. Agencies must be cautious, however, about the claims made and avoid overstating account wins and status of relationships with other clients.

A very effective way of gaining insight into an agency is to speak to existing clients. The RFI should include a reference section requesting the names of at least two or three existing clients with similar account size and services. This type of conversation can prove to be the most valuable part of the screening process. The team will learn much about the strengths and weaknesses of the agency as seen from another client's perspective. Another way to gather information is to visit the agencies' websites. Given the increasing importance of digital, the quality of the website may tell you quite a bit about their abilities in this area. Are they practicing what they preach? Have you ever heard the story of the shoemaker who didn't wear good shoes? Or the hair stylist with terrible hair? Not a confidence-builder, is it? A website can provide very helpful information about the agency's ability to talk about itself and gives access to press releases that speak to major events in the agency's history and annual reports for publicly traded companies, providing much insight on how each agency within the network is doing overall.

Instructions will need to be provided to the agencies on how to fill out the RFI. Clients will want to make sure to remind agencies of the confidentiality of the information exchanged between the two parties, that any news release or any disclosure regarding any aspect of the selection process cannot be made without the client's written approval. Whether or not the client will be responsible for any of the costs the agency will incur during this process, as well as the client's policy regarding document retention and disposal, how to submit questions and to whom, how to treat any pre-contract discussions, how one plans to treat intellectual property and any other similar considerations. The RFI fills a major gap in information gathering and it is highly recommended during a review. Still, some companies will bypass this step and go directly into the Request for Proposal (RFP) stage. The purpose of the RFP is to describe the way the agency would meet the needs of the brand advertiser, how they would structure the team to serve the account, what resources would be involved, how they would approach the business overall, and what their proposed financial arrangements would be. It provides deeper insight into the strategic approach taken by the agency. It is very specific to this client situation and therefore requires a bit more prep work for the agency. The RFP will include questions such as:

- "What specific actions would you suggest we take to meet our marketing objectives?"

- "How would you characterize our marketing efforts today?"

- "What would you propose we do differently?"

- "What do you see as the key issues, challenges, and opportunities faced by our brand?"

- "What are your views and opinions on our industry?"

- "How would you structure your team to most effectively serve our account?"

- "How would you propose to collaborate with other roster agencies?"

- "How would triage the work?"

- "How would you measure the performance of our work together?"

- "How would you stage your growth to meet our demands?"

Finally, the agency should be asked to provide the most compelling reason for the client to choose it over another (arguably equally capable) agency. Given the amount of information covered in a typical RFP, a client will want to minimize the number of agency candidates at this stage of the process to avoid crawling under pounds of carefully organized paper reports that may, unfortunately, never be read. As in prior stages, the agencies may have clarifying questions about the RFP. I strongly encourage advertisers to invite questions from agencies. As the 18th century French philosopher and writer Voltaire suggested: *"Judge a person by their questions, rather than their answers."* Advertisers will learn tremendously about the agencies by the way they formulate their questions and the type of questions they ask. Some clients choose to answer their questions, and then share those with every agency candidate. This is really up to the client. In my humble opinion, if an agency is not asking the right questions, they shouldn't benefit from getting answers to questions other agencies were clever enough to ask. There are different schools of thought about whether a client should level the playing field. In my opinion, clients should not attempt to artificially level the playing field to save themselves time and effort. Once the information has been carefully reviewed, the Consultant or Project Lead may require every team member to fill out a scoring sheet to then aggregate all the responses on a simple table or scorecard so that agency responses can be evaluated side by side.

If you are using a consultant, they will provide you with a standard template that has been customized for your individual needs. Summarizing the data supplied into a readable format is imperative to help the team evaluate the responses provided. It requires everyone to use common taxonomy and definitions. In addition to the table, a simple scoring methodology will facilitate the ranking and sorting of agencies. The scoring methodology can vary from scoring each attribute on a 1 to 5 scale. For example, 1 being "the lowest" and 5 being "the highest" for each question on a similar scale, or 1 being "strongly disagree" and 5 being "strongly agree." Each attribute or question should be weighted and agreed upon by the team. Then the results can be tabulated and calculated based on the score and weight. The analysis can be conducted in many different ways to evaluate the strengths and weaknesses of each candidate. After this initial rating, a first cut can be conducted, and the list of agency candidates reduced to the final few.

SEARCH PHASE V: PRESENTATIONS

The RFI/RFP phase misses a vital component: the human experience. This is what led Linda Boff, CMO at GE, to invite marketers to say, "RIP to the Media RFP." The marketing team at GE rallied behind a no-RFP stance, and instead, put the time in to get to know its media partners and platforms.

AGENCY VIEWPOINT

"In a post-RFP world, agencies and publishers don't waste time on proposals that will never go anywhere, and brands don't devote resources to sifting through cookie-cutter submissions. Instead, time and talent can be invested where it matters: In identifying breakthrough experiences that are good for users and drive attention—the only metric that really matters. It also opens the door to deeper, more dynamic partnerships between brands, publishers, and agencies." [83]

—LINDA BOFF, CMO, GE

It's incredibly difficult to get a feel for what it would be like to work with an agency based only on the way they answered questions and without getting to know the individuals that provided them. Some would argue good agencies can be particularly bad at filling out RFI/RFPs. Perhaps. It's almost certain that those good at filling out RFI/RFPs are not always the best agencies to work with. The point here is that the RFI/RFP phase is about collecting meaningful information that can be used to inform the face-to-face discussions that will result from this phase of the process. It's rarely sufficient to form a decision at this phase, and marketers should be wary of making one now. The next logical step is meeting with the agency to check the chemistry between the agency and client team, clarifying any potential gaps in the RFI/RFP, and giving both parties the opportunity to ask questions, and ultimately assess their understanding of your business and their ability to think about it strategically. The chemistry check is a critical component, as it says much about the future partnership from the outset. This opportunity obviously goes both ways. During the stage of "courtship," both parties find each other very engaged, willing, and positive about the future, sometimes at the risk of de-emphasizing negative perceptions and magnifying positive ones. The agencies will need a reasonable amount of time to get prepared for the final stage of the review process, especially if it involves a creative shoot-out, which is more time-consuming.

AGENCY VIEWPOINT

"The best ideas and results usually come from rethinking the problem statement, but most RFPs don't provide the respondents with the chance to reframe, rethink, or reposition the brand problem." [84]

—**A.J. MEYER**, CO-FOUNDER AND PARTNER, GOKART LABS

CREDENTIAL PRESENTATIONS

The credential presentations may be taking place at each agency, sometimes in multiple locations per agency for global clients. It is highly recommended to conduct the meeting at the agency's office rather than at the client's corporate headquarters. It's always tempting for advertisers to conduct the meeting at their office to minimize the burden of travel and coordination. Visiting agency offices, however, gives clients the opportunity to experience firsthand the true personality of the agency and validate whether it is consistent with the materials they provided. There is nothing like seeing how they treat a client at the front desk. Check the atmosphere and layout of their workspace, get a feel for the culture and energy level, and see how they interface with others in their own element. It is of utmost importance to meet the Core Team that would be actively engaged in your business at the meetings, not just the management team that you may not see much of after the selection process. Agencies tend to put their best talent up front for this type of meeting, even if those resources won't be involved as you move forward. Make sure the folks that will work on your business are the ones presenting. Half a day is a standard time allocation for these onsite visits, giving everyone enough time to participate, usually followed by a smaller group dinner to become more familiar with the key people involved in the business.

Give the presentations time and space to sink in. The review team is encouraged to take notes on the presentations, but their feedback should be requested only when all agencies have presented to give them a chance to compare all presentations before stack-ranking them. It's now time for the "pony show." There are two types of meetings: credential presentations and creative shoot-outs. Some clients may require both, if time and budget allow. If a creative shoot-out is expected, the credential presentation is unlikely to be a decisive factor in the selection process. So, it makes sense to schedule those within proximity to get a full picture of the agency candidate.

For credential presentations, the objective is to go past the documentation and ask questions about the information that has already been submitted. It also gives the agency an opportunity to show their proprietary tools and solutions, some of their work, and client case studies that speak to the hot buttons and pain points experienced by the prospective client. The review team should judge both the content and the form. The content will include questions about their ability to understand their client's business, to provide strategic insight and create impactful ideas, to leverage the brand, to find innovative ways to speak and engage their audiences, and to measure, optimize, and analyze performance. The forum will include questions about their ability to present their work effectively, to leverage each skill, seek buy-in, invite input, and manage client feedback. It also includes more subjective criteria like passion and energy level expressed by the agency during the presentation, as well as how approachable the team members are, and whether people would feel comfortable working with them.

AGENCY VIEWPOINT

"The issue of spec work is polarizing within the industry ... Many agencies refuse to do it in many circumstances. A lot of agencies will do it, but they don't think it's appropriate, and then there are some agencies who, for significant pieces of business, think it's a good part of the process for various reasons." [85]

—TOM FINNERAN, EVP OF AGENCY MANAGEMENT SERVICES, THE 4AS

CREATIVE SHOOT-OUTS

The purpose of the creative shoot-out is to assess how the agency would address a real client marketing challenge and demonstrate how they would apply their skills in a real-life scenario. It gives the advertiser a better understanding of the agency's listening and reasoning capabilities, how the agency likes to engage with a client, and how they communicate their ideas and receive input. The participation in "creative shoot-outs" is a highly debated topic since some agencies do not believe that this type of creative real-life assignment, sometimes referred as a "beauty contest," is conclusive. It's a worthwhile argument.

CLIENT VIEWPOINT

"In my 20-plus years of marketing, I have yet to see a truly creative idea come from a standard RFP... RFPs favor off-the-shelf, fill-in-the-blank, template-based recommendations. They don't inspire new thinking or give fledgling ideas room to grow." [86]

—LINDA BOFF, CMO, GE

But what other options do clients have besides credential presentations? How would they get to know the team and see them perform? Hiring a couple of agencies and giving them different paid assignments is not only unrealistic, it would be even less objective. Typically, the same marketing assignment would be provided to the agencies, allowing the Core Team to compare the respective approaches and creative solutions. A creative shoot-out usually requires more time and resources, since it will require the advertiser to brief the agency and be available to answer any follow-up questions. The specific assignment should be relatively well-defined and well-contained to help the advertiser assess the candidate agencies based on their most important criteria. Therefore, it is common for the creative shoot-out to be limited to rough concept to avoid the often unnecessary production expenses to bring it to life. Some agencies (most of those are independent) refuse to participate in competitive pitches requiring contenders to foot the bill for speculative creative work, allowing them to focus on expanding relationships with clients already on their rosters. Independent agencies like Zulu and High Wide & Handsome passed up dozens of invites and added assignments from Audi, Corona, Google, and Puma.

It is recommended to put the emphasis on the idea development process and less on the tactical execution process, which is typically not a differentiating and therefore deciding factor in agency reviews. Although the client will need to allocate enough time to answer any questions about the assignment, unlike a real assignment, the Project Lead is likely to shield internal contacts from the barrage of questions an agency would usually ask. A briefing document will be submitted with all appropriate supporting documentation. Once again, the way the agency interacts with the advertiser during that time will be very telling, a close approximation to how both parties would work together, and should ultimately be reflected in the end product delivered by the agency. Equal time (say one or two conference calls with the client) and access to information should be provided to the agencies. For global accounts, the client may require the candidate agencies to demonstrate their capabilities on a global scale as well as in-market, with their ability to adapt a global concept into specific markets. This is what Visa requested of TBWA before the company decided to appoint the agency as its creative global agency around its global brand campaign "Life takes Visa." Perhaps the most common issues faced by the industry are related to the ownership of ideas and whether agencies should be compensated for all or some of their expenses, regardless of whether the work will be used by the client. Agencies like Euro RSCG Life have been known to decline participation in reviews where the client wants to keep pitch ideas and materials. No agency wants to give away work.

AGENCY VIEWPOINT

"Statistically speaking, clients don't use the work that was presented in the pitch. So, they're buying the team and the people. It's like dating someone."[87]

—LAUREN CRAMPSIE, SENIOR PARTNER, GLOBAL CMO,
OGILVY & MATHER WORLDWIDE

Participating in a creative shoot-out can be an expensive proposition for an agency, as it will require many resources to work on the project and out-of-pocket expenses. Some clients will offer to compensate for the agency's travel expenses; some will offer to compensate for a portion of the expenses associated with the assignments. This is commonly known as "pitch fee." If the advertiser offers to compensate the agency for some of their time and/or expenses, a written agreement should be signed by the agency and the client that stipulates ownership of the work. This type of compensation issue is typically addressed early in the review process. Although most agencies consider business development a "cost of doing business," the most prestigious agencies may still decline to participate in the overall review if the client won't agree to compensate the agency for all or some of its expenses. They certainly have a point. For many of them, it can turn out to be a wasteful and expensive exercise. And it might distract their team from servicing existing paying clients.

In advance of conducting search meetings or presentations, it is recommended that the client and participating agencies discuss how ownership, license, or usage rights of agency-developed ideas, plans, and work will be handled. It's insane for a client to assume that an agency would agree to enter a pitch if the client can own the work of that agency and hire another one to launch the campaign. Unless specified otherwise, the agency keeps ownership of the work presented, regardless of whether a fee is paid to the agency. Once again, the Core Team will be asked to provide feedback about the presentation(s) and about the agency's ability to perform in the context of a real business scenario.

SEARCH PHASE VI: SELECTION

The assessment of the credential presentations and creative shoot-out (if applicable) complements the RFI/RFP already conducted. Further conversations may be needed to address any outstanding questions or concerns by the Core Team. The methodology has already been defined and agreed upon, the qualitative and quantitative information has been collected, so it is now only a matter of consolidating the assessment of the various team members and analyzing results. Trust and integrity are highly important throughout the process. The now infamous honeymoon of DraftFCB with Wal-Mart Stores, Inc., which hired DraftFCB in October 2006 after a comprehensive review, only to re-pitch the business two months later amid concerns over the handling of the review by Wal-Mart Store's SVP of Marketing Communications, Julie Roehm, will probably remain the most publicized agency review of all times. The lawsuits that followed between the company and its former SVP shed light on the importance of strict adherence to corporate policies (not accepting gifts from candidate agencies, for example) and code of conduct during the decision process.

INDIVIDUAL SCORING SUBMISSIONS BY INDIVIDUAL CORE TEAM MEMBERS

CORE TEAM MEMBER: JOHN SMITH

MAIN CRITERIA	WEIGHT	AGENCY A	AGENCY B	AGENCY C
STRATEGIC THINKING	15%	5	3	4
UNDERSTANDING OF OUR BUSINESS/INDUSTRY	10%	3	1	5
CREATIVITY	10%	2	5	3
INNOVATIVE	5%	4	4	2
ETC.	ETC.	ETC.	ETC.	ETC.
TOTAL	100%	3.5	2.8	3.2
KEY OBSERVATIONS AND COMMENTS				

CLIENT VIEWPOINT

"It only gives you a point-in-time view of an agency's creative capability. The creative work that's done for a pitch is usually done in a very short period of time, and often the agency chooses a team to work on a pitch that happens to be available, which might not be the team that you would have working with your brand on an ongoing basis."[88]

—**DEBRA GIAMPOLI,** FORMER GLOBAL DIRECTOR, STRATEGIC AGENCY RELATIONS, MONDELEZ INTERNATIONAL

Using the same scoring methodology and taxonomy for the credential presentations and a creative shoot-out allows for consistency and builds trust in the fairness of the evaluation.

The Core Team adds their scores against the weighted attributes and any appropriate commentaries as in the example on the previous page. The results will be compiled and summarized (anonymously or not). The reason for potentially keeping results anonymous is to save face for team members who may not have picked the lead agency and to avoid putting them into a defensive position that could derail the process. Once the results are available, the Core Team should meet again to discuss the findings. If everything went according to plan, the team has reached consensus, and a winner has emerged. If not, the Project Sponsor may need to arbitrate the decision. The discussion is centered on remaining gaps or weaknesses that the agency will be asked to address. The advertiser then contacts the selected agency to congratulate them, pending signing of an agreement. By that time, the advertiser has gathered enough detailed information about costs to finalize terms. An advertiser is in a much stronger position to negotiate favorably when the final decision is contingent on mutually agreeing on terms. The prospective agencies should not be contacted yet since failure to reach an acceptable agreement with the lead agency candidate may require the advertiser to pursue an alternative solution.

Once the agreement is signed, the decision is then communicated internally (email announcement, newsletters, etc.) and externally (press release, articles). Internally, the company will need to provide context for the decision and how it was reached and what transition activities are expected. At the very least, it should provide a rudimentary Q&A for everyone concerned. The non-selected candidates will need to be notified prior to any internal or external communications, preferably by phone, followed up by a formal communication from the company. The agencies that were not selected may understandably ask for feedback about where they fell short on meeting expectations, especially considering the numerous hours they invested to get to this point. This may be a highly sensitive topic, and your legal department will likely advise you to keep it high-level and focus on tangible criteria the agency didn't meet to the client's satisfaction. If handled professionally, the defeated agencies might gain some insight that would be applicable to future reviews. It's critical to avoid burning bridges. You may be reaching out to them a few years later to pick up another piece of business or participate in a new agency review. Be decisive, be direct, and be fair.

INDUSTRY VIEWPOINT

"I'm proud to say that never, in all the pitches I've run, has the cheapest agency been chosen on the basis of cheapness. In many cases, the more expensive option on paper becomes the winner. Price is important, sure—and I'm not suggesting that you inflate your numbers; but it is a component of value, not the other way around."[89]

—DAVID ANGELL, GENERAL MANAGER AND HEAD OF MEDIA, TRINITYP3

ENDING AN EXISTING RELATIONSHIP

Studies show more than 85 percent of American adults have experienced a break up at least once in their lifetime. When it comes to the world of marketing, it's safe to assume that a break up is something that EVERYONE on the agency and client sides have experienced at least once, if not multiple times, in their career. Advertisers and agencies are breaking up at an increased pace, and relationships are being reduced to months, sometimes years, but rarely decades as once was typical. Hiring a new agency as a result of a well-orchestrated agency review often implies that the incumbent agency lost the account. The search and selection process, although demanding, is often benign compared to what's coming next: transitioning the prior agency and preparing to work with a new agency partner. This process, known as agency transition, is critical to the combined success of the client and agency. It's not quite as glamourous and probably won't be the subject of much media interest, but it will determine the ultimate success of a process that started months prior and is at risk of creating more downside than upside, unless properly managed. Both parties enter the honeymoon phase of the relationship, realizing that the entire agency team must be onboarded to take on the work and quickly ramp up. As the incumbent agency phases out, the work is piling up quickly, putting incredible pressure on the partnership with high expectations from the client looking for improved performance. How long will it take the new agency to perform at the expected level? What options are available to brands looking to accelerate this process?

No matter how many breakups you've been through, they never get easier. Through my years of giving agencies and clients relationship advice, I've seen many CMOs highlight extremely frustrating problems as the reason for ending a relationship. Sadly, none of these scenarios have to be a reality—my hope is that you're never on the receiving end of this kind of letter:

CONFIDENTIAL

February 14, 2018

ACME
11536 Maple Blvd., Suite 500
New York, NY 10038
John Doe, CMO

Agency X
Jane Roe
CEO

Dear Jane,

Short relationships are increasingly the norm.

After a thorough review, we have made the decision to terminate our relationship with your agency. Over the past six months, we have enjoyed a successful relationship together. Although we didn't get the opportunity to provide your team with any usable onboarding or training information about our company's organization, processes, policies, guidelines, budget or marketing priorities, your team blindly jumped in with great eagerness and enthusiasm. For that, we are most grateful.

AGENCY ONBOARDING IS ESSENTIAL TO GET THEM CLIENT-READY QUICKLY AND EFFICIENTLY.

★ Lack of process rigor or briefing sets the agency up for unnecessary challenges.

Given the extended 150-day payment terms and low margin agreement we negotiated over the prior three months before a contractual agreement was reached, I can't tell you how grateful the marketing teams are for your support. Your agency was willing to staff our business with your best people, and start project work without a formal PO in place or brief of any kind. Your commitment to our business was most appreciated, even though we were unable to effectively return the favor.

Unreasonable contract terms can negatively impact the agency's ability to staff well or perform optimally.

RECIPROCAL EVALUATIONS ARE ESSENTIAL FOR CLIENTS TO UNDERSTAND THEIR ROLE IN CONTRIBUTING TO TOP OR WEAK PERFORMANCE.

Our decision is irreversible. Although we didn't conduct any formal 360 relationship assessment, we feel that we captured enough random, confidential, anecdotal feedback from our internal teams to inform our decision. We realize that your feedback about us as a client would have been helpful, as we are likely contributing to some of these relationship issues. If we'd had enough time to capture this information, all of our marketing stakeholders would have considered it valuable. As you know, our aggressive deadlines and go-to-market efforts leave little time for post-mortem reviews or discussions.

WITHOUT ANY FORM OF PERFORMANCE EVALUATION, ADVERTISERS CANNOT IMPROVE THE WORK RELATIONSHIP WITH THEIR AGENCIES.

In the end, the decision to terminate our relationship was based on an assortment of considerations. In the spirit of partial transparency, here are the primary ones:

- Despite overlooking our standard scope of work process and therefore, our inability to provide you line of sight into the work and type of deliverables needed, we hoped that our arrangement would have turned into a positive, flexible, unstructured approach to serving every team differently. Instead, it led to inconsistencies, endless negotiations, off-the-chart budget proposals, scope redundancies, gross staffing inefficiencies, and random execution.

A STREAMLINED, STANDARDIZED SCOPE OF WORK PROCESS DRIVES ALIGNMENT AND PRODUCTIVITY.

- Too many failed creative concepts leading to extensive reworks and delays. Your teams were unable to accurately guess our underlying strategy or objectives. Because of this your team required and would write a client input brief that ultimately slowed down our efforts, as it required internal consensus and identification of a single decision maker.

Agencies cannot perform well without role or goal clarity.

CONFIDENTIAL

- Kick off meetings were attended by significantly more agency staff than internal team members. The result was unnecessary travel costs to our HQ offices and led us to believe that no consideration was given to the careful use of our resources and travel budget.

Cost-cutting efforts must be conducted in collaborative ways.

THE RESPONSIBLE STEWARDSHIP OF CLIENT BUDGETS IS AN IMPORTANT AGENCY ROLE.

- Our decision to suddenly decouple production and all things digital from the original scope to cut our costs led to more complications than we expected. In turn, we encountered unexpected territorial issues with some of your direct competitors that had a negative impact on collaboration and undermined our cost-saving efforts.

- Although we never committed to a retainer or a predictable set of project work, we were disappointed in your agency's ability to secure, assign to our business, and retain Team A quality staff. We thought our brand's name and reputation would have helped your agency attract top talent for our business over your other client retainers. Instead, we experienced over 50 percent staff turnover (although we are not quite certain about the actual numbers as we had no access to staffing plans).

HOW THE RELATIONSHIP IS MANAGED FINANCIALLY GREATLY IMPACTS THE AGENCY'S ABILITY TO STAFF.

EXPECTATIONS MUST BE REASONABLY SET AND BALANCED.

- A lack of innovative, out-of-the-box ideas for our last minute, time-sensitive tactical assignments led us to question your agency's creative prowess to reach our audience, and move us forward, despite our constant budget constraints.

Due to some isolated evidence of quality work and an overall positive experience with your team, we may indeed work together in the future, but for the time being we will need to end our relationship. Effective April 1st, we will terminate our agreement with your agency. Of course, we will ask that you strictly honor the non-compete clause in our contract and refrain from working with any company in our category for the next 24 months.

TRANSITION TERMS MUST BE SENSIBLE AND ALLOW FOR A SMOOTH PROCESS.

We have many projects in the works with your agency. As our incumbent agency, we will ask you to kindly and collaboratively partner with our new agency and commit to smooth project transitions. Please contact me directly once you receive this termination letter, so we can begin the extended 15-day transition process together as stipulated within our contract. It has been great working with you and your team, and we wish you the best for your future business.

Sincerely,

John Doe, Chief Marketing Officer, ACME

PS: I am told we have a good chance to win a Lion at the Cannes Festival of Creativity, as we are nominated in a few categories. If we do, please extend my thanks to the entire team.

This letter—yes purely fictional and borderline irritable at times—is inspired from real stories and pain points between advertisers and agencies that I've witnessed over the years. For some, this letter might be a painful reminder. However, for most, I hope it highlights the many ways advertisers and agencies inadvertently create unproductive environments which undermine their relationships if those are not addressed proactively. Thankfully, many aspects of the client/agency relationship can be significantly improved by applying best client/agency practices, and yes, common sense. If we learn from the unnecessary breakups and poorly-managed relationships that are flooding our industry, we can instead build high-impact and lasting partnerships that flourish and get celebrated year after year.

Let's take a more intimate look at what the client and its agencies, the incumbent one and the newly assigned one, are up against, and let's reveal the secrets of effective, smooth agency transitions. Here are 10 critical steps to a successful agency transition:

10 CRITICAL STEPS TO A
SUCCESSFUL AGENCY
T R A N S I T I O N

| **Terms** Review and comply with the termination terms of the agreement. | **Resource Managment** Set up a transition v-team composed of internal and external stakeholders; actively monitor talent activity. | **Noise-handling** Over communicate; ensure everyone is operating on the same plan. | **Intellectual Property** Ensure the immediate transfer of all client documents, research and confidential materials. | **Investment** Minimize transition costs and duplication of expenses. | **Next** Look forward, focusing on setting up the new agency for success while gracefully transitioning the prior one. |

Assets Identify and transfer all creative and production assets held by the incumbent agency to the designated repository.

Stability Avoid work disruptions, delays, duplicative efforts, wasteful activities.

Timeline Set realistic timelines and checkpoints.

Onboarding Provide access to key resources and accelerate ramp- up time with training.

1) Terms: Review and comply with the termination terms of the agreement

The first step is to consult with the Marketing Procurement team on the specific requirements for termination often captured in the Master Service Agreement. Having a comprehensive termination clause and detailed language articulating expectations provides a much-needed framework to prevent unnecessary headaches and difficult conversations. Most termination contracts have a 90-day period. All terms are effectively negotiable, so it might be longer or shorter based on the nature of the work relationship. It should give ample time for both the client and the agency to handle the transition in a way that is mutually satisfying. As soon as the decision is made and shared with the agency, the clock is ticking. Relying on the precise termination terms will accelerate the process and reduce potential friction.

2) Resource management: Set up a transition v-team composed of internal and external stakeholders; actively monitor talent activity

Shortly after the decision has been communicated, the priority is in setting up a virtual team composed of major stakeholders: 1) The client team will designate a transition manager who can draw resources from procurement, legal, and the marketing organization and report progress made or escalate issues to senior management; 2) The new agency will assign a key contact to manage the responsibilities associated with onboarding and getting "client" ready; and 3) The incumbent agency will assign a lead individual to handle all agency communications and updates, as well as coordinate all activities back at the agency. Keeping an eye on talent is also vital. The incumbent agency might be required to lay off resources, move key individuals, or may simply lose employees looking for other, more stable opportunities, considering the termination. The new agency—even the brand advertiser—might be tempted to poach and hire top performers and key staff from the incumbent agency to accelerate its ramp up. Although some of it might happen organically, it remains an ethical issue. No solicitation or explicit inquiries should ever be conducted as this could lead to mistrust and additional costs detrimental to the brand's working relationship with its agencies.

3) Assets: Identify and transfer all creative and production assets held by the incumbent agency to the designated repository

For agencies that produce assets, creating such a list and making sure it gets transferred to the client can be a daunting task. Assets may include broadcast (talent agreements, music contracts, stock footage as well as reels, list of supplies, masters, and production elements), print advertising (art studio, art buying, etc.), digital advertising (all creative and production elements, copies of all contracts, list of client-specific IDs and passwords used with various vendors), and the list goes on, based on the services provided. As the process of moving physical and digital assets unfolds, and these are sent to a new storage vendor or the client's designated repository, the v-team must also initiate the reconciliation and closing out of any outstanding jobs, reviewing and signing off on final invoices. A brand may choose to hire a specialized production consultant or firm—if they don't really have one—to handle this labor-intensive, detail-oriented process of transferring all assets (money well spent if you ask me).

4) Noise-handling: Over communicate; ensure everyone is operating on the same plan

No matter how hard brands try to handle this process, agency transitions are turbulent times. It can be a noisy procedure with too many people playing deaf out of convenience. I've seen too many agency transitions fail with disastrous, undesired consequences due to a lack of proactive communications by the client, with the concerned agencies and internal teams all left to their own devices. Everyone on the client and agency side must be well aligned from the start and operate with a firm timeline and clear responsibilities. It's important that everyone becomes familiar with those to ensure full compliance with the contract terms and conditions. Additional resources can come handy, such as FAQs (what are the implications of this announcement, when is the change effective, what support will I receive, how do I get answers to my questions, etc.), a portal, email alias, or phone number for anyone to ask questions or raise potential concerns, allowing for immediate course correction and escalations as needed. Under no circumstances should anyone initiate communication regarding this transition to the press or anyone outside of the brand or key agency partners unless authorized. Most brands prefer to see limited-to-no communication on this topic to avoid any potential leakage to the press.

5) Stability: Avoid work disruption, delays, duplicate efforts, wasteful activities

The responsibilities of the agency are usually spelled out in the termination clause, during which the agency will continue to be compensated. The termination clause typically states that the rights, duties, and responsibilities of the agency and client continue during the notice period, which is the time between providing notice of termination, and the date that termination becomes effective. So, both must continue to abide by all terms of the agreement until the termination is effective. Often, the transition is a highly emotionally charged period with many moving parts. Despite all good efforts, it can easily lead to the disruption of work already underway or imminent. It can delay campaign work, suspend current activities, and create tremendous tension and unwanted frustrations for all involved. Whenever the work is delayed or suboptimal, it effectively turns into huge inefficiencies or a waste of time, energy, and funds.

6) Intellectual property: Ensure the immediate transfer of all client documents, research, and confidential materials

Once assets have been transferred, the focus must be on returning any relevant confidential documents, research materials, and reports. The brand needs to work with the incumbent agency to determine the specific IP that should be transferred pursuant to the agreement and to identify any contracts or other documentation that needs to be assigned or transferred to the brand or another agency to facilitate the client's use of the content developed by the agency going forward. Non-assets may include documents and data that include IP such as marketing and media plans, training materials, creative works in progress (storyboards, scripts, concepts), vendor contracts, input briefs, financial records, consents, licenses, releases, presentations, and memos, including transcripts and reports of any kind created by the client or by the agency on the client's behalf. Needless to say, the confidentiality provisions in the contract must be honored at all times by both parties and, often times, for years post-termination. Until the IP is returned, the agency should be reminded to take all reasonable precautions to safeguard any of the client's property entrusted to it, as it remains responsible for any loss, damage, destruction or unauthorized use by others of any such property caused by or arising out of negligence or willful misconduct.

7) Timeline: Set realistic timelines and checkpoints

The agency transition must be carefully orchestrated and timed properly so that everything is where it needs to be by the time the effective termination date is reached. That's easier said than done. The timeline must be realistic, and all parties must commit to deliver, especially during the hand-over period when responsibilities are transitioned between the incumbent agency and the client, and then from the client to the new agency. Now imagine the possible implications for a global brand with regional and local offices dealing with such complexity in a short 90-day window while juggling other important daily responsibilities. Setting regular checkpoints like monthly and weekly meetings is a must-have to proactively address potential roadblocks or unexpected issues along the way. Those are inevitable, and if they occur frequently, can significantly derail the transition plan. The brand marketing leadership must be kept in the loop as any hiccup could impact its campaign goals or commitments.

8) Investment: Minimize transition costs and duplication of expenses

Going through an agency transition is a significant investment of time and resources. As such, the expected benefits must outweigh the potential risks and resource commitments needed. Most termination agreements will stipulate that the brand will pay the agency for all services provided, prorated to the date of termination. It's quite possible that the incumbent agency might remain involved on a project basis or be considered down the road as an AOR. It happens more often than you might think, and it's in everyone's best interest not to burn bridges. Look at automaker American Honda Motor Co., which yanked its media planning business from advertising agency RPA four years ago to give it to MediaVest, only to return to RPA as its agency of record for media planning and ad buying for its Honda and Acura brands. No matter what the outcome, the brand and the agency are expected to fulfill their respective duties and obligations through the termination period and complete the work. As the new agency is ramping up, it's likely that a small overlap in time may occur. That overlap might create a duplication of resources (and therefore expenses) as one is rapidly winding down while the other is quickly ramping up. Any materials or services the agency has committed to purchase for the brand or any uncompleted work previously approved by the brand shall be paid for.

9) Onboarding: Provide access to key resources and accelerate ramp-up time with training

There is a clear need for a rigorous approach to training for speedy onboarding and a more effective use of agency resources. How long does it take for the average individual to be up and running efficiently in a new role? 60, 90, perhaps 120 days? It takes three to four times longer than it should for them to be "client ready" as they waste valuable time (read "your fee budget") trying to find relevant documents, learn new processes, and comply with brand guidelines. Do the math. If it takes someone new six weeks to get up to speed on your business, and you could have it done in two, that's 1/12 of your retainer that is potentially underutilized. In a fast moving and competitive environment where clients change agencies regularly and agency personnel attrition reaches astronomical figures, brand advertisers see new agency staff come on to their business at a much faster speed than ever before. These countless hours turn into large budgets of wasted efforts and resources due to the lack of effective training and onboarding resources.

According to a 2013 ANA study, only 39 percent of brands have a standardized process when they hire a new agency. That was then, and this is now. Brand advertisers are awakening to the under-tapped opportunity of streamlining and automating the training and onboarding of their agencies on the new frontier of improved client/agency engagement efficiency and effectiveness. All client organizations have spent a fair amount of time and resources defining their internal processes and establishing well-articulated brand guidelines to ensure consistency for the work they produce with their agencies. They expect their own team members and their vendor community to fully comply with these important requirements but rarely have the resources in place to support adoption and consistent compliance. During an agency transition, the costs of a knowledge gap couldn't be greater. The new agency is likely to struggle ramping up as quickly as it needs to, training its staff on everything from understanding the client's business and the way it is organized, to adhering to its brand, privacy, and legal standards, procedures and policies, as well as various campaign workflows and approval processes. It's a bit like drinking from a firehose . . . and trying to keep smiling.

Organizing training content and delivering it through a Learning Management System (LMS) can make a remarkable difference and ensure your new agency is ready sooner to take on the work. By implementing online training solutions for agencies, brands can create training modules, which can be customized by agency type or agency role (account, creative, production, media, digital, etc.). All agency staff members receive a personalized email with their training credentials. The training can be interactive in nature, allowing users to fully comprehend the content and interact with it for stronger content recollection. Once completed, the agency leadership team and the client receive training reports showing the results, enabling them to monitor progress and adoption of the training among their teams. The result: Agency teams are trained immediately on the right content, and these resources can then be assigned to projects with the confidence that they have the necessary knowledge to execute. That's a gift that keeps on giving.

10) Next: Look forward, focusing on setting up the new agency for success while gracefully transitioning the prior one

As the transition period nears the end, an important shift in focus must occur. Setting up the new agency for success is of paramount importance and must take precedence. Having a 30-60-90 day plan encourages the new agency to align behind a set of tangible milestones and metrics that simply improve its chances to successfully build a strong partnership and deliver great work. The lessons learned from the prior relationship should be applied to the new one, so the same mistakes won't be repeated. Productive client/agency relationships can't escape the occasional tension experienced by close partnerships. However, no brand advertiser wants to get burned by working with the wrong agency or by going through painful agency transitions.

MARRIED AT FIRST SIGHT?

Across the globe, a popular reality TV show, *Married at First Sight*, features three couples, paired up by relationship experts, who agree to marry when they first meet. The experts include a clinical psychologist, a sexologist, and a sociologist/marriage counselor, working together to find matches. When they do, the chosen couples meet for the first time, get married, and leave for a honeymoon. Upon returning home, they live together as a married couple for eight weeks. Thereafter, they choose to divorce or stay married. While certainly entertaining, the program tests an experimental concept, which includes how effective these experts are at finding the right people to match and tracking the married couples who ultimately stay together. The American version of the show monitors these results and found the following: After five seasons, 10 out of the 15 couples stayed married after the experimental period. Of these 10 couples, only three remained together as of November 2017. Compared with the oft-cited statistics that half of all marriages in the US eventually end in divorce, the results do not seem, at first glance, to be overwhelmingly positive. But given that each of these individuals effectively marry a perfect stranger, one could have expected a significantly lower marriage success rate and a much higher divorce rate than the results indicate.

The concept of this show begs the questions, is the science of love a reality or a scam? How do these findings correlate to the world of advertising and agencies? How can we predict the likelihood of two partners coming together to realize greatness and build a lasting relationship? Challenging the traditional system for finding service agencies (RFPs), a new business matchmaking company called Agency Geek uses an algorithm created by computer engineers to match clients and agencies using a 28-question survey that clients fill out on what they are like to work with and what they want from a potential client. The client/agency relationship is too demanding, too complex, and under too much pressure to thrive without relying on a carefully orchestrated alignment of expectations based on objective criteria like the ones we reviewed earlier in this chapter. Relationships and love, especially at first sight, may never be fully understood by science. But why not use relevant insights to improve its chances and turn a spark into a lasting fire?

As in personal relationships, always stay true to your values and you will find the pearl you deserve. Conducting an agency search has become an incredibly valuable skill set for advertisers to acquire. A well-managed agency search is a demanding process that requires considerable time and resource commitments. Having a rigorous process mapped out and assembling a dedicated team will improve the outcome: The right partnership to take marketing efforts to the next level. Having clear expectations and defined criteria is a must before investing any time and resources. Executive buy-in and support is also vital. Transparency and communication are key throughout the process.

Advertisers must also remember that agencies pay close attention to the way they handle reviews and searches. The way they conduct themselves and the way the process is handled says a lot about the type of client they are. It's easy to get the word out these days, shedding bright lights on good and bad search practices. Advertisers will continue to experiment and find more effective, streamlined ways to find and hire the best agency partner for their business—an agency partner that hopefully brings a unique and distinct offering that complements and strengthens the company's core marketing muscle. Some, like Mountain Dew®, are even turning over the selection of their agency to brand advocates and fans, asking them to review video postings and cast their vote online for the agency of their choice. No matter how much time and resources have been invested in this process, finding a new pearl and hiring that agency is only the beginning. The overall success of an agency search should also be measured by the quality of the on-boarding, staffing, training, scoping, and briefings that will follow that selection. It's now all about getting the agency quickly up and running. As an advertiser, only time will tell if you've found the right agency pearls for your business.

TOP 3
BEST PRACTICES
for Advertisers

① Before conducting a search or agency review, given the investment in time, resources and potential work disruption, make sure that there is a fundamental business need to initiate it as well as a sound understanding of what led to it.

② Follow industry principles, best practices, and methodologies to conduct an effective, fair, and expedient search process that sets the new partnership up for success.

③ In the event of a contract termination, prepare carefully and manage the transition to minimize risk, disruption, and costs, while conducting a thorough onboarding of the new agency partner.

6

PACTA SUNT SERVANDA

Setting up a rock-solid agency contract

"There is no such thing as inclement weather, only inappropriate clothing."
—**BEN ZANDER,** BOSTON PHILHARMONIC ORCHESTRA CONDUCTOR

I am no attorney. Chances are you're not one either. Not to worry. You don't need a law degree to have a basic understanding of agency contracts and to play a vital role in setting up one for your company. Yet there are many legal factors to consider. It is critical that you have a contract in place that clearly outlines the obligations of both parties. If you ever took Latin in school, you may have picked up that Pacta Sunt Servanda means "agreements must be kept." If you operate with a well-constructed contract, both parties are more likely to keep up their end of the bargain. Simply put, a contract helps define what is expected of us and holds everyone accountable. It's crazy to think that so many clients and agencies are getting "married" so eagerly that they don't even read the fine print of their prenuptial agreement. It's even more insane when they wake up with a headache months or years later, dazed by what was so quickly agreed upon when their current circumstance seemed to be a remote possibility. What do advertisers *really* need to know about agency contracts? What risks are they trying to minimize? How do they ensure no stone has been left unturned? How should they approach intellectual-property? How should they handle the termination of a contract or competitive conflicts should they arise? What are some of the most common mistakes and best practices in contract negotiations today? I debated whether I should include a chapter dedicated to this topic. Legal-related matters have the unavoidable effect of sleeping medication on most advertising people. Yet, without them, both parties can expose themselves to disastrous and unintended results. I decided to take on that challenge and provide an overview of the fundamentals of agency contracts. So, go ahead and grab a large cup of coffee. This chapter highlights common pitfalls both clients and agencies must avoid before tying the knot.

THE ROLE OF CONTRACTS IN STRENGTHENING RELATIONSHIPS
A well-structured contractual relationship is more likely to yield positive results and strengthen the partnership. In its purest form, a contract is a legally binding exchange of promises or agreements that both parties are expected to follow. At the most basic level, it covers the core commercial elements of the relationship: What is expected of the agency (services provided) and what is expected of the client (compensation) and how that exchange of value is conducted. Although there is some consistency from contract to contract, the terms and conditions (T&Cs) vary based on the

type of services provided (digital, media, creative, etc.) and the nature of the contractual relationship being established. A large and complex engagement is likely to raise more questions that must be addressed in the final agreement. The advertiser is also more likely to be open to negotiating the terms, something hard to justify with smaller agreements.

Contract terms and conditions are established at the outset of any work relationship but may be revised occasionally. There is much that is critical to any relationship that cannot be captured in a legal document, to most attorneys' despair. Albert Einstein was right when he said that *"Not everything that counts can be measured, and not everything that can be measured counts."* That applies to agency contracts. This section provides an overview of key issues and considerations before a solid contract is put in place. This is not, however, a substitute for the legal counsel required to successfully finalize a contract. Too often, advertisers are tempted to jump in and start work without a contract in place.

AGENCY VIEWPOINT

"Scratch the surface of any long-term agency/client relationship and you'll find trust. Trust in people and their integrity. Trust that the ideas are great. Trust that financials are handled fairly." [90]

—**MARTY STOCK,** CEO, YOUNG & RUBICAM AND CAVALRY, CHICAGO

HOW TO GET A ROCK-SOLID CONTRACT IN PLACE

No one should underestimate the time, cycles, and effort required to get a sound contract signed. It's not uncommon to see this process accelerated to accommodate pressing business needs, which in turn may lead to missed expectations and challenges down the road. It's wise to invest the time to get it right the first time around. This end-to-end process can take anywhere from a few weeks to over three months. The time frame is directly impacted by the willingness of both parties to move decisively and agree to concessions. Here are the steps advertisers should follow:

GET A ROCK SOLID CONTRACT IN PLACE

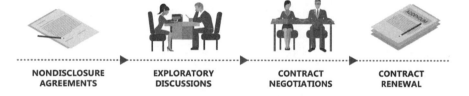

| NONDISCLOSURE AGREEMENTS | EXPLORATORY DISCUSSIONS | CONTRACT NEGOTIATIONS | CONTRACT RENEWAL |

Throughout this process, both parties are actively negotiating to ensure their interests are being successfully represented in the forming partnership. Let's walk through each step.

Step #1: Nondisclosure Agreement. A non-disclosure agreement (or NDA) is designed to protect the confidentiality of any information shared between the parties at the early stage of their discussions. This is often established in the initial phase of the relationship, during the "meet and greet" between an advertiser and an agency. This type of reciprocal agreement is straight-forward, rarely requiring significant edits before getting signed. This is a prerequisite before any advertiser can share any useful information with the candidate agency about their current efforts, priorities, or challenges. Conversely, an agency may be asked to disclose information about their exclusive approach, tools, and proprietary resources, many of which it may consider highly confidential in nature. An NDA is designed to protect both parties until a decision has been made to push forward and explore a business relationship which will require a more detailed agreement.

Step #2: Exploratory Discussions. This next phase typically involves internal discussions with management about the nature and scope of services the agency will be asked to provide. The more specific, the better. There is no point going further into contract negotiations until those have been clearly defined by the client and adequately communicated by the agency. It will be the basis for any follow-up conversation and therefore of paramount importance to avoid confusion. If the intent is to limit the services (e.g., digital media planning and buying services) to avoid territorial issues with other partners, then having absolute clarity about what's in or out of scope is important. Yet, in the absence of complete clarity, using broad service definitions (e.g., services for both traditional and digital media) would prevent boxing in an agency unnecessarily until these details have been adequately fleshed out. When agency services are too restrictive or too narrowly defined, often adjustments are required which delay otherwise time-sensitive projects.

Step #3: Contract Negotiations. Most organizations have dedicated marketing legal resources with extensive agency contracts experience. They have boiler plate templates to start from, incorporating common advertising related terms and conditions often associated with such services. When these resources are not available, hiring outside counsel with relevant category expertise will ensure a successful outcome. Similarly, agencies bring years of experience working on similar contracts and can be expected to drive their own agenda. They too may use their own legal resources or subcontract these services to specialized law firms. Both parties will go back and forth until they reach consensus or make concessions. The draft contract and redlined versions are reviewed and discussed extensively by both parties. This is where negotiation skills come in handy. This process is generally led by attorneys with close input by the business, helping to inform important contract decisions. Some compromises might be necessary on both sides to get closure. Once both parties have reached an agreement on the totality of the contract, it can be signed by the individuals with appropriate decision-making authority. The contract is not effective until signed, so both parties should get it signed before any work is initiated.

Step #4: Contract Renewal. Agency contracts are typically set to auto-renew on a yearly basis. Advertisers do not, however, need to revisit the standard terms of the master service agreement every year. As such, many agreements remain in effect until terminated by either party or are renewed with minimal changes. Any change must be captured in writing and submitted once again for signature. The renewal contract will likely include many important addendums such as scope of work and staffing plans, financial and compensation terms, affiliated companies, and other contract details that may be revised on a periodic basis but wouldn't necessitate a full contract review. While these terms may appear in an addendum, they are the most important terms in any contract since they define what the agency will do and how much it will be paid. For this reason, these terms are often segregated in separate addendums from the basic terms and conditions governing the relationship. This way, addendums can be revisited annually without requiring a potentially lengthy or costly legal review of the entire agreement.

INDUSTRY VIEWPOINT

"With every passing year, there is less and less trust between advertisers and agencies, and it's been going on for decades." [91]
—**BRIAN WIESER,** SENIOR RESEARCH ANALYST, PIVOTAL RESEARCH GROUP

STANDARD T&CS (AND WHY YOU SHOULD CARE!)

Every relationship is different. So, every relationship will require unique consideration when deciding which terms and conditions (T&Cs) are most suitable for that relationship. A client may appoint the agency to be its agency of record for all or a portion of the business (also known as "exclusivity"), either domestically or internationally. A client may contract with an agency only on a project basis and with several other agencies under non-exclusive agreements. These nuances impact the nature of the agreement and the terms that will need to be negotiated. In principle, both parties are agreeing to enter negotiations to establish fair and equitable terms for the relationship. But unless they both work hard at it, where they end up may not hold up to their original goals. The number of legal considerations in an agency contract is enough to make anyone's head spin a few times. Fortunately for us, there are several standard contract terms that apply to virtually any client/agency relationship. The following summary highlights the most critical sections and T&Cs of an agency contract and key client considerations. And if by now, you are running out of coffee, I added a brief explanation as to why agencies or advertisers should care about them.

COMMON ELEMENTS OF CONTRACT

FOR AGENCY SERVICES

SERVICES PROVIDED

COMPENSATION, PAYMENT TERMS & BILLING

APPROVAL OF EXPENSES & SUB-CONTRACTORS

MEDIA INCENTIVES & OPEN PAYABLES

INDEMNIFICATION & INSURANCE

PRIVACY & DATA PROTECTION

NON-SOLICITATION

AUDIT RIGHTS & PROCEDURES

IP, COPYRIGHT, OWNERSHIP & TRADEMARKS

CONTRACT TERMINATION

COMPETITIVE CONFLICTS

SERVICES PROVIDED

What it is*: A description of the services performed and delivered by the agency. These services will vary based on the type of services provided. A typical contract, for example, may include the following top-line description: analyze market

conditions; provide account planning services; develop and produce communication strategies; formulate and submit concepts
for approval; prepare recommendations and detailed media
plans, track and analyze campaign results, and so forth. It may
also include a list of additional agreed-upon services provided,
such as social media, PR, promotion, merchandising, analytics,
and the range of media used, such as television, radio, print,
digital, programmatic, and so forth. I suggest aiming broadly at
first. The list must be exhaustive enough to not limit the range
of services covered by an agency to the point where it is overly
restrictive. But it should also be limited to core competencies.
Such language can be added to avoid confusions: "Any work
above and beyond what is detailed here will require a separate
SOW [scope of work] as addendum and, until then, no work
should be started without client authorization." The list can
always be updated as the relationship evolves, or if the agency
decides to expand its service offering, or the advertiser transfers
responsibilities from one roster agency to another. This is also
where the client must state clearly whether the agency is acting
as an independent contractor or as an agent, based on the type
of services rendered.

Why should you care? This is where the scope of services provided is defined. Perhaps more importantly, it can also define
what's out of scope, to avoid any confusion in the relationship
moving forward. If the list of services is too broad, it is not
prescriptive enough and can lead to scope creep or false expectations on both ends. If the list of services is too narrow, it may
slow you both down and not be flexible enough to accommodate ever-changing and growing client needs.

AGENCY VIEWPOINT

"The moment a client pushes you to provide certain assurances and guarantees, it affects your neutrality. It forces you to think in ways an agent doesn't think. And it evolves the relationship in a different direction. And by the way, we're grownups. We willingly accept the terms. But you can't have it both ways. Once you assume business risks, things change." [92]

—IRWIN GOTLIEB, CHAIRMAN, GROUPM

COMPENSATION, PAYMENT TERMS, AND BILLING

What it is: This is the section where the overall compensation terms, payment schedules, and approval process will be laid out. It may also include any bonus or incentive plan as well as cost allocation methodology like overhead, profit margin, direct labor, and other fee-related expenses depending on the type of agreed compensation methodology. This section of the contract also explains how production, media, and out-of-pocket expenses are handled. It answers frequent questions: What should the payment schedule be? How much of the costs should be paid upon award of the project or at its completion? Is the client requiring a non-use fee clause for music and talent contracts? Is there a policy for talent exclusivity? What information should be submitted to budget owners for approval? How will we handle taxes and exchange rates, and other important financial provisions? It also states the frequency and type of financial reporting required.

Why should you care? The most critical and most debated part of a contract is often the one about compensation terms. Prepare well for these negotiations and consider contracting with a consultant before having in-depth pricing discussions with your agency. This is the section that usually gets the most attention from both parties, since it deals with financial transactions and impacts cash flow and payments. Detailed payment and billing terms are most important to ensure clients and agencies establish the back-end processes and operating guidelines for prompt and timely payments. Tax liabilities can add up quickly, so having clarity on who pays certain taxes is important from the start of the relationship. Tax provisions are often complicated, so it is highly recommended that the tax and finance department weigh in on these provisions. The next chapter covers agency compensation in greater detail.

AGENCY VIEWPOINT

"The surplus of readily eager agencies and an industry trend towards constant price scrutiny has led clients to dictate pricing to their agency partners. . . . The relationship between marketer and agency has to be respectful and copasetic, otherwise one or both will always feel disadvantaged." [93]

—**ED LU,** VP FINANCE, QUESTUS.

APPROVAL OF EXPENSES AND SUBCONTRACTING

What it is: This section stipulates which expenses are covered by the contract, what information is deemed necessary by the client, and how these expenses should be approved and by whom. There are several expenses associated with doing business with an agency that must be detailed in the contract from media to artwork and production (e.g., artwork, mechanical, printing, proofreading, digital distribution,), talent (talent and production rights, including right to use names, voices, music, and so forth), collateral support and merchandising material related to campaigns, packing, shipping, delivery, research (competitive analysis, advertising concept testing), and media reports/ratings. Some expenses like production may require the agency to competitively bid the work to multiple vendors. The agency may expect pre-payment to minimize cash flow for large expenditures. Payment terms may vary based on the type of expense and will need to be agreed upon. Penalties may be sought by the agency for continued past due payments since these can represent a serious financial burden. If expenses end up higher or lower than budgeted, a financial reconciliation process should articulate how those are to be handled. Typically, the agency is not allowed to subcontract any part of the work to any subcontractor without the client's prior written permission. If the client approves it, then the agency is held responsible for the performance and obligations of the subcontractor. This section should also specify how travel expenses will be handled. The client may have a detailed travel policy that it wants employees and vendors to adhere to. The travel policy might include specific guidance on allowable expense categories.

Why should you care? It's in everyone's best interest that there are no surprises about what's included and what's not when the first invoices land on the client's desk. How to best manage cash flow is an important consideration for the agency as well as for the client. No one is expected to profit from it and if set up properly, a neutral cash flow (aka "float") position is in everyone's best interest. What information is needed and clarity about who approves expenses should make the approval process smooth for all involved. Travel can be a sizeable expense item when dealing with remote or international offices. If a client spends a fair amount of its budget on travel expenses, it should be as prescriptive as possible about its travel policy.

MEDIA INCENTIVES AND OPEN PAYABLES

What it is: Trust and transparency in media planning and buying activities remain high on advertisers' list of top concerns. The most significant media-related issue of the past few years was the release of the seven-month study commissioned by the ANA revealing that senior executives across the agency ecosystem were aware of, and mandated, some non-transparent business practices. The results of the study stem from confidential interviews with 150 individual sources representing "a cross-section of the US media-buying ecosystem." Major agencies such as GroupM, Omnicom, Publicis, and Interpublic Group of Cos. disputed the report findings. The lack of visibility, transparency and disclosure about media activities had significant impact on agency contracts. The World Federation of Advertisers reported that, as a result, most advertisers amended their media agency contracts. Many of them included terms that define agency status as agent or principle at law and added specific audit right clauses to their contracts as well as language calling for the return of incentives (i.e., rebates) from media vendors. Advertisers must clearly spell out how any discounts, rebates, incentives, paybacks, barters, credits collected by the agency, whether directly or indirectly related to the agreement, are credited back to the client within a specific timeline. They must also define how media incentives must be tracked and reported, along with open payables and media purchases that have not been invoiced by the third-party media provider for more than one year. This is something historically more common in digital media, which still lacks the rigor of traditional media operating efficiencies. Although the client indemnifies the agency and remains liable for any funds, these funds should be returned to the client once that time window has passed.

Why should you care? Media incentives and credits are earned by the agency based on the total volume of spend. As the client, you are therefore entitled to those credits. Having clear rules on how those are treated ensures a smooth process for processing credits and open payables associated with aged media buys.

INDEMNIFICATION AND INSURANCE

What it is: This is a standard contract clause stipulating who is financially responsible and must defend the other party in any suit or proceeding against the client or its contractors, vendors, agents, and other roles, holding the client harmless against any costs, damages, or settlement awards which arise out of or are related to the breach of the contract. Mutual indemnification regarding claims of implicit or explicit breach of duties guarantees that each party will fulfill its obligations. This section also lists all insurance the agency must obtain and maintain throughout the entire term of the relationship. Insurance requirements may include a commercial general liability policy, automotive liability, workers and employers' liability, professional liability/ errors and omissions liability, workers' compensation, and full compliance with all applicable laws, statutes, and regulations. The contract often requires the agency to provide certificates of insurance. These insurance policies can quickly add up to millions of dollars a year. For international contracts, exchange risks and responsibilities will need to be spelled out based on the currency in which the agency will invoice the client.

Why should you care? There are increasingly more examples of costly litigation over advertising and marketing activities these days. It's better to be safe than sorry. An indemnification clause is a prerequisite. Your attorney shouldn't let you sign a contract without one. If you are lucky, you will never have to find out why it was so important to include in the contract. The bottom line is that agencies must obtain the appropriate insurance policies to put the client at ease and to protect themselves.

PRIVACY AND DATA PROTECTION

What it is: Data protection is of paramount importance, especially when dealing with "personally identifiable information" (PII), something increasingly more common in a digital world. The clause clarifies the agency's responsibilities as they relate to the collection, storage, usage, monitoring, security, and eventual destruction of client data. Giving a third-party vendor like an agency access to sensitive customer data is a risk that can be mitigated with the appropriate level of disclosure and information sharing. This section must reference any relevant corporate guidelines the agency must follow.

Why should you care? When providing PII, customers trust that the information is adequately safeguarded. Privacy laws around the world require clients to apply vigilance and rigor to the handling of customer data. It's especially important when the agency is responsible for handling large volumes of customer data on the client's behalf. Because a growing share of advertiser marketing budgets include digital assignments where consumers are invited to provide their contact and profile information for promotional purposes, or to access certain services and offerings, the handling of PII is something that must be managed properly.

AUDIT RIGHTS AND PROCEDURES
What it is: It's important that an advertiser has full access to transactional and payment data handled by the agency on its behalf for a given period. The type of documentation and records required should be listed (payroll records, timesheets, media placements, production bids, and books of account, to name a few). Another important disclaimer is how audits will be paid for, especially if discrepancies are revealed

through this process, and how any overcharged or undercharged amount will be handled. It also clarifies who is authorized to conduct such audits. Some data such as individual agency salaries is typically off limits and any audit of related data can be conducted through an independent third party to avoid compromising the sensitive and confidential nature of this information. If the audit reveals discrepancies (usually 5% to 10%) of the total audited amount, the agency can be made responsible for paying for the cost of the audit.

Why should you care? Clients will want to conduct an audit from time to time and having the requirements spelled out from the beginning will expedite the process when the time comes. It will also reduce any possible confusion and uncertainty around the way the audit will be conducted.

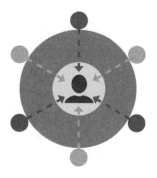

NON-SOLICITATION

What it is: The client and the agency agree to not solicit employees of the other party. Because a no-hire clause is generally not recommended based on labor laws, a non-solicitation clause is considered its second-best cousin. A non-solicitation clause may continue for several months following an employee's termination or resignation to avoid having folks potentially "gaming" the system.

Why should you care? It presents several benefits to advertisers. It's not unheard of for some clients to excessively hire from its agencies, depleting them of their raw talent. Agencies find such practices to be potentially destabilizing for their operations and very costly (recruiting, on-boarding, and training costs of replacing that talent). And what is not financially sound for the agency over time is likely to impact the client relationship one way or another. There are three common clauses that are particularly important to advertising and marketing communications contracts and require special consideration from a business and relationship perspective: intellectual property ownership, competitive conflicts, and contract termination.

AGENCY VIEWPOINT

"Clients should first ask if the agency has a standard contract. Many clients insist that their contract be used, without seeing what the agency typically uses. Most common roadblocks are about ownership of intellectual property. Clients want to own the agency's work; so do the agencies." [94]

—MARC A. BROWNSTEIN, PRESIDENT AND CEO, BROWNSTEIN GROUP

INTELLECTUAL PROPERTY, COPYRIGHT OWNERSHIP, AND TRADEMARKS

What it is: There are also different concepts of ownership. For example, the contract clause may give the agency access to all names, marks, logos, and designs for the sole purpose of performing the services already defined. The agency is not held responsible for the information provided by the advertiser, but the agency is held responsible for getting licenses, permits, and other usage rights that fall within the agreed scope of work. As far as trademark standards are concerned, this section insists that all materials be reviewed by the client for explicit approval and how that process should be handled. From a client perspective, this section should stress that the work created by the agency is considered "work made for hire" by default for copyright purposes, including inventions, ideas, techniques, software, and such. Whether or not an idea or a concept is ultimately produced should not alter its ownership.

Although different agreements can be pursued (such as rejected ideas that can be repurposed by the agency on another client, software, and application), most advertisers are retaining ownership of any work produced, regardless of its outcome. This remains a controversial topic in the industry. I expect continued tension on this subject in the years to come as the line between branded content and creative continue to blur and agencies build innovative customer experience-enhancing applications and tools they might want to repurpose for other clients. Due to the popularity of labor-based compensation models, most advertisers want to maintain full ownership of the work, even if concepts and materials are not being used immediately. The 4As issued guidance to address ownership, IP, and indemnification provisions when creating digital, online, and mobile content. They believe agreements should be written to *"preserve agency ownership and agency right to use agency-developed software and tools."* They assert that unlike a creative asset or commercial, which is only of value to the client for which the agency created it, software and software-related materials often produced by agencies as a by-product of services provided to the client have applicability and significant value to other potential agency clients. The issue tends to come up frequently during a pitch. It is common practice for the agency to keep ownership of the ideas produced during a new business pitch until the advertiser hires the agency to execute the work or some reasonable financial arrangement can be made to use the idea without formally hiring the agency to execute the work.

AGENCY VIEWPOINT

"Agency [intellectual property] will be business rules and algorithms we create. I still see us working on an FTE basis, but potentially getting paid royalties from IP, from an algorithm perspective we have." [95]
—SCOTT HAGEDORN, FOUNDER AND CEO, HEARTS & SCIENCE

Why should you care? The concept of ownership in advertising is increasingly more sensitive as digital and mobile experiences are rising exponentially. Should all content created by agencies be treated equally? Are current agreements unnecessarily restrictive, inadvertently prohibiting the agency from using software that is not a specific stand-alone client deliverable? Should agencies and advertisers re-evaluate the standard ownership and intellectual property provisions of their contracts to end up with more equitable agreements? Most agencies are willing to explore creative financial arrangements that give them skin in the game, pushing the limits of "ownership" in the work produced for a client.

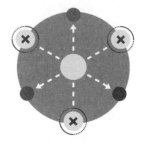

COMPETITIVE CONFLICTS

What it is: Setting clear expectations about the companies that the agency is restricted from working with is an important consideration when both parties agree to work together. Too often, the contract doesn't clarify with enough specificity the level of exclusivity the clients seek to enforce, leaving it to personal interpretation or prolonged, painful after-the-fact negotiations. Both parties attempt to find the right balance between an agency's desire to grow business where it has relevant experience and a client's desire for exclusivity. Clearly, agencies working for Burger King are very unlikely to also work for McDonald's or Taco Bell. For the agency, agreeing to limit its business to one client in each category is often a difficult decision. Agencies will consider this type of competitive conflicts clause when the client's account is large enough to warrant such restrictions. There is no true industry standard on how to handle competitive conflicts, which often results in vague contract terms, subject to interpretation. How restrictive is the relationship? Is the conflict defined at the company, category, or brand level? Is the agency handling the client's entire business (packaged goods) or a specific brand or category (cereal brands X and Y)? Is conflict defined globally or on a country-by-country basis? How often is the list updated? In the past few years, this type of policy has become increasingly more flexible and less restrictive, especially among large multi-brand companies that potentially compete broadly. It may be that the agency is already working with their key competitor and would need to resign the account upon a signed contract. Or it may be that the agency is planning to expand its client's portfolio in an industry segment. It might even be accidental on the part of the agency, as the result of mergers and acquisitions, for example, making it impractical for agencies and their holding companies to run their business.

Some exceptions are now commonly granted by the client at the agency's explicit and written request as long as certain criteria are adhered to: Dedicated team structures, so no staff can work for both accounts at the same time; restricted staff movement from one account to the other for a minimum period of time; housing of staff—in different offices or different floors; establishing proper technology firewalls and User Rights Management to secure access to documentation, directories, and servers; and setting policies to ensure the strictest levels of confidentiality and security. There are expectations in global accounts as well, where direct conflicts on a country-by-country basis are tolerated and competitors can co-exist under one agency banner because the global client has limited billing in that office. According to the 4As, "Conflicts are in the eyes of the beholder. Executives place high value on relationships and might endorse arrangements that less senior management might not feel empowered to approve." Ultimately, the client, defined as the relationship owner, must be comfortable (and that goes both ways). An agency should expect some latitude to pursue client opportunities that do not directly compete with their existing client. Those criteria should be defined and agreed upon for inclusion in the contract. Agencies typically will reach out to clients before entering a pitch to clear the way or decide to walk away. After all, relationships are based on mutual trust, which both parties play a role in defining when drafting a competitive conflict clause.

Why should you care? This issue can occasionally be a deal breaker. There is a lot at stake, so advertisers are understandably worried about the potential information leakage or conflict of interest an agency may have by servicing competitive businesses under the same roof. Although client rules may have relaxed a bit about competitive conflicts, the concerns that led to this type of clause must be addressed by the agency to the client's satisfaction. Or the agency must decide if dealing with it is worth the trouble and run the risk of potentially losing the account. Agencies gain deep industry experience when working for a client, which could easily be offered to another client in a similar category, eager to tap into a knowledgeable agency partner who can immediately deliver value to their business. Are you willing to chance seeing your confidential work, all your past efforts and campaign learning, research, and best practices exposed to the competition? Similarly, a client must decide if they want to run the risks of having the agency resign the account. Once again, it is about finding the right balance between being vigilant and flexible.

CONTRACT TERMINATION

What it is: Any business relationship eventually comes to an end. The termination clause describes the protocols and procedures associated with termination of the agreement and the transition period that follows. This includes, but is not limited to: prior written notice, number of days for termination to be effective, the rights, remedies, duties, and responsibilities in the event of termination, the transfer of client work, property, materials and assets, and how to deal with non-cancelable commitments such as production and media reservations, and contracts and arrangements with advertising media and vendors. Other standard clauses worth mentioning include code of conduct, business and employment practices, confidentiality and adequate safeguarding of proprietary information, contract survival, procurement and subcontracting policies (related to non-discrimination, off-shoring, etc.), record retention and disposal, and how agency staff should conduct themselves when interacting with clients or on the client's behalf with third party vendors, freelancers, and subcontractors. Clients should decide which ones are most relevant to their situation and ensure compliance with all relevant client policies and applicable governing laws. Issues such as insolvency, for example, tend to be more important with less established or small agencies and should be given some consideration. A 60-90 day termination notice is the norm for most contracts, giving everyone enough time to transition out of the relationship with minimal disruption. The actual terms vary based on the nature of the relationship and its overall scope. Naturally, large, retainer-based, global contracts tend to offer more cushion than small, local project-based relationships.

For the client whose agency walked away, it gives it enough time to look for another agency to pick up the work where the incumbent agency left it. For the agency whose client walked way, it gives it enough time to replace the account with a similar-size client or reduce operating expenses at a speed that doesn't prevent the agency from transitioning the work without unforeseen hiccups. The client's new agency will often leverage for as much time a client is willing to agree to, giving them a safety net that allows them to hire key talent where it's needed. Clients with labor-based agreements have been pushing for even shorter notice to reduce the financial constraint of having to pay for a new agency to ramp up while paying for the incumbent to exit. Advertisers should carefully weigh the financial benefits of short termination periods against the potential waste or opportunity losses that can result from overly aggressive and potentially messy transitions. An extended termination date can be granted at the agency's request if the given termination takes place within the first year of the relationship. This additional protection invites the new agency to move aggressively with staff hiring without having to worry about return on their long-term investment.

Why should you care? It's a semi-sour topic, a bit like putting in place a pre-nuptial agreement with your soon-to-be spouse. Unlike a marriage, however, an agency agreement will inevitably end as it has a preset duration. It's simply irresponsible not to agree what will happen when the time comes. The larger the account, the greater the pressure agencies are likely to exert to convince advertisers to agree to lengthier termination notices to minimize their financial exposure. Clients should apply good judgment to find the right balance point. A lengthy termination notice can prove to be expensive at the time of separation. A short termination notice might be financially beneficial to clients but represent a disincentive for the agency from making staffing commitments that in turn benefit the relationship and the work itself. Several exhibits or addendums will need to be incorporated into the main contract to address these issues.

AGENCY VIEWPOINT

"The only reason for lines in an agency world is for clients to give you budgets. One of the things I hate in the business are the terms we are given to define ourselves. They are based on how clients put budgets together. It's ridiculous. We are problem-solvers, and that's what good clients understand." [96]

—JON HAMM, GLOBAL CCO, GEOMETRY GLOBAL

CONTINUOUS IMPROVEMENT: CONTRACT ADDENDUMS

These exhibits and attachments should receive equal attention before being included in the final draft. They typically cover contract clauses that must be revisited or updated on an annual basis including, but not limited to, annual scope of work: fees and staffing plan, competitive businesses, list of designated countries (for global accounts) or affiliated agencies covered under the agreement (if applicable), rate cards, service level agreements (SLAs), and more. Service level agreements help articulate expectations for how client and teams should engage and provide more details about expectations such as campaign process and creative approvals, various agency reporting requirements, the mandatory use of tools like digital asset management and CRM systems, as well as relevant company guidelines (production, media, social, etc.) agencies are expected to fully understand and comply to. Contract addendums are meant to be updated on a frequent basis. The type of information found in the addendum is by far most practical to those on both the client and agency side who end up working together day in and out. It spells out the practical aspects of the relationship.

Hopefully, by now, you too realize the importance of these contractual terms and how they significantly impact the dynamic of the relationship between advertisers and their agencies. As with any contract, everything can be negotiated, within reason. Remember, if an advertiser brings up T&Cs with an agency, he/she's negotiating with them. Whether as a client or as an agency, if you are not ready to do that, just don't. You can't fake it until you make it. Ask the opinion of a specialized attorney. And yes, the answer is likely to be: "*It depends!*" Well, you know what? It does depend on a lot of things, as there are many nuances. There is no magic agency contract template and no silver bullet either.

CLIENT VIEWPOINT

"Not long ago, we discovered one of our agencies was using media money as float. We were incensed—they're supposed to be an agent. How could they use this money as 'principal'?...So we are now poring over every agency contract for full transparency by the end of 2017 to include terms requiring funds to be used for media payment only, all rebates to be disclosed and returned, and all transactions subject to audit." [97]

—MARC S. PRITCHARD, CHIEF BRAND OFFICER,

PROCTER & GAMBLE CO.

TOWARD FULL TRANSPARENCY: AGENCY AUDITS
Agency audits allow advertisers to do a better job of protecting themselves against non-transparent business practices and

improving their overall relationships with agencies. Advertisers often ask themselves: Are the terms of our contract being followed to a "T" by our agencies? Where is our greatest exposure as a company, and how should we best manage that risk? Audits often reveal inconsistencies, discrepancies, and wasteful activities. These issues may result in financial restitutions to the advertiser, in addition to improved process and controls. Compliance audits and risk assessments tend to be performed—to ensure full agency compliance to T&Cs—and as a result, minimize risks and take immediate course-correction actions. Transparency, trust, and an open-book policy are key to the long-term viability of any partnership. There have been several scandals in recent years about the lack of transparency provided by agencies about their dealings with publishers and media companies. Specifically, whether agencies should be entitled to profits from negotiated discounts and credits when acting as brokers rather than agents on their client's behalf. For example, large global advertiser and French dairy Danone Groupe, accused Aegis Media's Carat of failing to pass on millions of dollars in discounts obtained from media buys. Because of this dispute, a highly publicized court battle followed in Germany where a judge asked to open Carat's books going back a few years.

Advertisers are encouraged to hire skilled auditors with intimate knowledge of the agency industry, Sarbanes-Oxley, and other industry specific practices, regulations, and tools. When an audit is kicked off, both the agency and the client must provide relevant data to the auditor. The auditor will determine the sample size and methodology, such as high spending areas, known issues, or potentially high-risk topics. Audit findings are reviewed and discussed with the agencies. Any findings that must be remedied are in timeframes determined by the severity and financial value of the findings. Higher risk and spend areas usually require remedies within 30-60 days. Although audit rights are clearly spelled out in the contract, advertisers must apply caution. Random or too frequent audits can potentially disrupt business, delay client projects, put a strain on the relationship, raise concerns about the agency's trustworthy nature, and can negatively impact the partnership if the audit is not managed properly. It is advisable to set an audit schedule that summarizes the type of audit conducted and the timing and countries involved. Advertisers often lay out a multi-year rolling plan—by agency, audit type, and geography—and procedural protocols. An audit plan does not prevent random ones from being conducted as needed.

CHOOSING THE RIGHT AUDIT

Audits are usually financial or operational in nature. Operational audits are designed to ensure operating guidelines and processes are adequately followed and executed to determine if information flows effectively and efficiently to the agency. Operational audits review procedures and test the approval of media plans, job reconciliations, and client reports, for example. In the case of pay for performance agreements they determine whether the agency achieved the performance objectives identified to earn a bonus contained in the agreement, whether the bonus was awarded, whether support for the decision to pay the bonus or not to pay the bonus was communicated in writing, and whether the bonus payment was paid to the agency in a timely manner. Financial audits are designed to ensure financial terms are applied consistently: Billings and other agreed-upon financial transactions are handled according to the contract. They help identify duplicate payments, pricing errors, missed media/

production credits and refunds never returned to the client, excessive costs, miscalculations of sales tax, commissions and other related costs, non-compliant travel expenses, payments not reconciled with actual costs, and excessive costs. Production, a large spend category estimated to be a $5 billion business in the US, has received much-needed attention.

The 2017 Justice Department investigation into production practices of major holding companies is putting the spotlight on concerns raised that agencies are increasingly conducting bad faith bidding processes for production assignments, favoring in-house capabilities, and failing to disclose mandated quotas or details pertaining to their ownership of production facilities. Financial audits are most common with media agencies since they may lead to sizeable client credits for over-payment or inaccurate billings.

There are three primary agency-related financial audit types:

- *Fees:* verify compliance to contract and pricing terms and conditions (revenue, staffing plans, fee calculations, over-head, margins, open payables, invoicing). Findings may reveal that the agency is charging fees resulting in profit levels in excess of that agreed to with the client.

- *Media:* verify compliance to media-related contract terms and conditions, as well as the quality and cost effective-ness of media placement done by the agency and other financial-related transactions (cash flow, billings, media spend, and related controls). Clients want their agencies to be cash neutral. Many agencies are not as diligent or timely when reconciling media credits, rebates, and discounts.

- **Production:** verify compliance to production-related contract terms and conditions and competitiveness of rate cards (production spend and related controls, production credits, and adherence to competitive bids).

How the audit is funded can significantly influence its outcome or even its integrity. Audits are typically funded by the client as a priced fee. But a typical agency audit can be priced differently: as a one-time fee to the client (the most common alternative), on a contingency basis (as a percentage of cost-recovery), or as a discounted fee and capped commission on recovery funds. In a cost-cutting environment, advertisers may not always be able to secure the budgets needed to conduct audits. The alternative is to conduct an audit on a contingency basis under which the auditor assumes the risk (no recovery means the auditor doesn't collect any audit fees) and any associated costs but is potentially paid a percentage of recovered funds. The last two compensation alternatives, although popular for those who want to have this cost fully recovered or don't have any room in their existing budget, may create some tension and be damaging to the relationship since the auditor is financially incented to aggressively find and recover funds to offset their own costs and hopefully make a profit. Advertisers tend to work with specialized audit firms.

INDUSTRY VIEWPOINT

"The opportunity [is] for agencies of all sizes to become guardians of clients' budgets against fraud and inefficiencies by mastering all the science behind ad tech; programmatic, content syndication, social, etc. By taking the side of transparency, agencies have an opening to reclaim their role as trusted advisors." [98]

—JUDY SHAPIRO, CEO AND FOUNDER, ENGAGESIMPLY

TYPICAL AUDIT PROCESS

Once the advertiser has notified the agency of its intent to conduct an audit, both parties will determine what data is needed, what sample size to use, and will identify key contacts. Audits must be fact-based, not opinion-based. A typical audit requires the exchange of information among three main parties: the advertiser, the agency, and the auditor. In the case of a financial audit, the advertiser provides a copy of the contract to the auditor while the agency provides access to all billings and accounts payable data. It typically doesn't make economic sense to audit all activities conducted by an agency. Selecting a sample size (say 20 percent of all jobs) is effective, minimizing time, efforts, and costs. The sample, once selected, can be provided to the agency for additional information gathering such as client bills, job detail reports, estimates, timesheets, authorized statements of work, invoices, and bids. The auditor will now proceed with the actual execution of the audit and conduct the fieldwork at the agency offices concerned. It will vary based on the audit type. For example, the auditor might verify that all vendor invoices were submitted to the client and the amount billed to the client all agree with the total amount paid by the client or paid to vendors. They may determine whether the agency collected any annual volume bonuses (AVBs), vendor rebates, or volume discounts and make sure those are passed back to the client in a timely manner. They may verify that any bid policy is followed, and exceptions are documented. They may track contract compliance and measure media-value delivery. They may investigate if the agency is regularly reviewing suppliers and how competitive their rates are. They may verify that the amount billed to the client does not exceed the total estimate amounts agreed to. They may also confirm the agency's time reporting policy, timeliness, and accuracy by reviewing staffing plans and ensuring reconciliations are conducted as planned. They may look for any cost elements prohibited per the contract.

Once the fieldwork is completed, the audit findings are reported back to the advertiser and agency, preferably in writing as a formal wrap-up and in a group meeting offering opportunity for discussion. It's recommended that the auditor review preliminary results with the agency so that findings are vetted, and the agency has a chance to provide additional input and clarify any outstanding issues. After the agency has a chance to provide additional input to the audit findings, a meeting is scheduled by the auditor to review the findings with both the agency and the client. By that time, there should be agreement on improvement areas and both parties should discuss an action plan with a specific timeline to address them. If restitution is required, the auditor will facilitate the process. Financial audits can lead to the restitution of various forms of payments, credits, sales tax, cash flow, and other possible over-charges.

THE NECESSARY FOUNDATION OF TRUST

In 2016, amid numerous allegations of misconduct related to media rebates and price-fixing and other bid-rigging activities in production, the Association of National Advertisers' members chose "transparency" as the word of the year. The media landscape became far more complex in recent years. The various methods of buying and selling media, combined with the rapid advent of programmatic advertising has contributed to contracts being increasingly complex and opaque.

Its study on media rebates[99] exposed a fundamental disconnect in the industry regarding the basic nature of the advertiser-agency relationship. It also provided substantial evidence of non-transparent business practices in the US market in the form of rebates, as well as problematic agency conduct concealed by principal transactions. It also exposed evidence of non-transparent business practices in the US market arising from agencies holding or soliciting equity stakes in media suppliers. The ANA then produced several key recommendations for advertisers to adopt, leading to better agency contracts. So did its European sibling, ISBA, which issued a framework agreement with recommended Contract Terms for Media Agency Services—ranging from content, viewability, click fraud, brand safety, impact of agency group deals, performance and financial audits, and data ownership to guide its members and encourage greater transparency in media operations. It's insane to think that some agencies had not established rigorous-enough processes internally to come out of this process clean. It's equally insane to see advertisers conduct audit after audit with little regard to the impact on the relationship or their agency resources.

However, audits were not originally designed to be punitive. If an advertiser doesn't trust the intentions of its agency, it's probably time to move on. Audits help refine compensation guidelines, improve contract language, limit litigation risks, promote transparency, and if managed properly, build long-term trust. The issue of trust in client/agency relationships is so deep that it even led the newly elected 4As President and CEO Marla Kaplowitz to write a compelling column titled "How to Rebuild Trust in the Agency-Marketer Relationship" only three months into her new role. We know that the rate of change in the advertising industry has been nothing short of phenomenal, and the number of heated media and marketing debates has skyrocketed as a result. So, for the new head of the national trade association representing US advertising agencies and over 164,000 agency professionals to choose the topic of "trust"—instead of talent, growth, innovation, or technology, for example—is a testament of the severity of the divide now created between two worlds. In agencies, advertisers no longer trust. In the column Kaplowitz brilliantly states, "Trust is the cornerstone of any good relationship." So far, so good. But then she goes on to say, "We encourage agencies and clients to discuss trust in the context of business expectations and requirements to ensure a successful partnership. These will differ based on the needs of the participants." That statement alone shows that although the issue is somewhat easy to point to, the answer on how to fix it is far more complex than meets the eye. The solution is complex because "trust" is, well, "subjective" and subject to interpretation. How you bring trust to life in various systems, procedures, operations, contracts, and financially may vary significantly relationship to relationship. Hence the challenge for both advertisers and agencies.

The agency industry has been challenged to come up with self-regulation and consistent agency practices, leading to a few highly-publicized cases that lit a match and started a ramping fire that no one seems able to contain. In the hope to avoid further reputation damage, the 4As took action and gathered top talent to address the problem. The 4As Transparency Guiding Principles of Conduct provides much needed recommendations, helpful guidelines about business terms, and agency compensation practices. But as Kaplowitz reminded us, "They do not represent mandates—but recommended courses of action." If you read between the lines here: great agencies are likely to stay great, but one bad apple can spoil the barrel for everyone else. In the meantime, marketers still must distinguish the responsible, good practitioners from the others. These transparency guidelines do provide a starting point for a productive dialogue to avoid any confusion, or worse, failed relationships and costly legal actions. These principles are centered around this notion of "agency" vs. "principle" and the contractual obligations to clients and agencies, such as opt-in agreements, reasonable audit rights, and well-defined protocols, providing proper and full disclosure about commercial relationships.

In some ways, these guidelines are common sense, yet you may wonder why such a vibrant industry has never had stricter transparency principles for everyone to follow. No wonder that advertisers occasionally refer to it as The Wild Wild "Waste." Wherever there is opacity, there is inefficiency. In his infamous inspiring quote, American industrialist and the founder of the Ford Motor Company, Henry Ford said, "Coming together is a beginning; keeping together is a progress; working together is success." Now, we all know from experience that's easier said than done. Working together is an ambitious goal in any situation where the interest of one party appears to be diametrically opposed to the other. At the center of any transparency debate are the agency financial gains and economic interests that often result in over-priced services, double-dipping, and conflicts of interest. Building trust requires both parties to foster a culture of honesty, integrity, and accountability, but also fully disclose and audit operating practices so there are no surprises or broken promises. That's the only way to work together effectively.

In addition to agreeing to solid contract terms, here are five practical ways advertisers and agencies can collaborate to earn mutual trust and strengthen the partnership:

1. Fully disclose your respective principles and controls. Without proper disclosure, both parties may not

understand their respective approach and expectations. I've seen it happen so many times. You think you are perfectly aligned until some event requires both parties to articulate with absolute precision how they operate, only to find out that there are discrepancies and misunderstandings. This is particularly important during agency reviews or at the inception of a new relationship. At the very least, marketers should ask their agencies if they follow the 4As Transparency Guiding Principles of Conduct.

2. Fully understand your agency's operating process: If trust must be earned, it must be earned over time. Having a reasonable audit plan is the best way for advertisers to establish that the practices are consistent with the agreed principles. Of course, don't audit your agencies to death, as that is counterproductive. However, conducting an audit of the financials in the first two years of a new relationship (reviewing billings, reporting, processes, etc.) is likely to establish a solid foundation and trust for the years to come.

3. Institute and socialize a partnership code of conduct: How you behave in the partnership will profoundly impact the trust and relationship you build. However, advertisers and agencies are often left to their own devices to figure out the right way to interact and collaborate. Having a code of conduct, a set of rules outlining the mutual responsibilities and proper practices for the partnership to live by, goes a long way toward building trust. The code of conduct can also be incorporated into a sort of service-level agreement between the two parties.

4. Make trust the central piece of cross-agency collaboration: Trust is not limited to the client/agency relationship. Advertisers ask and expect their roster agencies to collaborate effectively together on their behalf. Yet when there are transparency issues surfacing often, such as differences of opinion and territorial concerns between the agencies, the work suffers. By having clear roles and responsibilities and conducting joint meetings with the agencies, an advertiser is building an environment of trust that is far more conducive to trust building and smart collaboration.

5. Be fully committed to providing and receiving feedback: No trust can be built based on a relationship where no one really knows how things stand. Post mortem meetings and annual or project-level performance evaluations provide the ideal forum for 360 feedback reviews. However, the process itself is not sufficient. The substance of the feedback must be productive and encourage open and direct discussions between client and agency teams that ultimately build long-term trust.

In the increasingly complex and opaque world of advertising, trust has become a rare commodity that cannot be substituted. It's a prerequisite to any successful partnership between a client and its agency(ies). Without full transparency, any relationship is deemed to fail over time. If you ever played the "trust fall" game as a group exercise, you know what I am referring to. In this game, a person with arms folded against the chest, deliberately allows themselves to fall, relying on other group members to catch them. Are you willing to close your eyes and rely on your business partner to catch you on the way down? If the answer is not a genuine "yes," then you must make building that trust a priority.

5 WAYS TO EARN TRUST
IN CLIENT / AGENCY RELATIONSHIPS

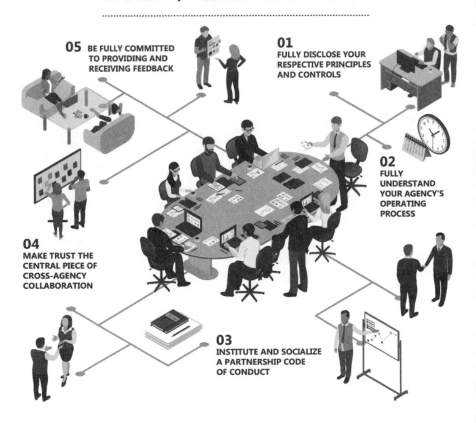

05 BE FULLY COMMITTED TO PROVIDING AND RECEIVING FEEDBACK

01 FULLY DISCLOSE YOUR RESPECTIVE PRINCIPLES AND CONTROLS

02 FULLY UNDERSTAND YOUR AGENCY'S OPERATING PROCESS

04 MAKE TRUST THE CENTRAL PIECE OF CROSS-AGENCY COLLABORATION

03 INSTITUTE AND SOCIALIZE A PARTNERSHIP CODE OF CONDUCT

In the end, Pacta Sunt Servanda implies more than saying contractual agreements must be kept or that one must always prepare for rainy days. It means that advertisers' and agencies' contracts and audits must be performed by each party in good faith, which is critical to establishing trust and strengthening partnerships.

TOP 3

BEST PRACTICES

for Advertisers

1 Use agency contracts to set clear relationship expectations and business parameters with the end goal of strengthening the partnership, not restricting it.

2 Review and carefully study the terms and conditions of your agency contract(s) so both parties adhere to the spirit of the agreement as well as the specifics.

3 Build trust by setting up reasonable and constructive audit terms that encourage transparency but also by adopting a more collaborative, open way to communicate, provide feedback and set expectations for the partnership.

7

JUST SIX NUMBERS

Determining the right agency compensation

"Fortune favors the prepared mind."
—**LOUIS PASTEUR,** CHEMIST AND MICROBIOLOGIST

Always complex, sometimes frustrating, often contentious are words people might use to describe their income tax return. Some might even use more colorful words. Well, the Internal Revenue Service (IRS) may have finally found its match. "Agency compensation" is a topic that stimulates similar feelings among high-ranking advertisers and agencies. This is due in large part to inconsistent and, from time to time, inequitable practices that have people pulling their hair out. Over the years, agencies have painfully discovered that negotiating agency compensation with clients feels a bit like what I fondly call the "hair loss syndrome:" You have less than you think, and you lose more each day. Trust me. Yet compensation, when it is done right and fairly, is known to be a critical part of any successful business partnership. Do you think you've already figured it out? That's what I thought. Few advertisers have the required knowledge, tools, or resources to assess the fairness of existing agreements or to anticipate what's next. As a result, they tend to rely on old-fashioned negotiation techniques like pressuring agencies to reduce overhead costs and shrinking agency profit margins year-over-year until, well, the whole thing implodes. Let's face it. Traditional compensation methods are, for the most part, obsolete. Luckily, novel approaches to successful agency compensation drive greater shared accountability and reward performance/results. These models focus on what matters the most: not cost alone, but the value realized from the agency multiplier effect.

ALIGNING THE STARS FOR MORE EFFECTIVE CLIENT/AGENCY RELATIONSHIPS

For the novices in agency compensation, the topic may at first sound like taking a class in astrophysics. In his ground-breaking book entitled *Just Six Numbers*, English science writer, cosmologist, and astrophysicist Sir Martin Rees, also known as Baron Rees and the Royal Astronomer of England, discusses how mathematical laws underpin the fabric of our universe. According to Sir Martin Rees, just six numbers govern the shape, size, and texture of our universe. And what's most amazing about his assertions is that if the values of these six numbers were only fractionally different, stars and galaxies would not form, complex chemistry would not be possible, and life could not evolve. In other words, we would not exist. What has a British cosmologist and astrophysicist to do with the controversial topic of agency compensation? I believe everything. I cannot help wondering if the logic that is true in astronomy could also be true in agency compensation: If a starting point is specified with clarity, is the outcome predictable? How many values or financial metrics, if changed slightly, would with most certainty alter the future of a client/agency relationship? As advertisers enter negotiations with their agencies, they must consider which of these numbers, whether it is margin, overhead, headcount, cost per unit of work, cost per qualified prospect, return on marketing investment, revenue targets, year over year sales growth, market share, or others will keep their relationship with the agency in balance and make it all worthwhile in the end. While agency compensation may not be rocket science, it certainly borrows from the world of logic and numbers: The right numbers can lift a relationship to excellence or keep it on the ground. As in astronomy, it encourages people to look up, not down. Why is it so hard, then?

AGENCY VIEWPOINT

"Probably the biggest source of derailment is the friction that develops from the misalignment of advertiser scopes of work, cost pressures, and budget constraints. Scopes of work have expanded as the number and complexity of marketing options has expanded while at the same time advertisers are cutting their budgets. Expecting more for less year-on-year has its limits, especially as agency talent costs and other operational agency expenses keep going up." [100]

—NEAL GROSSMAN, CHIEF OPERATING OFFICER—AMERICAS AT EG+ WORLDWIDE AND THE DESIGNORY

Both parties enter discussions in good faith, but soon negotiations derail for several reasons: mistrust, friction, misunderstandings, or the absence of industry standards. Both sides get caught in circular arguments, pulling the bed sheets to their side, and trying to extract further tiny concessions from each other. Yet they are often missing the big picture and getting lost in the minutia. At its core, the process of securing the right compensation agreement assumes that both parties will reach a consensus on the value that is being created and reach a fair and equitable contract. As Molière, the 17th-century French playwright and actor, so rightfully captured: *"Things only have the value that we give them."* Value is highly subjective by nature. Clearly, "fair and equitable" is in eye of the beholder. Do clients know what they are truly getting for their money? And if they did, would they compensate their agencies any differently?

The chronic pressure on "non-working" budgets in the past few decades, mainly from agency fees and profits, combined with increasing client demands in a far more challenging business environment, the industry has been forced to pause to reexamine how much advertisers pay for agency services. It has a tremendous economical and operational impact on their relationship. It is commonly accepted that the era of commission-based compensation is flat dead, with the exception of the digital space. And the existing era of labor-based compensation is slowly eroding, after years of shrinking agency profit.

Another significant shift is the move away from AOR retainers to project-based work, creating much greater risk for agencies having to provide continuity of quality staff to service clients in a timely manner and affordably. The significant growth of digital as one of the most complex, high volume disciplines in the media mix is also a paradigm shift that has broad implications on how budgets are set and how agencies are compensated. In lieu of these changes, clients and agencies alike are scratching their respective heads wondering what's next in compensation. Leading advertisers such as The Coca-Cola Company, Verizon, and Procter & Gamble are challenging the status quo, experimenting with innovative compensation approaches. They are hoping to find more effective ways to compensate and motivate agencies. But are we anywhere close today? Certainly. If you look in the mirror, you will realize that we've certainly come a long way from compensation historically based on how much advertisers spend (that is, commission-based) to current practices. Yet it worked for a long while.

There was logic to the madness of the time. It's crazy that it is now, for the most part, based on the agency's time and labor, irrespective of performance or the value realized from the work. It's crazy to think that most advertisers still pay today whether or not the work is any good or accomplishes its intended objectives. It's also insane to think that so many agencies still don't have skin-in-the-game. And when they do, they are eager to share any upside, but are far less enthusiastic about sharing the risks. Hmm. That was expected. This is not the way successful organizations manage their valuable human capital. When agencies exceed expectations and find creative ways for their clients to drive measurable business results, agencies don't necessarily get paid more, either. It's equally insane. But how exactly do they define performance or value? Frankly, advertisers haven't always made it easy for agencies, allowing cost-cutting efforts to take center stage and often undermining themselves in the process. They have negotiated aggressively, pushing agencies to apply unusual operational and financial pressure on their organization to eliminate inefficiencies. There is nothing wrong about that at face value. But too often, they went as far as forcing fees down to unsustainable levels, allowing scope creep, and shooting themselves in the foot by negatively impacting their agency's ability to hire/retain the right talent. Advertisers hire agencies to be effective at driving performance, not costs.

Sadly, agencies often found themselves unable to deliver value-add ideas that advertisers most desperately need. Steamrolled by some overly-aggressive cost-cutting efforts, unaware of the counter-productive effect of their actions, many agencies ended up on their back, weakened and with bruises, broken bones, and unwanted talent attrition. As Jean-Marie Dru, Chairman of TBWA Worldwide once declared *"We are paying the price of belonging to an industry which has not learned how to protect its own interests. We are our worst enemies."* Jean-Marie is dead on right. What will compel the right behavior and make it a true partnership? What is truly equitable? What will make advertisers feel good about what they get for their money, yet allow agencies to invest in technology and talent and improve the value they provide? It's time we demystify common beliefs and explore more effective compensation methods.

AGENCY VIEWPOINT

"The current way of being compensated is misery, and it's unfair, because we are compensated for time, and what we are bringing has more value than time." [101]

—MAURICE LÉVY, CHAIRMAN OF THE SUPERVISORY BOARD AND FORMER CHAIRMAN, PUBLICIS GROUPE

OVERCOMING THE INHERENT COMPLEXITY OF AGENCY COMPENSATION

Michael Farmer's book *Madison Avenue Manslaughter* provides an insightful perspective on the history of agency compensation—from the golden age to today's challenges faced by our industry. Why has it gotten even more complicated in the past few years? Figuring out what to pay an agency is not a simple task. The stakes are great. And it's not getting easier, either. For advertisers that require resources around the world or have multiple agencies in their roster, the added complexity is unavoidable. Unless managed centrally, such services may have to be provided by entering one or multiple contracts with potentially different compensation agreements. The specialized and labor-intensive, and therefore costly, nature of digital forces us to reset expectations while eliminating waste in marketing budgets. The complexity and often expensive and scarce technical talent along with the tools required for digital cannot be accommodated by existing rigid and linear compensation agreements. The rich set of technologies, the service-providers needed, and the high number of creative assets and content that must be produced, placed, refreshed, tracked, and continually enhanced in a vast number of ad sizes and platforms make digital a drastically different advertising environment than traditional. However, many advertisers recognize that as agency fees might be slightly higher, lower digital media costs generally offset those.

CLIENT VIEWPOINT

"We see over $2 billion in savings opportunities in marketing spending, with half or more coming from media rates or eliminating supply-chain waste." [102]

—JON MOELLER, CHIEF FINANCIAL OFFICER,

PROCTER & GAMBLE CO.

Advertisers and agencies won't realize these cost efficiencies until significant improvements in industry standards, modern technology, and innovation in processes enable greater automation at every step, from workflow and traffic management, to asset development and campaign analytics. A more effective use of agency resources also requires client behavioral changes and productivity gains: better briefs, fewer layers of approval or decision-makers, fewer stakeholders that need agency support, more centralized marketing structures. Agency resources are tighter than ever before. Expectations for cost reduction and innovation are greater. Qualified talent is scarce. Work volume is increasing exponentially. Speed to market is accelerating. How should advertisers deal with these challenges? How do they know if they are compensating their agencies fairly? Where should they start? Compensation agreements vary based on the nature and complexity of the work, real or perceived value, geography, and the respective company cultures. Frankly, the quality of a compensation agreement is often more a reflection of how organized or knowledgeable an advertiser or an agency is, than any other variable. Both parties must first discuss their respective goals, philosophies, and expectations about compensation. All of that should be done prior to selecting a compensation agreement. Then both parties can choose the right approach to meet their requirements. This is perhaps why it remains such a popular and highly debated topic at industry events: not paying the agency too much or too little, rewarding for the right outcome, and yielding the greatest possible value out of the partnership. Advertisers ask themselves:

- Are terms competitive relative to industry norms?

- Do both parties feel that the agreement is fair and equitable?

- Are the terms of the agreement allowing the agency to assign the right talent?

- How much compensation should be put at risk? Based on what metrics?

- What should the payment terms be?

- What level of transparency is needed to build and maintain trust?

- How much time and effort should be spent on administrating the compensation plan?

AGENCY VIEWPOINT

"Agencies need to also have a meaningful and collaborative relationship with procurement. This means quarterly meetings with clients, including all procurement teams, to track what work is flowing through the system versus the fees being charged. No surprises."[103]

—**SOPHIE KELLY,** SENIOR VP OF NORTH AMERICAN WHISKEYS PORTFOLIO, DIAGEO AND FORMER CEO, THE BARBARIAN GROUP

Although savvy advertisers are addressing these questions head on, compensation remains a multifaceted code that is not likely to be deciphered anytime soon.

EMBRACING COMPLETE TRANSPARENCY AND EQUITABILITY

In compensation agreements, one should never assume that agencies will subordinate their interest to their client. But again, why should they? Agencies know too well that the reverse is true as well. The chosen method is less important in the end than making sure the parties' interests and priorities are completely aligned. A compensation agreement must be designed to align the financial commitment to the goals of the client. It must also satisfy the needs of the agency to earn a fair profit and grow its business. Without it, the agency is unlikely to attract and retain the right talent. Today, many CMOs hide behind their procurement team, allowing them to choke their agencies by cutting margin to the bone without realizing that they are undermining their own value.

To be a great client, and more importantly an excellent partner, one must have a basic understanding of the agency business: how agencies generate revenue, bill for their services, manage expenses and ultimately yield a decent profit like any responsible for-profit organization. Understanding and even acknowledging that simple fact will go a long way with agencies and will set the right mindset for internal groups involved in these negotiations. After years of commission-based pricing, this form of controversial compensation is, for the most part, gone. The growth of non-traditional channels combined with the continued cost increases of media placements have increased the perceived—and sometimes real—gap between what agencies delivered and what they got paid for it. In the end, it has led the way for labor-based fee agreements in a concerted effort by clients to more closely link resources with compensation, by paying for the actual resources needed plus profit.

Greater marketing accountability at the boardroom level and the laser focus on return on marketing investment (ROMI) has put pressure on the way agencies are compensated. This has led to the growing involvement of procurement in agency negotiations. CFOs are now openly challenging CMOs: Are we over-paying our agencies? Are we getting enough value for what we are paying them? Agency fees are often the largest marketing spend category in advertisers' budgets, so it's no surprise that they have received growing attention in past years. Why is it now such a focus? Advertisers' trust in agency billing and cost accounting has been shaky to say the least. It has been fueled by agencies' (perceived or real) lack of financial disclosure and a few well-publicized cases of unethical practices, such as over-billing and other fraudulent behavior. Naturally, advertisers asked for more transparency and accountability, effectively driving costs down and reducing margins to a visible, known entity. The United States federal law, Sarbanes-Oxley Act of 2002, also introduced a set of new or enhanced standards for all, which certainly impacted the way holding companies manage and report revenue/expenses, improving internal controls and increasing confidence.

Any compensation agreement must be equitable to both parties. Yet advertisers and agencies often differ on what constitutes a reasonable profit and overhead. Clients want the best of the talent the agency can offer, but are they always willing to pay for it? Terms that are not sustainable will eventually derail the relationship and lead to wasteful litigious discussions about the long-term viability of the partnership. But the concept of equitability is known to be quite subjective. Clients and agencies are naturally coming at it from different angles and have divergent definitions for what is *"fair."* Not all agencies are created equal and therefore command different agreements based on their unique capabilities and cost models. Advertisers want to give the agency a reasonable deal without breaking the bank. Agencies naturally want to increase the profitability of their client accounts. All parties have good and valid intentions. Negotiations will take place to move the needle somewhere close to the middle of the range, allowing both parties to find a healthy and sustainable compromise. They all want something "fair."

Experience shows that if one party walks away feeling that it has lost, it means both parties have lost in the long run. Occasionally, advertisers are tempted to play on agency insecurities, threatening to put their account in review to land a better deal. And agencies may under-resource their clients to meet short-term profit targets or come up with other ways to make up for their past concessions. "Fair" is also in the eyes of the beholder.

AGENCY VIEWPOINT

"The executives on the front lines of your firm must understand that you're in the business of providing solutions, not services. Services can be procured from a lot of other sources, often at lower cost, and the professional buyers in client organizations know that. But if you present your offerings as effective solutions to business problems, you're putting your real value in perspective." [104]

—TIM WILLIAMS, FOUNDING PARTNER OF IGNITION CONSULTING GROUP

DID YOU SAY, "INDUSTRY STANDARDS?" WHAT INDUSTRY STANDARDS?

I am sorry, but we must start this discussion with sad news. So here it is: There are no universal compensation agreements advertisers can pick up from the template rack of their local Office Depot store. This is a sweet spot for cost consultants eager to help clients sail through these unfriendly waters. Compensation agreements vary widely in nature and scope as do cost accounting methodologies they often rely on. Experts on either side still debate what is deemed acceptable—what reasonable profit margins are, what should be included in overhead and pass-through expenses, and ultimately what constitutes a fair deal. Compensation is often based on scope of work, staffing resources, real or perceived value, or a combination of the three. Yet ill-informed procurement teams may sometimes focus on inputs/costs instead of scope or deliverables as the primary determinant of compensation. They do so because their own charter and performance is evaluated on cost savings instead of achieving marketing results. The scope of work is—and should be—the initial basis for determining the required agency resources and agency fees. Although all compensation agreements inherently include all the same financial elements—labor, overhead, and margin—their definition and the way they are calculated will vary significantly from one advertiser and agency to another, often dictated by the advertiser, leaving everyone scratching their heads for comparability and benchmarks.

I was reminded by the former Chief Compensation Officer of TBWA/Worldwide and my longtime friend, Neal Grossman, that beyond definitions there are other factors that will make things like labor and overhead difficult to compare. For example, two unique agencies may look like they have identical compensation, but the components vary based on an agency's philosophy and structure, which have a big impact on the resultant direct labor cost per employee or overhead factor comparisons. One agency might opt for lower salaries but provide much greater benefits and incentives than another agency that prefers to pay higher salaries and lower benefits and incentives. This can have a significant impact on the metrics even though the agency's costs in total between the two agencies are the same. Neal insists that other variables can also impact metrics resulting in higher overhead costs, but that's not necessarily bad. An agency that invests in research and technology helps themselves and, in turn, advertisers to achieve the advertisers' goals and objectives. However, that same agency might be perceived as inefficient compared to other agencies that do not invest in research and technology. Which would you rather go with? The lowest cost is not necessarily the best choice. Advertisers feel that they are likely to overpay when they are not sure what things should cost. They want standards or guidelines, especially in contentious areas such as IP and digital.

Digital typically calls for lower media investments (earned and owned) but higher fees and production budgets. Digital requires more creative units than traditional media due to its higher refresh rate and rotation of creative across a wider range of channels. Campaigns tend to change frequently, requiring greater upfront, and also more flexible media planning and buying, analytics, trafficking, designing, and programming services to refresh and update. There is ongoing tracking, reporting, and analysis to optimize campaign performance. Programming and back-end requirements are far greater as well. Production-related costs are often embedded into agency fees, contrary to traditional media. As a result, digital is more labor-intensive for agencies. There is tremendous momentum to shift client/agency relationships to a more outcome, performance-based approach. As marketing dollars are shifting to specialized agencies, the need for alternative approaches becomes more obvious. All these reasons contribute to increasing costs exponentially, creating huge tensions among clients and agencies.

Thankfully, the ANA and 4As have collaborated to remove some of the guesswork. They've come up with guidelines to help their members with better arrangements that result in stronger relationships. Ultimately, compensation agreements significantly impact the way an agency services an account, what talent and resources are assigned to it, how responsive they are, how they perform, and the level of investment they are willing to make to grow and nurture the relationship. Have no doubt about it. Whatever compensation has been chosen, it will deeply affect the dynamics of the relationship.

AGENCY VIEWPOINT

"Short-term thinking is all about cost and it encourages zero based growth in budgeting. At the same time, you have research showing that CMOs just last two or three years now and CEOs just a little longer. So, there's far too much short-term thinking and focus on cost, which isn't healthy for our industry." [105]

—SIR MARTIN SORRELL, FORMER CHIEF EXECUTIVE OFFICER, WPP AND EXECUTIVE CHAIRMAN, S4 CAPITAL

HOW TO FIND THE RIGHT COMPENSATION METHOD

Negotiating and managing compensation is an incredibly important competency for Agency Management teams to develop and master. They must rigorously structure their approach and get internal buy-in. They must develop pricing benchmarks and cost databases to better inform their decisions. They must develop training and guidelines for internal budget owners. And to do so equally as well, advertisers must first acquire a rudimentary understanding of the way agencies operate and look at the way they generate revenue, manage costs, and yield profits. Conversely, clients must educate their agency on their business, existing challenges and opportunities, and give a detailed description of their short and long-term objectives with clear metrics for success. They must explain the type of talent and competencies needed, levels of service expected, budgets/resources available, and the nature of the involvement of other roster agencies involved. Finally, they need to discuss what constitutes, in their opinion, a successful partnership. This exchange of information establishes the framework on which negotiations, trade-offs, and compromises will be made. Then, they need to determine what the most suitable compensation model for their needs is. The type of compensation may vary based on account size, client expectations, duration of the agreement, and type and scope of services provided. Each model has pros and cons, with varying degrees of sophistication and administrative requirements that clients must carefully evaluate before deciding on the most appropriate one. Some clients may use a hybrid of different compensation approaches for different marketing services, geographies, or business units.

CLIENT / AGENCY COMPENSATION DEVELOPMENT PROCESS

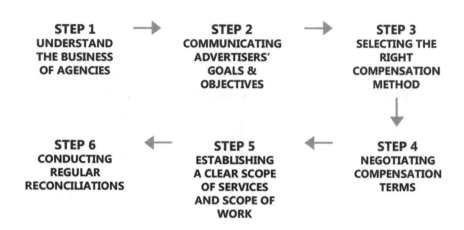

STEP 1
UNDERSTAND
THE BUSINESS
OF AGENCIES

STEP 2
COMMUNICATING
ADVERTISERS'
GOALS &
OBJECTIVES

STEP 3
SELECTING THE
RIGHT
COMPENSATION
METHOD

STEP 6
CONDUCTING
REGULAR
RECONCILIATIONS

STEP 5
ESTABLISHING
A CLEAR SCOPE
OF SERVICES
AND SCOPE OF
WORK

STEP 4
NEGOTIATING
COMPENSATION
TERMS

AGENCY VIEWPOINT

"In the agency world, though, our clients tend to buy the stuff our people produce. The what is more important than the who. Unfortunately, because much of what agencies produce has been commoditized, clients have squeezed agencies on costs. This has driven profit margins down and pitted agencies against one another in a 'how low can you go?' game that doesn't have a winner."[106]

—**STEVE RADICK,** VP, DIRECTOR OF PR AND CONTENT
INTEGRATION, BRUNNER

STEP 1: UNDERSTANDING THE BUSINESS OF AGENCIES

The agency's primary asset is its talent base—how to find, retain, and motivate it. So, relentlessly increasing the quality, output, and productivity of employees is vital to their success. The agency economic model is relatively simple in concept. Agencies often use a combination of revenue sources to grow their business. For the most part, agencies generate revenue for their services through fees and, in some cases, commissions. Newer revenue sources include IP licensing and revenue-share. Agencies then subtract their operational costs, namely salaries and benefits. They also subtract their costs of doing business, aka overhead, leaving them a profit margin or markup. Profit margin is expressed as a percentage of revenue (including agency compensation), while markup is expressed as a percentage multiplied by all-up operating expenses. There are nuances between disciplines, especially in those where media is an important part of the relationship. Understanding how agencies turn a profit and manage costs is a prerequisite to clients effectively negotiating with agencies. Large publicly traded companies like WPP, Omnicom, IPG, and Publicis do a decent job at making their revenue predictable to Wall Street. Here is a summary of their revenue and profitability in recent years:

HISTORICAL REVENUE
in billions
2000 - 2015

— WPP   — OmnicomGroup   ...... PUBLICIS GROUPE   ---- IPG

Source: earning reports

The four giants of advertising have increased revenue year over year, capturing a larger share of the advertising industry over time. They managed to do this at varying degrees of profitability and profit margin. Profit margin represents the percentage of revenue that a company keeps as profit after accounting for fixed and variable costs. It is calculated by dividing net income by revenue. Displayed as a percentage, profit margin can be thought of as the amount of profit that a company keeps per dollar of revenue. For example, if a company has a profit margin of 10 percent, the company keeps $.10 of each dollar of revenue. Between 2000 and 2015, the average profit margin has ranged between a low 1.89% in 2002 to a high 8.27 percent in 2011, with Publicis Groupe and WPP leading in terms of high profitability. The Interpublic Group struggled to stay on par with their peers in the industry with some difficult years in the early 2000s amid an accounting scandal, restated financial statements and earnings, and many loss-making international affiliates that the company eventually disposed of. It's important to note that when purchasing as an agent on behalf of a client, the largest third-party costs (media and production) are generally treated as pass-through costs and do not flow through the P&L as other businesses might reflect (i.e., as part of revenue and cost of goods sold). As a result, when comparing profit margins to other companies, advertising agency profit margins may seem higher than they would if these pass-through costs were grossed up and included in revenue and expense/cost of sales.

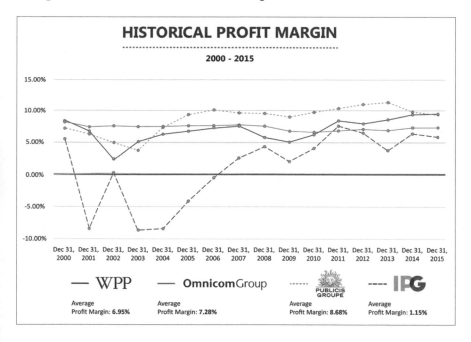

Despite agencies' efforts to avoid volatility, a large client loss or win can have a drastic and sudden impact on revenue and profitability as history has often shown. Furthermore, marketing expenditures are rather subject to economic conditions. In a growing and healthy economy, a client's marketing budget will be adjusted upward to stimulate demand. In a declining economy or recession, budgets tend to shrink to keep operating at minimal cost. And when marketing budgets are reduced, so are agency expenditures. It is also a highly competitive industry. Agencies must compete to grow and protect existing client relationships. That often means making short-term profit concessions for long-term revenue gains.

AGENCY VIEWPOINT

"We believe contracts should be simple and straightforward, with bonuses offered only if the agency outperforms very specific goals. There's still nothing wrong with charging by the hour, with overhead congealed in the hourly rates." [107]

—JEFF GOODBY, CO-CHAIRMAN AND CREATIVE DIRECTOR, GOODBY, SILVERSTEIN & PARTNERS

Thankfully, most agencies are efficient at doing capacity resource planning; they have designed and implemented strong time, media, and production tracking systems, with a billing and financial reporting infrastructure giving them timely, accurate, actionable information to manage costs, and, therefore, profitability. Some agencies ask staff to fill out timesheets to help them run their agency as effectively as possible, even if the compensation agreement is not hourly based. It allows them to measure productivity and client profitability and whether agency staff is at full capacity, or they have the bandwidth to take on another client. One of the indicators they look at is revenue per employee. Revenue per employee is a ratio that is calculated based on the company's revenue divided by the current number of employees. It is often considered a good indicator of efficiency and the effective use of a company's resources. However, a low revenue per employee ratio could also be an indication of a revenue problem; for example, the fees have been too heavily discounted. In the past 15 years, that ratio for holding companies (based on total employees) ranged from $124,000 to $166,000, starting on average at $124,000 in 2000 and increasing to an average of $159,000 in 2015 for the top 4 holding companies (WPP, Omnicom, Publicis, and IPG). Anecdotal evidence suggests a typical revenue per employee ratio of $200,000 to $300,000 per FTE based on direct staff alone.

Another important aspect of agency profitability is submitting billings to clients on a pre-determined schedule and making sure clients are paying their invoices when they are supposed to. Whenever they can, advertisers will push for extended payment terms. Reviewing the profitability of a given account is standard practice for the agency (and, in some cases, jointly with the client), regardless of the chosen compensation agreement. This information proves to be useful to run their business more efficiently, deciding which relationship is profitable and which one is not, and what actions must be taken to improve profitability without impacting the quality, speed, or effectiveness of the work produced. Profitable agencies attract top talent. Non-profitable agencies are undesirable to both prospective employees and clients, in the long run. As agencies lose or fail to attract talent in critical roles, they run the risk of eroding work quality and effectiveness.

AGENCY VIEWPOINT

"We don't do timesheets because they drive the wrong behavior." [108]

—**CARL JOHNSON**, FOUNDING PARTNER AND GLOBAL CEO,

ANOMALY

COMMON SOURCES OF AGENCY REVENUE

Fees: By far, fees have been the most common source of agency revenue in recent years. "Fees for services performed" are paid in return for the delivery of agency services. Fees are typically calculated based on negotiated or estimated hours at approved hourly rates (cost per hour). A retainer (committed fee budget) can be set to secure dedicated agency resources to the account or fees can be paid on a project-basis. Whether agency compensation is retainer- or project-based, hourly rates are expressed by dividing agency revenue by the number of workable hours per year (ranging between 1650 to 1800 in most countries but varying based on local labor laws). The compensation is negotiated based upon estimated hours at market-based hourly rates and/or based on the notion of full recovery of the agency costs and a fair and equitable profit. Direct labor and overhead are considered pass-through expenses (benefits can either be included in overhead or direct labor, based on the chosen methodology).

INDUSTRY VIEWPOINT

"It is hard not to conclude that the pricing and profit pressures on creative agencies have led to a deterioration in their capabilities. But not all of the price declines had to happen. For reasons best known to senior agency executives, agencies do not routinely plan, document, or negotiate their remuneration based on a measurement of the growing SOW workloads they carry out. In too many cases, declining fees are set by clients and growing workloads happen on an unplanned, ad hoc basis throughout the year." [109]

—MICHAEL FARMER, CHAIRMAN, TRINITYP3

The markup, or profit margin, is negotiated independently with the agency. Most of compensation agreements are likely to fall within an 8 to 25 percent effective profit margin range, based on various considerations (the reputation and popularity of the agency, the services provided, the scope of the work relationship, the size of the account, the longevity of the account, the risk level, performance bonus potential, and so forth). Large advertisers have so much buying leverage that they can demand preferential profit margin rates, extended payment terms and advantageous contract terms. Ultimately, profit margins are subject to the laws of demand and supply: what both parties are willing to live with and the value advertisers feel they are getting from their agencies. If the agency is paid based on time and materials, tracking time accurately becomes critical. A growing number of agencies now rebel against timesheet reporting. While it may be relevant to certain professions like attorneys or accountants, they argue it is not relevant in advertising services. Most agencies feel strongly that compensation should not be determined based on time or activity level but rather be determined based on performance or value, allowing them to generate additional revenue when they meet or exceed expectations. At the end of the day, what are advertisers really buying from their agencies? Are they buying time? Or are they buying outcomes, results, and business performance?

Commissions: Agencies pay for the media placement for advertising time or space that they place on the client's behalf. Historically, agencies made a standard commission of 15% as a primary form of compensation. The agency would handle 85 percent of the media payments, a pass-through expense, and bill the client for an additional 15 percent pre-determined commission, considered agency revenue. Today, commissions are no longer a very common form of compensation, with the exception of digital spend where there has been renewed interest for a simpler methodology. The 15 percent commission was a lucrative way for agencies to generate revenue, as commissions were loosely tied to the resources required to effectively plan, buy, and place media, leaving much room for agencies to be creative on how they managed the work. If traditional media used to generate commissions in the 15 percent range, digital media typically required an effective commission rate ranging from 25 to 30 percent. To reduce the risk associated with a small client not fulfilling its contractual payment obligations, some agencies will require pre-payment in advance of placing the media or paying the media after they have received payments from the client—a method often referred to as "sequential liability," whereby the client is solely liable to the media until such time as good funds have been placed in the hands of the agency after which the agency becomes solely liable to the media. Agencies generally won't buy media as a primary obligator except for agencies that are able to buy media, inventory it, and sell it to advertisers at market rates. Although rare among large accounts, examples like BBDO's position as second-largest unsecured creditor because of Chrysler's Chapter 11 bankruptcy, which added up to $58M, have served as painful reminders of the agency risks involved. These payments, made on behalf of clients, are commonly referred to as billings. Commissions can also be generated from clients paying a gross rate billed by media and the agency paying for media at a lower rate, generating a net difference commonly called commission. The nature of the agreement will dictate whether the agency is keeping the commission as part of its revenue or whether commissions are paid separately.

Production Markup: Markup is a percentage allocation on top of pass-through production costs that is passed on to the client. Marking up production was a common form of compensation for agencies for years. In fee-based compensation agreements, however, the agency is not permitted to markup production. Today, this form of agency compensation is rarely adopted in practice. Agencies are now seeing that production in a digital world has another source of potential revenue, creating their own production studio vs. contracting production through third party production suppliers. However, most agency in-house production studios charge based on an agreed upon rate card or bid, and under that scenario, there is no additional markup added by the agency.

OTHER DERIVATIVE BUT CONTROVERSIAL SOURCES OF REVENUE

Agency Volume Bonification (AVB): AVB is a credit, rebate, or bonus received by the agency from media vendors. It can take the form of free airtime/space in media, media upgrades, cash, or credit notes, typically negotiated on an annual basis and paid the following year. The practice has been in existence in Europe for a few decades and exists in many countries around the world, with a few exceptions. AVBs are not client specific. AVBs are earned by the agency based on the total agency volume of media-spend with a vendor and may vary based on a variety of criteria (performance, timeliness of payment, and key relationships). For agencies handling large media buys, this may represent a substantial volume of credit (from 1 percent to 3 percent on average), and therefore, a sizeable financial benefit to the agency if the client is not diligent about requesting it.

Float/Account Receivables: Most clients will seek a float-neutral situation with their agencies. Cash management is an important part of effective financial management for agencies. Most agencies will perform a risk analysis for every client on their roster before deciding if they agree to float media expenditures. Agencies are not banks. Agencies are not expected to turn a profit (or a loss) from having a sizeable amount of cash at their fingertips when clients prepay media (or when they don't). The reality is that some media and production firms have payment terms that are less preferential that those negotiated by the agency, giving the agency the opportunity to sit on a pile of cash until payments are due to their third-party providers. When they do this, they are simply generating interest from any large pre-paid media or production expenses sitting in the agency's bank account.

The reality, however, is that clients are now asking for delayed payments to media owners, requiring media agencies to take on the added expense risks on their client's behalf. Furthermore, production companies often require 50 percent to 75 percent up front significantly reducing the potential for float on production dollars. Regardless of the approach both parties agree to take, the larger the client budget, the more knowledgeable both parties must be about how to handle float. AVBs and float are rare sources of revenue for agencies whose clients have adequately addressed them contractually. Finally, the nature of the work provided by the agency will dictate whether one source of revenue or multiple ones apply to a given client/agency relationship. Payment terms (for example, net 30 days) are another important consideration. An agency's lifeblood is in its cash flow. It must be satisfactorily addressed in the financial flow between the client and the agency, so it minimizes the agency's potential exposure. Agencies have identified alternative sources of revenue over the years, going outside of traditional forms of compensation such as incentive-based agreements and revenue-sharing deals.

Now that we have reviewed the many ways agencies generate revenue, let's examine how they manage costs and, ultimately, profitability.

INDUSTRY VIEWPOINT

"Cheap doesn't mean effective: If reducing the cost of a service has a negative impact on the effectiveness of that service to the business, you've shot yourself in the foot." [110]

—DANIEL JEFFRIES, FOUNDER, JEFFRIES CONSULTING

STANDARD AGENCY COSTS

Typically, agencies incur "direct" and "indirect" costs as part of running their business. Direct costs tend to be mostly labor-related and include direct labor (salary base, bonus, benefits, merit, vacation, payroll taxes, and any other employment related expenses related to time of direct staff working on clients' businesses). Indirect costs include overhead costs required to run the agency. Overhead is comprised of all agency operating expenses which range from insurance, space/facilities, maintenance, and utilities to office supplies, IT, hiring fees, property taxes, severance, and indirect non-billable salaries (indirect departments such as human resources, accounting, IT, etc. as well as non-client time of direct staff spent on general office administration and new business). The list goes on. Overhead, however, excludes direct labor and direct client costs. Direct client costs (travel, materials, couriers, etc.) are usually billed to the client as pass-through expenses. It's important to note that agencies use different accounting methods to calculate overhead rates. Because there are no industry standard overhead rates or cost accounting methods, for labor based agreements, it is recommended that both parties first agree on what should be included in direct labor and what should be included in overhead. ANA and 4As publish a list of standard overhead expenses. Actual costs vary by discipline (such as advertising vs. PR), geographic location or city, and ultimately, by agency. Overhead typically is allocated to clients based on their pro-rata share of client direct labor (for example, a 100 percent overhead rate means that for every dollar in direct labor, another dollar in overhead is charged to the client).

A few overhead expenses are occasionally debated by clients. "New business" falls under that category along with "bad debt" (billings not paid by advertisers). In the case of new business expenses, agencies argue that these costs ultimately benefit clients: By having a healthy and diversified client portfolio, they are in a better position to make preemptive investments, hire talent, share agency resources, and in the end, make their offering more valuable to existing clients. Further, given the short tenure of client agency relationships (partially influenced by the short tenure of CMOs), if agencies are not able to replace lost business, then overhead rates will increase to the ultimate detriment of clients (either in higher overhead passed on to the remaining clients or in damaging the agency's ability to service its clients). As far as bad debt is concerned, some agencies are asking for up-front payment of media and production expenses to minimize risk. In early 2009, Omnicom Group standardized its contracts with suppliers, including a sequential liability clause, to insist on the fact that they won't assume financial liability until a client pays. Overhead should not be considered independently of other cost elements when negotiating with an agency and is often benchmarked by advertisers for negotiation purposes. How far should clients go in terms of understanding agency costs? Tim J. Williams, Founding Partner of Ignition Consulting Group suggests that "Transparency is for Windows, Not Pricing Professional Services" (per the article by the same name)[80]. "You are under no obligation to be 'transparent' about your costs any more than Samsung is compelled to disclose their margin when you buy a new mobile phone," Williams writes. This is a reasonable concern from the agency world. This being said, it is my belief that a basic understanding of the agency's business makes a better, more informed client. However, clients are always better served by focusing on the performance and value created from the relationship than by scrutinizing costs to death.

STEP 2: COMMUNICATING ADVERTISERS' GOALS & OBJECTIVES

There are many venues by which agencies can grow their business and generate profit. There are many ways compensation agreements can be structured and implemented by advertisers with their agencies. To align the two requires clear articulation and communication of the advertiser's core objectives. Compensation must be aligned to the advertiser's business goals and enable the relationship to perform at its absolute best. A poorly designed compensation agreement can add complexity and tension in the relationship and distract from focusing the teams on producing great work together. Mutual expectations and compensation philosophies must be shared and clarified if needed. These conversations must lead to both parties feeling well understood and respected. At the onset of this process, they must all feel that there is a deep and real sense of partnership and mutual accountability.

CLIENT VIEWPOINT

"In the end, there is no silver bullet to compensation. Client/agency compensation should be first and foremost aligned to a company's philosophy. It's about identifying what's important to you then managing the agency relationship fairly and consistently." [111]

—**JAMES R. ZAMBITO,** SENIOR DIRECTOR GLOBAL CORPORATE AFFAIRS, JOHNSON & JOHNSON

STEP 3: SELECTING THE RIGHT COMPENSATION METHOD

Compensation methods are typically organized around the primary driver by which compensation will be established. These drivers are grouped in four major categories: spend, time/labor, output/deliverables, and performance/value. Large advertisers tend to use a combination of methods, often based on the type of marketing discipline, but sometimes based on a region or market as practices and regulations differ. Smaller advertisers naturally consider compensation agreements that are simple to set up and administer. All are encouraged to explore the pros and cons of various compensation models before deciding on the one that leads to the best outcome. Let's take a close look at the most common forms of agency compensation:

COMMON AGENCY COMPENSATION AGREEMENTS

PERFORMANCE / VALUE

Value-based, Equity Sharing

Pay for Performance

Commission-based

SPEND

PRIMARY DRIVER

TIME / LABOR

Retainer/Staffing/ Talent-based

Fixed Fee

Deliverable-based

OUTPUT / DELIVERABLES

COMMISSION-BASED AGREEMENTS

Although there are different types of commission-based models, such as fixed percentage or variable percentage based on volume of spend (aka sliding scale), they are all based on the concept that agencies are compensated based on a commission applied to the cost of media. Commission-based agreements are naturally limited to relationships where media plays a big role in the services provided. They therefore have more limited applicability than fee-based or incentive-based agreements. The oldest form of agency compensation, the commission system, presented some unique benefits: simple, easy to understand and administer, and clients only spent media dollars on campaigns that performed well. Arguably, agencies were highly motivated to produce successful campaigns that would be in media outlets, since they were paid a commission on all media placements. The commission system has limited applicability and more questionable value today. Clients do not want to subject themselves to the potential bias of agencies promoting higher-spend or media-based activities when other alternatives might be more appealing. Given the fragmentation of the media landscape and the growth of digital and earned media that result in smaller but more targeted media buys (or no buy at all), commission-based agreements are too precarious for agencies. Although commission-based agreements are facing rapid extinction in most developed countries, calculating commission rates is still a common metric for check-and-balance purposes. Commission based agreements made a comeback in recent years, as a result of advertisers looking for simpler methodologies in the context of programmatic buying. However, fee-based compensation agreements (fixed or variable) are the most common, because advertisers have a reasonably sound understanding and full visibility into the tangible resources agencies are assigning to their account.

AGENCY VIEWPOINT

"Financial structures changed dramatically when we went from a commission base to an hourly base. ... My guess is we'll continue on hourly base with more of a performance component."[112]

—HARRIS DIAMOND, CHAIRMAN AND CEO, MCCANN
WORLDGROUP

Let's explore the different types of fee-based agreements:

FIXED-FEE AGREEMENTS

Under this type of agreement, the client agrees to pay a fixed amount to the agency to deliver according to a specific project or an agreed scope of work for a given period. The fee is fixed regardless of whether the agency will require slightly more or less (or a different set of) resources to get the job done. So, payment is pretty much guaranteed, pending completion of the work. Fixed fee agreements are perhaps the simplest form of compensation, and the most common one for advertisers with "open source" agency models that emphasize choice and flexibility, sometimes at the expense of cost efficiencies that can be realized by the economies of scale of retainer-based agreements. A project is priced for a set of deliverables. The negotiated fee does not vary. There are no strings attached on either side. There is no reconciliation in the backend. If the agency uses resources to get this done, they will either pick up the difference or drop it to the bottom line.

Project-based relationships are the least preferred by most

agencies. There is no upfront financial commitment and limited line of sight into resource allocation. However, if the fixed fee is a labor based fixed fee (based on a staffing plan without reconciliation), there is still pressure for the agency to provide top resources, as it will impact the project work and, eventually, whether the account becomes a longer-term relationship. Top resources are usually the most visible, and advertisers can tell if they aren't getting the amount of attention from them that was committed. "Upon completion" agreements also put much pressure on agencies, as payment is made when the services have been fully completed. Fee revenue recognized on a completed contract basis contributes to higher seasonality.

Straight-lined contracts are usually preferred by agencies as they guarantee a predictable revenue flow. It also helps agencies to meet their cash flow needs as most agency expenses are paid currently, including payroll, taxes, rent, utilities, insurance, equipment leases, and software licenses. This type of compensation is mostly common with agencies that are on a trial basis before a client further commits. Like project-based agreements, the negotiated fee in fixed agreements does not vary, no matter what the circumstances. Considered relatively more simple than variable labor-based agreements, once the fixed fee has been agreed upon, no reconciliation is needed to track individual cost elements or resource utilization. This is particularly popular among agencies that do not believe in asking employees to fill out timesheets. Simplicity is one of the main benefits here. It doesn't, however, allow much flexibility, which proves to be challenging for advertisers in highly volatile or unpredictable industries, requiring them to set bare minimum staffing and fees with their agencies. Fixed-fee agreements come in different flavors and can be set up several different ways, including a labor-based fixed fee, a negotiated fixed fee, or a fixed fee built on staffing at hourly rates.

RETAINER/STAFFING/TALENT-BASED AGREEMENTS

The most common form of payment for professional services of all types is in the form of billable hours. Time and labor-based type agreements have been in place for many years. This model has received the favor of many advertisers who, under cost and financial pressure, realized that the commissions paid were, in large part, an unjustifiable and excessive agency cost to deliver these services that ultimately would provide agencies a disincentive to be media agnostic. The concept is well understood, as it is standard in other professional services. The advertiser agrees to a fee amount to deliver against an agreed scope of work, for a given period, in return for a forecasted number of agency resources at a given hourly rate. The scope of work includes a detailed description of the deliverables, schedule, and other agency responsibilities. Variable labor-based agreements are based on the notion that an annual financial commitment by the client enables its agency to staff the account with the best resources while realizing economies of scale, which are then passed on to the client as discounted rates.

Full Time Equivalent (FTE) is a term used to express a unit of client labor that is equivalent to one full time employee or multiple shared employees adding up to the equivalent of one individual. The hourly rates by function (Creative Director) or by individual (Joe Smith, Account Director) are calculated based on direct labor, overhead, and the agreed profit margin. A rate card is produced that summarizes rates by job function, which is used by the agency to determine staffing plans based on set budgets. Some may use average functional (vs. individual) salary or blended rates to simplify an already complicated approach. The number, type, and percentage of time allocated per individual (whether dedicated or shared resources) are determined based on scope of work requirements. The number of FTEs required is based on an agreed baseline of annual work hours (which typically exclude vacation, sick time, and holidays).

AGENCY VIEWPOINT

"Retainers can keep creativity stuck in a swirl. It's not that retainers are evil, but they often lead to unclear briefs, unnecessary meetings, misbehavior, noise, and frustration on all sides." [113]

—**MARK POLLARD,** STRATEGY CEO, MIGHTY JUNGLE

For global relationships, the denominator for annual work hours may vary as the contract must comply with local laws. For example, France and Germany have more restrictive labor laws than most countries. Agencies can generate additional profit to the bottom line when a billable employee works more than the typical average work hours. For that reason, clients typically request that the agency not pass on charges to the client for more than the determined number of hours per year for an individual, which would equate to 100 percent of billable time for that individual. Any time spent over and above a typical work day benefits the client. The agency and the client monitor utilization of billable hours against the contracted number and decide if some type of financial reconciliation is required. Staff utilization is traditionally defined as the percentage of billable hours utilized relative to the number of hours contracted. Typically, an allowable band is determined, and if staff utilization falls within that band (plus or minus a few percentage points), no financial adjustment is needed.

Unlike the fixed fee compensation model, both parties agree to monitor utilization of staff resources and reset staffing and fee resources based on pre-agreed reconciliation terms. The actualization of costs or resources used typically takes place at the completion of a project or a determined contract period (often annually or quarterly). The annual reconciliation is conducted to ensure the client is getting what it paid for and that no one unfairly benefits from the arrangement: A client could request higher paid employees once staffing and fees have been determined; an agency could delay hiring of key talent or bring lower-paid employees onto the account, effectively improving margin. For agencies, tracking and reporting actual time by individual resource is a necessity. Getting staff to fill time sheets accurately (especially creatives) is also challenging, adding to the skepticism shared by clients about the accountability of time-based arrangements that often result in financial audits. Furthermore, many agencies push back on or refuse to use time sheets altogether, arguing against variable based fee agreements that put too much emphasis on time and labor instead of performance and value. Advertisers must also take into consideration that these agreements require greater administrative efforts and, in turn, higher administration costs for advertisers and agencies. Some might argue that the significant time and resources an agency spends in recording, tracking, and reporting labor utilization might be better spent servicing clients and driving results.

In a fee-based agreement, clients typically spread payments evenly throughout the year. With recurring monthly payments, the agency is benefiting from a predictable revenue flow from the client, regardless of potential "peaks and valleys" in terms of agency workload. Fees should be reviewed periodically and adjusted based on material changes to the scope of work and associated staffing plan. Both parties must agree on the number of acceptable change orders and restatement periods. Finding the right balance between revenue/fee predictability for the agency and scope of work flexibility for the client is at the core of typical agency fee negotiations. Advertisers and agencies have increasingly challenged this fee model because it is based on the notion that the clients pay for time, regardless of how effectively that time might be spent and regardless of performance. Rance Crain, former president of Crain Communications and editor-in-chief for *Advertising Age*, said it best: "So nowadays, agencies get paid for their work like accountants and attorneys do, based on a negotiated fee. They get paid whether their ads run or how much their client spends. In most cases, they get paid the same for good or bad advice—just like lawyers do."

CLIENT VIEWPOINT

"Mutual accountability means everyone must have skin in the game. At J&J, we have been proponents of pay for performance type arrangements with our agencies since 2001. Agencies respect and want that accountability." [114]

—**JAMES R.** ZAMBITO, SENIOR DIRECTOR GLOBAL CORPORATE AFFAIRS, JOHNSON & JOHNSON

Another disappearing form of labor-based compensation is "cost-plus," implying that the client will compensate for actual (vs. estimated) agency expenses plus an agreed upon margin. This is mostly beneficial to agencies, as they're guaranteed to be compensated based on actual costs, even if those increase unexpectedly. This is unpopular among clients due to the lack of budget predictability and lack of incentive for cost-control.

DELIVERABLE-BASED AGREEMENTS

Advertisers are increasingly moving away from AOR-type committed models to more output/deliverable and project-based work. Per a survey[81] by RSW/US in 2017, 35% of agencies stated that most of their work is project-based compared to 20% the year prior, showing a trend towards more flexible arrangements for advertisers and therefore less predictability for agencies. Project work is often associated with deliverable-based pricing as the focus is on the output rather than on agency staffing and agency fees. However, output/deliverable-based pricing is occasionally found in AOR type relationships. Those are often split into two types of compensation methods: tactical, with output/deliverable-based pricing for what needs to be produced, and strategic, a retainer that covers the most valuable agency resources assigned to the account. Project-based relationships assume a set menu price per deliverable (e.g., $5,000 for deliverable type A) or a sort of bidding process (often based on an agreed upon hourly rate card) by which advertisers submit a proposal for clients to evaluate. Set menu pricing addresses the most common deliverables or assets produced (sometimes referred to as unit-based pricing) but requires a solid taxonomy. The pricing menu is often set and mandated across multiple agency relationships for consistency purposes. In other cases, under the bidding approach, the agency can submit their proposal based on pre-agreed rates, but the actual cost per deliverable may vary significantly from one agency to another.

Pricing typically varies based on the type of deliverable (e.g., 30s TV spot, print ad, etc.) and the complexity of that deliverable. The client then either selects the most compelling proposal, in the case of a bidding scenario, or compares the proposal to their "should-cost model," which compares the cost per asset to a benchmark database, to ensure the deliverable has been priced competitively. This approach is gaining momentum, because it finally allows clients to use comparable data to make better informed decisions about costs. There are inherent challenges associated with output/deliverable-based pricing. It's clearly geared toward a more production-type relationship, as more strategic engagements that may not lend themselves to explicit deliverables are harder to price using this methodology. The unpredictability of project-work relationships, when combined with the rigor of output/deliverable-based pricing, raised several concerns from the agency community around pricing fairness. Many agencies questioned the relevancy and credibility of clients using benchmarking data to construct fee schedules for non-deliverable-based services like strategy and ideation. They also face the challenge of providing consistent staffing and resource allocation without a revenue commitment from clients. Project work relationships and conflict policies often collide. Should conflict clauses go away and clients be more accepting in project-based agreements? Are advertisers really open to working with constantly changing agency staff or resource allocation issues? In 2016 4As and ANA released new guidelines titled "Agency Reviews for Project Work Guidance Considerations,[82]" outlining best-practice recommendations designed to bring greater consistency to how competitive reviews for project assignments are conducted by marketers and agencies.

AGENCY VIEWPOINT

"The model of the future will be an output-based model where agencies are compensated based on agreed-upon deliverables. This way, the scope of work is defined and staffed and planned against, but agencies are free to find the most efficient and innovative way to deliver against the mandate." [115]

—ALISTER ADAMS, VP DIGITAL, PUBLICIS

In recent years, we've seen new and creative models emerge from innovative agencies and advertisers who pave the way, from Pay for Performance to IP-sharing or sales-based royalties. Such models already exist in other service industries such as the music business, software development, and photography. They challenge conventional wisdom and traditional compensation methods in which a company operates as "agents" on the client's behalf. They are simply rejecting what they consider to be the "ancestral" principles of hourly billing and labor-based agreements that reward regardless of business output. They are viscerally opposed to the notion of agencies contributing only time and effort to their clients. Agencies want more ownership. Ultimately, agencies want to see radical changes in the way they are to be compensated for their work. They want compensation to be based on the results they help produce, the value they provide, and the intellectual property they create, not the time they spend or the costs they incur. For the most part, clients concur, but it often sounds better on paper than in practice, as this compensation model is harder to set up and administer. Let's take a closer look.

PAY FOR PERFORMANCE AGREEMENTS

The idea behind Pay for Performance (aka PFP or P4P) is quite simple in theory, but putting it into practice can prove to be challenging. It comes from having any part of the client/agency compensation, above and beyond the baseline compensation, contingent on meeting or exceeding agreed upon performance metrics, like the way a sales organization might be compensated. Or an attorney hired on contingency, hoping to receive a percentage of the damages awarded in favor of his client, a concept that is far from being new to the business world. It was new to the agency community until P&G pioneered the idea of tying client/agency compensation to business results based on principles familiar to the packaged goods giant. As a matter of fact, P&G introduced a profit-sharing program giving employees an ownership stake in the company as early as 1887. Today, P&G's P4P agreements are reported to be split between quantitative measures (sales and share) and qualitative measures (performance evaluation), with sales being the biggest driver. Also, commonly known as "Payment by Results" or "Performance-Based" agreements, these bonuses are now common to many relationships. Variable pay outcome is mostly about getting active involvement in driving toward the desired outcome. Failing to reward employees, or even vendors, for outstanding performance and superior results might be one of the greatest missed opportunities of all time in business management.

When compensation and results are disconnected, and there is no upside for agencies going above and beyond, why should they? Arguably, at the essence of any business partnership is risk taking and upside sharing. At least, in principle. The fear of losing a client should motivate agencies, but it may not be enough on a consistent basis to ensure it meets or, better, exceeds expectations. Frankly, agencies can become compla-cent knowing that seeking a new agency can be an expensive endeavor and a major distraction for a client's core business. They need different motivation to provide added value effort. Many agency leaders believe that holding this "stick" over an agency's head isn't the most effective. Linking a portion of compensation to bonuses can provide greater alignment of interests. The concept of partnership is doubtful until both parties have skin in the game and the financial success of the agency is tied to client results or service levels. Giving agencies a stake in the performance of the work itself or the company's performance encourages "media-neutrality" and "discipline-neutrality" among specialty agencies, perhaps overtly focused on what they do vs. what's needed. It also encourages agencies to focus on what truly matters to the client. Clients typically rely on business metrics such as revenue growth or market share, leading indicators such as brand awareness, perception change, and relationship metrics, like those captured in performance reviews. For the most part, those companies who use perfor-mance incentives report that it does result in greater agency performance or getting alignment on important success metrics for the partnership.

I say for the most part that the rapid adoption of this type of agreement has led to some inherent challenges for smaller adver-tisers who are ill-prepared to successfully implement changes to get the intended benefits. These challenges often include the following: the link between agency and business results is often hard to establish, or blurry at best, unless scorecards are activity-based instead of focused on tangible value; the finan-cial upside is often not material enough to drive meaningful behavioral change; the risk/reward equation is not balanced (i.e., risk is too great for the upside potential); the advertiser's bonus budgeting is too complex (how much should they set aside to pay the bonus the following fiscal year once assessment is complete, etc.); and the third party costs associated with tracking brand metrics is often prohibitive for smaller clients. Lastly, the efforts to set up such agreements and the ongoing monitoring and sometimes tense or even contagious dialogue with agencies often is perceived as outweighing the benefits.

AGENCY VIEWPOINT

"A baseball player that hits over .300 is considered a star and yet seven out of 10 times they effectively 'strike out.' Similarly, in the agency business we don't always hit home runs (especially considering the variables out of our control). But it's a player's batting average that counts that allows them to command higher pay until they no longer consistently deliver. Agency compensation, like a sports athlete, a movie star, photographer, director, or other creative services, is based on PAST performance and FUTURE EXPECTATIONS. If they no longer perform over time, they are either fired or no longer hired." [116]

—NEAL GROSSMAN, CHIEF OPERATING OFFICER—AMERICAS AT EG+ WORLDWIDE AND THE DESIGNORY

I asked for the opinion of agency leaders. They believe that advertisers should first and foremost recognize that they are dealing with creative services and, as is often the case in creative services, the hit/miss ratio varies. They believe that the downside risk has not been compensated by sufficient upside reward to warrant having much "skin in the game," and that this compensation model has yielded limited rewards even when an agency hits a home run. This might be due to a number of factors including: 1) Junior staff are often given equal weighting in determining an agency's score; 2) Meets, exceeds, ... "satisfaction" is inherently biased as "meets expectations" is a more common score in evaluations than "exceeds expectations," since everyone's normal expectations are for better than average results—so the bar is set so high that achieving a full bonus is often difficult, even when hitting a home run; 3) Advertisers often don't budget for full bonuses, which makes the evaluations more biased and the higher scores difficult to achieve; 4) So many variables are beyond the agency's control such that agencies may not get rewarded fully. On the other hand, when things go badly beyond the agency's control, then the agency often feels the full brunt of that.

According to the *ANA Client/Agency Compensation Guidebook*, "A major impetus for the use of performance incentives has come from advertisers challenging the idea of having to pay the same for mediocre work as for outstanding work. Looked at another way, many advertisers are willing to pay a premium for work that proves itself in the market." Just how much of a premium is often the hard question to answer. They make an excellent point. Marketers want to reward excellent work, if that work is yielding the desired results. Who wouldn't? P4P programs are set up based on the principle that a noticeable and impactful shift in interest, attitudes, and behavior can be expected from the agency when operating under this type of compensation agreement; there is a greater level of focus on things that matter most. As a result, the client is not taken for granted. Everyone on the account seems to try harder, everyone is well informed about their contribution to the business, and so forth. Simply stated, paying more is fine when you are getting more as well. For any potential upside, there is a potential downside, balancing rewards and risks accordingly. Advertisers and agencies must ultimately agree on the objectives, the risks and potential earn out, and the measurement and evaluation system. Setting up this type of compensation agreement is a collaborative process that must be based on complete transparency and trust. Given the growing importance of this type of agency compensation agreement in years to come, we will go slightly deeper and I will articulate here some of the best practices every brand advertiser should consider:

KEY SUCCESS INGREDIENTS TO PERFORMANCE-BASED AGREEMENTS

| DEFINE REALISTIC AND ACHIEVABLE OBJECTIVES FROM THE OUTSET | METRIC AND MEASUREMENT NEED TO BE MUTUALLY AGREED UPON | DETERMINE PROFIT TARGETS AT DIFFERENT LEVELS OF PERFORMANCE IN GOOD FAITH | CONDUCT REGULAR CHECK POINTS TO MEASURE PROGRESS | SET AN ADEQUATE BUDGET AND PAYMENT SCHEDULE |

Define realistic and achievable objectives from the outset.
Typical objectives are: 1) quantitative, based on business performance (sales, profits, growth, share, stock value, customer satisfaction, etc.) AND marketing communications metrics (awareness, perception shifting, recall, engagement, site traffic, profiles, response and conversion rates, cost per click, cost per lead); or 2) qualitative, such as thought leadership, creative, innovation, and customer service; or ideally 3) a combination of both to provide a comprehensive view into how well the agency is performing. Most common brand criteria are sales awareness, perception shifting, and response rates. These are more easily attributable to the agency's performance compared to metrics such as company profits, stock value, or brand equity that can be, in some industries, outside of the direct span of control of the agency. If the performance evaluation includes multiple metrics, these should be prioritized and weighted accordingly. Stay away from intangible metrics that might be too vague or arguable, leading to endless,

wasteful debates with the agency as to whether the objectives were accomplished and the agency should be paid. Give yourself enough time to measure progress by the time you must determine what the agency is entitled to. Not all agencies are comfortable with business metrics weighted so heavily, many of which are out of their control. While agencies are not responsible 100 percent for sales results, advertisers significantly influence the direction of the agency work—so the agency's compensation is tied to the performance of work that may or may not be 100 percent supported as the agency's recommended strategy.

Other relevant questions advertisers should ask themselves are: Should agencies be penalized for the massive recall and product quality issues of their clients? Probably not. Advertisers should ask themselves: Are the objectives clear and specific enough? Are they realistic? Do they stretch the agency enough? Are those objectives within the agency's control or influence? Are they promoting shared accountability? Can they be effectively and accurately measured? Are the goals time-bound, so performance can be assessed within a time-window during which the agency can positively impact them? Is there an inherent bias in the chosen qualitative metrics? Is the agreement flexible enough that goals can be reset if mutually agreed?

AGENCY VIEWPOINT

"We're not lawyers or accountants. We are creative people. We need to assert the principles of partnership. To do away with time sheets means we have to radically change our traditional agency philosophy of work to revolutionize, improve, and invigorate the way business is done today." [118]

—KERRY GRAHAM, FOUNDER, THE BRAND HOTEL, LLC

Metrics and measurement need to be mutually agreed upon.
Too often metrics are dictated to agencies without a lot of choice
given to the agency other than to agree to them or walk away
from the business. Consideration should be given not only to
the metrics that will be used and to specific target goals, but how
the information will be collected, by whom, for what period,
when it will be reported, and how it can be validated. For
qualitative objectives, determining who makes the final call on
whether a goal was met or exceeded expectations is also critical.
The computation of results may vary based on the level of specificity sought: Some criteria may be weighted more heavily than
others (business metrics such as sales might represent one third
of the incentive budget, marketing communications metrics
such as favorability might represent another third, and qualitative assessment such as customer service or collaboration might
represent the remaining third). The qualitative assessment must
be conducted as objectively as possible, even though the qualitative measures are inherently subjective. The agency's incentive
can then be calculated and distributed based on a basic scoring
system (e.g., needs improvement, achieved, or exceeded).

**Determine profit targets at different levels of performance
in good faith.** It assumes that the advertiser already has a solid
understanding of compensation benchmarks across the industry.
It also assumes that the incentive is meaningful enough to
positively impact the relationship. For this discussion, if you
assume 15 percent margin as the industry norm (numbers tend
to vary significantly by type of agency and client), the agency
might be willing to risk all or some of its profit (typically in the
5 percent to 10 percent range) in return for a potential uplift
deemed appealing enough (typically in the 20 to 25 percent

range) upon meeting jointly agreed objectives. Most agencies feel the potential bonus in exchange for the downside should be higher, a sensitive topic to this day. And the reality is that agencies only earn a portion of the bonus potential. So, for example, if an agency is at 15 percent profit and gives up 5 percent so the base compensation is 10 percent in exchange for a bonus that would get them to 20 percent. Agencies on average would likely achieve 50 percent of the PFP or 5 percent of the 10 percent, which would just get them back to the 15 percent. So, in effect, agencies end up with a 5 percent downside with the likely potential to just get back to the 15 percent where they were before. Not much of a reward if you ask agency leaders, some of them doubtful of the true upside.

Clients should set a base level compensation that is fair relative to industry standards. McDonald's Corp. reviewed its consolidated US creative account, inviting holding companies Omnicom Group and Publicis Groupe, owners of its existing shops (DDB and Leo Burnett, respectively), as well as WPP to pitch the account. Yet less than two weeks later, WPP withdrew from the contest without explanation. Ad Age reported that the terms of the pitch might be the reason: the RFP stipulated that the agency would operate at cost, essentially breaking even. There was the potential for some profit incentives should the shop meet certain market metrics (likely sales-based) but also more subjective metrics established by McDonald's. The brand was also reportedly insisting on a restrictive conflict clause—that any agency in the pitch cannot have conflicts in food retail, including convenience stores. It didn't seem to work for WPP. Make sure that the terms get established in good faith. Typically, a minimum margin level is guaranteed to the agency, preventing agencies from staffing at the bare minimum to reduce expenses in the event it is unsuccessful. But some clients have been pushing for all profits to be based upon performance. Some may risk all their profit, but few will risk doing work at less than break-even since it effectively threatens the viability of the agency. Are the trade-offs commensurate with the risk taken by the agency? Some agencies have found that clients with a P4P compensation can be less profitable than clients without it. So, to work effectively, the upside must be somewhat proportional to the risk taken and vice versa. More importantly, it must be perceived equitable and fair by both parties.

AGENCY VIEWPOINT

"With accounts turning over more frequently and the trend toward more project-based work, having to make longer term commitments to costs such as real estate and equipment when client contracts can be terminated on relatively short notice, etc., these inherent risks already in place should not be overlooked. While costly for advertisers to change agencies, the relative cost impact to agencies is much greater." [119]
—NEAL GROSSMAN, CHIEF OPERATING OFFICER—AMERICAS AT EG+ WORLDWIDE AND THE DESIGNORY

Conduct regular check points to measure progress. Setting up a regular cadence to monitor performance gives the agency an opportunity to react and course-correct before the end of the period if results are not trending positively. It clearly takes special meaning when the agency's profitability is at risk. No one wants to be surprised by the outcome. Furthermore, if the

KPIs do matter, they should be part of the way the business and the agencies are managing their efforts. If both parties agree to reset on the metrics or targets due to significant scope of work changes or material events (acquisitions, economic conditions) it can be done at such time. Communication and transparency are key, from start to finish.

Set adequate budget and payment schedule. Advertisers should budget assuming the maximum payout and have the reserve in place if/when full payment is due. They can effectively pay the full amount on the regular payment schedule and ask for a credit at the end of the year if the agency didn't earn all the incentive. Or the client can set aside the incremental budget to pay for the incentive at the end of the year, a preferable scenario from a cash flow perspective. P4P models are always challenging to implement for clients without prior experience in this area. But it should not deter you from implementing it or at least experimenting to get a feel for it. Agencies are likely to question aggressive, even punitive, P4P models where all or a sizeable portion of the agency's profit is at risk. Advertisers are often concerned about bonuses that do not get systematically passed on to the actual staff working on the account instead of being added to the agency's bottom line, which defeats the purpose of these incentives.

However, it's difficult for agencies to guarantee staff bonuses for various reasons: not all accounts are the same, some accounts may be profitable with or without the P4P, etc. Agency leaders ask: "Should the agency reward the staff on the less profitable account and not the ones on the more profitable account, just because the less profitable one has a P4P component? Also, if someone does award-winning work but the account is not as profitable as others, should they not be rewarded?" They believe that the P4P is just one part of the overall agency compensation and it should be up to the agency how to distribute rewards to its staff, regardless of the compensation methodology. Once objectives are set, to work effectively, the agency must have a seat at the table whenever important decisions are made that might impact the performance of the program they have shared accountability for.

New relationships benefit the least from P4P agreements because they usually require a certain degree of familiarity with the account. Agency performance is highly subjective without quantifiable metrics, exposing agencies unduly to risks due to mergers or acquisitions, or frequent changes in management. Regardless of the level of rigor and integrity applied to this process, it requires a fair amount of trust between the client and the agency. After all, the client is often on point to collect and to report and compare results with objectives. Trust is earned over time; so well-established client/agency relationships seem to be best positioned to use P4P. This is the reason why it is often recommended that for new client relationships, a fee is agreed to for at least the first 6 to 12 months before instituting P4P, so that the new agency and client can become more familiar with each other, the goals and objectives that matter most, how they'll work together, etc.

In my experience, this type of compensation model also tends to work better with advertisers that have implemented a similar bonus program for employees and/or upper management based on company and/or individual performance for two primary reasons: 1) It demonstrates that the company has already bought in into the concept of P4P, which is that the work will generate a measurable business benefit, and 2) It indicates that the company has already identified the metrics by which performance will be measured, making this a shorter ramp up for everyone involved. For the most part, it is a philosophical approach that typically is anchored into a company's culture and ways of doing business. If a company hasn't set an incentive pay program internally for its employees, the chances for such an incentive program for vendors to work are limited. P4P agreements are also more commonly found among large advertisers. It has nothing to do with risk tolerance but has to do with complexity and client bandwidth. Large companies are more likely able to afford the time and resources to set up, manage, and administer this type of elaborate compensation agreement than small ones.

This type of agreement has been challenged by some in recent years, questioning its impact and highlighting the common challenges expressed by both advertisers and agencies in making this work. It's true that unless these performance-based agreements are set up properly, they are likely to create headaches and disappoint. The benefits must outweigh the time, resources, and costs required to manage it. So, do it right or don't do it at all. An independent consultant might be a valuable resource to busy clients for the heavy-lifting, facilitating the selection of goals and metrics, as well as reporting results and payout. Bad, good, or excellent work should not be compensated the same. As labor-based agreements grew in popularity, so did the perception that agencies are in the business of selling time by filling timesheets.

We know however that agencies are in the business of driving measurable results for clients. Clients prosper or die based on a few key performance metrics. So should their agencies. P4P compensation is recalibrating the relationship to be results vs. activity focused. It encourages agencies to engage with clients upstream and more strategically about what they can control and what they might be able to influence, including timing, pricing, and retail and channel distribution. The reality is that it requires agencies having a seat at the table, which advertisers often are reluctant to provide. The greatest value realized from P4P is clarity of goals, aligned priorities, and stronger synergy. In the end, P4P agreements are intended to increase accountability and strengthen the strategic relationship between clients and agencies. Keep it simple. Advertisers and agencies want to focus their energy on driving business performance first and foremost, not in endless agency negotiations or distracting and overcomplicated compensation agreements. According to the ANA Agency Compensation study titled "Trends in Agency Compensation, 17th Edition[83]," the use of labor-based fees has decreased for the first time since 2006, along with the use of performance incentives, while traditional (non-incentive-based) commissions seem to have gained popularity among brands trying to simplify their agency compensation practices in an increasingly complex digital marketing landscape.

AGENCY VIEWPOINT

"CMOs claim they don't know how to budget for an agreement, the cost of which could not be accurately predicted. My own answer was: Set your budget on the assumption of success. If we don't deliver the results, then you've got extra money at the end of the year, so you'll look good either way." [120]

—KEITH REINHARD, CHAIRMAN EMERITUS, DDB WORLDWIDE

VALUE-BASED, EQUITY-SHARING AGREEMENTS

What do lip balms, newborns, and marijuana have in common? They're markets taken on by agencies who are not only helping clients advertise products, they're developing brands of their own. The agency Anomaly helped develop and incubate a new, modern line of global skin and beauty care focused on lip balms and shaving products. In 2013 its EOS line became the best-selling lip balm in the US, outselling market leaders ChapStick and Blistex.[84] Talk about having skin in the game! Anomaly also helped create/launch a cannabis company's product, which uses science to deliver specific doses and targeted health benefits for consumers. It was named by *Time* as one of the 25 Best Inventions of 2016. Anomaly has a history of incubating and creating joint ventures, ranging from skin care products to fashion and music. They are not alone. Agency Schafer Condon Carter created and sold Hogwash, a low-carb, low-calorie, kids' juice drink brand to a bottling company.[85] IPG's digital agency R/GA and its Accelerator team helped create/fund new technology: a newborn wearable device called Owlet, awarded for their innovation at the Cannes Lions. As part of its IoT Venture Studio UK initiative, the agency selected 10 IoT startups to receive funding, guidance, and access to the agency's roster of clients and services (e.g., smart light switches, contactless payments, pay-as-you-fly drone insurance, in-home beacons, smart photo capture for live events, and a food-waste tracking system).

A new type of compensation agreement has recently emerged, suggested by agencies looking for creative ways to overthrow traditional cost-based compensation philosophies considered flawed and grossly inadequate. They argue that the ingenuity of what they do is in the approach they take and the value they create as a result, not how many bodies they assign to the account. Staples's "Easy Button" idea developed by McCann Erickson was so successful that the company ended up producing the buttons and selling them in their store. Agencies are licensing technology and applications they built for some clients and now offering them to others. Entrepreneurial independent agency Mother New York created and sold a hot-dog business called Dogmatic, inspired from their travel through Europe. Other agencies like Euro RSCG, who create songs for their clients, also generate revenue from in-house record labels. For agencies willing to go outside their core offering, the revenue opportunities seem endless. These innovative concepts are putting emphasis on value, not cost, answering a fundamental desire by clients to see their agencies laser-focused on what matters most to them.

Value-based: If P4P is predominantly focused on results, another form of compensation is making waves centered on the ultimate end goal of any partnership: "value." Value is the worth expressed in monetary terms of the benefits (however it is defined) a client receives in exchange for the price it pays for a given market offering. Advertisers genuinely know that their agencies add tremendous value to their marketing efforts. But how is that value defined? By whom? And how is it measured? Naturally, it comes in different flavors depending on who is defining it. Here's the challenge: for agencies, it is based on the principle that they should be entitled to a portion of the value they create on their clients' behalf. For clients, it is based on the principle that clients should pay for the value they believe they are receiving from their agency, which may or may not be based on in-market results. They might receive a royalty for the life of the work produced. It is a highly subjective measure and works best when the value created can be sustained over time. It is therefore extensively debated and difficult to agree on. Some call it Utopian: admirable but impracticable. For that reason, it will take time for this type of compensation to go "mainstream." To date it seems to work better with smaller, more entrepreneurial advertisers that may lack funding to invest in additional new products or even marketing services. Larger advertisers tend to be much more averse to this approach. Similarly, agencies that are more independent have been able to experiment with this more than holding company agencies because Wall Street does not yet recognize revenues from these sources as recurring but rather one-offs that are not given added valuation to holding company stocks.

Consultants like Ronald Baker and Alan Weiss have published books about value-based pricing (*Professional's Guide to Value Pricing* and *Value-Based Fees* respectively), promoting an alternative to existing compensation methods and moving beyond the old "time plus materials" concept employed by so many professional services. Although their views are not specifically focused on advertising, marketing, and communication agencies, they are emphasizing the need for anyone in professional services to change their views on how to price their services, from selling time to generating profit from their intellectual capital, and in the process, permanently getting rid of time sheets. It's important to distinguish value from price in this concept. Raising or lowering price does not in effect change value but, instead, provides an incentive or disincentive to purchase. So, the incentive to purchase must exceed the one from the competition, which implies that clients must gain visibility into market rates.

Value-based compensation is based on a powerful idea. In 2008, The Coca-Cola Company (TCCC) designed an elaborate value-based compensation model[86] with deliverables prices based on historical pricing and perceived value and with profitability solely contingent on meeting performance goals. The company piloted the model and the following year rolled it out to key markets, hoping to replace its labor-based approach and create incentives for agencies. Previously TCCC agencies were guaranteed a profit, which now must be earned. TCCC compensation model is based on two principles: investing in outputs based on scope of work deliverables and rewarding outcomes that are based on actual performance. The pay for performance component, which replaces discretionary bonuses, adds a 30 percent or higher bonus markup onto the base fee. The scope of work is broken down into discreet creative and media deliverables by various campaign development stages, from research and brand strategy to proof of concept, adaptation, trafficking, and measurement. A database of cost per deliverable is helping TCCC figure out what things have historically cost them and the highest and lowest they would be willing to invest in per deliverable. TCCC model assumes a base value range is determined per deliverable based on historical cost per deliverable (the price paid for similar work in the past) and value perception based on past work and project parameters (budget, strategic nature of the assignment, talent requirements, and so on).

Over time, Coca-Cola built a comprehensive database of spend information based on different types of assignments that allows them to determine the "value" of a project. Once the value has been defined per deliverable, then the pay for performance amount is defined along with metrics and weighting. Although the model has received mixed feedback (who ultimately defines "value?"), it has certainly generated much interest. To this day, TCCC approach by Coca-Cola has been challenged by agencies claiming that the 30% profit markup is actually a 23 percent gross profit margin. As a result, under the model where base compensation has zero profit, agencies effectively give up 15–18 percent gross profit margins (guaranteed downside) in exchange for a 5–8 percent upside. To them, it doesn't seem like a fair exchange since agencies need to earn 70 to 78 percent of the bonus to be at the same base compensation gross profit margin they were at prior to the change. And earning more than 70–78 percent of a bonus (for reasons already articulated) is highly unlikely.

AGENCY VIEWPOINT

"[There's] a sigh of relief from the CEO or CMO when they hear that we're willing to share their risk. We want to do great work, but we're no longer walking in with a preconceived notion of what's right." [121]

—STEPHEN GOLDBLATT, FOUNDER, PARTNERS IN CRIME, LLC

Revenue and profit-sharing: Sales-based royalties or profit-sharing agreements are fundamentally transforming the nature of the client/vendor relationship into a business partnership. They introduce the notion of risk- and reward-sharing by giving the agency an opportunity to invest in building value that can be monetized or in sharing sales associated with the activities driven by the agency. Or the agency might introduce a new product line on the client's behalf by giving up its time in return for a share of the revenue and profits. It might also consider being compensated by taking ownership into a new business venture, officially becoming a business partner to the client as Haggar Clothing did with its agency Crispin Porter + Bogusky. The concept was based on whether an agency and its client were willing to incorporate a certain level of risk and reward in the compensation that tied back to not only to performance, but to business ownership and long-term profitability. The possibility in this area is endless. I suspect, however, that advertisers will not move in that direction on their own, or if they do, they'll do so very cautiously. Agencies might find it possible to monetize the value of their engagement with consumers, above and beyond their client assignment, developing and distributing surplus entertainment content. Smaller advertisers who want to subsidize some of their agency costs might be more open to this type of arrangement.

Another type of related compensation approach is shared ownership, also popular in the corporate world where employees are eligible to earn stock or ownership shares in the company. As in profit-sharing agreements that are based on sales, the potential earn-out is based on how well the company is performing (or is perceived to be performing in the case of public companies). Once an employee or an agency has equity in a company, it suddenly changes the nature of the relationship, as both parties share the financial outcome, good or bad.

AGENCY VIEWPOINT

"The agency of the future does more than provide sheer services and makes money from more than just tracking hours and getting paid for that. It means creating your own IP and your own products. It means behaving a little more like an investor. It means creating your own content, legitimately." [122]

—ALAIN SYLVAIN, FOUNDER AND CEO, SYLVAIN LABS, INC.

IP-based: Agencies are now challenging the client's outright ownership of intellectual property rights and pushing for alternative limited-ownership licensing arrangements that give them skin in the game. IP-sharing agreements tend to focus on the value of the intellectual property generated by the agency as part of a client assignment. Under the concept of IP-sharing, an agency might develop a Web experience with functionality (e.g., an automated reminder service) that it intends to resell to other clients or customize for them at a profit. In this instance, the agency would agree to restrictions by agreeing to not make this solution available to companies in the same business to protect their client's interest without limiting their ability to profit from it. In a digital world where agencies are asked to write code to develop engaging digital experiences, the temptation for agencies to fully or partially own the IP is increasingly higher. Advertisers are not likely, however, to agree to sharing the IP of innovative, creative ideas that are natural extensions of the brand identity or brand assets for which they want to retain full ownership. I also suspect that digital agencies are more likely to seek this type of partnership opportunity. This type of compensation agreement is far more complex to set up and presents higher risks for business conflicts with continued pressure on the relationship. It is, however, likely to become the norm, especially for client assignments that require a fair amount of development and innovative applications. Agencies are driving tech and IP investments and solutions for clients.

The agency Anomaly, mentioned earlier for developing the EOS lip product line, continues to challenge our understanding of what it means to be in the agency business by branching out into intellectual property creations such as a joint venture with street-culture brand Mighty Jaxx, which creates limited-edition

3D art figures out of 2D sketches from street artists around the world and sells them online and in retail. Some of these agencies are changing their business models and offerings. Many agencies like NextTECHnow (Starcom MediaVest) are increasingly establishing partnerships between startups and their clients. R/GA, named Ad Age's "2015 Agency of the Year," was acknowledged for its efforts in wearables and 3D printing. R/GA secured equity stake in more than 70 companies as part of its connected-device startups.[87] Its consulting arm, called "business transformation," accounted for a growing and sizable part of the agency's revenue.

STEP 4: NEGOTIATING COMPENSATION TERMS

CLIENT VIEWPOINT

"Too many clients cut into the bone and don't realize that they get what they pay for. If you've been cutting fees the last three or four years, it will directly correlate to the level of talent on the business and the level of satisfaction you have with the work from the agency." [123]

—KEN ROBINSON, OWNER, ARK ADVISORS

As Chester L. Karrass's book title explicitly states: "In business as in life, you don't get what you deserve. You get what you negotiate." Negotiations often start with familiar rituals: The advertiser insists on laying out their company policies, with justifications based on vague or inconclusive competitive benchmarks, boilerplate terms and conditions, and other non-negotiable issues. Agencies counter with "we are unique" arguments, guesstimates, case studies, references, and pages-long disclaimers. Both parties operate with little insight or trust. They do know how to align to their mutual interests. We've all seen this movie before. There is a better way. Let's start with a set of principles:

- First, agency compensation must be based on the total cost of the ownership, which means going beyond the typical agency costs, calculated by a fair and equitable profit margin, to also take into consideration the overall investment made by the client, the real and perceived value of the services received, and the potential long-term value of the relationship.

- Second, negotiations must, for the most part, be finalized before any internal or public announcement is made about the selected agency in the case of a search, or before any work gets initiated in the case of a contract renewal. An advertiser runs the risk of losing a strong hand at the negotiation table if it fails to lock on compensation early on. Once the announcement is made public or the work has started, all bets are made, and leverage has been lost. In some unfortunate cases, endless, wasteful negotiations by individuals that have not been empowered to make decisions may shorten the honeymoon and perhaps even deteriorate the relationship.

- Third, both sides must assign that responsibility to someone with adequate authority to make decisions. Most client contracts are individually negotiated and therefore, the terms and conditions, engagement profile, and the basis on which they generate revenue and profit vary significantly from one relationship to another, making it hard to apply best practices for clients in search of guidance.

- Fourth, if a cost-based compensation arrangement is selected, advertisers must have a clear understanding of the expense classification, definitions of compensation terms, direct and indirect agency costs included, and the cost accounting methods.

- Fifth, agreement to contractual terms other than agency compensation should not be overlooked before any internal or public announcement is made, including the need to lock on payment terms, reporting, year-end reconciliation, audit requirements and associated administrative costs, as well as ownership and indemnification.

- Finally, reporting requirements must be comprehensive enough to satisfy clients' need for agency transparency and reasonable costs. The agency financials related to a client should be reviewed annually. A financial reconciliation of payments ensures that the compensation model is adhered to and gives the opportunity for modifications of compensation terms in subsequent years if appropriate. Anything more frequent may not be needed.

"Negotiation is not a bad word. Through the years, we have learned that if we didn't lobby for fair agency fees, no one else would. Procurement's goal is to get the best possible price from vendors, and your goal should be to get the money you need to do the job properly and keep your business alive and healthy. These two worldviews are not mutually exclusive." [124]

DEACON WEBSTER, OWNER AND CCO, WALRUS

and

FRANCES WEBSTER, OWNER AND CEO, WALRUS

In healthy relationships, transparency and trust are critical success factors and signs of longevity. An open book approach builds trust in the relationship and shows that both parties want to establish a fair and equitable partnership. How often should you revisit compensation agreements? The short answer is how often you deem it is necessary. If the client or the agency experience major changes in business conditions that justify reevaluating terms, then it might be appropriate to do so. Otherwise, it is recommended to review those only every couple of years. In a period of economic uncertainty, advertisers may feel justified in revisiting some elements of the compensation terms annually to keep them market competitive. The process can be a major resource tax for both the agency and client, so more frequent re-evaluations might be wasteful and distracting for everyone. Compensation by its own nature is never static. It is subject to change based on the evolving nature and requirements of the relationship. The reality in is that every dollar in their bottom line is a dollar not ending up in yours. Advertisers are justifiably being diligent about finding the right compensation agreements. Unless a dollar in their bottom line has a multiplier effect on yours. In that case, it's worth the investment you are getting back. Advertisers must work with agencies in very close partnership to identify potential efficiency improvement. It is known that conditions of scarcity often produce more creative and innovative results than conditions of abundance. Any efficiency improvement should be mutually beneficial to the relationship.

STEP 5: ESTABLISHING A CLEAR SCOPE OF SERVICES AND SCOPE OF WORK

Once the compensation terms have been negotiated, the next logical step is providing the agencies absolute clarity about what outcome is expected and what assets must be produced. In our next chapter, we will go through the delicate but critical process of establishing a clear scope of work.

STEP 6: CONDUCTING REGULAR RECONCILIATIONS

There are at least three million burn cases every year in the United States. Yet burns are highly preventable. In the advertising world, "burn" has a vastly different meaning, and a controlled burn is more the focus. The large majority of client/agency relationships are retainer-based agreements: The advertiser/client commits to a budget for the year that covers fees for all agency staffing resources required to deliver against an agreed scope of work. The agency tracks and regularly reports back to the client on the productive utilization of their resources, effectively known as "FTE burn" or "retainer burn." In that context, "burn" is expected. What must be prevented however is excessive variance from the original committed budget. In deliverable-based agreements, the agency reports on the status of these deliverables, i.e., "open," "completed," "delayed," "in progress" with relevant commentaries. No matter the type of agreement a client may choose, a regular actualization or reconciliation process to ensure that the deliverables and/or the resources assigned were effectively provided remains critical. It serves multiple purposes. First, as discussed previously, advertisers are held accountable internally (as they should be) and must show that they are good stewards of the budgets they are managing. Second, the reconciliation exercise may show low or high usage of agency resources or under- or over-delivery of deliverables relative to the original target. Understanding the nature of the variance and its origin allows both parties to course correct and make important, timely decisions. To illustrate this process, let's take a closer look at various scenarios and decisions based on a retainer-based agreement (i.e., the agency is reporting on retainer and FTE burn):

MAKING EFFECTIVE USE OF AGENCY RETAINER FEES

RETAINER AND/OR FTE BURN	ON TRACK AS PLANNED	LOWER THAN PLANNED	HIGHER THAN PLANNED
SUGGESTED CLIENT CORRECTIVE ACTION	IF FTE & RETAINER ARE MISALIGNED Understand root causes IF FTE & RETAINER ARE ALIGNED Seek potential inefficiencies in initial planning	SCOPE INCREASE OR BUDGET LOWER	SCOPE LOWER OR BUDGET INCREASE

- Scenario 1: Burn is lower than expected in this scenario, the agency is using fewer resources than expected. If this happens in the first half of the year, it's quite possible that the work is back-loaded or some projects were delayed. If this is likely to change as you approach the tail end of the fiscal calendar, no immediate steps may be required. However, if the burn is low and expected to remain lower than originally estimated, then a scope of work and retainer reset may be required to realign expectations with the agency. Suggested client corrective actions: increase scope or reduce fees. The scope can be increased by identifying new assignments, or the retainer budget can be proportionally reduced, effectively resetting the retainer to a more appropriate amount.

- Scenario 2: Burn is higher than expected in this scenario, the agency is using more resources than expected. If this happens in the first part of the fiscal calendar, it's quite possible that the work is front-loaded or some assignments were moved up. If the forecast indicates that the burn will end on target, no action is needed, and you might in a good spot. However, if the burn is trending high and expected to remain higher than planned, then a scope of work and retainer reset may be required. Suggested client corrective actions: reduce scope or increase budget. The scope can be reduced by eliminating a project or two (or more) that were lower priority, or the retainer can be increased by having the client add to their budget to cover the gap.

- Scenario 3: Burn is on target. Good news. The agency seems to be right on track, or at least within a few percentage points from the original forecast. All set, right?

Wait; not so fast. The "FTE" burn might be on track, but if the "retainer" burn is higher, it indicates that the agency is using more senior resources than originally planned. Or the "retainer" burn might be on track, but if the "FTE" burn is higher, it means that the agency is using far more junior resources to handle the work. Even in the event where both the "FTE" and "retainer" are reported to be on track, you might not be off the hook. There is always a possibility that whatever inefficiencies may have existed in the relationship up to that point were factored in by the agency and built in to the new plan. Suggested client corrective actions: an open conversation with the agency to understand the root causes so these findings can be incorporated into future staffing discussions. Always be on the lookout for potential inefficiencies and opportunities to right-size or ensure that team members with the right level of seniority are aligned to assignments.

Look for outliers and discrepancies and use this time to make more informed decisions about resource allocations. Some of the reasons for high burn might be agency-driven: off concepts and reworks, excessive turnover, lack of account management rigor, etc. In this instance, the agency must also take accountability for their role and decide which part of the burn they are willing to take on and absorb. Addressing the root causes behind any type of overage is essential to maintaining a productive partnership. Retainer-based agreements still represent most agency contracts today. Regularly reviewing agency burn should not distract clients and agencies from delivering magnificent work. Rather, it should instill more rigor in the ongoing account management to keep client and agency expectations aligned. By giving more attention to these details, you'll have a system for controlling the burn. Chances are that you have plenty of fires to tend already.

PAY FOR RESULTS—NOT ONLY TIME—WHENEVER POSSIBLE.

The compensation model of the past is no longer suitable to either party. Clients pushing for further margin-squeeze, while the agency workload becomes more complex and more demanding, are preventing agencies from hiring and training great talent. There has been too much abuse for too long. As a result, there is too little transparency and virtually no trust. The micro-focus on the component of agency costs is unlike any other industry. It loses sight of the fact that the focus should rather be on the outputs and performance than on the inputs and costs. It has led to the continued weakening of relationships between clients and their agencies, which as a result undermines a client's ability to succeed in the marketplace. Clients no longer want clock-watchers on their business. Agencies no longer want to die by a thousand paper cuts. Too few are getting what they want from their existing relationship. As advertisers moved swiftly from commission-based agreements in the late 1990s and early 2000s to labor-based agreements and agency retainers, time sheets became vital to agencies and clients: Agencies would commit to completing time sheets to keep an eye on their client billing ratio. No agency CFO wants to see an excessive amount of non-billable agency personnel on their books. And brand advertisers would review time sheets to ensure the effective use of the agency resources they committed to. No client CMO wants to commit massive retainer budgets to an agency without having a mechanism to show they're a responsible budget steward and that they honor their fiscal responsibilities to their organization. I have yet to meet someone at an agency who likes doing time sheets.

In his article "F***king Time Sheets," Rick Webb, angel investor, consultant, co-founder of The Barbarian Group, calls them "a joke," "an outright lie," and "a massive fraud, content-edly performed and affirmed by all parties in the ecosystem," and also accuses them of killing creativity. Providing a more balanced perspective, Marc Brownstein, the CEO of Philadelphia-based Brownstein Group, highlighted the upside and downside of timesheets in an article titled, "Timesheets: Necessary? Evil? Or Both?" He pointed out a commonly stated downside: "Garbage in, garbage out. Too many people fill out timesheets with a broad, inaccurate stroke. No one benefits from that." So, timesheets are far from being a perfect tool on either side.

But are timesheets dead? If time sheets aren't quite dead, they are seriously injured. Non-conformist but highly publicized agencies like MDC Partners' shops Anomaly and CB&P are known to challenge clients who ask for timesheets, claiming that there is a better way to serve clients than keeping an eye on the clock. Instead, they advocate focusing on measurable business and marketing objectives to evaluate whether they delivered to the client's satisfaction, and they tie compensation to their performance whenever possible. Most agencies would agree. But incentive-based compensation typically represents a small portion of the total retainer, so the need for time tracking and reporting is not completely obsolete. The timesheet may occa-sionally seem like a washed-up clown: a bit dated and slightly annoying at times. But timesheets serve a reasonable purpose when brand advertisers favor staffing-based compensation and must hold themselves and their agencies accountable for their budgets. If you are collecting data from your agency, make sure to collect the right type and take action, or, as a client, you are potentially wasting agency resources. Whether you like the idea of killing time sheets or you believe they're a necessary part of agency life, consider how some clients and agencies are making changes, but please don't shoot the messenger.

It is time for change. It's time to end the debate, move toward a bi-partisan approach and change compensation agreements to focus on the sheer measurable value and results produced by agencies. It's one thing to pound our chests with pride that we cracked the code when at industry events. It's another to make it an effective and sustainable way of driving greater value from the partnership every day. Compensation must reward results and value, not activity, efforts, labor, or costs. It's just easier said than done. The agency community is enthusiastic about new forms of compensation that no longer set a ceiling on a profit indexed to cost. Some agencies have established incubating departments/teams to collaborate with clients on creating new products and services. They range from new lines of consumer products such as skin care, shaving cream, juice drink brands, books, and candles, to paid services and tools such as virtual conference software, analytical tools, and games. In addition to these, there are many other potential sources of revenue outside of conventional client assignments that can be sold directly to consumers or even licensed to other agency clients.

Agencies like Anomaly created departments to incubate IP and invest in new business opportunities and joint ventures like i/denti/tee, its fashion and music joint venture involving iTunes, and another business partner, Hard Rock Café, so music lovers can buy t-shirts that allow them to wear their favorite lyrics; Avec Eric: A joint venture creating TV series, book, and licensing opportunities with Eric Ripert, chef/co-Owner of Le Bernardin, MIGHTY JAXX: A joint venture with creator Jackson Aw. Nontraditional agency businesses over the past year have grown to about 30 percent of R/GA's revenue. The agency reports five revenue streams: R/GA Ventures (accelerators, investments), Business Transformation (consulting, outcomes, and deliverables), Agency (retainers, projects), Studios (design and production), R/GA IP (software licensing, partnerships). The agency had stakes in 56 companies, with 20 more on the way in early 2017.

INDUSTRY VIEWPOINT

"The right question is usually more important than the right answer to the wrong question." [125]

—ALVIN TOFFLER, AMERICAN WRITER AND FUTURIST

The list of opportunities appears endless. In return, the skepticism expressed by some clients about the entrepreneurial nature of some agencies is understandable: Where does an agency start and end? The concept of partnership clearly takes on a new meaning. These concepts introduce a new level of complexity that often make them impractical to negotiate, set up, and administer, at least until industry standards and best practices emerge and lead the way. Advertisers must consider many criteria that will play heavily in their decision: How predictable, measurable, simple, scalable, flexible, and equitable is the proposed compensation plan? Large clients or ones with established agency relationships can have privileged compensation models that are measurable, predictable, and scalable. Predictability and scale are both critical for securing discounted rates based on economies of scale. Small to medium size clients or new relationships may pursue simple, yet proven, models with a high degree of flexibility. Large companies might be able to deal with the administrative requirements of more complex compensation models. Does it allow agencies to be adequately rewarded for the risks they are willing to take? Are interests and priorities clearly aligned? Mature client/agency relationships are often considered to be well positioned to experiment with P4P and value-based models, but it's often the smaller and more entrepreneurial advertisers who are more willing to pilot those than the well-established ones.

Global clients typically work with multiple agencies to accommodate scale and coverage that may not be available through a single relationship. A few global agencies have access to a network of local offices in the countries their clients operate. Unfortunately, the level of sophistication or uniformity of compensation practices is still widely spread around the world, making it challenging for global agencies to operate under the chosen standard compensation model for a given client. Typically, the global agency takes on the challenge of coordinating the various accounting systems under a single profit and loss management of the account, making it seamless to the client. The client still can gain visibility into these practices by conducting occasional audits. Most global accounts are handled as labor-based agreements. Those agreements are popular as they greatly simplify the engagement for clients. However, global, labor-based agreements are complex to administer for agencies as they require a huge, coordinated effort across multiple countries, currencies, languages, and teams with varying degrees of sophistication (e.g., reporting, systems, processes). The contract stipulates the requirements that must be followed by all offices to avoid any confusion or misalignment. Once the profit margin is agreed upon for the relationship globally, overhead and labor costs for each geo concerned must be negotiated, often with the assistance of local agency and client resources. The result is a global rate card that is the basis for staffing decisions and billings. As expected, P4P is harder to manage in global contracts because of cultural differences and business practices. IP-sharing agreements are even fewer on global accounts given the added complexity of multinational offices.

CLIENT VIEWPOINT

"We're going to continue to fund increases in spending that matter with reduction in spending that doesn't." [126]

—JON MOELLER, CHIEF FINANCIAL OFFICER,
PROCTOR & GAMBLE

CLOSING THE DIVIDE AND FINDING COMMON GROUND

The level of budget pressure has never been greater, as evidenced by recent moves by leading advertisers. Procter & Gamble Co. announced in 2017 it will cut $2 billion in marketing spending over five years as part of a broader $10 billion cost-cutting plan launched the previous year. The marketing spending cuts included $1 billion or more in media and around $500 million in agency fees, which came on top of $600 million of cuts in prior years. The advertiser believes that half of the $2 billion will be coming from media rates or eliminating supply-chain waste. Marc Pritchard, its Chief Brand Officer, warned the agency industry at the 4As Transformation conference in 2017: "There is too much complexity, crap, and cost." In 2013, Unilever's CFO told analysts that he expected to find more than $470 million in marketing savings that year, in part from reductions in "non-working media," or what the company spends on such things as agency fees and commercial production. It led to the subsequent consolidation of agency resources, followed by many other brand advertisers looking to right size their agency expenses.

Zero-based budgeting (ZBB) is becoming increasingly more popular as a cost-cutting method rather than using historical benchmarks. According to a January study by Deloitte, 22 percent of consumer-packaged goods (CPG) companies, including Unilever, Kraft-Heinz, Mondelez, and Kellogg's, have adopted zero-based budgeting models. Only 16 percent of Fortune 1000 companies used this in the last 24 months. However, ZBB is typically more resource-intensive than traditional budgeting and contributes to tough conversations with agency partners. In addition, procurement is playing a more active role in compensation agreements.

For example, Kraft Heinz kicked off a procurement-led review of its creative accounts as part of a cost-cutting measure following the recently completed Kraft Heinz merger. Following the review, agencies were no longer able to handle production, which is now outsourced to production houses. To assist its members, the 4As developed guidance and benchmarks in client compensation (best practices dos and don'ts, billing practices and payment terms, and more). Ideally, agencies want to be paid based on their strategic or operational value, not their time or headcount. The misalignment of advertisers and agencies about compensation has contributed to the erosion of the spirit of partnership and shared value creation so essential to the fabric of that unique relationship. Advertisers must invite agencies into that conversation about driving efficiencies. Advertisers and agencies must set joint objectives and actively address the many respective areas of waste, low productivity, and inefficiencies. This includes advertisers identifying improvement opportunities in the relationships with agencies and improving briefing and client work approvals that are often considered top inefficiency contributors.

AGENCY VIEWPOINT

"Recently, several client executives have referred to reducing or capping the ratio of their "non-working" marketing expenditures and increasing their "working media" spending in investor earnings calls. These client sound bites play well with Wall Street because they appear to reflect prudent business practice and an emphasis on efficiency. Unfortunately, the appearance is an illusion and the sound bite is a myth." [127]

—TOM FINNERAN, EXECUTIVE VP-AGENCY MANAGEMENT

SERVICES, THE 4AS

One of the most controversial topics among advertisers, C-suite executives, and agency leaders is no doubt the infamous "working" and "non-working spend" ratio. It often makes the headline in investor calls when the CFO or CMO announces major cuts in non-working spend, leading to budget reductions or reinvestment in media budgets. At the core of this discussion is a fundamental desire of marketing leaders to demonstrate both a responsible and efficient use of their marketing spend in an increasingly cost-cutting business environment. "Working spend" represents the amount of marketing budget allocated to the actual distribution and optimization of marketing content (i.e., media spend) across different channels of communication

(TV, print, outdoor, digital, etc.). "Non-working spend" is pretty much anything that doesn't fall into "working spend" as defined previously but is essential to enabling "working spend" activities to take place—that is, the effectiveness of media spend is only as good as the creative work ("non-working spend") behind it. So squeezing "non-working spend" to the point where it affects the effectiveness of the creative work could result in wasted spending on media. "Non-working" spend is often associated with the budget allocated to pay for agency talent (agency fees), assets, and other third party production costs associated with developing and producing content. The ratio of working to non-working, or vice versa, is the metric used to determine how efficient the advertiser is at managing its budget. Yet, the reality is that there is no real industry benchmark for working vs. non-working.

Most clients have their own definition of what they consider "working" and "non-working." Comparing your marketing spend allocations to another brand might be like comparing apples and oranges. Different brands have different go-to-market strategies, various approaches to production and content development, and different ways to allocate their media mix. For example, some clients rely heavily on paid media while others invest aggressively in owned and earned media such as the company's website properties, brand content vehicles, or social platforms. If an advertiser is shifting spend from mass-reach paid advertising channels to a more content-rich, highly targeted, high-rotation type of execution, it will spend more in production and agency fees, but it doesn't mean that it's a bad thing in that context. The value of establishing benchmarks between companies with such diverse approaches to marketing strategy and execution is highly questionable.

Years of experience as a client has taught me that following these principles guarantees more efficient use of marketing budgets and improves the quality of decision making: If you are evaluating agency fees and production expenditures, incorporate the financial value of owned and earned media channels into the spend allocation analysis. It will provide you with a broader, more holistic understanding of what's needed in terms of content development and production to support maintaining and feeding these channels. Set internal benchmarks and monitor the impact of your efficiency initiatives. Most companies focus on tightening marketing spend because it is based on a set of reliable expense categories that can be easily tracked and reported on. Although everyone wants marketing to be more ROMI (return on marketing investment) driven, the reality is that the "R" part of ROMI is much harder to define and measure. However, no one will dispute the fact that spending more to gain exponentially more is reasonable. Most CFOs would gladly allocate more spend to marketing if they could ensure a certain return on their investment. Advertising is an investment to make and to maximize, not a cost to be minimized.

AGENCY VIEWPOINT

"One of the challenges we have is, 'How do you invest enough in training while still being able to pay the bills?' That's still one of the challenges with everything that's happening with cost cutting and procurement and fees." [128]

—BRYAN WIENER, EXECUTIVE CHAIRMAN, 360I

Aligning compensation philosophies is common sense, so it's a good place to start. If the agency is simply an extension of the client's marketing team, whatever compensation agreement you contemplate should ideally be aligned to the way the client handles employee compensation. It's easier to implement client/agency compensation based on the guiding principles of a client's approach to compensation, and it's easier to explain because everyone in the company is fully aware of it and hopefully supporting it. If it's a good idea for employees, it's probably a decent idea for agencies. There shouldn't be a double standard. I am not implying that it must be identical. But it can be based on a common set of principles. For example, advertisers with a strong culture of accountability, that also offer bonuses to employees based on the company's performance (business, financial, marketing), are more inclined to institute P4P pricing than those who don't. Similarly, advertisers that foster an employee culture of long working hours may not be receptive to client/agency compensation that is hourly-based. The compensation agreement will need to be tailored to the needs of both parties, but essentially cannot be diametrically opposed to a client's philosophy on employee compensation if it is to be successful and take root within that relationship. Finding and implementing the right compensation agreement is critical to the success of that relationship. In the end, advertisers must face the legendary "fast, good, and cheap" triangle, well known in software engineering, which states that it's virtually impossible to get all three and that one must choose just two: If you pick good and cheap, you might compromise speed. If you pick fast and cheap, you might compromise quality. But if you pick good and fast, don't expect it to be cheap.

"The mix of marketing-related expenditures should be evaluated individually and in aggregate in order to derive an accurate assessment of the components that are working hardest and contributing demonstrably to optimal marketing ROI." [129]
—**TOM FINNERAN**, EXECUTIVE VP-AGENCY MANAGEMENT SERVICES, THE 4AS

There are several scenarios to pick from, so advertisers must carefully evaluate their options. In the end, clients and agencies must share some risks and rewards, and pick just the numbers that matter if we are to truly end the debate. Agencies are creating Chief Compensation Officer roles to lead fee and contract negotiations with advertisers, exploring ways to create greater value while protecting an agency's ability to grow and prosper. Advertisers must also play their part. CMOs must reaffirm their commitments to healthy agency relationships that emphasize value over cost and results over efforts, which is not much different from the way they want consumers to buy from them. They must enable agencies to invest in the talent they need to succeed and focus their resources and energy on delivering great work that drives business growth. To do so, they may need to stand up and vigorously push back against unfair payment terms and unreasonable cost-cutting demands targeted at agencies from Finance and Procurement. CMOs and business leaders must advocate for their agencies as drivers of growth, protecting these valuable resources as they do internal ones, and keeping their goals and respective economic interests aligned.

WHAT MOTIVATES AGENCIES—BEYOND FINANCIAL INCENTIVES

For years, advertisers have used extrinsic motivators like incentives and fear (the carrot-and-stick approach) to motivate agencies to perform well on their business. Compensation is often about intrinsic motivation. Yet today, many agency leaders find the notion of "motivating" agencies using compensation as misguided by advertisers. There is no greater motivation for agencies than the risk of losing the account, often on a relatively short notice. Even today, advertisers incentivize agencies to consistently meet or exceed certain expectations of value to them. But is that sufficient? Besides the leadership team, are the many agency people—across seniority levels and departments— working on their business even aware of the financial incentives agreed to in the compensation agreement? The answer is often "no," assuming they even care, in the case of creative talent typically less interested in financial rewards than in accolades.

Drawing on four decades of scientific research on human motivation, including experiments in behavioral science, Daniel H. Pink in his book *Drive: The Surprising Truth About What Motivates Us* shows a different way to motivate and achieve high performance. Dan argues that the reward-and-punishment approach so popular in routine, rule-based, yet essential left-brain type of work, doesn't work any longer and can even do harm in today's fast growing right-brain type of environments where cognitive thinking is prevalent. Why? In his memorable speech at TED he suggests that *"reward narrows our focus and restricts our possibility,"* especially in a business environment where there are no clear set of rules and no single solution to a problem. To sharpen our big-picture thinking and accelerate creativity, are material, financial incentives the way to motivate?

Pink proposes intrinsic motivators organized in three major elements: "autonomy, mastery, and purpose."

I've come to believe that his argument also applies to client/agency relationships, especially among agencies where cognitive thinking, creativity, and innovation are core to their offerings. I would add another one: "acknowledgement." Agencies are motivated by clients who acknowledge their efforts and their commitment to success. A simple "Thank you" message, a bottle of wine, or some flowers can make the day of anyone working their ass off, often the leaving the office late, to deliver great work. Agencies also want some autonomy and creative freedom to think proactively about a client's business, something many of them feel challenged to do in an environment where they are asked to manage a narrowly focused scope of work and tight budget that leaves little room for anything else. They want to be rewarded with work that allows them to refine and master their craft. And finally, they are motivated first and foremost by assignments, because those are what truly matter and have strong emotional relevancy or significance to the agency. Purpose is a powerful motivator for agencies as well. They must be inspired by the brand they serve. They must be believers. Not every client assignment can meet all four criteria, but thinking in these terms is a new way of looking at what motivates agencies and leads to higher performance. There are many other ways to motivate agencies. Advertisers can also contribute to developing greater talent at the agency by assigning agency staff to the right projects, developing new skills, attending internal trainings or events, or even partnering closely with internal teams on innovative concepts and ideas.

CLIENT VIEWPOINT

"Having agencies that don't make money is not a sustainable business practice. So, we're refining our compensation to make sure we're paying for the work that you do and the talent that you bring to our brands, especially the creative talent." [130]

—MARC S. PRITCHARD, CHIEF BRAND OFFICER,
PROCTER & GAMBLE CO.

If the value exchange is not only about financial incentives and is also not solely transactional, there are other ways to motivate an agency beyond pure compensation. When done properly, compensation can turn into a powerful tool to motivate and restore confidence in client/agency relationships. The value exchange may be based on less than just six numbers. Whatever right number might keep your client/agency universe in balance, keep in mind that pursuing equitable terms ultimately motivates people, builds trust, mutual respect, goodwill, and translates into outstanding success.

TOP 3
BEST PRACTICES
for Advertisers

1. Embrace a transparent and equitable approach to agency negotiations by finding a compensation methodology that best aligns with your mutual objectives and philosophies.

2. Learn the intricacies of the agency business model to be a more informed and effective negotiator and a better business partner.

3. Pay for results, not time, whenever possible and conduct regular reconciliations to create a culture of absolute accountability and to focus on what matters most.

It was six men of Indostan
To learning much inclined,
Who went to see the Elephant
(Though all of them were blind),
That each by observation
Might satisfy his mind.

The First approached the Elephant,
And happening to fall
Against his broad and sturdy side,
At once began to bawl:
"God bless me! but the Elephant
Is very like a WALL!"

The Second, feeling of the tusk,
Cried, "Ho, what have we here,
So very round and smooth and sharp?
To me 'tis mighty clear
This wonder of an Elephant
Is very like a SPEAR!"

The Third approached the animal,
And happening to take
The squirming trunk within his hands,
Thus boldly up and spake:
"I see" quoth he, "the Elephant
Is very like a SNAKE!"

The Fourth reached out an eager hand,
And felt about the knee
"What most this wondrous beast is like
Is mighty plain," quoth he:
"Tis clear enough the Elephant
Is very like a TREE!"

The Fifth, who chanced to touch the ear,
Said: "E'en the blindest man
Can tell what this resembles most;
Deny the fact who can,
This marvel of an Elephant
Is very like a FAN!"

The Sixth no sooner had begun
About the beast to grope,
Than seizing on the swinging tail
That fell within his scope,
"I see," quoth he, "the Elephant
Is very like a ROPE!"

And so these men of Indostan
Disputed loud and long,
Each in his own opinion
Exceeding stiff and strong,
Though each was partly in the right,
And all were in the wrong!

—JOHN GODFREY SAXE,
WRITER AND POET

8

THE BLIND MEN AND
THE ELEPHANT

Successfully scoping work and briefing agencies

In his poem "The Blind Men and the Elephant" John Godfrey Saxe warns about common misperceptions when looking at the component parts and not the whole. Without stretching the imagination too far, but to bring this home, one might think of the Elephant as a client and the Blind Men as the agencies. Playing on the metaphor, the agencies are simply seeking to understand the client, approaching it from multiple angles. However, without explicit guidance from the client, they are indeed blind. They are likely to misread the signs or make false assumptions, misinterpret the client, and ultimately, miss the mark and all be *in the wrong!* The powerful lesson of this emblematic story is that agencies cannot deliver outstanding work without solid, comprehensive guidance and direction from clients. Period. A comprehensive annual scope of work planning and management process, combined with the use of solid client input briefs, provides the agency with a complete picture of the client opportunity they need to serve and staff for. It also guarantees absolute alignment by focusing on what truly matters in the work relationship. This exercise involves adjusting the marketing lens from big to small, from strategy to execution. Or more specifically, from the initial scope of work process—an aggregate, holistic view of all marketing campaigns and activities commissioned by the advertiser *(or the whole)*—to the many individual client input project briefings, the details behind each individual project or assignment *(or one of the many parts)*. Scoping work and briefing agencies are the most impactful activities an advertiser must do well to yield strong work.

QUALITY SCOPING AND BRIEFING

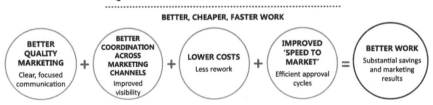

When done properly, it contributes to clear, focused communications, improved visibility, less rework, efficient approval cycles, substantial savings, and marketing results. Effective scoping and briefing is so important to building strong client/agency relationships that it deserves its own chapter. To use the popular English idiom, now that the elephant is in the room, let's take a closer look at how advertisers can use scope of work and client input briefs to successfully direct their agency partners and make the best use of them.

CLIENT VIEWPOINT

"Developing an emotional connection is the ultimate objective of marketing. In the digital era of infinite impression and multichannel noise, you must breakthrough or become irrelevant. Brands that are able to transcend the rational dimension of their product and build a place in consumers' hearts will remain relevant for a long time. The first step in driving emotion is to approach our customers with empathy; we need to walk in our customers' shoes to feel the world as they feel it." [131]

—ANTONIO LUCIO, FORMER GLOBAL CHIEF MARKETING & COMMUNICATION OFFICER, HP, GLOBAL CMO FACEBOOK

All advertisers seek the right agencies, doing the right type of work, at the right investment level, and in the most efficient ways to meet their marketing objectives. Yet, getting there proves to be far more challenging than expected. The 2015 ANA study called "Enhancing Client Agency Relationships" emphasized that most agencies (73 percent) do NOT believe their clients do a good job at guiding them. The lack of solid scope and briefing practices continues to be a major source of tension and waste for advertisers. Thankfully, several industry best practices have arisen over the years that have enabled them to provide more clear guidance.

SCOPE OF WORK ("THE WHOLE")

A new fiscal year is around the corner. Everyone can feel the energy and excitement building up. The CEO sets the vision and business priorities for the company. The CFO provides financial guidance and sets budgets. The CMO articulates the overall marketing strategy and announces key initiatives to deliver against it. Everyone is ready to get started. Now what? The answer: developing a scope of work and using it to determine specific campaigns, projects, deliverables, and their associated staffing plans and agency budgets. Budgets are somewhat easy to define. Defining how they will be used with some specificity is far more challenging. Scope of work planning and management is just that. It's about defining key marketing priorities and expectations for an entire fiscal calendar. It plugs right into the tail end of the marketing planning process during which goals are set and budgets locked. That's the "planning" part of scope of work. Scope of work "management" implies that scopes are rarely static and that the resources assigned to them may fluctuate. It is therefore the process by which reconciliations—of deliverables, staffing, and financials—will take place on a quarterly or monthly basis. This end-to-end process, illustrated here, is increasingly automated, allowing both agencies and client teams to partner more effectively and more rigorously on the management of scope. The scope of work can be tracked and measured. Internal and external benchmarks can be used to inform the diligent review by clients of agency estimates. The automation of scope of work also simplifies an otherwise already-complicated workflow and approval process and allows the collection and analysis of critical scope, staffing, and financial data. It ultimately helps remove inefficiencies and redundancies.

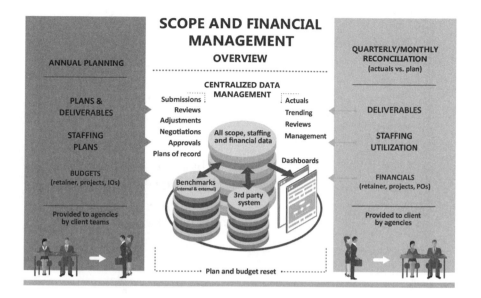

The scope of work includes details about all the marketing initiatives, campaigns, and activities planned for the year. As a result, redundant efforts can be spotted early on and eliminated. This critical planning process ensures agencies are working on the right priorities, have adequate line of sight into the volume and complexity of the work they are tasked to do, and as a result, can make accurate staffing decisions to carry out these activities. This alignment of scope activity to staffing and agency fees is what agencies typically refer to as "agency resourcing," "agency capacity planning," or "resource forecasting." It enables the effective planning and utilization of agency resources, anticipating what's needed to successfully support a well-defined set of work priorities. Based on that information, resource plans will be determined by the agency and submitted to the advertiser for approval. Anecdotal feedback over the years has shown that there is a direct correlation between the degrees of involvement of an agency in the early phase of the advertiser's planning process and the agency's ability to deliver strategic value and breakthrough ideas to that client. This is common sense: When agencies are involved early enough in the planning cycle, they can offer insight and recommendations that shape or strongly influence client decisions. Rather than being treated as "order takers," agencies seize the opportunity to shape the objectives that they will be asked to support. The result is an agency better integrated into the company's overall strategy and objectives, more knowledgeable about what needs to be done (and why), more engaged with senior leadership, and better prepared to tackle their client's marketing challenges.

CLIENT VIEWPOINT

"It's much easier to make brave decisions if you have the right information. But it's very stupid to make brave decisions without data." [132]

—ANDREW CLARKE, CHIEF MARKETING AND CUSTOMER OFFICER, MARS

A robust scope of work process requires process discipline, a strong taxonomy, streamlined workflows, and a centralized approach to data management to allow for various scope, staff, and cost analysis. Often, the strategy has not been fully baked; the decision as to which agency is doing what may not have been made, priorities may be conflicting or unclear, budgets may still be in flux, and yet work may need to start immediately. Sound familiar? The myth of agencies with unlimited supply of top talent standing by, waiting by the phone for the advertiser to call, is hopefully long gone in people's minds, even in the most clement economic times. Agencies do not have endless resources or cash on hand. It's especially important to realize this as agencies today face increasing demands, greater complexity, and higher expectations. They must work with their clients to map the effective use of their valuable but limited resources. Doing so requires them to actively engage in the process of setting objectives and coming up with ways to meet them.

This is what a partnership is all about. The level of scope of work detail provided is likely to vary advertiser to advertiser— what level of budget information they will provide, what level of specificity they will provide about the type of deliverables that must be produced, etc. Agencies are not only on the receiving end. They must be an integral part of scoping. They must be sitting at the table where priorities are set. A certain amount of flexibility is often necessary as the scope of work changes to respond to rapidly changing market conditions. The process allows marketers to open and lock scopes throughout the year, always keeping a current view and updating agencies of scope (client teams may cut, change, or add scopes) or budget changes. And yes, expect those to change frequently. The process also allows the agencies to update the marketing teams on a monthly or quarterly basis on where they stand with deliverables (project status), and how much of their resources have been utilized (FTE/retainer). Scope of work planning and management is not easy. No matter how challenging it might be at times for advertisers to scope activities for a full fiscal calendar year, providing line of sight into the immediate future is the least advertisers can do to best prepare their agencies. By doing so, they can ensure expectations are well understood and resources are in place to support them.

CLIENT INPUT BRIEFING ("ONE OF THE MANY PARTS")

If I ask you if your briefs are tight enough, I am not referring to briefs as the style of close-fitting, short, snug underwear commonly known as "jockey shorts" in the US. Instead, I am referring to the number one contributing factor to wasted marketing dollars and troubled client/agency relationships: briefs that are often way too loose, incomplete, and seriously lack the necessary process rigor and discipline that effective brand advertisers and their agencies should expect.

Most relationships cannot handle the highly stressful process of assembling IKEA furniture, especially when the directions are unclear or simply missing or lost. If you ever shopped at IKEA and attempted to put together any large piece of furniture without directions and with countless individual pieces that must carefully be assembled in the right sequence, you will know exactly what I mean. This kind of IKEA breakdown has been the subject of many psychological studies and has been featured in many YouTube parodies as well as an episode of the NBC comedy *30 Rock*, where Tina Fey's character, Liz Lemon, ends up breaking up with her boyfriend. In advertising, the IKEA metaphor highlights the critical nature of the input client brief, aka creative brief, in providing direction and inspiration to the agency. The briefing is a multi-step bi-directional process between the client (originator) and the agency (receiver) as illustrated in this creative assignment example:

OVERVIEW OF THE BRIEFING PROCESS

BRIEFING DEVELOPMENT	BRIEF DELIVERY	CREATIVE DEVELOPMENT	CREATIVE PRESENTATION	CREATIVE FEEDBACK
Developed in partnership with agency	If this is an integrated campaign, all agencies must be briefed at the same time	Managed by each agency based on their own internal processes	Concepts and creative presented to client	Feedback (decision and rationale) must be communicated formally (ideally in writing)
Any disagreement requires resolution	Must ensure clarity of purpose and encourage dialog		Concepts and creative must be "on brief"	
Internal approvals may be required				

When handled poorly, it leads to too many rounds of revisions, missed expectations, frustrations, and wasted efforts. Luckily, best practices have emerged to address this issue head-on and make clients more accountable, providing better guidance and direction to their agency partners. Do you want to subject your relationships to the IKEA meltdown? Jag trodde inte det! ("I didn't think so!" in Swedish). Writing better briefs is about better work. It's also about avoiding waste that results from poor guidance and projects that zig-zag unnecessarily in agency hallways. In the many client/agency evaluations I have been exposed to over the past few years, we have heard agency comments like:

- "We rarely receive briefs."

- "Briefs should be more concise and have fewer, clearer objectives."

- "Briefs are written as order forms instead of strategic assignments and stifle creativity."

- "Our client often uses the brief to figure out his/her objectives."

- "We (the agency) were asked to write the brief for a client too busy to write it."

- "We often get asked to start work before getting any brief."

- "The brief was not written or didn't get approved by those who will ultimately review the work, and it changed once the project started."

And the list goes on and on. The result is a tragedy of Shakespearean measures: hundreds of millions of advertising dollars are going down the drain at a time when brands are pressured to do more with less.

AGENCY VIEWPOINT

"The client-agency relationship needs to start way upstream of the communications brief. Clients need to invite agencies into the depths of their business, to share all of their data, and to welcome a fresh point of view on their business, marketing, and communications problems." [133]

—**KOFI AMOO-GOTTFRIED,** HEAD OF BRAND CONSUMER MARKETING, FACEBOOK—FORMER CHIEF STRATEGY OFFICER, FCB GARFINKEL

HOW ADVERTISERS BENEFIT

AGENCY VIEWPOINT

"The briefing process is critical. It's not about giving a 30,000-foot brief and sending the agency along its way. We want the agencies to have the latitude to create, dream and push the barriers. But at the same time, we want to make sure the objectives are very clear, so they are not wasting their time." [134]

—OLIVIER FRANÇOIS, GLOBAL CHIEF MARKETING OFFICER, FCA

Occasionally, you run into these overly simplistic, yet essential questions. *"What makes a good brief?"* is one of those. The answer is priceless. Tom Bassett, CEO of Bassett & Partners, created a series of video interviews ("Briefly") to understand how some of the world's most consistently exceptional creative talents (in design, advertising, architecture, etc.) used the brief to deliver exceptional creative results. The benefits of a brief are universal. In its most basic definition, a brief is the initiating point, the blueprint for providing the agency with all relevant insight needed to drive to the desired business outcome. Through the brief, the advertiser is providing clear objectives and vital information on how to accomplish them. It is the single most important phase of a working relationship with an agency. It is where it all starts. It facilitates the process of exchanging critical information with the agency, addressing the "what," "who," "where," and "why" of an assignment but not the "how." The "how" a project gets conceived and executed is for the agency to define. One thing is certain though: The better the brief, the greater the outcome. A good brief informs, but more importantly, inspires, motivates, and stimulates creative ideas from the agencies. If it doesn't get the agency hugely motivated, it's unlikely to ignite their creative juices and result in the best work they can produce. Providing clear and consistent direction, objectives, and success metrics for an agency assignment helps reduce waste significantly. Even small improvements in this area can easily translate into millions of dollars in increased effectiveness or reduced expenses.

So, advertisers are wise to invest the time and energy required to produce the best possible brief before sharing it with their agencies. This investment will pay itself back over and over. Every creative review meeting with the agency should start with a review of the brief. The brief must always serve as a reference point in the evaluation and approval of the work. A great brief exponentially increases the agency's ability to do excellent work. Perhaps no differently than a surgeon would. Imagine yourself for a second being wheeled into an operating room, dreadfully hoping the surgeon was properly briefed about the procedure. As a client, you carefully selected the hospital and the surgeon, your service providers. The surgeon is competent, no doubt. But was he or she provided all the information needed to do the job? Are you both on the same page as to what a successful outcome is? Next time you brief an agency, think about it as if you were briefing a surgeon. You don't need to tell him/her what to do or how to do it. State the problem clearly. Give some background and focus on what's essential. Supply meaningful, actionable information. It's probably best he/she is aware of your allergies, has seen your lab results, and is going in well-informed. But once you agree with his/her recommendations, get out of the way, and let him/her do the job.

INDUSTRY VIEWPOINT

"The brief is a clarity of purpose."

—FRANK GEHRY, PRITZKER PRIZE-WINNING ARCHITECT

WHAT IT ISN'T

Let's demystify common beliefs about what a brief IS by defining what it ISN'T:

WHAT A BRIEF IS NOT

| A BRIEF IS NOT AN ORDER FORM. | A BRIEF IS NOT A ONE-WAY DIALOG. | A BRIEF IS NOT "WAR AND PEACE" OR A CANDIDATE FOR THE PULITZER PRIZE. | A BRIEF IS NOT A SUBSTITUTE FOR THE COMPANY'S MARKETING PLAN. | A BRIEF IS NOT ABOUT GATHERING DATA, IT'S ABOUT PRODUCING INSIGHT. | A BRIEF SHOULD NOT BE DOLEFUL OR STERILE. |

A brief is NOT an order form. Often the solution has already been established upon briefing or is so baked that it leaves little room for the agency to play its role as a strategic partner. Many briefs are used as order forms, rather than inviting the agency to come up with solutions to the core business or communication challenge. Both parties may have to concede to find common ground. The agency wants to provide thought leadership and they should be encouraged to do so. A brief is more than a check box.

AGENCY VIEWPOINT

"The challenges that all agencies face are the same. Attracting and retaining talent is difficult. Getting clients to truly brief well is one more. Brief the problem and not the deliverable. In the nutshell, that's the biggest problem that all agencies face." [135]

—JON HAMM, GLOBAL CCO, GEOMETRY GLOBAL

A brief is NOT a one-way dialogue. A brief is not just a physical object or a document. It is only a means to an end. The end is an agency that is highly engaged, excited about the assignment, knowledgeable, focused, and ready to get work started. It is a way to efficiently structure a rich and lively dialogue between an agency (or multiple ones) and a client. A brief is usually best informed when agencies are given the opportunity to have direct conversations with the client. Advertisers must set up a formal joint process requiring a review of the brief immediately after the brief has been submitted. A written brief submission alone is never sufficient to allow for the agencies to capture the intent of the project and can result in brief defects and additional costly review cycles. If multiple specialty agencies are involved, roles and responsibilities must be clearly defined out of the gate to avoid confusion. The opportunity for all agencies to be briefed simultaneously and to interact with each other is likely to produce better ideas that have far greater impact. They might even bounce ideas off each other. Embrace the two-way dialogue. This is a healthy process.

A brief is NOT "The Provincial Letters" or a candidate for a Pulitzer Prize. As the name implies, great briefs are brief. Keep it succinct. It's not about the quantity, but the quality of information. Advertisers have the tendency to cram the brief with way too much information. Obviously, larger, complex assignments require lengthier briefs. But advertisers must spend more time on culling down to pertinent information before sending it to the agency. To paraphrase French, and Blaise Pascal, *"If I had more time, I would have written a shorter letter."* Take the time. I've see advertisers produce very lengthy briefs coupled with lengthy and detailed research material and presentations, leaving it up to the agency to figure out what matters instead of making the tough choices themselves about what's relevant and actionable. If you have pertinent support documentation to provide, add it to the appendix. But keep the brief laser-focused on what needs to be done.

AGENCY VIEWPOINT

"Rapid-fire content creation [is the single most significant change you need to make in your agency in the next 12 months]. It's now an always-on cycle driven by opportunities to connect with customers. The 'we always brief in December' days are gone." [136]

—PAM SCHEIDELER, CHIEF DIGITAL OFFICER, DEUTSCH LA

A brief is NOT a substitute for the company's marketing plan. Too often, advertisers are tempted to incorporate all their marketing priorities into the brief instead of being specific about what is expected of the agency. The brief should go through multiple internal reviews before it is ready to be used as directional input to the agency. It is important to incorporate all internal input before the work has started. Too often, a brief will go through multiple rounds of revisions after it has been approved, adding unnecessary frustration, delays, and costs. Advertisers often use the brief process to solidify their own strategy, test various ideas, and brainstorm with the agency for weeks, before the brief is finalized and work can start. Although that process can yield tremendous value, it can also turn into a costly investment for the agency if not adequately budgeted by the client.

A brief is NOT about gathering data, it's about producing insight. Often some sections have not been well thought out or the brief is used as a data dump. Avoid the "copy and paste" from other documents. The brief is sometimes missing critical information like clear objectives and success metrics as well as important background on the core audience. The brief should provide customer insight—insight that can get the agency thinking about how to best tackle the project. Otherwise, it is nothing more than garbage in, garbage out. Advertisers must provide meaningful, actionable insight, not raw, undigested data.

Finally, a brief shouldn't be doleful or sterile. The briefing process is more involved than filling out a template and sending it to the agency. It must ignite and inspire the agency. It must be truthful and authentic. It needs to invite an open, direct, honest conversation. It may also include videos, customer visits, testimonials, the participation in an event, or a prototype or demo of a new product giving greater depth to the assignment. If it doesn't get the agency energized, what are the chances they will, in turn, energize the target audience? A brief is not supposed to read like a company's earnings report or a grocery list. Spice it up. It must sell right off the page.

CLIENT VIEWPOINT

"A bad brief is a road to nowhere." [137]
—**DANA ANDERSON**, FORMER SENIOR VICE PRESIDENT AND
CHIEF MARKETING OFFICER, MONDELEZ INTERNATIONAL,
CMO, MEDIALINK

WHAT'S IN A BRIEF

Although briefs are likely to vary from advertiser to advertiser, from discipline to discipline (e.g., media, social, and digital have unique information requirements), a typical client input brief is likely to include the following building blocks:

Brief essentials: This section includes general project information and basic details about the assignment such as the project name or ID, the date the brief was created, and the date of last modifications (for versioning control), PO number or related budget information, or geographic scope, just to name a few. It also identifies key client and agency leads and their contact details. If specific internal resources are needed (Privacy, Legal, Finance, and so forth), this is where they should be listed as well.

Business and marketing objectives: What are the key business objectives and/or goals? How is success defined? Objectives must be defined in the broader context of the marketing strategy. Typical objectives include business metrics such as market share or sales, as well as marketing metrics such as increasing unaided or aided awareness, brand perception, etc. However, the list of objectives shouldn't be a laundry list. One or two core objectives should be sufficient. Only the most critical objectives should be listed and then prioritized. The objectives cannot be too broad or unattainable. The timeframe should be clearly stated as well. Nothing else matters unless this is clearly spelled out, as it sets expectations for the work. What potential sources of tension are we facing in achieving our objectives? It sets expectations for the role communications will play in meeting the objectives of the assignment and identifies a challenge for the agency to get excited about solving.

Target and key insights: Who are we targeting with this effort? It includes a description of the most important people the client wants to engage with. It includes a description of the highest value opportunity and relevant demographics, psychographics, lifestyle, and behavioral data. It defines their attitude, motivations, and barriers as it relates to the category, but also clarifies their relationship with the brand. The insight helps identify a human trust and tension the agency can pivot from.

Communication strategy: The communication strategy articulates the FROM (what the target audience might think or feel about, or do with the brand currently), the PROMISE (the single-minded proposition), and TO (what the advertiser wants the target to think, feel, or do). It also specifies the Reasons to Believe (RTB), or why the target audience should believe what is being communicated to them. This section clarifies what action the audience is expected to take (what do we want them to do?), or what perception or behavior is expected to be changed because of this assignment. It also includes a description of the key benefits—rational and emotional.

Mandatories: These guardrails are important to the agency. It may include campaign tenets, channel guidelines, mandatory creative and brand guidelines (use of logos, trademarks, tag lines, assets), legal reviews and required sign offs, the required use of brand assets or images, certain time dependencies (sponsorships, events), the use of specific vendors, privacy policies, etc. Don't confuse considerations for mandatories, and remember that too many mandatories can become too prescriptive and limiting.

Other relevant brief sections:

- **Deliverables:** What does the agency need to deliver to meet the objectives of the brief? It may provide guidance for asset creation and storage.

- **Milestones:** What are the key milestones and dependencies, including reviews and approvals? Advertisers should be specific about any critical milestones (including in-market dates), campaign or product-related milestones (release date for a new product or an important corporate event), key milestones that will dictate the timing and tempo of communications and deliverables.

- **Success metrics:** What are the key performance indicators the team will use to evaluate whether the business and marketing goals were successfully achieved?

- **Budget guidance:** A specific budget number or a budget range is often provided. Providing some budget guidance prevents agencies from coming up with ideas that their client cannot afford. If applicable, it should include a breakdown of production, media, and agency fees. For media, budget phasing might be added.

- **Competitive landscape and market conditions:** Any relevant competitive intelligence should be included in this section of the brief. Market conditions might be specific to certain regions or countries.

- **Approvals and signatures:** Several stakeholders might be invited to provide input. Everyone must have a specific role, but there should be only one final decision maker. The formality of a signature block on the brief for both the agency lead and final decision-maker confirms the document has been carefully reviewed and formally approved.

HOW TO CURE THE ROOT CAUSES OF INEFFICIENCIES

Agencies emphatically believe that clients do not provide clear assignment briefings. It is amazing that one out of every three client briefs today is considered weak and, consequently, wasteful. Bad briefs are frustrating to agencies and cost clients both time and money—for agency rework and the resulting agency fees—and this is likely to be a focus area for many clients. Bad briefs are a lose-lose proposition from unnecessary meetings and conflicting direction to pointless complications and delayed decisions—all resulting in significant waste. Over the years, briefs have gotten better, through trial and error and continued dedication, for those clients who understand the value of efficient briefings. But it can still be a clumsy process and advertisers universally agree: There is still plenty of room for improvement.

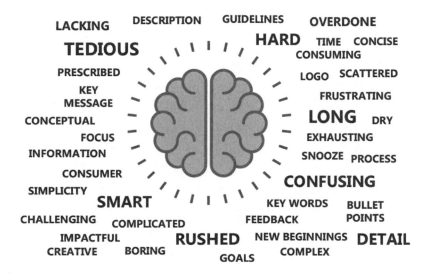

WHAT COMES TO MIND WHEN YOU THINK ABOUT

CLIENT INPUT BRIEFING?

Thankfully, clients can follow a few simple steps to eliminate common root causes of briefing inefficiencies.

INDUSTRY VIEWPOINT

"At its best, the brief is a provocation." [138]

—DAVID ROCKWELL, FOUNDER AND PRESIDENT, ROCKWELL GROUP

ROOT CAUSE #1: INADEQUATE PREPARATION LEADING TO UNCLEAR OBJECTIVES

Solution: Invest time up front

Time is of the essence and a new campaign must be put in market as soon as humanly possible. The client is willing to cut corners, sometimes at the expense of providing a solid brief. Too many clients jump into submitting the brief before having done their due diligence, seeking internal input from decision makers and other stakeholders, and send a brief only half-baked to the agency. Relying on "What we discussed over coffee the other day" is no longer acceptable. But providing too little too late is the equivalent of changing tires on a car that is still moving. Or asking a contractor to start pouring concrete while the floor plans are still being drawn by the architect. The goals are still vague, perhaps contradictory, somewhat confusing, or are missing all together. As a result, the brief is likely to change frequently, requiring several costly revisions—the equivalent of "defects" in the manufacturing world, far exceeding what would be considered an acceptable number of brief revisions (two or three at most).

Engaging an agency without having properly and clearly defined objectives is likely to delay the campaign and increase costs. The solution: Advertisers should invest the time up front and be 100% clear about the objectives of the assignment before engaging an agency. Do not pick up the phone or schedule a meeting with the agency until the objectives are somewhat clear and the brief is reasonably complete. The more time, effort, and information invested upfront, the better the time savings throughout the entire process itself. Abraham Lincoln once said: "If I had six hours to chop down a tree, I'd spend the first four sharpening the axe." It doesn't matter how small the assignment or budget might be. Advertisers should sharpen their axes and be clear about what they really are asking the agency to do—and not wait until the work is well under way to figure it out.

CLIENT VIEWPOINT

"The role of the agencies is to stimulate our internal creative process. The best ideas are not created by briefs; they are found. A brief means boundaries, so you don't want to put creativity in a cage. What is in a brief? It's the product detail, the features. What are the demographics of the people that we are going to sell to?" [139]

—OLIVIER FRANÇOIS, GLOBAL CHIEF MARKETING OFFICER, FCA

ROOT CAUSE #2: LACK OF DIALOGUE AND COLLABORATION
Solution: Develop the brief collaboratively

Sloppy or unilaterally developed briefs always fail to deliver. The brief is a powerful communication and discovery tool between the client and the agency, not an email in someone's inbox, a piece of paper on someone's desk, or a checkbox on a client to-do list. The brief is not meant to be a static, formal document, but rather a dynamic, iterative, collaborative exchange. As such, it should be conducted in person as often as possible, but at the very least, should be accompanied by a phone conversation to answer any outstanding questions from the agency. It's meant to actively encourage strategic dialogue and creative collaboration from the outset, communicate the client's opportunity, and provide clarity of purpose to the agency. Briefs are not meant to be written in seclusion. Being open to collaborating on a brief requires trust and mutual respect. Talk about your ideas for the brief with your agency, exchange ideas and develop a stronger brief together. Sarah Williams, partner and creative director at Beardwood and Co., suggests the use of a "visual creative brief" which involves getting all key decision-makers in a room to build the brief together, leveraging typography, graphic forms, illustrations, photography, etc.

As the ultimate decision-maker, the advertiser must lead the creation of the brief and invite the agency to provide input or even collaborate in writing it. No matter how involved the agency is, make sure to give adequate time to the agency to absorb the information, seek clarification, and participate. They must have enough time to challenge the brief or even reject it if it doesn't feel right or something is missing or unclear. Often, the agency is hesitant to challenge it because of tight deadlines. Briefing must be approached as a collaborative process to ensure both teams are feeling accountable.

ROOT CAUSE #3: TOO PRESCRIPTIVE CLIENT GUIDANCE
Solution: State a challenge, not the solution
The brief must invite the agency to solve an exciting human or business challenge. Too often, advertisers default to writing a list of marketing tactics for the agency to execute. For the most part, the brief shouldn't mandate the type of deliverables the agency is to produce. The brief must encourage the agency to challenge any of the assumptions and give it room to think creatively about ways to get to the desired destination. The objectives must be SMART—specific, measurable, achievable, relevant, and time-bound. It should be, well, "brief," too, and not drown the agency in useless or borderline relevant information. Finally, the brief and the process surrounding it must convey the passion and convictions of the client and inspire

those who are engaged with the project. As a result, the brief must be the conduit for insight-rich, inspiring conversations throughout its creation and up to its completion.

Is the agency jazzed about the assignment? Is the brief simple, yet audacious? Is it inspiring? Advertisers should think of themselves as music composers who set the vision and tempo but rely on orchestra leads to decide on how to build the best arrangement, which instruments are needed, and how they come together for the music to come alive. At best, a client might recommend specific deliverables or media vehicles. Unless of course, this agency's sole purpose is pure execution and nothing more. Advertisers who are too prescriptive end up burning people out and eroding the partnership, which then leads to reduced quality of staff. Clients should focus their efforts on accurately and comprehensively stating the communication challenge, providing all relevant data, and then giving space to the agency to brainstorm and come back with recommendations on the most efficient and effective ways to accomplish that objective. This is their expertise and the client shouldn't do their job. As David Ogilvy once said, "Why keep a dog and bark yourself?"

AGENCY VIEWPOINT

"Many years ago, we were regarded as being an investment; today we're regarded as being a cost … If you invest in innovations and brands you win. Fundamentally I do believe that what we do adds value, when harnessed with innovation."[140]
—SIR MARTIN SORRELL, FORMER CHIEF EXECUTIVE OFFICER, WPP AND EXECUTIVE CHAIRMAN, S4 CAPITAL

ROOT CAUSE #4: LACK OF ROLE CLARITY
Solution: Ensure clear decision-making

Advertisers that are known to often change direction midstream, or who have inefficient approval processes with too many stakeholders involved, or require excessive rework cycles, are staffed more generously by their agencies in anticipation of these inherent inefficiencies. Agencies are more likely to build buffers to avoid having any shortage of agency talent. Having clear guiding principles on how the brief is vetted and approved is critical. Ideally, the brief requires the formal signature by the brief owner to be considered "final." Seeking internal alignment or dealing with potentially conflicting guidance by teams with various agendas can quickly complicate and confuse the agencies. The briefing process must allow enough time for that process to successfully unfold. Roles and responsibilities within a client organization, between the client and the agency (or even among multiple agencies working on the same assignment), may not be clearly defined from the outset. There shouldn't be any ambiguity about who is on point to approve the brief and ultimately the work itself. Is it Matthew, the CMO, who occasionally drops in last minute during creative reviews and is known to have veto power? Is it Angela, the strongly opinionated brand manager, responsible for writing most of the brief but doesn't seem to ever find time to attend meetings scheduled by the agency? Or is it Oliver, the director of marketing, considered the budget owner, but who often delegates to his team? This lack of clarity around who does what can be a major source of confusion and frustration for all involved. Keep the team small: Too many clients will likely create confusion and slow things down. Be clear about the role of all internal clients participating in the briefing. As a large advertiser who shall remain nameless put it to me humorously: *"We often have many final decision makers."* Every brief must have a single decision maker or approver.

ROOT CAUSE #5: LACK OF CONSISTENCY AND EFFICIENCIES
Solution: Standardize, streamline, and automate

The lack of consistency and the manual, labor-intensive nature of briefings can also lead to slowing down the process from initiating the brief internally to finalizing it with the agency. The type of information required, regardless of marketing discipline, must be simplified and standardized so an advertiser has an expedient way to work with multiple agencies. If the brief is iterative, it requires a more dynamic way to handle versioning control, approvals, and effective exchange of information between the client and the many agencies potentially involved. Thankfully, new technology platforms enable a more fluid and flexible flow of information that keeps everyone in the know and overcomes natural human obstacles associated with many moving parts, projects, and large teams. It also keeps the process simple. With so many moving parts, the brief is here to help, not slow down or create more complications.

Advertisers must regularly benchmark and carefully monitor

the quality of briefs submitted to agencies. They must initiate regular audits of submitted briefs to determine what they can do to improve the quality and clarity of their direction to agency partners. They can leverage their client/agency performance evaluation process to ask questions related to the briefing process. Advertisers must also track the number of brief revisions and the number of creative rounds and benchmark those internally to identify marketers who brief superbly and those who consistently do so poorly. Those individuals struggling to brief well probably never received formal training on it. Yet some companies expect their marketing teams to do this well consistently. Those who do it well should provide their teams with training, playbooks, and other helpful resources to determine what is a great SOW or brief vs. what is not.

AGENCY VIEWPOINT

"Many clients are simply trying to settle petty differences within their marketing department when they brief agencies. ("See? I was right. They agree with me.") Try to set the agency up to teach you something new. To break new ground." [142]

—JEFF GOODBY, CO-CHAIRMAN AND PARTNER, GOODBY, SILVERSTEIN & PARTNERS

ROOT CAUSE #6: LACK OF CONCISE AND ORGANIZED CLIENT FEEDBACK

Solution: Provide actionable creative feedback to agencies

I couldn't finish this section without addressing an important part of the information exchange between the advertiser and the agency: the creative feedback. Creative evaluation is the natural extension of the input brief and creative development process. Providing actionable creative feedback to the agency is another important client responsibility, yet so few do it well. The agency presents its creative concepts, typically in a meeting setting, and the client provides feedback on the concepts presented. Advertisers often struggle with this: They have the tendency to get too granular too early, lack an open-minded perspective, or provide conflicting feedback, especially if there are too many voices in the room without clear authority, or worse, the right decision maker is painfully absent. Sometimes, they do not give themselves enough time to step away and reflect before coming back to the agency with a unified point of view. Advertisers should ask clarifying questions during this process and answer the following questions: Is it on brief? Is it a big idea? Is it unique and memorable? Is it likely to stick/last? Does it work broadly, across multiple media/channels? Is it likely to be shared? And is it on brand? Advertisers should start the meeting by reviewing the brief. Give feedback, don't jump to conclusions. Ask for the agency's top recommendation and their rationale. Be transparent and share your thoughts openly and respectfully. Start with the positives and avoid the temptation to focus on details. Be decisive when everyone's input has been provided. Focus on a clear outcome: go, no go, or rework.

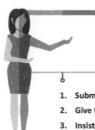

20 EFFECTIVE WAYS TO PROVIDE ACTIONABLE CREATIVE FEEDBACK

1. Submit a clear, concise client input brief
2. Give time for the agency to prepare
3. Insist on an in-person meeting
4. Prepare before showing up
5. Review the brief and project objectives
6. Set clear meeting expectations
7. Let the agency present all its ideas first
8. Evaluate the work based on three simple criteria
9. Ask for input from other participants but be clear about decision making
10. Determine if more time is needed
11. Assess the work objectively
12. Do not focus on executional details
13. Ask clarifying questions
14. Ask for the agency's top recommendation
15. Challenge assumptions or gaps in a productive way
16. Show genuine appreciation for the work
17. Always start with the positive
18. Summarize key feedback points
19. Make a decision — Go, no go, redo
20. Close with clear next steps

To get better work from agencies, advertisers must provide better work from agencies, advertisers must provide better briefs. This universal, ageless principle has never been timelier as advertisers move at light speed. That's also the conclusion of the ANA whitepaper, "Better Creative Briefs," which provides guidance for developing stronger briefing practices to address alarming trends. Any improvement in the quality of agency briefs yields significant impact on the effectiveness of the work and the efficiency of the process to get there—this can be the equivalent to millions of dollars in savings and upside opportunities that few advertisers can ignore. Agencies also play an important role in setting high standards and not compromising: They shouldn't settle for mediocre input; they should push back if the goals are not clear enough; they should challenge any assumptions; bring their own research and insight to the conversation; use their client's team wisely and raise the flag if client responsibilities are not well defined. A good brief doesn't guarantee success. But it significantly improves a client's chances. Advertisers should invest the time to properly define scope of work and brief agencies. There is no room for compromise here. Exceptional work never happens without a solid scope of work and briefing process. So, go ahead now, scope and brief your way to marketing excellence. Agencies and clients perform better when everyone knows what is expected and each player is clear about their role, is clear about the process, understands the boundaries and parameters of any assignment, is provided and provides ongoing feedback, is held accountable for the performance of their work, and is communicating openly and with full transparency. Then both parties might look back, and like the blind men of John Godfrey Saxe's poem, joyfully conclude that both parties are in the right.

TOP 3
BEST PRACTICES
for Advertisers

1. Institutionalize a rigorous planning process to define scope requirements and ensure the optimal ongoing alignment of marketing plans and priorities with agency resources and/or financials.

2. Master the client input briefing process to boost work quality and performance and ensure an effective collaborative process with key stakeholders on both ends, as well as a single client decision maker.

3. Learn to avoid the root causes and common traps of client scope and briefing inefficiencies.

9

THE LOMBARDI RULES

Conducting productive client/agency

performance evaluations

"If you are able to state a problem, it can be solved."
—EDWIN H. LAND, American Scientist and Inventor

Ask "Who is the best sports coach of all time?" and you are likely to get very different answers. In locker rooms around the world, you will hear names like Phil Jackson, Paul "Bear" Bryant, and many others, all equally worthy of this noble title. Regardless of who makes it to the top of your list, what they all have in common is a vibrant, resilient commitment to win as a team. Vince Lombardi is considered a legend in the NFL and a role model for his coaching philosophy and ability to motivate players. Born in Brooklyn, New York, in 1913, Vince Lombardi is known for his infectious drive, perseverance, hard work, and dedication to the sport. Lombardi had a remarkable work ethic that led him to graduate cum laude with a business major, work full time and take night classes in law school and play semi-pro football. In his book *The Lombardi Rules: 26 Lessons from Vince Lombardi, the World's Greatest Coach*, he shares what principles he taught to motivate and lead teams to success:

- Ask yourself tough questions.

- Look the truth straight on.

- Lead with integrity.

- Build team spirit.

He led the Green Bay Packers who dominated professional football under his acute leadership to nine winning seasons, three NFL championships, and two Super Bowl wins. He asked for dedication and commitment from each player. He gave nothing less to his team. His words of wisdom became legendary and his commitment to team success made him one of the most admired and respected coaches in the history of American football. These simple yet powerful ideas apply to virtually any competitive team environment, whether in sports or in business. The best sports coaches are known to be catalysts of team performance. They know that optimal performance can be accomplished only as a team and as a team only. They know that the whole is greater than the sum of its parts. And as a result, they expect much from each other and hold everyone accountable to do their part. Clients and agencies can learn a great deal from sports legends like Vince Lombardi who mastered long before us the art and skill of building high performance teams through structured performance management, direct, timely, and actionable feedback, self-criticism, trust, and mutual accountability.

The fundamental shift in the way agencies and advertisers must engage in this increasingly fast moving, complex marketing world is only reinforcing the critical need for ongoing, direct feedback that fosters a renewed sense of risk-taking, accountability, and partnership. Performance, work quality, and efficiency can be dramatically influenced by reasonable changes in client and agency behaviors, which performance evaluations enable. In the world of Vince Lombardi and sports in general, we are used to countless statistics about team and individual performance. The world of advertising should be no different. My experience working on both sides of the table, derived from an empirical study of high-performing relationships, gives me a unique and balanced understanding of the challenges that clients and agencies face while working together. I am excited to share with you how formal performance evaluations can have significant positive impact on these client/agency partnerships.

INDUSTRY VIEWPOINT

"I used to think that great work led to great relationships. Now I think the opposite: great relationships lead to great work." [143]

—ROBERT SOLOMON, FOUNDER AT SOLOMON STRATEGIC

EXAMINING OURSELVES

FROM GOOD TO GREAT

PUTTING OURSELVES UNDER THE MICROSCOPE

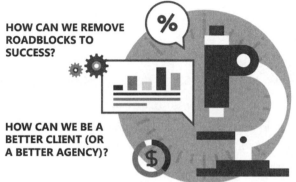

HOW CAN WE REMOVE ROADBLOCKS TO SUCCESS?

HOW CAN WE GET THE MOST VALUE FROM THIS RELATIONSHIP?

HOW CAN WE BEST RECOGNIZE AND FUEL PERFORMANCE?

HOW CAN WE BE A BETTER CLIENT (OR A BETTER AGENCY)?

HOW CAN WE AMPLIFY OR REPLICATE WHAT'S WORKING BEST?

Every advertiser and agency should ask themselves these simple yet essential questions. Given that both are investing a considerable amount of time, energy, and resources to perform up to each other's expectations, building on existing strengths, overcoming weaknesses, and improving the partnership is of utmost importance. Yet relying on anecdotes and hearsay is not reasonable. Formal client/agency evaluations are now common practices. According to a WFA study, 96 percent of brand advertisers have a formal agency evaluation program in place, and the majority feel that those help build and maintain strong client-agency relationships. 30% of CMOs are now directly involved in providing input on agency performance. Providing or accepting feedback is the best way to show that we care. Agencies, and in many cases advertisers, are receptive to the opportunity of receiving (and sometimes providing) constructive input. After all, it makes the relationship more predictable. Performance data is a fundamental resource for brands looking to make better decisions and improve the performance of their work. The effective use of data for managing agency relationships delivers stronger relationship outcomes: According to a 2016 ANA study of advertisers entitled "Using Data to Manage Agency Relationships: What's Important to Marketers,"[144] 82 percent of respondents see it contributing to better overall client/agency relationships; 90 percent see it improving agency efficiencies; 78 percent see it improving internal efficiencies at the client's organization. Early signs of dissatisfaction in the relationship can be detected and formally addressed. It is common sense that identifying issues early on, before they get to be majorly disruptive to the relationship, is in everyone's best interest. Too often, either side goes on, leaving unresolved issues to grow like bacterial infections that eventually end up killing the partnership. There are many examples of long-term relationships that ended abruptly for similar reasons.

Here are the main reasons for evaluating the health of the client/agency relationship:

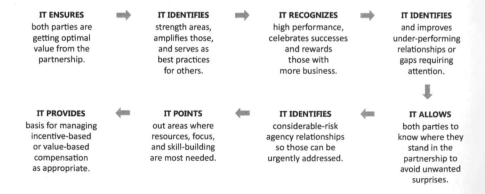

PRIMARY REASONS TO EVALUATE CLIENT / AGENCY RELATIONSHIPS

IT ENSURES both parties are getting optimal value from the partnership.

IT IDENTIFIES strength areas, amplifies those, and serves as best practices for others.

IT RECOGNIZES high performance, celebrates successes and rewards those with more business.

IT IDENTIFIES and improves under-performing relationships or gaps requiring attention.

IT PROVIDES basis for managing incentive-based or value-based compensation as appropriate.

IT POINTS out areas where resources, focus, and skill-building are most needed.

IT IDENTIFIES considerable-risk agency relationships so those can be urgently addressed.

IT ALLOWS both parties to know where they stand in the partnership to avoid unwanted surprises.

AGENCY VIEWPOINT

"We had an incredible relationship with the client for five years. We completely restructured their campaigns, doubled revenue, and totally dominated the competition. The results were so good that the client was finally able to afford a pricey CMO. A month after joining, without even meeting with us once, the CMO sent us a curt letter telling us he was terminating our contract in favor of an agency that had no experience in the client's vertical!" [145]

—DAVID RODNITZKY, CEO AND FOUNDER, 3Q DIGITAL

When performance evaluation is done at the onset of any new relationship, it sets up a baseline to compare future evaluations against. It encourages both agencies and advertisers to be accountable to each other from day one. Most clients have established a formal performance evaluation program and have set clear performance targets for the relationship. They evaluate the work—the **what** *gets done,* expressed as measurable business or marketing outcomes, and the relationship—the **how** *things get done,* expressed as the quality of the delivery and the degree of satisfaction in the partnership and—the **why** *things get done a certain way,* expressed as underlying drivers that impact how people collaborate or behave the way they do. These dimensions, the "What," "How," and "Why" are natural complements. All these views are valuable. Advertisers make the most out of their agency partnerships by investigating, and diagnosing what's working and what's not, to yield positive change and improve mutual satisfaction, strengthen the partnership, and produce more impactful work. Then both parties need to act upon these findings decisively, so their investment in time and dollars pays off, a requirement in a fast-moving world where campaigns are launched within weeks, even days and hours, and results known in real time. A solid performance evaluation program should be built on quantitative and qualitative criteria. These performance metrics will speak not only to the end goal of what must be accomplished, but also to how the work should be conducted. Relying solely on the end goal without setting expectations about how things get done may lead to inefficient behaviors and bad precedents that could be damaging to the relationship or to the work.

The Key Performance Indicators (KPIs) must be exclusively composed of metrics that are under the agency's control. Common quantitative KPIs include campaign results such as gains in awareness and consideration. They also often include business results such as market share and revenue growth. However, it absolutely shouldn't include metrics that agencies have limited ability to impact or are simply outside of their scope, such as stock performance. The metrics used are likely to be part of the company's own regular overall business metrics. The weight assigned to each type of performance metric varies by client. Typically, quantitative metrics make up half of the performance evaluation, of which half of this is related to marketing communication metrics and half to business metrics.

Qualitative metrics represent the other half. The quantitative aspect of performance evaluations is typically core to the way a company runs its business and measures success in the partnership. It varies significantly by client. Most advertisers use a structured survey to capture 360-degree feedback on each other's performance. It typically involves these distinct but complementary dimensions: 1) Feedback from the client assessing its agencies, 2) Feedback from the agencies assessing the client teams, 3) Agencies self-assessing (and sometimes clients conducting a self-assessment) and 4) Agencies assessing other agencies they are collaborating with on the client's behalf.

TYPE OF EVALUATIONS

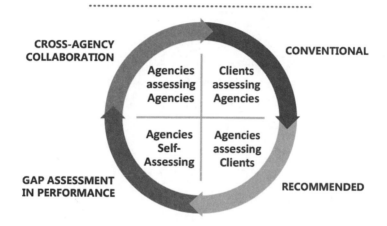

CROSS-AGENCY COLLABORATION

CONVENTIONAL

| Agencies assessing Agencies | Clients assessing Agencies |
| Agencies Self-Assessing | Agencies assessing Clients |

GAP ASSESSMENT IN PERFORMANCE

RECOMMENDED

This data will be used to inform findings-based conversations about how to improve the partnership. It might even be used to determine incentive-based payments if such an agreement is in place. Everyone involved should have a clear understanding of how they will benefit from the evaluation. Both parties must trust the information captured will be used in a constructive and reasonable manner. Then both parties analyze it, review it together, and agree on immediate actions they can take to leverage this insight or course-correct if needed. I've highlighted earlier that agencies are natural extensions of their client's team. So, it is no surprise to find similarities in the way employee performance is evaluated within the client's business and the way they evaluate their agencies. If a client conducts employee performance reviews twice a year, then it makes sense to align to the same schedule. Similar objectives would apply. Even the methodology itself, familiar to the client, can be easily picked up and replicated for agency evaluations.

CLIENT VIEWPOINT

"We've been able to build a robust evaluation process around the world that encourages more productive dialogue, greater accountability, and contributes to better quality work, higher performance, and stronger partnerships with our agencies." [146]
—**STORI WAUGH**, MARKETING DIRECTOR, CONSUMER AND SMALL OFFICE, DELL

Advertisers like Dell rely on the capabilities and performance of talented agency partners in various disciplines and regions around the world to successfully promote its solutions portfolio. To deliver top notch results requires constant refinement and a mutual commitment to collaboration, innovation, creativity, and executional excellence from these partnerships. They rely on a comprehensive feedback process called Dell Agency Performance Evaluation. To get the most value from this evaluation process, Dell focuses on the analysis and set of recommendations that contribute to relationship improvements and better work. With 800 people participating across 27 countries, with an average 85% completion rate and 1,600 thoughtful comments provided, Dell has access to great insights to drive action plans that improve the partnership and work quality. The strong participation is due in part to the great communication around the program as well as Dell Performance Assessment online training, which is completed by hundreds of individuals globally. Holding itself and its agencies accountable to certain performance standards allowed Dell to set the bar high and encourage conversations on how to reach new levels of productivity and performance together.

FIVE EASY STEPS TO EFFECTIVE PERFORMANCE EVALUATIONS
If we can't improve what we can't measure, it's no surprise that advertisers are focusing on putting in place better metrics and up-leveling their agency evaluation programs. They are evaluating their agencies several times throughout the year, and tailor their evaluations to address the different agency types. To conduct a productive client/agency evaluation, advertisers must follow these simple steps:

#1
STRATEGIC AND
OPERATIONAL PLANNING

#6
CONTINUOUS
IMPROVEMENT

#2
COMMUNICATION
AND TRAINING

**PERFORMANCE
EVALUATION
PROCESS**

#5
ACTION
PLANNING

#3
SURVEY FIELDING

#4
REPORTING AND ANALYSIS

STEP 1: STRATEGIC AND OPERATIONAL PLANNING

To be as effective and impartial as possible, expectations must be set, and questions agreed upon early on. In the common reflection areas below, I will share typical survey categories and questions agencies and clients are asked to answer. Both parties will achieve greater results from the exercise if fully transparent during the initial strategic and operational planning phase. At the very least, agencies should validate the criteria and associated client and agency survey questions, so everyone is bought in and therefore, receptive to the feedback received. It would be highly unproductive to have anyone arguing about the legitimacy of the results after the fact. The survey may need to be adjusted annually as the relationship or expectations evolve. Who should participate and provide feedback? Preferably individuals directly working on the account and ultimately accountable for the relationship as well as senior leadership. Although senior client leaders don't work with the agency day to day, their perspective is still incredibly valuable. To facilitate the gathering of names, a scrubbed list is created as a starting point to compile names, typically spread across different geographic locations and/or business units. Less is often more. Participation should be limited to those who interface with each other frequently. Those who do not should be excluded. Their limited exposure can potentially skew results. It is also best not to invite individuals who have been working together less than six months. Don't make it a company-wide proxy vote. Pick a scale and stick with it to measure year over year improvements. Most advertisers use a similar 5-point scale. Here is an example and the definition of each rating:

COMMON RATE SCALE

IMMEDIATE ATTENTION	**BELOW EXPECTATIONS**	**MEETS EXPECTATIONS**	**ABOVE EXPECTATIONS**	**OUTSTANDING**
Unsatisfactory. Is failing to meet expectations and should be placed on a performance plan immediately.	Requires improvement. If improvement is not forthcoming, partnership may be at risk.	Consistently meets expectations	Consistently meets expectations, occasionally exceeding in some areas.	Best in class. They set an example for others.

Advertisers should communicate the implications for falling under an acceptable score. This is particularly helpful in some parts of the world where cultural norms may lead participants to either score on the higher or on the lower end of the scale. It will set expectations for the level at which the agency is expected to consistently perform. Top advertisers are looking to enhance the value of their agency evaluation process to make it as productive as possible. At the 4As Transformation conference, Marc Pritchard of Procter & Gamble Co (P&G) highlighted a problem described by one creative director as "P&G polites you to death." He described how P&G's 5-point rating scale has "devolved" into 1.5 points, where 4.5 is "true love," under 4 is "you're in trouble," and anything below 3 means "you're dead." Feedback can only be useful if it's specific and actionable. One can reasonably suspect that BBDO once fell in the 'you're dead' rating zone with the brand. In 2013, P&G moved the global Gillette men's grooming business to another agency (Grey Group), ending a relationship with its agency Omnicom-owned BBDO that spanned over 80 years. That's right, the two companies worked together over 80 years before one of them decided to pull the plug, something few companies would do without adequate measures. Advertisers must go beyond the scoring exercise. A comment box should be provided with each survey question, or across a category of questions, to generate meaningful, actionable insight. Understanding why something was suboptimal or deficient will make it less likely that the mistake is repeated in the future. Simple, open-ended questions will help illuminate the rationale behind particularly high or low scores. In today's business environment, it's always best to keep the survey to a manageable length. In general, the survey should be designed to take no more than 15-20 minutes to complete to avoid survey fatigue, and to produce statistically valid results from enough participants. The survey length is typically a function of its frequency (higher frequency surveys should be shorter than lower frequency ones) and the company's client culture and management style.

CLIENT VIEWPOINT

"Smart advertisers understand that good advertising comes from a partnership. It doesn't come from an agency just delivering work, and it doesn't come from clients trying to do it on their own. Models will shift; maybe we'll do some specialization around digital and social, and maybe the pendulum will swing back. But people will recognize that the only way to stand out in any of these categories is to have a very strong partner." [147]

—JOHN INGERSOLL, VP OF BRAND AND CUSTOMER EXPERIENCE, CSAA INSURANCE GROUP—FORMER HEAD OF BRAND, FARMERS INSURANCE

STEP 2: COMMUNICATION AND TRAINING

Once the survey has been finalized, clear guidelines and instructions must be provided to the participants. At this stage, it's important to set expectations about the way the information will be used once the survey has been completed. Having a robust communication plan laid out for all participants and stakeholders ensures everyone is clear about the purpose of this exercise and the role each one of them plays. Executive air cover on both sides goes a long way to reinforce the commitment of the organization and the importance of everyone's participation. When senior leaders are involved and provide advocacy for the program out of the gate, participation is higher and commitment to productive feedback improves significantly. Put your marketing hat on. Why is this exercise important to them? What is their expected role? How will results be used? When will the reports be available and who will see them? An online training module can help get everyone up to speed, answer the most commonly asked questions, and encourage participation. It can set clear expectations and ensures survey participants are trained on how to provide useful comments that can yield improvements. Common tips to participants may include:

- Ask participants to apply a balanced point of view. If one circumstance in a full year was especially poor, avoid over-penalizing for that one transgression.

- Similarly, don't give inappropriate overly-glowing ratings.

- Don't place all your ratings in the middle of the scale. We need to tease apart the strong areas of performance from the weak.

- Give credit where due: If they've done a really good job, don't hesitate to use the higher ratings.

- Conversely, if performance is especially weak in some areas, use the lower end of the scale.

- Ask them to devote the time necessary to provide thoughtful, accurate, and actionable feedback.

STEP 3: SURVEY FIELDING

The survey is then sent to the participants. Using an online survey is the most effective way of collecting or organizing input. The link to the survey contained in the invitation email is customized to the invitee's profile, making very clear which agencies or client groups the participant is reviewing. The survey should allow the participants to save their responses if they are interrupted during the appraisal process. They should be able to save their work if they cannot complete it during one session and come back to the survey during the allocated time window and make changes they deem appropriate. It also allows them to take some time to step back and think about the points they want to make. A clear deadline should be provided with ample time to participate. Giving participants two weeks to respond should be sufficient, giving everyone the opportunity to reflect and provide meaningful feedback. Multiple reminders should be sent to non-responders as the deadline nears. Assuming normal conditions and sufficient time for the surveys to be completed, participation rates should be at least 75% on both sides, but ideally 100%. The level of survey participation (especially if low or high) might also provide some useful insight on the level of commitment to the relationship. However, low participation may compromise the analysis, so make sure to rally the troops so they complete their evaluations. Without adequate participation from the right individuals on both sides, the results are skewed and the value questionable. Individual follow-ups with any non-respondents may be needed to understand the underlying issues they face.

STEP 4: REPORTING AND ANALYSIS

Once the input has been gathered, organized, and reviewed, insights gained from the results of the summary synthesis and analysis are shared. Both parties should simultaneously receive summary insight into overall aggregate results and information about which performance attributes were given the highest and lowest scores. Results should be provided within a reasonable timeframe, so they remain actionable and relevant. The actual timing may vary based on the survey's complexity, scope, and reporting requirements, especially if extracting actionable insight is a big part of that process. Analyzing such a vast amount of information—especially non-structured data like comments—can be intimidating. The results should be summarized to highlight key takeaways and high/low ratings. Verbatim should be easily searchable and sortable to inform the analysis. Evaluation results are often analyzed based on several criteria (by topic, agency and agency type, geography, business unit) as well as historical views (year over year), comparative views (client vs. agency, self-assessments), by category, by low or high scores, and several pivots (seniority, job function, type of agency, etc.). The level and depth of reporting may vary significantly from one relationship to another. These reports allow participants to review comments/verbatim, as well as, by attribute or score. Consideration about the way the information will be distributed within the client organization or to the agency should be given before the process kicks off. Failing to do so will erode trust. Using a third-party vendor to conduct the assessment can help.

CLIENT VIEWPOINT

"I've heard a lot of talk about relationships falling apart, but the agency partnership is just like any other relationship. It's important to stay close and be in constant communication. If both parties are willing to work together, most problems can be sorted out." [148]

—**CHERYL CALLAN,** CONSULTANT AND INTERIM CMO, PIER 1 IMPORTS—FORMER SVP AND HEAD OF MARKETING, MARKETING WEIGHT WATCHERS

STEP 5: ACTION PLANNING

Giving feedback isn't enough without a plan. Tying performance feedback with a plan and action items helps to give direction for areas that need improvement and provides guideposts for both parties. Once the information has been collected, it will help inform a findings-based conversation between the client teams and agencies about major themes in the relationship and action plans for improvement overall. Creating an open, collaborative forum to review the results and agree on next steps is critical. Holding a formal, face-to-face meeting to review these findings and come up with a joint action plan will go a long way in establishing a strong foundation for the relationship. This evaluation process is a big waste of time and resources, unless both parties are 100 percent committed to act. Mutually-agreed corrective action plans should include two to three key areas of focus (e.g., improving the quality of input briefing), some of those jointly owned (e.g., create a culture of mutual accountability and respect), with clear owners and due dates, as well as metrics for measuring success and potential roadblocks or dependencies. Here are some examples of common points in action plans:

EXAMPLES OF ACTION PLANS

EXAMPLE OF AGENCY ACTION PLANS	EXAMPLE OF CLIENT ACTION PLANS
Improve timeliness (within 24 hours) of recapping details of agency meetings and calls. Create talent retention plan to reduce staff attrition among senior talent by 25% in Q4. Assign senior copywriting resources with a minimum of five years technical experience and category knowledge.	Improve quality of SOW submitted during planning, especially goals and metrics. Improve accessibility and availability of key client decision-makers during and post- client input briefing. Reduce number of client contacts to decision-maker(s) during creative feedback process for Tier 1 campaigns.

STEP 6: CONTINUOUS IMPROVEMENT

Both agencies and client teams are now working on their respective plans to drive improvements. Performance feedback is useful when it provides detailed, actionable recommendations to improve. Useful performance feedback relies on some sort of roadmaps with predefined dates to check in on progress. This will help ensure that there is improvement. Some of these improvements are short-term fixes while others are long-term commitments. To ensure progress is being made against these agreed-to action plans, a monthly or quarterly review might be necessary to maintain momentum and allow for unexpected roadblocks to be addressed collaboratively. Most advertisers will leverage their existing agency Quarterly Business Reviews (QBRs) to assess how well they are respectively doing in addressing these top relationship issues.

COMMON REFLECTION AREAS

What information should agencies and advertisers share with each other to improve performance? What's important to the partnership drives what will end up in the actual survey. The questions focus on whether each party is fulfilling its obligations. They must be worded to encourage constructive feedback. Each question invites feedback on how any change in behavior, attitude, or engagement can significantly improve the quality of the partnership, and ultimately, the quality and effectiveness of the work itself. Most advertisers tailor their evaluation approach for different agency types. Logically, the approach and questions must reflect the type of agency (creative, media, digital, etc.), size/scope, and strategic nature of the relationship. Several questions should remain identical no matter the type of agency considered to allow advertisers to conduct comparative analysis. These questions can be weighted (by the advertiser alone or jointly with agencies) based on their relative importance at a moment in time. For example, innovation might be a particularly important attribute this year as the advertiser is entering a highly competitive segment. Multi-facet relationships are likely to expose a range of areas of improvement. These topics are organized by categories. Clients may want to evaluate their agency(ies) based on their abilities in these areas:

CLIENTS EVALUATE THEIR AGENCY(IES)

TYPICAL CATEGORIES	TYPICAL SURVEY QUESTIONS
STRATEGY	• Demonstrates solid understanding of the client's business • Proactively presents new angles and opportunities • Conducts post-campaign analysis and incorporates learnings into plans • Considers longer-term considerations of proposed strategies • Etc.
ACCOUNT SERVICE	• Are responsive despite shifting of priorities and budgets • Demonstrates accountable stewardship of client budget • Executes on brief, on time, and on budget • Follows up in a timely manner, providing fast turnaround when needed • Etc.
CREATIVITY	• Understands how to translate business objectives into creative solution • Leverages research to inform creative recommendations • Creates ideas that break through and have lasting impact • Develops channel-agnostic ideas • Etc.
INNOVATIVE THINKING & MINDSET	• Provides clear, insightful recommendations that push the envelope • Considers other points of view to arrive at breakthrough ideas • Challenges assumptions and pushes back constructively • Demonstrates ability to leverage new trends and innovative concepts • Etc.
COLLABORATION	• Approaches project collaboratively with internal teams and stakeholders • Openly shares information with other agencies • Acts impartially, no matter where input comes from • Proactively seeks to establish strong relationships with other agencies • Etc.
STAFFING	• Prioritizes workload and manages resources effectively • Assigns the right talent (type, seniority and number) • Minimizes talent attrition • Handles staff transitions smoothly • Etc.

Agencies may want to evaluate their client(s) based on their abilities in these areas:

AGENCIES EVALUATE THEIR CLIENT(S)

TYPICAL CATEGORIES	TYPICAL SURVEY QUESTIONS
GUIDANCE	• Produces quality scope of work and briefs • Provides clear strategic thinking and direction • Shares actionable data and information • Sets reasonable goals and timelines • Etc.
FEEDBACK & DECISION-MAKING	• Provides constructive and honest feedback to agencies • Reviews agency work and recommendations with an open mind • Delivers consolidated input and approvals from internal stakeholders • Secures buy-in and makes cohesive and timely decisions • Etc.
COLLABORATION	• Creates a culture of mutual accountability • Fosters an environment of group collaboration • Ensures clarity of roles and responsibilities for all involved • Incorporates input and shares direction among all roster agencies • Etc.
SUPPORT	• Shows appreciation for the agency work and gives credit for efforts • Values and respects the agency's point of view and perspective • Supports successful roll out of ideas and projects internally • Challenges agencies productively to tease out better work • Etc.
PARTNERSHIP	• Treats agencies as partners, not vendors • Takes accountability for mistakes • Provides time and resources necessary to produce great work • Sets realistic expectations for the relationship • Etc.
COMMITMENT TO INNOVATION	• Encourages and rewards innovative ideas • Enables agencies to push teams outside of their comfort zone • Takes calculated risks • Demonstrates willingness to fund and support out of the box ideas • Etc.

EVALUATION CONSIDERATIONS

There are several important decisions that a client must make prior to implementing an evaluation program, including the type of questions asked, who should participate, how often it should be conducted.

KEY CONSIDERATIONS FOR CONDUCTING A PERFORMANCE EVALUATION

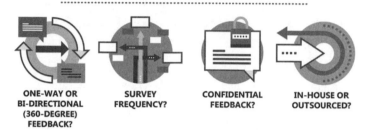

| ONE-WAY OR BI-DIRECTIONAL (360-DEGREE) FEEDBACK? | SURVEY FREQUENCY? | CONFIDENTIAL FEEDBACK? | IN-HOUSE OR OUTSOURCED? |

One-way or bi-directional (360-degree) feedback? A one-way evaluation means that only the advertiser is providing feedback to the agency. It implies that areas of improvement are limited to the agency and fails to acknowledge the role played by the client in influencing the performance of its agency partner. Some advertisers do not have an effective way to process and handle feedback from agencies, or simply don't find as much value from it as they do in providing feedback. In practice, most advertisers understand that reality and use a 360-degree evaluation process. In the prior common reflection areas, you may have noticed that these are logically paired: For example, an agency's ability to come up with innovative, breakthrough ideas is highly influenced by a client's willingness to take risks. Advertisers willing to take accountability for their role in driving certain behaviors in the relationship should implement 360-degree evaluations that give both parties the opportunity to share constructive feedback. From ballrooms to boardrooms, it always takes two to tango. Self-assessment questions can also be insightful. The inability to see performance issues signals perception gaps and misaligned expectations.

CLIENT VIEWPOINT

"It all comes down to trust. If you trust your partner, you can talk frankly with one another, you can get the most value from the relationship. People who understand the agency business have better relationships with agencies. It's a collaboration of ideas, a sort of give and take, and a safe relationship where people can say things and not fear to be being penalized for it. My best agency relationships are those who tell me when I am being unreasonable." [150]

—SUSAN MARKOWICZ, GLOBAL ADVERTISING AGENCY MANAGER, FORD MOTOR COMPANY

Survey frequency? How often should you conduct this evaluation process? As often as deemed necessary is the best answer. However, industry best practices point to the following: Most advertisers are evaluating their agencies several times throughout the year. Once a year is a minimum to keep a pulse on the relationship. Twice a year is increasingly more common, allowing for a light mid-year pulse. Semi-annual reviews are also common for incentive-based compensation models, giving everyone time to course-correct quickly and avoid unpleasant surprises by year end. The French say that bad news is like bad wine: it never improves with time. An open line of communication is most important to any partnership. No one wants to wait six months to find out if the partnership is delivering to everyone's satisfaction. Ad-hoc, automated, or trigger-based evaluations are also acceptable, especially in the event of unexpected performance concerns. Performance feedback has a greater impact when it pertains specifically to a situation that has just occurred or is occurring in the present. If it gives a team the opportunity to course-correct in the moment, so much the better. Shortly after a project is completed, or a new ad produced, the advertiser and the agency should meet to conduct a post-mortem. This type of real-time feedback process should be completely automated and limited to a few, short questions. Advertisers and agencies should be comfortable having open, frank conversations regularly and informally, on an ongoing basis, as often as needed, in addition to a more structured, rigorous approach.

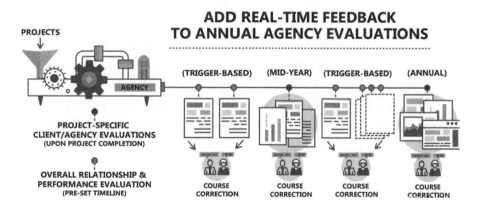

CLIENT VIEWPOINT

"Today we have qualitative metrics to conduct performance evaluations. We also have an open discussion every six months with our partners to review how they did. This is also a time to learn if we as a company are providing our partners with the tools for success." [151]

—CARLA GIOVANNETTI DODDS, BUSINESS AND MARKETING CONSULTANT—FORMER HEAD OF MULTICULTURAL MARKETING, WALMART

Confidential feedback? For most clients, this is a tough question to answer. There is no real relationship without trust. How you gather input and how you use it will either reinforce or weaken it. Can agencies and clients be candid in their feedback? It also has much to do with the company culture and management style. Most prefer surveys to be confidential, like employee surveys, encouraging more open feedback without having to fear potential retaliation or retribution. Confidential feedback tends to skew results towards the negative as people take a chance to vent on issues. Some argue non-confidential surveys encourage more balanced feedback and make it easier to address improvement areas when you know precisely where to find them. There are certainly pros and cons to either scenario. Either way, both parties must be assured of their respective commitment to work on improving the partnership. They must trust that the information will be used constructively.

In-house or outsourced? Thankfully, the years of rudimentary internal IT solutions, basic survey tools, Word or Excel-based rating documents sent as email attachments, manual data collections, and disorganized and informal feedback are over. Hallelujah! We all deserved better. Specialized performance evaluation solutions are now mainstream and enable this end-to-end process to go smoothly and effectively, reducing time and effort while improving our ability to extract more useful, actionable insight from the results. These robust, secure, scalable, and customizable solutions are designed to be simple, quick, and engaging to use. They allow advertisers to spend more time on value-add activities such as diagnosing issues, internalizing core insights, and developing meaningful action plans that up-level the value of this process. Using a neutral party to coordinate these evaluations and analyzing the results builds trust in the process and the outcome. Consultants with deep professional expertise about client/agency relationships can add tremendous value to advertisers looking for help in setting up and/or managing these evaluations. These experts can draw from their vast experience to objectively review results, tease out actionable insights, and make recommendations to strengthen the relationship.

CLIENT VIEWPOINT

"I often get asked whether longevity in client/agency relationships is important to us. An advertiser can be with an agency for 10 years. Or only 10 months. In the end, it's all about performance. Are you getting a high performing agency team on your business? This is what's truly important. If your agency delivers consistently for 10 years, then longevity is a great thing." [152]

—MARTINE REARDON, FORMER CHIEF MARKETING OFFICER, MACY'S

AS TWO FAMILIES ARE BECOMING ONE. WE ASK THAT YOU CHOOSE A SEAT, NOT A SIDE. J+L

WHAT DO HIGH-PERFORMING EVALUATIONS HAVE IN COMMON?

Misunderstandings and misalignments are quite common in all relationships. Expectations are not clearly communicated, and the absence of timely, direct feedback only makes things significantly worse. Well-designed and orchestrated performance evaluations significantly reduce the likelihood of a partnership falling apart. However, despite concerted efforts on everyone's part, sustained high-performance relationships are rare.

Too many advertisers still fail to get a good read on the relationship before it deteriorates to the point of no return. A few things can get in the way of a productive relationship. Both parties may not be asking the right questions to the right people. They may not extract actionable insight or focus on what matters most. They may not be clear on what actions to take. They may not know where to start. They may not trust that the information will be used in a constructive manner. They may fear the process will end up being a finger-pointing exercise. They may feel that they must pick a side instead of a seat at the table. Thankfully, client/agency performance evaluations have been around for a while now and industry best practices have rapidly emerged, removing the guesswork and improving the value of this process. Successful client/agency performance evaluations share the following characteristics:

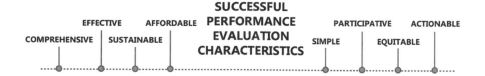

SUCCESSFUL PERFORMANCE EVALUATION CHARACTERISTICS

COMPREHENSIVE — EFFECTIVE — SUSTAINABLE — AFFORDABLE — SIMPLE — PARTICIPATIVE — EQUITABLE — ACTIONABLE

- Comprehensive: They must provide a holistic view of the relationship and its multiple facets.

- Effective: They must drive positive change and justify the time/resource investment.

- Sustainable: They must help identify trends over time, across geographies, or across agencies.

- Affordable: They must be reasonable in cost and time commitment.

- Simple: They must be simple to set up, and roll out, with effective training and communication.

- Participative: They must be considered conclusive and get adequate participation.

- Equitable: They must foster active collaboration, respect, and trust. They must also be balanced.

- Actionable: They must generate actionable insight that can translate into tangible improvements.

CLIENT VIEWPOINT

"Successful relationships are based on trust, respect, and accountability. As accountability grows in a partnership, so does trust and respect." [153]

—JAMES R. ZAMBITO, SENIOR DIRECTOR GLOBAL CORPORATE AFFAIRS, JOHNSON & JOHNSON

As we all know from experience, evaluating employee performance is one of the most crucial roles played by responsible employers. It's about driving individual excellence and developing high-performing teams. Similarly, a relationship between an advertiser and its agency(ies) is a significant investment in time, effort, and resources. It's therefore imperative to evaluate the return on that investment and continuously fine-tune it. Every relationship deserves and benefits from a constructive, honest feedback-loop process. Coach Vince Lombardi summarized it best: "The achievements of an organization are the results of the combined effort of each individual." When clients and agencies take accountability for their shared responsibilities in an open, collaborative, transparent, respectful, and self-critical environment that strives for excellence, they create a shared vision, and the partnership flourishes.

TOP 3
BEST PRACTICES
for Advertisers

1. Commit yourself to provide actionable feedback and be open to receive feedback as well, and spend quality time selecting a set of questions that will draw meaningful insight.

2. Set up a regular performance evaluation process to capture, analyze and share the results, with the end goal to identify specific action plans on both sides to improve the work and relationship.

3. Focus your efforts on making sure these actionable plans are being successfully implemented and progress is regularly monitored for course correction and continuous improvements.

10

GOTTMAN'S PAPER TOWER TEST

Partnering towards mutual success

"Great things are done by a series of small things brought together."
—**VINCENT VAN GOGH**, POST-IMPRESSIONIST PAINTER

Success is said to be vastly contagious. Leading advertisers have relationships with successful agencies because as the saying goes: behind every great client is a great agency. Agency executives have long known that the secret of profitability is through the success of their clients. They also know that partnering with the right client is essential. That's right: behind every great agency is also a great client. There has been a great deal of debate on how to build better relationships, considering frequent reviews and constant turmoil in the industry. I am sure you will agree that building strong, lasting relationships takes concerted effort, commitment, and compromises in both our personal and professional lives.

John M. Gottman, PhD, the author of a *New York Times* best seller *The Seven Principles for Making Marriage Work* (Three Rivers Press, 1999) has been studying what makes relationships stick at the Love Lab in Seattle, an apartment research laboratory at the University of Washington. The lab features state-of-the-art technology and proprietary software derived from mathematical models integrating nonlinear differential equations. Their team can pinpoint the strengths and challenges in any relationship and provide specific recommendations to positively adjust the course of a couple's life together. The couples being analyzed are connected to the lab's wireless, state-of-the-art physiology equipment that measure heart rate, pulse transit time, respiration, and facial movement. They are guided through two brief conversations with each other, which are video recorded for analysis.

After many years of scientific research and experiments, John and his wife, clinical psychologist Dr. Julie Schwartz-Gottman, co-founded The Gottman Institute in 1996 to bring decades of research to the public and help improve relationships by leveraging reliable patterns in observational data to discriminate happy from unhappy couples. They have come up with a proven scientific-based methodology to determine with great accuracy which relationships are most likely to succeed and those which are doomed to fail. The Gottmans can tell with an average of 90 percent certainty whether a marital discussion will resolve a conflict after the first three minutes . . . and the couple's chances to stay together in the long run. They could even predict not only if a couple would divorce but also when.

BEHIND EVERY GREAT CLIENT
IS A GREAT AGENCY
AND VICE VERSA

Among Gottman's many exercises, one of them is called the "paper tower" test where a couple is tasked to build a free-standing paper tower using scotch tape, a stapler, markers, newspaper, a ball of string, paper, and colored cellophane. What the participants ignore is that the result of this exercise is far less important than the way the couple interacts during that experiment. The way a couple partners on accomplishing the task provides remarkable insight into the health and strength of that relationship—as well as its ability to last over time. Sure, some couples might complete their paper tower project but at what cost? Will the relationship survive the next exercise? According to Gottman, successful relationships tend to follow several interaction styles that are producing positive outcomes and feelings. But it doesn't mean that these fruitful relationships are conflict-free. Conflicts are not bad if those are handled productively. The answer to conflict is rarely problem solving but rather mutual understanding. It is true of any kind of business relationship as well. Client/agency relationships are no exception to that rule. Through mutual understanding, clarity of purpose, and aligned expectations, both agencies and clients can produce better work together. Gottman also observed that unsuccessful relationships fall into negative interaction styles that undermine collaboration and performance.

We have plenty of examples of negative behaviors in the client/agency environment. Let's be frank. It's worse than negative . . . it's sometimes harmful and incurable. Agencies often drive their clients mad. And clients drive their agencies crazy. Let's see how:

HOW AGENCIES DRIVE CLIENTS MAD

Based on years of research and experience working with brand advertisers and agencies, I identified 20 primary ways advertisers drive their agencies crazy, and in the process, sabotage their own efforts. Experienced advertisers know better; they know how to turn these agency relationships into productive partnerships that deliver outstanding work. However, it takes two to tango. Agencies also play an important role in cultivating successful or failed relationships. Sorry agencies, you are not off the hook. Yes, agencies can drive clients equally mad, and they often do. Let's take a closer look at the things agencies say and do that undermine a sense of true partnership, and what can be done about it:

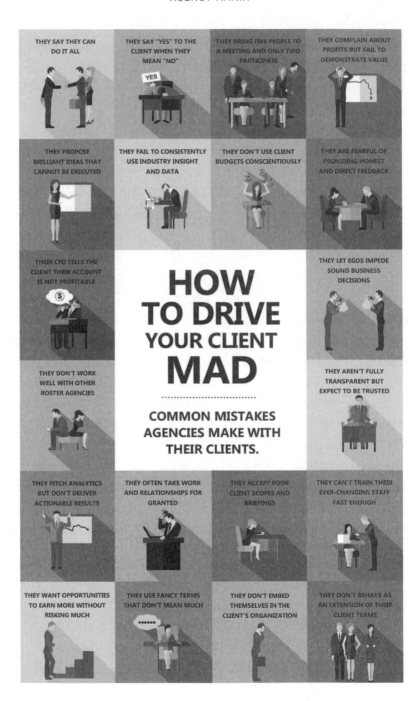

#1: They say they can do it all.

Agencies have the tendency to claim they can do it all when an opportunity arises, for fear of losing a new business opportunity. By doing so, they over-exaggerate the true capabilities they have and set themselves up for failure when the work suffers down the road. Advertisers have no choice but to challenge their agencies as a normal course of action to fully understand what they can really do well. Agencies should always be clear about what they do and don't do. Expect clients to require demonstration of core capabilities, conduct pilots, and set very clear parameters for the type of work agencies are officially approved to do on their behalf after they prove themselves.

#2: They say "yes" to the client when they mean "no."

The agency business is a service industry. As a typical service industry, the tendency is to please customers at all cost. That cost is often too high, frankly. Clients value agency partners who know how to say "no" if they disagree with the approach, or believe it is not in the best interest of their client. It takes integrity and courage, but then again, as strategic advisors, this is what is expected of agencies.

#3: They bring five people to a meeting and only two participate.

Have you ever attended a meeting in a room full of people that do not seem to have a clear role? Rather than taking account-ability for debriefing other team members accurately and in a timely manner, some agencies default to bring everyone that might be involved in a project. It turns out to be very expen-sive for clients, and they often wonder why so many attended when, so few actively participated. Clients and agencies should set clear guidelines for travel and meetings, so they can work together efficiently.

#4: They don't work well with other roster agencies.

Advertisers expect their roster agencies to work together collaboratively. Everyone seems to say the right things when they commit to share information and collaborate. Yet the reality is often a series of territorial issues with agencies more preoccupied with protecting their turf than looking for ways to best support their client efforts. They are not to blame at times. Advertisers should clarify the roles and scope of their agencies, so territorial concerns are minimized, and the focus is on the work itself.

#5: They propose brilliant ideas that cannot be executed.

Agencies thrive on coming up with new, breakthrough ideas that clients love and that earn them awards at shows. However, their out-of-the-box ideas are not always grounded in real, pragmatic execution. The budget requirements are too great, the scalability of the idea is not realistic, or there are various brand constraints or regulatory restrictions that get in the way. Agencies must concentrate their efforts on reasonable, actionable recommendations. Clients can also provide clear parameters in the briefing process to minimize potential waste.

#6: They fail to consistently use industry insight and data.

There are many aspects of what agencies do that are based on experience and instinct. Some agencies regularly shoot from the hip. After all, this is a big part of what advertisers are seeking from agencies. Yet agency recommendations must be based on meaningful consumer insight and research. W. Edwards Deming once said, "Without data, you're just another person with an opinion." An opinion informed by data is simply a better opinion.

#7: They don't use client budgets conscientiously.

And they should. Advertisers look to their agencies to be fiscally accountable, steering their budget and exploring ways to drive cost efficiencies on their behalf. How often are agencies coming back to their clients with recommendations on how to drive costs down? Not often enough, most clients would agree. Advertisers should provide feedback to their agencies on how good they are at providing financial stewardship and being accountable to the resources made at their disposal.

#8: They are fearful of providing honest and direct feedback.

If they are challenged to say "no," one can only imagine how likely they are to provide honest, straight-forward feedback to their clients. We see it in 360 performance evaluation surveys where some agencies are naturally shy to provide feedback. The fear is quite legitimate. Some clients don't have the backbone or appetite to receive feedback and act based on it.

#9: They want opportunities to earn more without risking much.

Incentive-based compensation is common in large client/agency agreements. Agencies eagerly consider opportunities to earn more, and that's a very legitimate expectation. However, when facing the potential downside associated with the upside they seek, the enthusiasm softens. The risk must be proportional to the opportunity, and agencies must be willing to take it on. Clients must also be reasonable by balancing the two carefully.

#10: They aren't fully transparent but expect to be trusted.
Trust is the cornerstone of relationship building. Recent issues in media and production have exposed business practices in the agency world that often lack adequate transparency. Agencies expect to be trusted. Yet trust is earned, not given. Providing full transparency is a critical first step in building a trustworthy relationship. Transparency is a two-way street and clients must also be transparent with agencies.

#11: They complain about profits but fail to demonstrate value.
From experience, I would say that most advertisers are willing to pay more when they get demonstrated value from their agencies. Many agencies often complain about the lack of profitability of their client account, yet too little of the focus is on finding ways to deliver greater, sustained value to clients. Focusing on value is the only way to address profitability concerns over time.

#12: They let egos impede sound business decisions.
If you have ever participated in creative review, you know how much passion the creative team puts into the work they do. That's all good. But egos can also get in the way of rational business judgement. Frankly, it's very difficult to remain impartial and unbiased when reviewing creative work. Agencies and clients must acknowledge that fact and produce the work that best supports the marketing objectives.

#13: They pitch analytics but don't deliver actionable results.
Advertisers can't go through a pitch presentation without extensive focus on analytics capabilities. Nothing wrong with that—to the contrary. But when it's time to operationalize

these ideas, agencies often fail to deliver strong analytics and actionable campaign results. It's either too little, too late, or too much data without meaningful insights. The agency should set realistic expectations and deliver results that clients can act upon.

#14: They often take work and relationships for granted.

Landing a new client often feels like a marathon for agencies. Once they win the pitch, the real work actually starts. A few years into the relationship, there is a natural tendency to take client relationships for granted. Agencies don't push the envelope as aggressively and become complacent over time. Regular performance feedback ensures expectations are clear and met.

#15: They accept poor client scopes and briefings.

Poor briefs lead to mediocre work. Clients often rush through new assignments and do not provide the necessary guidance agencies need to deliver great work. Too many agencies accept this as their everyday reality, trying to compromise and make trade-offs, which ultimately lead to the demise of the relationship. Don't allow for work to start without strong scopes and clear and comprehensive briefs.

#16: They can't train their ever-changing staff fast enough.

Agencies have a very tough time attracting and keeping talent. It means the agency is a revolving door and new folks often join the client team without proper training or onboarding. When agencies fail to communicate these changes to the clients, it doesn't look good. Clients don't always make it easy for new agency personnel to get trained on the basics of the partnership (the company's overview, brand standards, operating guidelines, etc.), requiring the agency's account team to be proactive in sharing the necessary details to get new talent up to speed.

#17: Their CFO tells the client their account is not profitable.
Has any client ever met an agency CFO who didn't complain about the lack of profitability on the account? I'm not sure—it appears that part of the negotiation process at agencies is to focus on poor guidance, scope creep, and budget reductions. There is no doubt that some agencies are not getting the return that they deserve or need to sustain a healthy business. Agencies must also be transparent about their level of profitability, so clients and agencies can find a fair and equitable balance between being competitive and being reasonable.

#18: They use fancy terms that don't mean much.
To impress clients, agencies often use fancy terms to describe their approach or their offering, which it turns out, might be rather conventional. They are masters of rejuvenating existing ideas and concepts and serving them up as new capabilities. By doing so, they can easily confuse advertisers who have to decipher what they say to understand what they are buying, instead of spending time and energy to bring the ideas to life operationally.

#19: They don't embed themselves in the client's organization.
Many client/agency relationships happen to be remote, as the main agency office might be hours away from the client headquarters office, forcing the teams to rely on technology to communicate. By failing to spend adequate time embedded within client teams, agencies miss out on the opportunity to learn and experience the business on a daily basis, lessening their ability to react in a timely manner to client needs. Some agencies are co-locating staff at client offices to address this concern, and advertisers often have "agency days" during the week.

#20: They don't behave as an extension of their client teams
Advertisers face growing challenges and pressure points internally. When their agencies come short of showing a level of commitment, dedication, and accountability on par with internal teams, they lose credibility in the eyes of their clients, creating a divide. Agencies that do behave as an extension of their client teams often blend in in such a way that it's even hard to tell who is whom in a meeting. Then and only then, the agency and client team are behaving as one.

Poor agency practices contribute to sub-optimized relationships and vice versa. There are many other ways agencies can drive their client mad. By acknowledging what those are, we can start driving positive change and help client/agency partnerships flourish. Don't get mad. Don't get even, either. Lead by example.

HOW CLIENTS DRIVE AGENCIES CRAZY

Many client behaviors guarantee you will fail your agency every time. Those who believe that common sense is not so common anymore are in for a real treat. American humorist, writer, teacher, television host, and journalist Sam Levenson said so brilliantly: "You must learn from the mistakes of others. You can't possibly live long enough to make them all yourself." Find out what so many have learned the hard way: 20 demonstrated ways brand advertisers set up their agencies for failure, drive them insane, and in the process, sabotage their own marketing efforts, GUARANTEED.

#1: They expect agencies to know their business as well as they do.

"Why should I take the time to educate them on my business?" Sure, agencies would benefit from having some understanding of the category or prior relevant experience before working on your business. But they will never know your business as intimately as you do, nor should they. Give them time and opportunities to learn your business but maintain this as your area of expertise.

#2: They keep information to themselves.

"I am busy enough. Do they really need more information?" All clients are struggling to keep up with the workload and demands placed on them. So, naturally, taking the time to prepare, organize, and share information with their agencies might not be high on their priority list. However, agencies cannot operate effectively without being well informed throughout the course of a project about the business context, marketing priorities, or creative mandatories. Help them help you by providing timely and usable information.

#3: They change their mind frequently for less than obvious reasons.

"We just need to go another route. It's probably for the best." Change is the new constant. We all know that. That means changing your mind occasionally is not only necessary, it's vital. But changing your mind frequently for no apparent reason leads to wasteful efforts and excessive agency fees. At the very least, make sure agencies are aware of the rationale behind the change of strategy so they too can benefit from it.

#4: They ask for strategic work to be rushed.

"I need it yesterday and it's got to be your best thinking!" Asking for strategic work to be rushed is like asking to prepare a gourmet cassoulet in two minutes. It's a recipe for disaster. Agencies need adequate time to think strategically to make sound, well-informed recommendations. When they don't, agencies cut corners and ultimately this contributes to failed execution, re-concepting or suboptimal work. Don't rush important work.

#5: They expect agencies to write the brief themselves.

"I am way too busy to write it. Can you quickly put it together, so we have a paper trail?" Much gets lost in translation and the brief is often weak. The results speak for themselves. Garbage in, garbage out. However, if you want great work from your agencies, set the example, take ownership of the brief, and spend the time to accurately capture the objectives of the assignment by providing actionable information.

#6: They pretend to be the final decision-makers (but are not!).

"It's my call … well, of course, unless I get overruled." Too often, the work is being challenged late in the process because the final decision makers are not involved early enough. Clients might suggest that they have final authority, only to realize that they are unwilling or unable to sign off on the final product. Agencies go back to the drawing board, and the project is delayed, and they are required to bill additional time to complete the work. Insist on getting the real stakeholders and decision makers involved early on.

#7: They jump into the work without clarity of goals or preparation.

"Let's get the team started. I don't have all the details, but we can figure out the objectives as we go." This is a common pain point: Clients ask agencies to jump in immediately. No brief has been submitted. The client has half of the information needed: objectives are vague, timing is still TBD, success metrics are unclear. A PO may not even be open. It means that the work has started and it's out of compliance with corporate policy. Clients too often use the brief process to clarify their strategy, instead of stating it. Prepare accordingly.

#8: They do not provide timely or actionable feedback.

"We should probably have said something earlier. Oh well, now you know." Who likes to be surprised? No one, really. When we fail to provide feedback, or the feedback is too late for someone to learn from it and act, we do ourselves and others a disfavor. How many times are agencies learning that they will miss their bonus, or the account is in review without getting a chance to address the issues? The feedback is not always actionable either. There is no better way to sabotage a relationship. Don't keep things to yourself. Provide feedback consistently so they can course correct if needed.

#9: They are always critical and never acknowledge great work.

"Although the agency team stayed at the office all weekend long to make up for our slow response, it feels as if I would write better copy if I did it on my own." Bad clients are always critical and do not see value in telling agencies when they do well. They believe that agencies produce better work when they are consistently pressured or criticized. It's far from the truth. Tell them how great the work is and make sure your feedback is balanced.

#10: They consistently threaten to take their business somewhere else.

"Once again, if you don't get this done by next week, I will give the assignment to another agency that is waiting for my phone call." Bad clients use fear as a technique, hoping to get the agencies to agree to their unreasonable requests. Clients can only pull this card so often before it completely loses its impact. This is not a viable long-term approach and ultimately backfires. Instead, build a culture of respect and collaboration.

#11: They make false promises and under deliver.

"I thought I could get you paid much sooner but it's really out of my hands." Agencies are not expected to over promise and under deliver. Nor should clients be. When clients make false promises, it sets up an environment of distrust and false expectations that are detrimental to any relationship in the long run. Set realistic expectations and lead by example at all times. Agencies appreciate it and will be more likely to go the extra mile when you need them to.

#12: They believe agencies are overpaid and expect them to operate at cost.

"Come on ... we know them to be very profitable with other clients, so they can take a loss on our business. Is being on their client list not good enough?" This is a sensitive topic on both sides. Are some agencies overpaid? Probably. Should agencies be expected to work for free? Absolutely not. When agencies are profitable, they hire better talent and become even better partners to their client. Transparency goes a long way to improve perception and get clients to understand that agencies, like them, are operating a business that must be sustainable.

#13: They treat agencies as order takers.

"We just need your agency to create two display ads and one magazine print ad! When can we get those?" Advertisers who treat their agencies like order takers are getting what they deserve: tactical execution and low value. If you want great work, treat your agencies as strategic partners and see the difference it can make. State the problem you are trying to address; don't impose the solution. If you are using agencies tactically, you are only getting a very small amount of value. If you are not getting strategic value, then consider other agencies. The best agencies won't let clients treat them as order takers very long. They too know better.

#14: They are rarely reachable or available to answer questions.

"I wish I could, but I really have no time to meet or answer any questions. Proceed with what you have." Some decisions must be made in a timely manner to keep projects on schedule and on budget. Some questions must be answered for the project to proceed. Yet too many clients don't make themselves available to their agencies, and the work suffers. They don't answer emails or phone calls in a timely manner and agencies are left making important decisions without the client's input to keep the project on time and on budget. As a client, make yourself or someone on your team always reachable to answer questions and keep things moving with agencies.

#15: They consistently drop in on Friday evening with Monday deadlines.

"So glad I was able to reach you so late on Friday afternoon. Something came up. Hope you didn't have any plans this weekend." Agencies understand better than most professions the need to be available to their clients in a moment's notice. The nature of marketing makes the work more fluid, and time to market shorter than ever. The agency business is a service industry and a certain level of flexibility is required. But when clients abuse their status repetitively, it creates unhealthy environments that lead to higher agency staff attrition and demotivated teams.

#16: They ask for strategic, innovative ideas but don't want to pay for or can't afford them.

"Although we significantly reduced budgets, we still want you to deliver innovative and breakthrough ideas on every project." If agencies are not appropriately funded to staff the account with the right individuals in strategic planning and innovation, they are likely to fall flat. Advertisers must give agencies the resources they need to deliver. Or set realistic expectations if they are not funding them well enough to staff important roles on the account.

#17: They are asking the agencies to hire ahead of revenue but won't commit.

"We won't agree to a retainer yet, but need your agency to guarantee us dedicated resources, even in down times." Agencies are often hiring talent ahead of revenue, but to do so, they typically need some line of sight into the near future to make these investments. Retainer-based relationships provide a buffer for agencies to invest in staffing the account and to minimize cash flow concerns. Project-based work might be the right approach at times, but clients should understand the inherent agency talent consequences.

#18: They kick off a review at the first sign of challenges.

"We will put the account in review. The last project was disappointing." There are many valid reasons for putting an account in review. Especially if the client and the agency have done their due diligence to address whatever challenges and mutual responsibilities they played in the downfall of the work relationship. However, some clients will rush to conclusions and find themselves to be "trigger happy." Relationships have hiccups and bumps along the way. Jumping ship too quickly is unlikely to provide the long-term fixes that are most likely needed.

#19: They ask the agencies to figure out how they should work together.

"You have extensive experience working with other clients. Tell us how we should operate." Most agencies indeed have extensive experience working with clients that might be leverageable in this relationship, but every client has unique requirements that must be clearly articulated for the work to flourish. These requirements are often captured and documented in a Service Level Agreement that ensures all agencies are working with clear engagement rules around campaign processes, approval processes, reporting and analysis expectations, and more. As a client, define these rules of engagement so everyone is aligned from the outset.

#20: They consistently ask agencies to compete on work and collaborate as well.

"Why can't you get along? If you do well, we might give you some of their business." Advertisers expect their roster agencies to collaborate well and play well together in the sand box. And they should. As long as they share common goals and have clear rules of engagement. Some clients, however, set up these agencies to fail by forcing them to compete against each other, making them territorial, and inviting them to do land grabbing and act paranoid as they fear losing work. It's impossible to do both. Set clear engagement rules so agencies know their specific role instead of having them figuring it out on their own, and agencies will operate in a trustworthy environment that benefits the client.

It doesn't take much to miss the mark. A little too much to the left or to the right, and you miss your target. The same applies to effective client/agency relationships. You don't need to fail agencies in all 20 of the above common mistakes to miss out on the opportunity to get great work. It just takes one or two, and clients fail to get the value these important partnerships can deliver. So, what are the prerequisites of strong client/agency relationships? What makes or breaks relationships? What's a true partnership and how should both parties behave? What's the recipe for success? What makes a good vs. a great client or agency? How do agencies produce such great work that they become an indispensable piece of the client wheel? When things turn bad, how do you patch things up and recover? How do you build on existing relationships and get the most value from them? Advertisers have asked these daunting questions for years. Many still struggle to come up with definite answers, but one thing is certain: asking these questions is getting you one step closer to answering them. In this chapter, we will explore key ingredients needed for a partnership between an advertiser and its agency to grow and flourish.

CLIENT VIEWPOINT

"What are the key ingredients for a great client / agency relationship that really matter? Mutual respect and a passion for creating business outcomes is fundamental, and that's fostered with on-going, authentic feedback. Like in any long-term partnership, clear communication and joint understanding are both critical ingredients for success. We look for the agency to deliver creatively and remain flexible— while celebrating success together and trying new things to keep the teams motivated." [154]

—PETER TORRINGTON, GENERAL MANAGER & MANAGING DIRECTOR AT COLGATE-PALMOLIVE

WILL YOU MARRY ME FOR JUST ONE NIGHT?

This is one of many popular pickup lines. But it's a lot more than just humorous. If you work in the advertising industry, this line is more likely to make you cry your eyes out than laugh. Endless client/agency reviews in prior years have exposed us to countless stories of failed relationships worthy of the script of the most popular drama shows. Some of the most notorious ones include: Fast food giant McDonald's let go its agency of 35 years, Leo Burnett. Fast-food chain KFC is replacing its nearly 10-year incumbent media agency MEC. Swarovski replaced its media agency of nine years, and I could go on and list hundreds of failed long-time client/agency marriages. According to Agency Spotter, the average agency of record relationship lasts fewer than three years. Many decade-long iconic relationships have come to an end in favor of what appears to be nothing more than one-night stands with new, sexy agencies. Some of these new relationships don't even survive a year. Let's look at the most significant contributing factors to this disastrous phenomenon and consider four wedding vows that will ensure yours will last longer than a Kardashian marriage:

CLIENT VIEWPOINT

"If you look at the trust with Wieden+Kennedy, they have longstanding relationships with a lot of partners throughout the world. Predominantly, of course, their flagship partnership with Nike. Those are the kinds of partnerships we want to develop, with agencies and all of those marketing partners throughout the world. We truly see this as a long-term relationship of like-minded organizations from a cultural perspective." [155]

—**JORN SOCQUET,** VP MARKETING USA,
ANHEUSER-BUSCH INBEV

Vow #1: Apply more rigor in selecting the right partner.
An expedited selection process and lack of thoroughness are the main reasons for failed client/agency relationships. As reviews are aggressively shortened to quickly select and onboard a new agency, clients often make compromises to speed things up. There is tremendous pressure to minimize the business impact of making

an agency change, so clients are forced to skip important steps like in-person chemistry checks with all agency team members or conducting reference checks. The result: the lack of process rigor leads clients to hire partners that are not the perfect match and are therefore likely to be short-lived. Similarly, agencies eager to get "in bed" with a new client might fail to properly assess how strong a fit it is and figure out as they go how to make the relationship work, despite some inherent gaps in mutual expectations. A cavalier approach or overly aggressive review process may endanger the outcome and create more inefficiencies and delays in the end. Do it right or don't get started at all.

AGENCY VIEWPOINT

"It's our responsibility to coach our clients on how to get the best work out of their agency. It's not an easy conversation but when it's warranted, delivering some tough love is critical in building a partnership. And remember, it's not one sided. Don't forget to check in internally and ask "What can I do to make this better?"[156]

—**IAN BAER,** CHIEF STRATEGY OFFICER, RAUXA

Vow #2: Commit to professional excellence in providing/receiving feedback.

As we saw in prior chapters, we can't improve what we can't measure. We can't fix what we don't know might be broken. It's surprising to hear that some brands still have not formalized a 360-degree performance evaluation process, which provides a much-needed platform for continuous improvement on both sides. The result: brand advertisers change agencies frequently without valid reasons. These decisions are too often made subjectively, without data to inform them, leading to a revolving door of agencies coming and going. Not to mention the significant time and effort associated with handling these reviews and onboarding new agencies. Even when brands conduct regular performance evaluations, they are too often using outdated, cumbersome, data-rich but insight-poor methods that fail to provide truly actionable insight. For some, it's like checking a box on a to-do list. Only those genuinely committed to regular bi-directional feedback and willing to invest in industry best practices are getting useful information to course-correct or improve the quality, speed, or cost associated with the work. When brands up-level the way they capture or share feedback with their agencies, they can proactively identify the root causes of some of the inefficacies and make sure they do what they can to set up their agencies and themselves for success in the long run.

CLIENT VIEWPOINT

"Oh, and for God's sakes, give them your gut reaction. React, laugh, grimace, anything. Do not give them a prepared polite response. If you say "I loved No. 3, hated No. 2 and think No. 1 has potential, they will come over and kiss you. If you don't know, say it and say why. Someone once told me the best clients are the ones who, if you walk into the room, you wouldn't know who the agency was and who was the client. Strive for that." [157]

—LESYA LYSYJ, PRESIDENT, US, WELCH'S

Vow #3: Build a genuine culture of partnership and collaboration.

We've seen this movie many times, haven't we? A new CMO gets appointed and a new agency soon after is assigned agency of record status. The relationship is being held at the executive level and is mandated from the top down throughout the organization without much consideration to encouraging or promoting a culture of collaboration from the bottom up. The significant turnover in marketing leadership has led to myriad reviews in creative, media, digital, and other disciplines. Much consideration must be given to set up the new partnership for success by investing in a robust onboarding process and a strong emphasis on a culture of collaboration at every level of the organization and among roster agencies. At the 2016 ANA Masters of Marketing conference, Verizon's Executive Vice President and Chief Marketing Officer Diego Scotti spoke to the power of collaboration: "We are stronger together than we are apart." According to Scotti, putting collaboration into practice is everything.

AGENCY VIEWPOINT

"Encourage and celebrate bravery. Taking risks, albeit calculated ones, is the best thing to break through in today's world. It also attracts and retains the right talent, as well as the right clients." [158]

—**BRENT CHOI,** CHIEF CREATIVE OFFICER, J. WALTER THOMPSON NEW YORK AND CANADA

Vow #4: Enable innovation, velocity, and impact through empowerment.

There is no greater contributing factor to vastly shortened client/agency partnerships than missed expectations or unclear objectives. When the goals and expectations are not clearly stated at the beginning of the relationship, it inevitably leads to disappointments, wasted efforts, and agency reviews. Setting up an operating model that is designed to foster innovation, velocity, and impact is empowering agencies to lead and excel. This is what Deborah Wahl, Senior Vice President and Chief Marketing Officer of McDonald's USA Inc. has built as part of the brand's new agency called "Cortex." It puts cultural insight, consumer insight, media data, market context, business data, and user journey at the center, all of which are driven by a roster of agencies like Omnicom's Annalect and sparks & honey, and supported by DDB, OMD, and others driving innovating thinking, moving at the speed of culture and focused on business impact. At the ANA Masters of Marketing, Wahl pitched "never ending transformation based on human intelligence at the speed of now," as an approach that is built to win and last.

4 VOWS FOR A
LASTING PARTNERSHIP

VOW #1
APPLY MORE RIGOR IN SELECTING THE RIGHT PARTNER

VOW #2
COMMIT TO PROFESSIONAL EXCELLENCE IN PROVIDING / RECEIVING FEEDBACK

VOW #3
BUILD A GENUINE CULTURE OF PARTNERSHIP AND COLLABORATION

VOW #4
ENABLE INNOVATION, VELOCITY AND IMPACT THROUGH EMPOWERMENT

Brand advertisers must consider the implications of constant agency reviews and apply more thoughtfulness to choosing the right partners, building the right model of collaboration, feedback-rich processes, and efficiency for these client/agency relationships to prosper and last. Agencies play an important role as well to adapt to the changing landscape that requires brands to move faster, innovate, build better content, and operate in a more streamlined fashion. Then, and only then, agencies and their clients can drop dated pickup lines like "Do you believe in love at first sight?" or "Should I walk by again?"

THE DNA OF A SUCCESSFUL PARTNERSHIP: THE APPLE AND TBWA\Chiat\Day EXAMPLE

Can you tell the difference between a vendor relationship and a business partnership? Hopefully you can. Business partnerships are few. Look at the Apple and TBWA\Chiat\Day relationship. Apple has been a remarkable business story that continues to inspire. In 2010, AdAge named Apple the marketer of the decade, celebrating the amazing brand the company built, which has contributed to its amazing commercial success, making it one of the most valuable companies on the planet. It's undeniable that Apple's marketing has been incredibly effective. Apple's influence on marketing and advertising is undeniable, ranging from the brilliant, breakthrough Super Bowl "1984" television spot for Mac to building legendary customer loyalty and an over-the-top customer service shopping experience with Apple stores. Its marketing success has much to do with the successful partnership between the company and its brilliant advertising agency, TBWA\Chiat\Day. What are the key ingredients of a successful partnership like the one between Apple and TBWA\Chiat\Day? Spending nearly two decades evaluating business relationships with the goal to improve them or yield better value has helped us identify the most common ingredients of a successful partnership between a brand advertiser and its agencies:

AGENCY VIEWPOINT

"Ken Keir, former head of Honda and one of the best clients in the history of clients, always said that he was only interested in ideas that scared him. . . . So next time you are in a review, look for the ideas that start to jar with you. Take notice of the idea that makes you uncomfortable or even nervous. You just might be onto a real winner." [160]

—**KEVIN CHESTERS,** CHIEF STRATEGY OFFICER, OGILVY UK

Provoking and demanding: Good clients and agencies expect this. These qualities foster strong bonds and help deliver better work. No doubt, TBWA's Lee Clow met the most demanding and thought-provoking client in Steve Jobs. In

1997, Steve reportedly gave the agency only 17 days to launch the entire "Think Different" ad campaign—TV commercial and billboards included. Not long enough for most agencies to even secure the rights to the images. The TV spots and print ads ran for five years after that. When you expect more, you get more. Good enough is never enough. And it goes both ways.

Adaptive, responsive, and culturally compatible: Having the right culture fit is critical to having both organizations come together and work together effectively. Even as CEO of Apple, Jobs met weekly with its agency partner TBWA. Both clients and agencies must be responsive to each other, invest the time required, collaborate well with all their internal and external partners, and adapt rapidly as circumstances or needs change.

AGENCY VIEWPOINT

"I learned lots of things during my 20 years at BBDO and one of them was that agencies are creatures of their clients. If you compared the quality and leadership involvement of the people who worked at one major account with those on another you would never think that both groups worked at the same agency." [161]

—ED PAPAZIAN, PRESIDENT, MEDIA DYNAMICS INC

Reciprocal passion and chemistry: Client and agency leadership need to genuinely share a common passion for their respective mission and purpose. And people need to like each other, especially under pressure, which is inevitable. The relationship of Lee Clow and Steve Jobs was based on a real friendship that ultimately helped them produce award-wining work. They shared a passion for disruptive ideas. Do people like working with each other? Will they get the best from each other? Will they be there for each other when things get tough? There is a reason why chemistry is such an important part of any search process. If it's not there, the relationship will ultimately fail.

CLIENT VIEWPOINT

"Mutual accountability means that you succeed together, or you fail together, as one. It's that simple. Client/agency relationships should be conducted more like joint ventures with business partners, with aligned goals and metrics, than as transactional buyer and vendor relationships." [162]

—MICHAEL E. THYEN, DIRECTOR OR PROCUREMENT, INTERNATIONAL BUSINESS UNIT, ELI LILLY AND COMPANY

Trust and transparency, commitment to feedback/open dialogue: No relationship can be built and flourish without absolute trust. Trust comes from full transparency—about client priorities, agency finances, and more—and can only be earned over time. An email exchange between TBWA Media Arts Lab CEO James Vincent and Apple CMO Phil Schiller in January 2013, then picked up by the media, showed how blunt and direct the two partners allowed themselves to be. So being committed to providing feedback and having open dialogues about any topic that might get in the way of the work or the relationship are essential to building good will that translates into outstanding performance.

CLIENT VIEWPOINT

"Communication is key. It's kind of trite, but it's the secret to any great relationship. BBDO and GE have a super open, very communicative relationship. We talk, we see each other, and we spend time together." [163]

—**LINDA BOFF,** CMO, GE

Nonconformist strategy and critical thinking: Advertisers want and need critical thinkers in their agencies who will challenge the status quo, never cease to ask "why?", and push clients outside of their comfort zone. Advertisers look to their agency to bring strategic ideas to the table and act as a trusted adviser, and, conversely, agencies want clients that articulate a clear strategic direction and are willing to think outside the box. The campaign "Shot in one day entirely on an iPhone," directed by Ridley Scott, illustrated the unconventional approach the two partners would entertain to break through in the marketplace.

AGENCY VIEWPOINT

"Smart marketers greatly increase their chances of breakthrough work through co-creation of their agency ecosystem, clarified roles and responsibilities, and selection of agencies that are adaptable enough to lead and succeed in a constantly evolving world." [164]

—**BRYAN WIENER,** EXECUTIVE CHAIRMAN, 360I

Expertise and executional excellence: When it's time to produce, the work must be impeccable and demonstrate the domain expertise of the agency in a functional discipline (creative, media, PR, social, etc.) or industry category. Apple's marketing is nothing short of a superb, high-quality, and flawless execution. Advertisers like Apple must institute streamlined processes for the work to flow internally and to allow for effective and timely decisions.

CLIENT VIEWPOINT

"Agencies are often hesitant to push clients. Great agencies should have the confidence to be heard, to say "no" to status quo if they truly believe it's the right thing for their brand. They get their senior people to engage with a clients' senior management. They make concerted efforts to stop doing work that is little value-add to clients." [165]

—JAMES R. ZAMBITO, SENIOR DIRECTOR GLOBAL CORPORATE AFFAIRS, JOHNSON & JOHNSON

Resourceful, collaborative, and innovative: Being innovative, finding creative solutions to complex challenges, and being resourceful are essential qualities that set apart the mediocre from the most brilliant in any business relationship. This is particularly true in a client/agency partnership that is destined to produce outstanding work. In 2006, TBWA created Media Arts Lab to exclusively serve Apple as a new type of ad agency that creates culture, not just commercials. They produced highly innovative work like the iconic "Mac vs. PC" campaign and 66 spots created by TBWA\Media Arts Lab between May 2006 and October 2009.

CLIENT VIEWPOINT

"Pitch us on an idea even if we didn't ask for it. That shows that you know and care about our business." [166]

—KIERAN HANNON, CMO BELKIN INTERNATIONAL

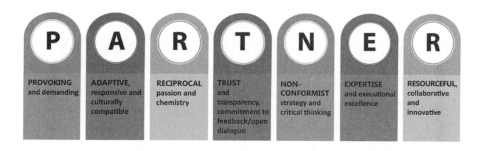

P	**A**	**R**	**T**	**N**	**E**	**R**
PROVOKING and demanding	**ADAPTIVE,** responsive and culturally compatible	**RECIPROCAL** passion and chemistry	**TRUST** and transparency, commitment to feedback/open dialogue	**NON-CONFORMIST** strategy and critical thinking	**EXPERTISE** and executional excellence	**RESOURCEFUL,** collaborative and innovative

Looking back, it seems to me that Clow and Jobs set new standards for what two companies can accomplish together when they choose to become long-term partners and produce amazing work. By the time you read this book, the relationship between these two brands may have strengthened or they may no longer work together. Who knows? Relationships are not static, leadership and priorities change. Open your eyes to the possibilities these best practices bring and follow these principles, so you too can realize the transformational value a well-managed partnership can bring to your marketing efforts. Nationwide's CMO Matt Jauchius at the Ad Age CMO Summit made a compelling base for a better approach to working with agencies if you aspire to get more from your agency: "Stop treating your agency like a vendor."

THOUGHT-PROVOKING PARTNERSHIPS

CLIENT VIEWPOINT

"I love it when one of my valued agency partners tells me
I'm wrong." [167]

—JOHN HAYES, CHIEF MARKETING OFFICER,

AMERICAN EXPRESS

As the Gottmans validated in their studies about marriage compatibility, not all disagreements in relationships are bad. Even good relationships are not free of conflicts. To the contrary. Tension and occasional conflicts are a healthy part of any relationship. It's not uncommon to see strong agencies and clients in prosperous partnerships embracing occasional thought-provoking and feisty conflicts that bring out the best of the partnership. A certain amount of tension is desired, as agencies respectfully question the client's strategy, seek to validate key research and business assumptions, ask challenging questions, or simply challenge the status quo because someone should. As a result, they often push them in new directions and unfamiliar territories. Can they disagree respectfully? They can do this in a constructive way, not for the sake of arguing, but to look at things from a multitude of angles. They can afford to challenge their clients because they've built enough equity in the "relationship" bank account that they can draw from it when things occasionally go sideways. Thinking differently is an asset that must be cultivated. This is an important part of the value realized by working with a third party. Let's face it. There is no shortage of "yes" people to support clients in their decisions.

CLIENT VIEWPOINT

"Openness is a must for a healthy partnership. And don't hesitate call BS on us when we deserve it. We're adults, and we can take it." [168]

—KIERAN HANNON, CMO BELKIN INTERNATIONAL

Agencies seek new perspectives that clients wouldn't consider unless challenged to do so. It takes a mature client to welcome a healthy dose of tension in the relationship without getting to the point where it becomes unproductive. There are good and bad conflicts. Good conflicts encourage clients and agencies to step outside of their comfort zones, and think constructively to deal with their differences of views and opinions. Bad conflicts are sources of strain in a partnership. Bad conflicts are those where no consensus or compromise can be reached and there is no positive outcome. Valuable resources are wasted.

Advertisers must encourage their agencies to come together as "Castellers" in Catalonia would ("castel" is the Catalonian word for "castle.") A castell is an 18th century tradition in the southern part of Catalonia where members of a team come together to form a human tower up to ten levels high and involve several hundred people.[169] It starts with a strong foundation of packed bodies, holding arms, and hands together. The base provides strength and stability to the structure. Then teammates climb on the shoulders of the ones below, one layer at a time, working together to build a unified, connected structure that is based on strength, coordination, trust, and balance. Without these team attributes, the structure would fall and break apart. Each party has a role to play to make the partnership successful. Most long-term partnerships are built on mutual respect, trust, and integrity. Gottman says that people who stay married live four years longer than people who don't. Something tells me it might be true in business as well. But who really wants to find out?

TOP 3
BEST PRACTICES
for Advertisers

1 Learn ways to turn client/agency relationships into productive partnerships by addressing what drives clients mad and agencies crazy.

2 Follow four vows of successful relationships: Apply more rigor in selecting the right partner, commit to professional excellence in providing/receiving feedback, build a genuine culture of partnership and collaboration, enable innovation, velocity, and impact through empowerment.

3 Encourage thought-provoking dialogue and occasional tension to get everyone out of their comfort zone and tease out innovative concepts and better work.

11

THE ERA OF
"PARTNERSHIP CAPITAL"

A glimpse at the future and what it
means to agency/client relations

"Coming together is a beginning; keeping together is progress; working together is success."
—HENRY FORD, AMERICAN INVENTOR AND AUTOMOBILE PIONEER

Born on July 12, 1895, in Milton, a suburban community 20 miles from Boston in Eastern Massachusetts that prides itself on a rich historical heritage, Buckminster Fuller had a reputation for coming up with ideas that were somewhat unorthodox and futuristic for his time. Ideas of this American architect ranged from flying cars to floating communities and geodesic domes. He invented words such as going "outstairs" and "instairs" (instead of "downstairs" and "upstairs") and "world-around" to acknowledge that movement is done in respect to the center of Earth. One of the most intriguing facts about Fuller, a frequent traveler, is that he was known to wear as many as three watches:

one for the current time zone, one for the zone he came from, and one for the zone of his destination.

Today, the advertising industry is at a critical inflection point. Like Fuller, we may need three watches on our wrists to keep us sane: one to remind us of where we started, one for where we are today, and one for what the future might look like. However, many of us would disagree about the nature of the events in the time each of these watches signifies. Especially the one that tells of the future. It's partially because the advertising world is profoundly changing, and your perception might be significantly altered based on where you sit. When I say change, I mean "big" change. Not small waves, but seismic, tsunami-style waves, enabled by technology and consumer behavioral changes. It affects how we speak to each other in everyday life. It also affects how brands communicate with consumers. We might as well call this transformation "client mania." And the pace of change is far from slowing down. No one knows with certainty what's on the horizon. The scale and speed at which these changes are taking place is whiplashing both agencies and their clients. As a result, there is chaos in the advertising, marketing, and communication world today. Advertisers do not have the luxury to watch their agencies fail to drive high impact results on their behalf. They cannot commit to agencies that are unable to anticipate their needs or address their challenges. They no longer want agencies that are exclusively paid by filling time sheets, without regard to business outcome or performance. They no longer have the patience to see agencies fight with each other over territorial issues when they need their entire marketing arsenal to work well together. In the end, consumers are too demanding, competition is too tough, financial pressure is too great, marketing is too important, and time and resources are too scarce, for advertisers to undervalue or underleverage their agency partners.

Conversely, agencies don't have the means to jump from one review to another in endless pitch situations. They cannot afford to give away their valuable work or ideas. They cannot build sustainable value when the CMO's office is a revolving door. They cannot act as banks for their clients. Agencies cannot rely on generalists to meet their clients' specialty needs. They cannot credibly be all things to all their clients. In a world of uncertainty, agencies don't always have the line of sight and commitment from their clients to make wise long-term investment decisions in talent and technology. Agencies cannot afford clients who fail to understand that only reasonably profitable agencies translate into stronger partners that will contribute to their own success. The clock is ticking. A fierce debate now rages about what the future looks like for client/agency partnerships. What becomes of advertisers that keep asking for more while expecting to pay less? What will get agencies to take greater risks with their clients? Will agencies risk more to earn more? Will advertisers invest in up-leveling their competency in managing agency partnerships? Under what circumstances will advertisers continue to in-source and build in-house agencies? What will it take to get advertisers to treat agencies as trusted advisors? If the world of advertising is moving in such fast and frantic motion, where is it going? How is the sensible advertiser-agency relationship evolving? How are disruptive technologies transforming the marketing value chain and agency offerings? How do we best leverage their competencies? What should agencies do less or more of to make themselves more valuable to their clients? What do the advertiser and the agency of the future look like? So many questions, so little time. It seems as if everyone is running fast to take the lead, with divergent opinions as to where this is all going.

Client/agency relationships are grossly undervalued and underleveraged. The opportunity is now to transform them into the powerful, fruitful, competitive assets they were intended to be. Only one thing is certain. Regardless of size or industry, savvy advertisers need the talent, creativity, perspective, know-how, and services/tools only agencies can provide. In the so-called "generation of conversation" where brands are also media channels, advertisers must leverage agencies as brand stewards, leading them in evolving, modernizing the way they reach, converse, interact, and exchange with consumers. Agencies, still shaken by the massive force of a business in continued transformation, are adapting to these new conditions by rein-venting themselves, not once, not twice, but as many times as needed to find the best way for them to deliver sustainable value. Agencies are now increasingly competing to own data, content, and technology, in addition to key talent. They are designing agile, responsive, nimble, results-oriented organizations. They can thrive in these new market conditions and can move quickly, change direction, take risks, adapt to ever-changing client needs, and operate cost efficiently. They cannot do this alone and clients must play their role. Advertisers must drive change internally to challenge the status quo in the tireless pursuit of excellence. Clients must empower marketing and procurement leaders to take full advantage of what their agencies can offer and turn those into valuable business partnerships that turbo-charge their business performance.

Advertisers must take ownership of managing agencies by setting up streamlined processes and easier ways to work together. They must carefully examine their needs to come up with the right agency model. They must apply rigor and discipline when searching for the right agency partners, transitioning prior ones and onboarding new agencies. They must set up contracts that are fair and equitable. They must rethink agency compensation to encourage the right behavior and foster shared accountability. They must continually provide and receive feedback to improve the partnership. They must scope work and brief agencies more effectively than they did before. They must prepare and train their marketing organization on how to work better with agencies and become better clients. The opportunity to turn these relationships into partnerships is considerable. Following years of economic progress driven by human knowledge and intellectual capital, we are now entering an interconnected period of "partnership capital" where our greatest company assets are our business partnerships. Clients and agencies of all sizes, from the boutique shop to the holding company, have heard the call. This is an opportunity to drive exponentially greater value from these relationships. This can only be done through mutual understanding, mutual goals and priority alignment, shared accountability, and thoughtful consideration about what makes strong partnerships deliver results repeatedly. How do we make the most of those partnerships in this new era?

Over the years, we will see new partnership models and best practices emerge. Regardless of their flavor du jour, they are likely to have one important thing in common: They will realize the transformational power of the multiplier effect that only strong partnerships can produce. *Agency Mania* is nothing more than a genuine wakeup call to embrace the madness rather than resist it or ignore it. An invitation to thrive in these challenging times and generate high-impact business results requires a guide on how to successfully navigate the disorienting world of client/ agency relationships. It suggests how agencies and advertisers can start this journey together, how to make the most of it and stay ahead of the competition. Advertisers must manage their agency investment wisely and commit to driving greater business value from these partnerships. There is no better time to reset our watches. The client/agency relationship model of the past decade is now obsolete. There is no business partnership more important to a company's success and longevity. Tick, tick, tick. Advertisers and agencies must change how they work together . . . or perish. Together, let's embrace this new era of "Partnership Capital" and harness the madness of client/agency relationships to deliver outstanding customer value and business results.

"One's destination is never a place . . . but rather a new way of looking at things."
—**HENRY MILLER**, AMERICAN NOVELIST AND PAINTER

Wouldn't it be great if we could predict the future accurately? Think about all the decisions you would make differently, as an agency or advertiser. We are living in fascinating times. The advertising business has never experienced such profound change in its entire history. Quality relationships between advertisers and agencies have never been a greater catalyst of effective brand building and business growth than they are today. Yet, they've never been under more scrutiny. The expectations are high on both sides. The pressure is mounting, and as we finish another great year, we all ponder: what will be next? French physician Michel de Nostredame, also known as Nostradamus, came up with a list of long-term predictions in 1555, which are often referenced to this day. Which of past trends will accelerate, stay on course, or change direction all together? If the past is a good predictor of the future, and we connect the dots, what will the future look like for advertisers and agencies?

Are you ready for a brave new world of advertising? "A brave new world" also happens to be the title of a book by Aldous Huxley published in the 1930s that speaks to new developments and technology that would eventually change society. In a way, the convergence of creativity and technology is changing society as well. The digital age has generously fed into a Western culture of togetherness, immediacy, and instant gratification to bring more change in the past decades than the ad industry has experienced in half a century. The digital age provides far more than a foundation for brand storytelling. The 24/7 availability of products and services at anyone's fingertips has accelerated customer realization that they are in control. Advertising is not only adapting to the technology-empowered consumer culture; it's leading it in many ways. Companies are finding ways to give customers choices about how they communicate with them, how often, and where. The dynamics of the advertiser/agency relationship are being disrupted by digital technology, marketing automation, financial pressure, and talent demands. Nostradamus's prophecies have often been associated with the idea of the end of the world being imminent. In a far less dramatic way, it's obvious that the world of advertising as we've known it for the past decade is coming to an end.

DEATH AT A FUNERAL

Consumers have learned to distrust advertising, the clutter, the irrelevance of messaging, and the constant interruptions it generates. They now proactively block advertisements, using technology such as on-demand streaming and pop-up blockers, even paying premium services to avoid disruptive, unwanted, contextually-poor advertising. Building and nurturing brands, even in the face of an advertising-averse audience is something that agencies do well by trade, and as a result, their unique perspective becomes increasingly more valuable to their clients.

CLIENT VIEWPOINT

"It's astonishing to me that we still have digital agencies. Do we have print, radio or out-of-home agencies? Of course not. We expect our agencies to be skilled at all mediums." [170]
—MARC S. PRITCHARD, CHIEF BRAND OFFICER, PROCTER & GAMBLE CO.

They know how to reach consumers in meaningful ways and make the brand an incredibly powerful asset on the balance sheet. The ability to embrace and energize brand principles and deliver solutions that bring the brand to life in every piece of communication has always been vital to an agency's success. But they are now facing unprecedented challenges. The traditional marketing model of mass production and analog marketing is obsolete. Advertisers can no longer rely solely on traditional media to move their business forward. Advertisers have been shifting their marketing spend to more effective disciplines. Marketing services have experienced tremendous growth in the past decade and the category is expected to continue to grow more rapidly than traditional advertising—or at the expense of traditional advertising during a slower economy. Holding companies have seen their revenues generated from marketing services rapidly exceed those previously dominated by advertising services. Advertising will continue to play an important role in the mix, now most frequently confined to driving awareness and buzz. These marketing services can best be characterized by the fact that their strength doesn't come from scale as in traditional advertising, but from applied insight and discipline execution; not from artists, writers, or big idea tanks, but from various specialty consultants, programmers, researchers, data analysts, engineers, and data scientists. The growth of marketing services has been fueled mostly by marketers' continued interest in more targeted, measurable, accountable marketing vehicles and by agencies finding inspiration in delivering creative ideas on new platforms as consumer habits and interactions continue to shift. Perhaps this trend is further accentuated by the higher cost of traditional media resulting from the increased fragmentation in broadcast media and a shift in media consumption habits, making marketing services attractive substitutes to advertising.

The years of the lavish TV production budget and standout 30-second spot placed in extravagant Super Bowl buys are now waning while advertisers desperately look for new ways to bring meaning to their platforms. It appears as if traditional forms of media are slowly dying. Years ago, prime-time network television had such broad reach that advertisers were pretty certain to hit their target audience, even with an inefficient buy. Now network television events of large scale—those in excess of 90 million viewers (such as the World Cup, the Olympics, and the Super Bowl) are in such limited supply that the cost has reached new heights: A 30-second spot reaching 90 million viewers like the Super Bowl will cost you more than ever before. Network cost per thousand continues to rise faster than inflation. Advertisers are shifting budgets to invest in videos and mobile. They are integrating these new tactics into their mainstream marketing plans. Agencies must now look for new flavors of skills and talent to compete and thrive. As agencies migrate to diverse marketing services, the number of specialized offerings is likely to increase, making it challenging for them to replicate the scale and cost efficiencies they enjoyed from their traditional services. Higher agency profitability will enable them to invest in R&D and talent, and as a result, develop even more powerful offerings. To stand out, advertisers will embrace these new capabilities, even at higher cost. It will require advertisers to apply thoughtful consideration, relying heavily on a highly-tuned discipline of agency management to select, manage, and optimize these rapidly evolving relationships. They need to deal with a richer, larger set of agencies, operating with different business models and with unique and distinct engagements.

TECHNOLOGY EVERYWHERE. FOR EVERYTHING.
Technology is a profound social and cultural force in today's economy. Digital is the reason behind the powerful and seamless blending of technology, branded entertainment, and media. Digital media

are pervasive and have revolutionized the way we talk to consumers, plan and execute campaigns, buy media, and measure results. Digital technology enables "always on" marketing compared to the traditional "campaign drop"-based approach, changing the way clients and agencies must work together. The way information reaches audiences today is equally as impactful as the message itself. Media is considered by many to be the new "creative." Digital media have forced us as advertisers to think differently about the timing, relevancy, and contextual nature of the multitude of communication channels and social networks in which messages are distributed or conversations are held. Often the medium dictates the nature of the message, gaining life organically in active social webs. Advertisers can no longer rely on behavioral assumptions and inferences developed based on viewer demographics. They now have access to rich predictive behavioral data about the actions of customers. The radical and lasting transformation of the landscape, propelled by the rapid growth of digital, has not given traditional agencies much time for reflection. It has pushed them into reactive mode as they attempt to defend their endangered client territories against sparkly new capabilities sported by small digitally-born shops. The phenomenal growth and dynamic nature of digital media in all facets of our lives (the digital lifestyle as you might call it), societies, and economies has opened remarkable new opportunities for brand advertisers to engage and influence their audiences and provide consumers with an immersive, convergent experience.

A new kind of agency is emerging, addressing a more demanding consumer and evolved marketing department. The agency of the future breaks the silos of marketing and technology, aligning priorities and erasing inefficiencies. They innovate constantly. They push the limit of what's possible. Advertisers find themselves having to do more with less, spending their budget more effectively on higher return, higher-accountability marketing vehicles. CFOs are asking CMOs to step up to greater fiscal accountability by investing in media outlets that allow them to test, scale, and optimize based on measurable marketing performance. In this convoluted ecosystem where there are increasingly blurry lines between software, media, and advertising, everyone seems to compete for marketing dollars. Ad tech companies are building increasingly efficient ad delivery solutions, producing customer data and rich analytics, generating audience insights and analytics, and automating virtually every step in the marketing funnel. Agencies will invest in R&D to incubate and experiment with new technologies. They will develop tools and applications on multiple platforms, identify M&A opportunities, depose patents, and secure strategic partnerships and alliances. Some of these agencies are turning into comprehensive software development entities, creating alternative sources of revenue. Consolidation will continue for years to come as agencies expand their offerings to stay competitive. As technology becomes omnipresent and everything is finally "digital," technical competencies will no longer be a relevant point of differentiation for agencies in the future.

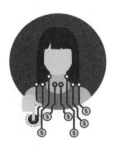

THE YOU ECONOMY

On its December 2006 cover page, *Time Magazine* surprised everyone by introducing the Person of the Year: "You." "You control the Information Age. Welcome to your world." The balance of power has permanently shifted from advertiser to consumer in what some call the "democratization of marketing." Technology is opening options to advertisers they never had before, turning the tables to talking less and listening more. Digital makes everything participatory and transactional. As a result, customers engage more as well, and companies are turning it into a competitive weapon. In the case of Doritos' annual ad contest, the brand's biggest fans get the opportunity to create and submit Doritos-themed commercials, then vote online to determine the few lucky ones that are to be aired during the Super Bowl. Advertisers gain immediate audience insight. They must be responsive, and agile, adapting their messaging in real time and treating consumers with a greater level of attention, leading to higher customer satisfaction and brand advocacy.

Today's knowledgeable consumers turn out to be willing programmers, media producers, publishers, and distributors all at once, using blogs, community forums, social networks and digital word of mouth vehicles to help brands tell their stories in authentic ways. What was once described as "the age of interruption," which was rife with methods used to grab attention to break through and stimulate unconscious desires in the consumer's psyche, is long gone. Companies are now looking to actively, continuously, and deeply engage consumers and influencers with their brand, establishing a unique and compelling brand connection through personalized brand experiences. This phenomenon doesn't come without challenges. The metaphor of a marketing funnel where the buying process happens in a very linear way is obsolete. This deliberate engagement is enabled through tools and vehicles that help advertisers generate value beyond transactions, based on their active involvement, interactions, and dialogues with the brand. The spread of mobile devices is accelerating the number of options for consumers, and therefore for advertisers, transforming the dialogue from a one-way monologue to a rich conversation with user-generated content and social networks of engaged customers weighing in. It's about marketing messaging as conversations. Social channels are now considered "mainstream." Advertisers are furiously scratching their heads as they wonder: At what cost, and at what return? We are witnessing both a cultural and business phenomenon of magnitude. Participation becomes the currency of customer value and a critical way clients are measuring marketing performance.

This new breed of agencies will need to adapt their hiring strategy to attract talent that is culturally immersed into these trends and develop deep knowledge on how to tap into them. They will continue to invest in knowledge sharing, advanced collaboration, and community-building tools, internally embracing new ways of working and adopting the rich tools and capabilities they are building for clients. In return, advertisers must carefully evaluate their agencies for their ability to embrace, master, and skillfully capitalize on these new participatory capabilities.

CLIENT VIEWPOINT

"We as marketers have to adapt and support these fundamental changes. We have to be evangelists. Business is more complex, customers are more demanding, budgets are constrained, agency talent is sporadic, traditional ways of doing business or compensating agencies are now obsolete. Everything has to be re-evaluated with a higher focus on accountability." [171]

—JAMES R. ZAMBITO, SENIOR DIRECTOR GLOBAL CORPORATE AFFAIRS, JOHNSON & JOHNSON

MAKING EVERY DOLLAR COUNT

You can't finish a presentation without someone asking about ROI and ZBB (zero-based budgeting). These three-letter acronyms are the most powerful in business and can make your CFO smile. It's about time. But many others frown. Marketing budgets are increasingly tight and CMOs struggle to effectively measure ROI or justify investments. In today's harsh economic climate, C-level executives are asking questions about the accountability of every dollar spent. The notion of accountability is now, more than ever, a priority area for CMOs eager to keep their desk position a while longer. Every marketing initiative is scrutinized and must be justified with a solid business case before getting funded, hence the growth of zero-based budgeting. John Wanamaker, the 19th century department-store business man warned us: "Half the money I spend on advertising is wasted. The trouble is, I don't know which half." The digital era makes everything more measurable. However, the sea of tools, service providers, and data sources is making it harder to discern what's important from what's interesting.

Thankfully, agencies are helping advertisers sort through and filter campaigns. At its core, the fusion of art and science gives birth to a new marketing life force that is highly traceable and measurable. At almost every industry conference, discussions turn to the evolution of advertising as a dependable, measurable discipline. What you can measure, you can improve, and herein lies a world of opportunities to optimize marketing campaigns and ensure every dollar is spent wisely. The most common concerns are related to the changing media landscape, which is uncertain, and therefore a source of confusion. Deeply rooted in internet media for which measurability is in the DNA, this level of accountability has clearly generated much interest in other areas of marketing communications less accustomed to such level of scrutiny. Standard ROI measurement tools for traditional media pale in comparison with digital. This explains how these have rapidly gained popularity among advertisers. Industry leaders such as Facebook, Google, and Amazon, are introducing new measurement tools and audit capabilities to gain the favor of CMOs concerned about rising fraud and deliverability issues.

This focus on marketing accountability has put many CMOs on the hot seat within their companies, with CEOs and CFOs demanding tangible proof that their marketing investments are paying off and that marketing dollars are ever-more efficiently spent. Because of this, the average CMO tenure is shorter than ever before. As a result, agencies are working hard to preserve existing client relationships, despite the revolving door of the CMO's office. With this amplified emphasis on marketing accountability and ROI, left-brained thinkers and their right-brained counterparts must come together to apply the right-brain creative process to the pursuit of measurable results. Agencies must also embrace these new methods and provide reporting and analytical services of their own.

As the lines between the various media channels continue to blur, clients are asking their agencies to address the intricacies of how one channel drives another, so they can track which marketing investment triggers what actions. Agencies more than ever share the burden of efficacy with their clients, applying the same procurement rigor to pricing and the contractual terms that clients are applying to them. The relentless and almost irresistible drive towards measurability will require some degree of moderation and careful consideration, however, since measurement of ROI for certain types of marketing objectives may be an elusive goal. Poorly applied, it can end up favoring cost-avoidance programs rather than high-impact campaign work, and it may not be a perfect panacea to measure results or decide where to invest marketing dollars. *Every dollar counts.*

As a result, agencies are pushed to experiment and innovate and are looking for ways to do more with less. Agencies will continue to be expected to play a critical role in advising clients when to apply the rigor and science of ROI and informing them what mix of marketing programs will drive business performance. Addressing these imperatives requires astute management of every expense, including marketing that's often one of the largest spending categories, and a scrutiny of every dollar spent by the company to ensure it provides a compelling return on investment. Advertisers must design systems to apply increasing rigor and accountability in tracking and measuring marketing and business performance as it relates to investments and big bets, which in turn, gives C-level executives and corporate boards more confidence in the company's ability to win and curry favor in the marketplace.

Companies are struggling to find new ways of doing things in these difficult times and are turning to their agencies to play an even stronger role in helping them weather economic uncertainties and business volatility. To win share and grow, advertisers now require two simultaneous approaches to agency management: a more focused and disciplined use of agency resources, and a more aggressive pursuit of models that motivate their agencies, encourage risk-taking, and link agency performance to business outcomes. Companies must make informed decisions about their capital expenditures based on these criteria. Discretionary expense categories such as advertising and marketing communication services are directly impacted by the moods of the world financial markets and the pressure experienced by CFOs looking to reduce operational expenses to stay competitive.

In a booming economy spurred by growth and expanding markets, agency services can thrive or shrivel. Since marketing spend is mostly seen as a necessary investment to grow market share and revenue (after all, it was commonly said that *"a product seen is a product sold"*), it's no surprise that the agency business enjoyed a successive number of years of overall expansion, characterized by a highly competitive business sector and fueled by new distribution channels and the growth of digital media. The recession that followed has forced agencies to move more cautiously as marketing budgets evaporated. In the wake of economic turbulence, the agency industry is finding ways to overcome budget cuts and tough clients eager to control costs, which in turn are fueling a drive for innovation and breakthrough thinking. The trend toward faster, leaner, and meaner is not going away. Outspending the competition is no longer the way to win. Clients are turning to their agency talent to help them navigate smartly and move decisively, and with the conviction that comes from data, extraordinary insight, and an understanding of what's working best.

SCARCITY OF TALENT
The lifeblood of the agency business is, and will remain, its people. No matter what technological advancements agencies are able to leverage to reduce labor dependencies and automate tasks, it's

likely to remain a labor-intensive business for years to come, as key talent makes or breaks agencies. For the most part, agencies struggle to staff accounts with senior talent who have sufficient tenure and experience to lead clients vs. simply serving them. Finding and retaining top talent is now one of the greatest challenges faced by agencies and a fundamentally limiting factor in their ability to grow. Especially when agencies have to compete with the 800-pound gorillas and digital talent grabbers like Google and Facebook. Thankfully, there is enough money at stake to motivate the entire industry to shake up and adjust. It has been a challenge. The talent hole, predominantly in digital but also in rich analytics, social, content, video, VR/IA, and other emerging competencies, is indicative of a generation gap in competencies and skills that will take time to close. The gap in these high-demand professionals is partially due to the fact that clients are hiring them faster than agencies are able to produce them. Clients have realized that they need highly capable and digitally savvy employees with sufficient knowledge and work experience to lead their organizations in the new world. Agencies also compete with their clients for the same talent.

There is significantly more human capital required to service the growing number of digital channels and the associated number of tactics that support it. And when clients start challenging how much they pay their agencies, it's not helping agencies fill the gap. It is generally true across all disciplines, but it appears to be having the greatest impact on media services. The fee and margin pressure felt across the agency industry has resulted in some agencies reducing, or worse, canceling training programs as well as reducing entry-level salaries. In some cases, the scarcity of talent has led to salary inflation in high-demand positions as agencies fight to attract and retain the best talent.

The resulting pressure on the bottom line has required nimble agencies to look for more cost-effective ways to produce work for their clients. Off-shoring and near-shoring of production work can be attractive solutions for agencies wanting to reduce costs and retain their margin.

As agencies staff for existing and future needs, they are hiring individuals from varying professional backgrounds than they have historically, pursuing candidates who may not have considered advertising or marketing agencies a career choice until now. It means that agencies are tapping into recruiting firms with a broader coverage than traditional advertising or marketing services. They are also increasingly reaching out more for international resources, importing talent from other countries as needed. They are using some of their offices as hiring hubs with the intent to develop their own best talent and disperse it to other offices around the world. Domestic-only agencies will eventually suffer from not having access to similar benefits: access to larger pools of audiences and technology-savvy resources, greater talent selection and training, and rotation of talent to develop skills and experience. Advertisers face similar recruiting challenges as their agencies, so they understand well the challenges being faced. As clients hire top talent to handle what they consider to be increasingly more critical business functions, agencies will need to keep up with their client needs, or better, lead them into the future. The savviest client/agency partnerships are experimenting with joint approaches to sourcing and managing talent. Ingenuity rarely comes from times of abundance but rather from scarcity.

EVOLUTION OR REVOLUTION ON MADISON AVENUE?

Agencies in marketing and communication services have evolved from a reputation of demonstrating strong creativity, ideas, and interpersonal skills to building upon a scientific body of knowledge and proven results. They have to, or they face the risk of being devalued in the eyes of their clients. But there is still a fair amount of chaos in both agency businesses and client organizations today. This complex world of marketing and technology convergence is allowing agencies to deliver greater value to clients in desperate need of maps and playbooks. The advertising industry of the future will be shaped based on the collective impact made by macro-level market business and social dynamics, as well as new socio-demographic and technology-based advancements. Agencies will lead by driving greater relevancy and value in their offerings. Today they are creating work styles that are more about partnership than vendor relationships. They are sharing office space with clients to be closer to the heartbeat and to reduce overhead. If not, they're using communication software and technology such as video conferencing to narrow the space/time gap between their and the client's worlds.

They are building virtual teams of top-notch subject matter experts by tapping into centers of excellence wherever they may be. They are creating, organizing, and assembling communities of like-minded individuals on their clients' behalf, a role previously played by media companies now struggling with the increased audience and media fragmentation. They are capitalizing on the growing sophistication and investment by clients to build customer insight and improve campaign performance. They are collecting rich customer data, embracing data management and analytics to enrich their targeting and optimization competencies. They are producing rich branded content vs. simple advertising. They are improving their senior to junior staff ratio by bringing in more experienced talent to the account to add value, not just push projects through the pipeline. They are building procurement-type functions within the agency to drive cost-efficiency with their own roster of outsourced suppliers. They are fighting shrinking profit margins by staffing their agencies with compensation officers who can stand up to clients and have fact-based conversations. They are pushing back on the notion that their value is defined by their time or resources. They are finding creative ways to monetize the value they create by negotiating financial incentives tied to performance. They are preserving and licensing more intellectual property, especially software and digital tools developed as a by-product of a client assignment, and developing and distributing original creative content at a premium. They are building innovative new services and delivery mechanisms. They are pursuing new revenue models from consulting services and software development to licensing new technologies. In the end, the agency model of the future will be more like an ecosystem of interconnected competencies. Agencies are waking up to their value, driven by a new accountability for success, and they want a piece of the action.

Advertisers are noticing a healthy change in agency attitudes and aspirations. Agencies understand that marketing strategy is first and foremost about business strategy. Their business models are now built on an understanding that marketing strategy must first and foremost be about business strategy. They are eager to show off their ability to go beyond the communication layer to deliver on customer experiences, build brands, and even invent new products and new distribution channels to drive new business opportunities. They want to tap into their rich and unique customer insight and communities to influence business strategy, product development and product design, fulfillment and distribution, and even customer service. They bring their clients solutions that demonstrate that smart marketing is about enabling meaningful end-to-end conversations and experiences between brands and audiences. It's an all-new game. If they play it well, they can more effectively address what clients need from their agencies. If they don't, they risk permanently becoming commodities. Some pundits venture to say that the changes that Madison Avenue has experienced in the past decade are truly revolutionary and have profoundly, and permanently, impacted its core nature. One cannot argue with the long-term economic and social impact of game-changing phenoma like technology-based digital lifestyles that touch the consumer 24x7x365—and how they are shaping the industry that feeds from it.

"Madison Avenue" as a homogenous phenomenon is per-haps an old and outdated icon that holds it place in the annals of the advertising industry of the 20th century, and nothing more. But the agency world is fundamentally its own catalyst in revolutionizing the business of how clients establish, maintain, and grow relationships with their customers. The future of the agency-client relationship is being played on a chessboard that looks more like a spinning, multidimensional globe than the flat map of Manhattan. This book provides advertisers and agencies the knowledge required for them to come together and collaborate more effectively. *Agency Mania* was written as a roadmap to producing more effective partnerships that keep delivering over and over. Put your sneakers on. This era of partnership capital, this brave new world, is a mad race. And we are only getting started.

RECOMMENDED READINGS AND RESOURCES

AdForum, search for 25,000+ agencies, 9,000+ production companies, 180,000 creative works, fully credited. http://www.adforum.com

Agency Mania Solutions, "Resources" section includes opinion papers, articles, industry updates. http://agencymania.com/resources/

American Association of Advertising Agencies (4As), "Client Essentials" section. https://www.aaaa.org/home-page/client-essentials/ (restricted to members only)

Association of National Advertising (ANA) Agency Management Playbook—February 1, 2018—http://www.ana.net/miccontent/show/id/dm-toolkit-agency-relations (restricted to members only)

Association of National Advertising (ANA), Marketing Knowledge Center, "Insights and resources" section. http://www.ana.net/mkc (restricted to members only)

Auletta, Ken, *Frenemies: The Epic Disruption of the Ad Business (and Everything Else),* New York: Penguin Press, 2018

Baker, Ronald J., *Implementing Value Pricing: A Radical Business Model for Professional Firms,* Hoboken: Wiley, 2010

Farmer, Michael, *Madison Avenue Manslaughter: An Inside View of Fee-Cutting Clients, Profit-Hungry Owners and Declining Ad Agencies,* New York: LID Publishing, 2017

In-House Agency Forum, leading professional association for in-house agencies. https://www.ihaforum.org/

Williams, Tim, *Positioning for Professionals: How Professional Knowledge Firms Can Differentiate Their Way to Success,* Hoboken: Wiley, 2010

NOTES

CHAPTER ONE

[1] At the time he was quoted in the first edition of *Agency Mania* (SelectBooks, 2010), Mr. Scotti's title was Chief Marketing Officer, Verizon.

[2] E.J. Schultz, "PepsiCo Exec Has Tough Words for Agencies," *Ad Age*, October 15, 2015. http://adage.com/article/special-report-ana-annual-meeting-2015/agencies-fire-ana-convention/300942/

[3] Alexandra Bruell, "21st Century Fox Finishes Bulk of Media Agency Review After a Year," *Ad Age*, May 18, 2016. http://adage.com/article/agency-news/21st-century-fox-finishes-media-agency-review-a-year/304068/

[4] At the time he was quoted in the first edition of *Agency Mania* (SelectBooks, 2010), Mr. Goodby's title was Co-Chairman, Goodby Silverstein & Partners.

[5] Tanya Dua, "What's on Martin Sorrell's Mind: 'We need to rename advertising'" *Digiday*, October 1, 2015. https://digiday.com/marketing/advertisingweek2015-sir-martin-sorrell-the-definition-of-advertising-needs-to-change/

[6] At the time he was quoted in the first edition of *Agency Mania* (SelectBooks, 2010), Mr. Lévy was Chairman of Publicis Group.

[7] Michael E. Thyen, Director of Procurement, International Business Unit, Eli Lilly and Company, interviewed by Bruno Gralpois, author, *Agency Mania*, 2010

[8] Alexandra Bruell, "IPG Beats Revenue Expectations," *Ad Age*, October 21, 2015. http://adage.com/article/agency-news/ipg-total-revenue-1-3-quarter/301001/

[9] Shareen Pathak, "Inside Deloitte's $1.5 Billion Ad Agency," *Digiday*, August 17, 2015. https://digiday.com/marketing/inside-deloitte-1-5-billion-ad-agency/

[10] Martine Reardon, Former Chief Marketing Officer, Macy's, interviewed by Bruno Gralpois, author, Agency Mania, 2010

[11] Sarah Vizard, "How Marketing Is Changing and Why Agencies Are Not Keeping Pace," *Marketing Week*, May 25, 2017. https://www.marketingweek.com/2017/05/25/marketing-changing-agencies-pace/

[12] Noreen O'Leary, "5 Agency Leaders on Which Industry Changes Keep Them Up at Night," Ad Week, December 23, 2014. http://www.adweek.com/brand-marketing/5-agency-leaders-which-industry-changes-keep-them-night-162072/

[13] Leysa Lysyj, "Your Agency Hates You and You Don't Even Know It," *Ad Age*, July 21, 2015. http://adage.com/article/viewpoint-editorial/agency-hates/299532/

[14] Jack Marshall, "Clorox Is Betting Big on Programmatic Advertising," *Wall Street Journal*, September 4, 2015. https://blogs.wsj.com/cmo/2015/09/04/clorox-is-betting-big-on-programmatic-advertising/

[15] Brian Braiker, "Q&AA: Publicis Groupe CEO Arthur Sadoun on His First 100 Days (And Next 20 Years," *Ad Age*, September 27, 2017. http://adage.com/article/qaa/publicis-group-ceo-arthur-sadoun-raison-detre/310455/

[16] Jeff Beer, "25 Predictions for What Marketing Will Look Like in 2020," *Fast Company*, March 4, 2015. https://www.fastcompany.com/3043109/25-predictions-for-what-marketing-will-look-like-in-2020

CHAPTER TWO

[17] Lindsay Stein , "Six Questions with New Hill Holliday President Chris Wallrapp," *Ad Age*, January 24, 2017. http://adage.com/article/agency-news/questions-hill-holliday-president-chris-wallrapp/307670/

[18] Sarah Vizard, "How Marketing Is Changing and Why Agencies Are Not Keeping Pace," *Marketing Week*, May 25, 2017. https://www.marketingweek.com/2017/05/25/marketing-changing-agencies-pace/

[19] Sarah Vizard, "How Marketing Is Changing and Why Agencies Are Not Keeping Pace," *Marketing Week*, May 25, 2017. https://www.marketingweek.com/2017/05/25/marketing-changing-agencies-pace/

[20] Lalita Salgaokar, "R/GA's Barry Wacksman on Philosophy, Strategy and Building an Agency," *Campaign US*, July 17, 2017. https://www.rga.com/news/articles/r-ga-s-barry-wacksman-on-philosophy-strategy-and-building-an-agency

[21] Maureen Morrison, "Martin Sorrell on Mobile: 'We Haven't Adapted'," *Ad Age*, February 24, 2016. http://adage.com/article/digital/martin-sorrell-mobile-adapted/302818/

[22] Peter Levitan, "The Lost Advertising Agency Client," Peter Levitan Blog, October 26, 2015. http://peterlevitan.com/the-lost-advertising-agency-client-7457/

[23] Megan Graham, "How PR Giant Edelman Made Its Paid-Media Play," *Ad Age*, November 7, 2017. http://adage.com/article/agency-news/pr-giant-edelman-made-paid-media-play/311071/

[24] Richard Whitman, "Accenture Interactive: Adland's Fastest-Growing Holding Company," *MediaPost*, October 22, 2017. https://www.mediapost.com/publications/article/309116/accenture-interactive-adlands-fastest-growing-ho.html

[25] Susan Markowicz, Global Advertising Agency Manager, Ford Motor Company, interviewed by Bruno Gralpois, author, *Agency Mania*, 2010

[26] Larissa Faw, "Publicis Groupe Posts Modest Organic Growth in Q2," *MediaPost Agency Daily*, July 20, 2017. https://www.mediapost.com/publications/article/304629/publicis-groupe-posts-modest-organic-growth-in-q2.html

[27] James R. Zambito, Senior Director, Global Corporate Affairs, Johnson & Johnson, interviewed by Bruno Gralpois, author, *Agency Mania*, 2010

[28] Patrick Coffee, "Q&A: Michael Roth Looks Ahead at 2016's Challenges, Trends and Opportunities for IPG," *Adweek*, February 12, 2016, http://www.adweek.com/brand-marketing/qa-michael-roth-looks-ahead-2016s-challenges-trends-and-opportunities-ipg-169653/

[29] Publicis Groupe website, www.publicisgroupe.com/en/the-groupe/about-publicis-groupe

[30] Brian Braiker, "Q&AA: Publicis Groupe CEO Arthur Sadoun on His First 100 Days (And Next 20 Years," *Ad Age*, September 27, 2017. http://adage.com/article/qaa/publicis-group-ceo-arthur-sadoun-raison-detre/310455/

[31] Andy Favell, "Why Mobile Video Is Massive and Other Lessons from Mobile World Congress 2017," *ClickZ*, March 15, 2017. (https://www.clickz.com/why-mobile-video-is-massive-and-other-lessons-from-mobile-world-congress-2017/110028/)

[32] Michael J. McDermott, "Digital Consultancies Are Making Inroads with Marketers Against Traditional Ad Agencies," *ANA Magazine*, July 21, 2017, http://www.ana.net/magazines/show/id/ana-2017-07-digital-consultancies-making-inroads-w-marketers

[33] Penry Price, "Why Creative Agencies Need to Think Like Consultants in 2017," *Ad Age*, January 11, 2017. http://adage.com/article/digitalnext/creative-agencies-consultants-2017/307400/

CHAPTER THREE

[34] Jack Neff, "Vitamin Powerhouse NBTY Selects Droga5 as Agency of Record," *Ad Age*, September 9, 2015, http://adage.com/article/agency-news/vitamin-powerhouse-nbty-selects-droga-5-agency-record/300273/

[35] Maureen Morrison and Mark Bergen, "4A's Transformation: Takeaways and Reporters' Notebook," *Ad Age*, March 27, 2015.

36   Marc A. Brownstein President and CEO, Brownstein Group, interviewed by Bruno Gralpois, author, *Agency Mania*, 2010

37   Tom Denford, "Good Marketing Needs Good Procurement Support," *MediaPost*, December 3, 2015. https://www.mediapost.com/publications/article/263916/good-marketing-needs-good-procurement-support.html

38   Jack Neff, "How P&G Hopes to Raise Creative Bar and Lower Costs: 'Cut The Crap'," *Ad Age*, June 20, 2016. http://adage.com/article/cmo-strategy/p-g-hopes-boost-creative-cut-fees-cut-crap/304770/

39   Jeff Goodby, Co-Chairman and Partner, Goodby, Silverstein & Partners, interviewed by Bruno Gralpois, author, *Agency Mania*, 2010

40   Marc S. Pritchard, "Turn The Page & Raise The Bar," (presented at 4As Transformation 2017 conference, Los Angeles, California, April 4, 2017

41   Susan Markowicz, Global Advertising Agency Manager, Ford Motor Company, interviewed by Bruno Gralpois, author, *Agency Mania*, 2010

42   Stuart Elliott, "Madison Avenue Sees Rough Times Ahead, Tempered by Growth," *The New York Times*, December 8, 2014. https://www.nytimes.com/2014/12/09/business/media/madison-avenue-sees-rough-times-ahead-tempered-by-growth.html

43   Jack Neff, "P&G Tells Digital to Clean Up, Lays Down New Rules for Agencies and Ad Tech to Get Paid," *Ad Age*, January 29, 2017. http://adage.com/article/media/p-g-s-pritchard-calls-digital-grow-up-new-rules/307742/

44   Sarah Vizard, "How Marketing Is Changing and Why Agencies Are Not Keeping Pace," *Marketing Week*, May 25 2017. https://www.marketingweek.com/2017/05/25/marketing-changing-agencies-pace/

45   Marla Kaplowitz, "Marla Kaplowitz Shares Her Takeaways from Advertising Week," *Campaign US*, October 2, 2017. www.campaignlive.co.uk/article/marla-kaplowitz-shares-takeaways-advertising-week/1446093

46   Erik Sherman, "Fearless Pursuit of Excellence," ANA Blog, May 14, 2015. https://www.ana.net/magazines/show/id/ana-2015-may-fearless-pursuit-excellence

47   Jeff Devon, Former Senior Director, Indirect Procurement, HP/HPE, interviewed by Bruno Gralpois, author, *Agency Mania*, 2010

CHAPTER FOUR

48   Bryan Wiener, "Outside Voices: Marketers Need to Modernize, Not Just Switch Their Agencies," *The Wall Street Journal*, August 21, 2015. https://blogs.wsj.com/cmo/2015/08/21/outside-voices-marketers-need-to-modernize-not-just-switch-their-agencies/

[49] Oliver Agency Blog, "The Traditional Agency Model is Going to Break." Accessed May 2, 2018. https://ie.oliver.agency/news/the-traditional-agency-model-is-going-to-break/

[50] Lauren Johnson, "McDonald's Is Creating 5,000 Pieces of Marketing Content This Year. Here's Why," *AdWeek*, September 26, 2016. http://www.adweek.com/digital/why-mcdonalds-will-create-5000-pieces-marketing-content-year-173711/

[51] At the time he was quoted, in the first edition of *Agency Mania* (Select Books, 2010), Mr. Pollard was SVP, Coca Cola. Now he is Chief Marketing Officer at General Mills.

[52] Michael E. Thyen, Director of Procurement, International Business Unit, Eli Lilly and Company, interviewed by Bruno Gralpois, author, *Agency Mania*, 2010

[53] Jack Neff, "Why Unilever is Halving Its Agencies and Investing in Strategy," *Ad Age*, June 30, 2017.http://adage.com/article/cmo-strategy/weed-root-waste-agencies-unilever-alike/309631/

[54] Alexandra Bruell, "Maurice Levy Talks About the Publicis Reorganization, Succession and P&G Review," *Ad Age*, December 3, 2015. http://adage.com/article/agency-news/publicis-maurice-levy-talks-p-ls-reorg-timing/301592

[55] Susan Markowicz, Global Advertising Agency Manager, Ford Motor Company, interviewed by Bruno Gralpois, author, *Agency Mania*, 2010

[56] James R. Zambito, Senior Director Global Corporate Affairs, Johnson & Johnson, interviewed by Bruno Gralpois, author, *Agency Mania*, 2010

[57] Jack Neff, "Verizon's Scotti: Agency Model Isn't Broken, But Lazy Marketers Are Screwing It Up," *Ad Age*, October 20, 2016. http://adage.com/article/special-report-ana-annual-meeting-2016/verizon/306382/

[58] Steve McClellan, "Horizon Media's Koenigsberg: The New Agency Model is 'AOC'," *MediaPost*, March 22, 2015. https://www.mediapost.com/publications/article/246120/horizon-medias-koenigsberg-the-new-agency-model.html

[59] Richard C. DelCore, Senior Advisor, The Boston Consulting Group—Former Director, Global Brand Entertainment & VP P&G Productions, interviewed by Bruno Gralpois, author, *Agency Mania*, 2010

[60] E.J. Schultz, "Frito-Lay's CMO: Agencies of Record Are Outdated, Lay's Brand Has Gone Project-to-Project," *Ad Age* , May 9, 2015. http://adage.com/article/agency-news/frito-lay-s-cmo-aors-outdated/298542/

[61] Erik Oster, "Hershey Adds CP+B to Core Roster," *AgencySpy*, January 26, 2016. http://www.adweek.com/agencyspy/hershey-adds-cpb-to-core-roster/101165

62 Meredith Verdone, "Turning an In-House Agency Best-in-Class," ANA Blog, October 18, 2017. http://www.ana.net/blogs/show/id/mm-blog-2017-10-boa-inhouse-agency

63 Tanya Dua, "Chobani CMO: The More You Outsource, the Less Creative You Get," *Digiday*, May 18, 2015. https://digiday.com/marketing/chobani-cmo-outsource-less-creative-get/

64 E.J. Schultz and Megan Graham, "Fair or Not, In-House Agencies Take Heat For Pepsi Gaffe, Ad Age, April 7, 2017. http://adage.com/article/agency-news/pepsi-gaffe-puts-target-house-agencies-fair/308604/?CSAuthResp=152562475 9179:0:2370067:0:24:success:AA94428395DAB4F23FF964C324278AED

65 Matthew Chapman, "Ad Week: Issues Around Insourcing And Marketers' Role Fuel Debates," CMO.com, March 22, 2017. http://www.cmo.com/features/articles/2017/3/22/ad-week-issues-around-insourcing-and-marketers-role-fuel-the-debates.html#gs.=IbFz6c

66 Amy Gesenhues, "A CMO's View: How Intel's Head of Creative Is Building the Brand Through Its In-House Agency," *Marketing Land*, November 18, 2016. https://marketingland.com/cmos-view-intels-head-creative-building-brand-house-agency-198344

67 Jeanine Poggi, "In New Era Of TV Ad Deals, Agencies Are No Longer Gatekeepers," Ad Age, January 11, 2016. http://adage.com/article/media/closer-marketers/302048/

68 Vince Bond Jr. and Charles Child and Larry P. Vellequette, "Oliver Francois on 'Game of Thrones' and Agency Tension," *Ad Age*, May 12, 2015. http://adage.com/article/cmo-strategy/olivier-francois-game-thrones-agency-tension/298564/

69 Hans Riedel, "Category of one: This Is not about 'we' and 'they'. This Is about 'us'," Spark44 Blog, accessed May 6, 2018. https://spark44.com/our-model/

70 Jack Neff, "The CMO's Guide to Agency Procurement," Ad Age, May 13, 2015. http://adage.com/article/cmo-strategy/cmo-s-guide-agency-procurement/298536/

71 E.J. Schultz, "Fiat Chrysler and Wieden & Kennedy Are Splitting Up," *Ad Age*, March 1, 2016. http://adage.com/article/agency-news/fiat-chrysler-wieden-kennedy-splitting/302901/

72 Ilyse Liffreing, "Chobani CCO Lee Maschmeyer on cutting out creative agencies: 'We can make our dollars work harder'," *Digiday*, February 13, 2018. https://digiday.com/social/chobani-cco-lee-maschmeyer-cutting-creative-agencies-can-make-dollars-work-harder/

73 Urey Onuoha, "Finding the Perfect Match," *ANA Magazine*, February 1, 2015, http://www.ana.net/magazines/show/id/ana-2015-feb-finding-perfect-match

CHAPTER FIVE

[74] Claus Wedekind et al., "MHC-Dependent Mate Preferences in Humans, *Proceedings: Biological Sciences*, Vol. 260, No. 1359. (Jun. 22, 1995), 245-249. http://www.coherer.org/pub/mhc.pdf.

[75] Jeff Goodby, Co-Chairman and Partner, Goodby, Silverstein & Partners, interviewed by Bruno Gralpois, author, *Agency Mania*, 2010

[76] E.J. Schultz, "New MillerCoors CMO Says Marketing Has Been 'Too Scattered'," *Ad Age*, July 17, 2015. http://adage.com/article/cmo-strategy/millercoors-cmo-marketing-scattered/299519/

[77] Lynne Seid, Partner Global Marketing Officers Practice, Heidrick & Struggles executive search firm, retired, interviewed by Bruno Gralpois, author, *Agency Mania*, 2010

[78] Stephan Argent, "Agency Relationship Deal Breakers (And What to Do About Them)," Argedia Group Blog, November 29, 2015. http://argedia.com/wp/10-agency-relationship-deal-breakers-and-what-to-do-about-them/

[79] James P. Othmer, *Adland*, (Doubleday, 2009)

[80] Susan Markowicz, Global Advertising Agency Manager, Ford Motor Company, interviewed by Bruno Gralpois, author, *Agency Mania*, 2010

[81] Michael Fanuele, "An Open Letter to Clients Considering an Ad Agency Review: Part 2," *Ad Age*, February 24, 2017. http://adage.com/article/viewpoint/open-letter-clients-ad-agency-review-part-2/308050/

[82] Urey Onuoha, "Finding the Perfect Match—Building Agency Relationships That Last," *Association of National Advertisers Magazine*, February 2015. https://www.ana.net/magazines/show/id/ana-2015-feb-finding-perfect-match

[83] Linda Boff, "Marketers: It's Time to Say RIP To The Media RFP," *Ad Age*, November 4, 2015. http://adage.com/article/cmo-strategy/time-rip-media-rfp/301195/

[84] A.J. Meyer, "Brands And Agencies: Is It Time to Kill The RFP?" *Ad Age*, October 2, 2015. http://adage.com/article/agency-viewpoint/brand-agencies-time-kill-rfp/300703/

[85] Urey Onuoha, "Getting Creative" *Association of National Advertisers Magazine*, December 2016, 14-16

[86] Linda Boff, "Marketers: It's Time to Say RIP To The Media RFP," *Ad Age*, November 4, 2015. http://adage.com/article/cmo-strategy/time-rip-media-rfp/301195/

[87] Shareen Pathak, "Inside the Agency New-Business Dating Game," *Digiday*, February 12, 2015. https://digiday.com/marketing/agency-new-business-dating-game/

88   Urey Onuoha, "Getting Creative" *Association of National Advertisers Magazine*, December 2016, 14-16

89   David Angell, "8 'Less Obvious' Reasons Why Agencies Lose Pitches," TrinityP3 Blog, May 26, 2017. https://www.trinityp3. com/2017/05/8-reasons-why-agencies-lose-pitches/

CHAPTER SIX

90   Marty Stock, "Calvary CEO on Losing a Major Account: Don't Cry in Your Beer—Just Move On," *Ad Age,* August 24, 2015. http://adage.com/article/ news/cry-beer-move/300048/

91   Lindsay Stein, "Survival Guide 2017: How Agencies Can Rebuild Credibility," *Ad Age*, January 9, 2017. http://adage.com/article/print-edition/ survival-guide-agencies-rebuild-credibility/307407/

92   Jack Neff, "GroupM Chairman Says Media Agencies Aren't Really 'Agents' Anymore," *Ad Age*, April 28, 2015. http://adage.com/article/agency-news/ groiupm-chairman-media-agencies-agents/298294/

93   Ed Lu, "The Secret to a Profitable Agency," *imedia*, July 22, 2015. http://www. imediaconnection.com/article/180443/the-secret-to-a-profitable-agency

94   Marc A. Brownstein, President and CEO, Brownstein Group, interviewed by Bruno Gralpois, author, *Agency Mania*, 2010

95   Alexandra Bruell, "How the Agency of the Future Will Be Compensated," *Ad Age*, May 2, 2016. http://adage.com/article/agency-news/ agency-future-compensated/303805/

96   Raahil Chopra, "If Technology Is Not Part of the Solution, It Is Part of the Inspiration," *Campaign*, July 15, 2015. https://www.campaignlive.co.uk/article/ if-technology-not-part-solution-part-inspiration/1356031

97   Jack Neff, "P&G Tells Digital to Clean Up, Lays Down New Rules for Agencies and Ad Tech to Get Paid," *Ad Age*, January 29, 2017. http://adage.com/article/ media/p-g-s-pritchard-calls-digital-grow-up-new-rules/307742/

98   Judy Shapiro, "The Disruptive Agency Model" Ad Age, November 16, 2017. http:// adage.com/article/agency-viewpoint/disruptive-agency-model-part-2/311252/

99   From the press release, "ANA Independent Study Finds Rebates and Other Non-Transparent Practices to be Pervasive in U.S. Media Ad-Buying Ecosystem," ANA website, June 7, 2016. Accessed May 2, 2018. http://www.ana.net/ content/show/id/pr-media-transparency

CHAPTER SEVEN

[100] Neal Grossman, Chief Operating Officer—Americas at eg+ worldwide and the designory, interviewed by Bruno Gralpois, author, *Agency Mania*, 2018

[101] Alexandra Bruell, "How the Agency of the Future Will Be Compensated," *Ad Age*, May 2, 2016, http://adage.com/article/agency-news/agency-future-compensated/303805/

[102] Jack Neff, "P&G Will Cut $2 Billion in Marketing But Spend Some Back to Become 'Irresistible'," *Ad Age*, April 26, 2017. http://adage.com/article/cmo-strategy/p-g-cut-2-billion-media-agency-costs/308811/

[103] Shareen Pathak, "What Agencies Want: Pay Us Fairly," *Digiday*, March 3, 2015. https://digiday.com/marketing/agencies-want-pay-us-fairly/

[104] Tim Williams, "Your Clients Hire You to Be Effective, Not Efficient," The Business Model Company Global: November 27, 2017. https://www.thebusinessmodelco.com/our-thinking/2017/11/27/your-clients-hire-you-to-be-effective-not-efficient

[105] Sean Hargrave, "Sorrell: I'm No Trump, But I'm Right About Everything, Especially Facebook," *MediaPost*, October 5, 2016. https://www.mediapost.com/publications/article/301904/mad-london-will-return-on-monday-june-5th.html

[106] Steve Radick, "Agencies Should Start Thinking More Like Consultants," *MediaPost*, December 28, 2016. https://www.mediapost.com/publications/article/291885/agencies-should-start-thinking-more-like-consultan.html

[107] Jeff Goodby, Co-Chairman and Partner, Goodby, Silverstein & Partners, interviewed by Bruno Gralpois, author, *Agency Mania*, 2010

[108] 4As (@4As), Twitter post, April 3 , 2017, 3:55 PM, "We Don't Have Time-Sheets Because We Think It Drives the Wrong Behavior." https://twitter.com/4as/status/849032674421428224

[109] Michael Farmer, "Agencies Struggle with Declining Prices," *MediaVillage*, June 28, 2017. https://www.mediavillage.com/article/agencies-struggle-with-declining-prices/

[110] Daniel Jeffries, "Great procurement is built on collaboration…," Jeffries Consulting Blog, April 29, 2015 http://www.jeffriesconsulting.com/blog/2015/4/29/great-procurement-is-built-on-collaboration

[111] James R. Zambito, Senior Director Global Corporate Affairs, Johnson & Johnson, interviewed by Bruno Gralpois, author, *Agency Mania*, 2010

[112] Alexandra Bruell, "Print—How the Agency of the Future Will Be Compensated," *Ad Age*, May 2, 2016. http://adage.com/print/303805

113   by Mark Pollard, "A New Agency Model," *Medium*, January 20, 2015. https://medium.com/@markpollard/a-new-agency-model-solving-slowth-ac9de5fbec13

114   James R. Zambito, Senior Director Global Corporate Affairs, Johnson & Johnson, interviewed by Bruno Gralpois, author, *Agency Mania*, 2010

115   Shareen Pathak, "What Agencies Want: Pay Us Fairly," *Digiday*, March 3, 2015. https://digiday.com/marketing/agencies-want-pay-us-fairly/

116   Neal Grossman, Chief Operating Officer—Americas at eg+ worldwide and the designory, interviewed by Bruno Gralpois, author, *Agency Mania*, 2018

117   Keith Reinhard, "'Time And Money': What DDB's Keith Reinhard Has Learned About How Agencies Are Paid," *Ad Age*, November 22, 2017. http://adage.com/article/opinion/ddb-s-keith-reinhard-agencies-paid/311390/

118   Kerry Graham, "Agencies: To Improve Your Business, Get Rid of Time Sheets," *Ad Age*, July 28, 2015. http://adage.com/article/agency-viewpoint/agencies-improve-business-rid-time-sheets/299664/

119   Neal Grossman, Chief Operating Officer—Americas at eg+ worldwide and the designory, interviewed by Bruno Gralpois, author, *Agency Mania*, 2018

120   Keith Reinhard, "'Time And Money': What DDB's Keith Reinhard Has Learned About How Agencies Are Paid," *Ad Age*, November 22, 2017. http://adage.com/article/opinion/ddb-s-keith-reinhard-agencies-paid/311390/

121   Patrick Coffee, "Agencies Are Remaking Themselves to Satisfy Client Demands," *Adweek*, November 13, 2017. http://www.adweek.com/agencies/agencies-are-remaking-themselves-to-satisfy-client-demands/

122   Brian Braiker, "Ad Age Ad Lib: Alain Sylvain of Sylvain Labs on Race, Creativity, The Talent Crunch and More," *Ad Age*, October 6, 2017. http://adage.com/article/podcasts/ad-age-ad-lib-alain-sylvain-sylvain-labs/310792/

123   Lindsay Stein, "How Much Are Agencies' Ideas Worth?" *Ad Age*, November 13, 2017. http://adage.com/article/agency-news/ideas-worth/311267/

124   Deacon Webster and Frances Webster, "Best Practices: Leadership for Small Agency Owners," *Ad Age*, July 23, 2015. http://adage.com/article/small-agency-diary/leadership-lessons-small-agency-owners/299603/

125   Alvin Toffler, *Future Shock: The Third Wave* (William Morrow, 1980)

126   Barrett J. Brunsman, "Here's how P&G Is slashing spending n advertising," Cincinnati Business Courier, November 5, 2015. https://www.bizjournals.com/cincinnati/news/2015/11/05/here-s-how-p-g-is-slashing-spending-on-advertising.html

127   Tom Finneral, "Dispelling the Myth of Working Vs. Non-Working Marketing Spending," *Ad Age*, January 7, 2016. http://adage.com/article/guest-columnists/dispelling-myth-working-working-ratio/302023/

[128] Tanya Dua, "360i's Bryan Wiener on agency talent development: 'Traning is overhead'," Digiday, October 27, 2015. https://digiday.com/marketing/360i-bryan-wiener-training/

[129] Tom Finneral, "Dispelling the Myth of Working Vs. Non-Working Marketing Spending," *Ad Age*, January 7, 2016. http://adage.com/article/guest-columnists/dispelling-myth-working-working-ratio/302023/

[130] Jack Neff, "Cuts Aren't Over, But P&G Wants to Restore Agency Profits," *Ad Age*, April 4, 2017. http://adage.com/article/special-report-4as-conference/cuts-p-g-restore-agency-profits/308559/

CHAPTER EIGHT

[131] Kimberly A. Whitler, "Developing An Emotional Connection With Customers: Insight From HP's CMO, Antonio Lucio," *Forbes*, February 14, 2016. https://www.forbes.com/sites/kimberlywhitler/2016/02/14/developing-an-emotional-connection-with-customers-insight-from-hps-cmo-antonio-lucio/#26bca6c71692

[132] Ben Bold, "Mars CMO Andrew Clarke: 'challenge orthodoxy, do the reverse'," *Campaign*, November 15, 2017, https://www.campaignlive.co.uk/article/mars-cmo-andrew-clarke-challenge-orthodoxy-reverse/1450239

[133] Kofi Amoo-Gottfried, "How the Ad Industry Can Be Truly Inventive (and Effective) Again," *Adweek*, May 18, 2015. http://www.adweek.com/brand-marketing/how-ad-industry-can-be-truly-inventive-and-effective-again-164803/

[134] Kathryn Luttner, "Fiat Chrysler's Olivier Francois doesn't expect agencies to do his job," *Campaign US*, February 21, 2017. https://www.campaignlive.com/article/fiat-chryslers-olivier-francois-doesnt-expect-agencies-job/1424663

[135] Raahil Chopra, "If technology is not part of the solution, it is part of the inspiration," Campaign, July 15, 2015. https://www.campaignlive.co.uk/article/if-technology-not-part-solution-part-inspiration/1356031

[136] 4As Member, "5 Questions for: Pam Scheideler of Deutsch LA," 4As Blog, July 11, 2016. https://www.aaaa.org/5-questions-pam-scheideler-chief-digital-officer-deutsch-la/

[137] ANA White Paper, "Better Creative Briefs," ANA, November, 2017

[138] ANA White Paper, "Better Creative Briefs," ANA, November, 2017

[139] Kathryn Luttner, "Fiat Chrysler's Olivier Francois doesn't expect agencies to do his job," *Campaign US*, February 21, 2017. https://www.campaignlive.com/article/fiat-chryslers-olivier-francois-doesnt-expect-agencies-job/1424663

[140] Erik Oster, "Sir Martin Sorrell Says the Advertising Industry Is 'Too Competitive'," *Adweek*, September 26, 2017. http://www.adweek.com/agencies/sir-martin-sorrell-says-the-advertising-industry-is-too-competitive/

[141] Giselle Abramovich, "ANA Study: CMOs Need To Get Involved Early In The Client-Agency Briefing Process," *CMO*, April 24, 2015. http://www.cmo.com/features/articles/2015/4/24/ana-study-cmos-need-to-get-involved-early-in-the-clientagency-briefing-process.html#gs.iGLx8k0

[142] Jeff Goodby, Co-Chairman and Partner, Goodby, Silverstein & Partners, interviewed by Bruno Gralpois, author, *Agency Mania*, 2010

CHAPTER NINE

[143] Robert Solomon, *The Art of Client Service: The Classic Guide, Updated for Today's Marketers* (John Wiley & Sons, 2016).

[144] ANA survey. "ANA Survey Shows Great Majority of Marketers Rely On Data To Manage Client/Agency Relationships," October 31, 2016. http://www.ana.net/content/show/id/41934

[145] David Rodnitzky, "Advice To The New CMO: How To Deal With Your Existing Agency," *Marketing Land*, May 5, 2015. https://marketingland.com/advice-new-cmo-deal-existing-agency-126446

[146] Dell Case Study. July 31, 2017, Agency Mania website https://agencymania.com/dell-case-study/

[147] CMO Council and ACE metrix, "Optimizing Marketing Partner Performance and Value in a Digital World," Copyright CMO Council, 2012. http://haiconsulting.com/wp-content/uploads/2013/04/CMO-Council-Study-on-Agency-Relationships.pdf

[148] CMO Council and ACE metrix, "Optimizing Marketing Partner Performance and Value in a Digital World," Copyright CMO Council, 2012. http://haiconsulting.com/wp-content/uploads/2013/04/CMO-Council-Study-on-Agency-Relationships.pdf

[149] Charlie Silvestro, Vice President Marketing and Communications Talent Development, MasterCard, interviewed by Bruno Gralpois, author, *Agency Mania*, 2010.

[150] Susan Markowicz, Global Advertising Agency Manager, Ford Motor Company, interviewed by Bruno Gralpois, author, *Agency Mania*, 2010.

[151] Carla Giovannetti Dodds, Business and Marketing Consultant—Former Head of Multicultural Marketing, Walmart, interviewed by Bruno Gralpois, author, *Agency Mania*, 2010

[152] Martine Reardon, Former Chief Marketing Officer, Macy's, interviewed by Bruno Gralpois, author, *Agency Mania*, 2010

[153] James R. Zambito, Senior Director, Global Corporate Affairs, Johnson & Johnson, interviewed by Bruno Gralpois, author, *Agency Mania*, 2010.

CHAPTER TEN

[154] Darren Woolley, "4 thoughts on advertiser/agency relationships—Colgate-Palmolive and GPY&R," trinityP3 Blog, January 21, 2015. https://www.trinityp3.com/2015/01/advertiser-agency-relationships-colgate-palmolive-gpyr/

[155] Kristina Monllos, "Bud Light Leaves BBDO, Moves U.S. Business to Wieden + Kennedy," *Adweek*, July 2, 2015. http://www.adweek.com/brand-marketing/bud-light-leaves-bbdo-moves-us-business-wieden-kennedy-165718/

[156] Ian Baer, "Stop Client Bashing And Start Client Managing Today," *Ad Age*, July 19, 2016. http://adage.com/article/agency-viewpoint/stop-client-bashing-start-client-managing-today/304937/

[157] Lesya Lysyj, "Your Agency Hates You And You Don't Even Know It," *Ad Age*, July 21, 2015. http://adage.com/article/viewpoint-editorial/agency-hates/299532/

[158] Jeff Beer, "How Marketing Will Change In 2015: The Creative Forecast," *Fast Company*, January 1, 2015. https://www.fastcompany.com/3040028/how-marketing-will-change-in-2015-the-creative-forecast

[159] Beth Snyder Bulik, "Best Practices: How To Handle Difficult Clients," *Ad Age*, June 29, 2015 http://adage.com/article/agency-news/practices-handle-difficult-clients/299246/

[160] Kevin Chesters, "Planners and account handlers, here's a little feedback on feeding back," *The Drum*, January 25, 2017. http://www.thedrum.com/opinion/2017/01/25/planners-and-account-handlers-heres-little-feedback-feeding-back

[161] Comment on Steve Smith, "Agencies Are Putting Themselves Out Of Business," *MediaPost* January 24, 2016. https://www.mediapost.com/publications/article/267355/agencies-are-putting-themselves-out-of-business.html

[162] Michael E. Thyen, Director of Procurement, International Business Unit, Eli Lilly and Company, interviewed by Bruno Gralpois, author, *Agency Mania*, 2010.

[163] Lindsay Stein, "Love Me Tender: Why Agencies And Clients Stay—And Why They Stray," *Ad Age*, February 12, 2016. http://adage.com/article/agency-news/longstanding-agency-client-relationships-highs-lows/302674/

[164] Bryan Wiener, "What You'll Need To Build The Agency Of The Future," *Ad Age*, September 23, 2016. http://adage.com/article/digitalnext/build-agency-future/305979/

[165] James R. Zambito, Senior Director, Global Corporate Affairs, Johnson & Johnson, interviewed by Bruno Gralpois, author, Agency Mania, 2010.

[166] Shane Atchison and Kieran Hannon, "An Agency CEO And Brand CMO Write Each Other's Resolutions," *Ad Age*, December 30, 2014. http://adage.com/article/agency-viewpoint/agency-ceo-brand-cmo-write-s-resolutions/296349/

[167] Janet Northen, "Three Things the Best Agencies Have Going For Them," *Ad Age*, November 21, 2014. http://adage.com/print/295947

[168] Shane Atchison and Kieran Hannon, "An Agency CEO And Brand CMO Write Each Other's Resolutions," *Ad Age*, December 30, 2014. http://adage.com/article/agency-viewpoint/agency-ceo-brand-cmo-write-s-resolutions/296349/

[169] Barcelona Yellow website, accessed May 5, 2018, https://www.barcelonayellow.com/barcelona/catalan-culture/catalan-traditions/castellers

CHAPTER ELEVEN

[170] Jack Neff, "Cuts Aren't Over, But P&G Wants to Restore Agency Profits," *Ad Age*, April 4, 2017. http://adage.com/print/308559

[171] James R. Zambito, Senior Director, Global Corporate Affairs, Johnson & Johnson, interviewed by Bruno Gralpois, author, *Agency Mania*, 2010.

ABOUT THE AUTHOR

Bruno Gralpois has been instrumental in establishing Agency Management as a central global discipline for many of the top 200 advertisers, utilizing strategies for ensuring efficient collaboration and driving high-impact results for advertisers and their agency partners. This dedication to improving advertiser-agency relationships has earned him the moniker: The Advertising Love Doctor.

Bruno encourages advertisers to focus less on managing their agencies, and more on working in tandem to build brands—and businesses—backed by a strong and trusting partnership. This belief led to Bruno both co-founding and serving as principal of

Agency Mania Solutions, a company dedicated to helping brand advertisers navigate change and drive better business outcomes with their agencies.

Bruno previously served as Head of Global Marketing and Operations at Visa Inc., leading global agency strategy and management, and building a first-of-its-kind agency management department driven by best practices. As Director of Global Agency Strategy at Microsoft, Bruno developed a company-wide approach to increase the brand's global strength through successful agency partnerships, which earned him the prestigious Marketing Excellence Award from CEO Steve Ballmer for his continued leadership. Bruno has also held leadership positions in pre-IPO high-tech companies AvenueA/Razorfish and Visio, served as Head of Relationship Marketing at Clearwire/Sprint, and as Chair of the Association of National Advertisers Client/ Agency Committee.

His experience as both the client and the agency has shaped this push for an industry-wide initiative, backed by industry associations such as the ANA and 4As, to improve understanding and practices in agency management. Bruno is an active member of the ANA Faculty of Marketing, facilitating training for the largest brand advertisers and their teams, and helping to build effective advertiser-agency relationships.

Visit www.agencymania.com to contact Bruno, share your story, or get more information.